ELIZABETH'S
ARMY

ELIZABETH'S ARMY

BY
C. G. CRUICKSHANK

SECOND EDITION

OXFORD UNIVERSITY PRESS
LONDON   OXFORD   NEW YORK

Oxford University Press
OXFORD LONDON NEW YORK
GLASGOW TORONTO MELBOURNE WELLINGTON
CAPE TOWN SALISBURY IBADAN NAIROBI LUSAKA ADDIS ABABA
BOMBAY CALCUTTA MADRAS KARACHI LAHORE DACCA
KUALA LUMPUR HONG KONG TOKYO

© Oxford University Press 1966

*The first edition, published in 1946,
appeared in the*
OXFORD HISTORICAL SERIES
Second edition 1966

First issued as an Oxford University Press paperback 1968

PRINTED IN GREAT BRITAIN

PREFACE TO THE SECOND EDITION

THE first edition of this book dealt principally with the organization and administration of the many military expeditions which left England in the second half of the reign of Queen Elizabeth I. The validity of the title *Elizabeth's Army* was therefore questionable. The present edition, however, extends to the whole reign the examination of the topics previously covered; and it examines more fully the army at home. It includes a new chapter on 'Drill, Training, Tactics, and Strategy', and gives greater scope to the engaging company of Elizabethan military experts to enliven the text with their own contribution to the understanding of contemporary theory and practice. Finally, it follows the forces on active service in three representative campaigns—the expedition to Scotland in 1560, to Normandy in 1589, and to Spain in 1596. These changes, together with a more detailed investigation of the constitutional basis of the sixteenth-century English army, make the title more accurate.

The present volume has benefited from a number of valuable studies in sixteenth-century English military history since the first edition—both in Britain and in the United States. I should like to mention in particular the work of Professor R. B. Wernham, whose guidance over a quarter of a century ago I still remember with gratitude, of Dr. A. L. Rowse (his chapter on military organization in *The Expansion of Elizabethan England*), and of Captain Cyril Falls.

I am indebted to the four scholars in my family for the toleration which they showed while the book was being written. I must also pay a tribute to the staff of the Public Record Office and of the British Museum Library, whose essential services are too often taken for granted. Nor can I resist expressing gratitude to the management of the latter institution for maintaining unimpaired through three decades of violent change the characteristic, and to me inspiring, aroma of the Reading Room.

Finally, I thank many unseen hands in the Clarendon Press for generous, expert, and patient help.

C. G. C.

PREFACE TO THE FIRST EDITION

THE credit for any merit which this study may possess is to be shared by Professor J. B. Black, who introduced me to Elizabeth, Mr. R. B. Wernham, who fostered the acquaintanceship, and Professor G. N. Clark, who has been generous with advice and encouragement.

I also wish to thank Mr. J. M. Wyllie, and my colleague, Mr. S. R. Raffan, who read drafts, and made valuable suggestions.

The substance of pages 45–47 and 100–4[1] has appeared in the *English Historical Review*, and of Chapter X[2] in *The Army Quarterly*. Acknowledgements are made to Messrs. Longmans, Green & Co., Ltd., and Messrs. William Clowes & Sons, Ltd.

I am indebted to my wife for preparing the index, and for helping with proofs; and above all to my parents, without whose sacrifices the research on which the book is based would not have been possible.

C. G. C.

[1] Pages 153–8 and 286 in the second edition.
[2] Chapter XI in the second edition.

CONTENTS

ABBREVIATIONS	xi
I. CITIZEN VERSUS CROWN	1
II. RECRUITMENT	17
III. THE CHAIN OF COMMAND	41
IV. MOVEMENT AND COMMUNICATIONS	61
V. RATIONS	76
VI. UNIFORM	91
VII. ARMS AND EQUIPMENT	102
VIII. MUSTERS	130
IX. PAY	143
X. DISCIPLINE	159
XI. THE MEDICAL SERVICE	174
XII. DRILL, TRAINING, TACTICS, AND STRATEGY	
A. Drill	189
B. Training	193
C. Tactics and Strategy	198
XIII. THREE CAMPAIGNS	
A. Scotland, 1560	207
B. France, 1589	236
C. Spain, 1596	251
XIV. CONCLUSION	280

CONTENTS

APPENDIXES

1. Levies in England and Wales for Service Abroad, 1585–1602 — 290
2. Origin and Destination of Troops levied in the Welsh Counties between 1585 and 1602 — 290
3. Origin and Destination of Troops levied in the English Counties between 1585 and 1602 — 291
4. Indenture for Troops — 291
5. Prayer for the Troops — 292
6. Soldiers' Oath — 293
7. An Admonition before the Musters — 294
8. Oath for Musters — 294
9. Examples for Musters Certificates — 295
10. Warrant for Payment — 295
11. Receipt for Payment — 296
12. Leicester's Disciplinary Code — 296

INDEX — 305

ABBREVIATIONS

PRINTED SOURCES

(a) SOURCE COLLECTIONS

A.P.C.	*Acts of the Privy Council of England (New Series).*
Birch	Thomas Birch, *Memoirs of the Reign of Queen Elizabeth, from the year 1581 till her death.*
Carew Cal.	*Calendar of the Carew Manuscripts.*
Dom. Cal.	*Calendar of State Papers, Domestic, Elizabeth.*
E.H.R.	*English Historical Review.*
For. Cal.	*Calendar of State Papers, Foreign, Elizabeth.*
Haynes, *State Papers*	Samuel Haynes, *A Collection of State Papers relating to affairs in the reigns of Henry VIII, Edward VI, Mary, and Elizabeth, from 1542 to 1570.*
H.M.C.	*Historical Manuscripts Commission Reports.*
Irish Cal.	*Calendar of State Papers, Ireland, Elizabeth.*
Sadler Papers	*The State Papers and Letters of Sir Ralph Sadler* (edited by Arthur Clifford).
Scot. Cal.	*Calendar of State Papers relating to Scotland, 1547–1603.*

(b) CONTEMPORARY BOOKS

Actions	Sir Roger Williams, *The Actions of the Lowe Countries* (Lond. 1618).
Allarme	Barnaby Rich, *Allarme to England, fore-shewing what perilles are procured where the people live without regarde of martiall lawe* (Lond. 1578).
Annals	Sir John Hayward, *Annals of the first four years of the reign of Queen Elizabeth* (Camden Society edition).
Briefe Discourse	Sir Roger Williams, *A Briefe Discourse of Warre* (Lond. 1590).
Certain Discourses	Sir John Smythe, *Certain Discourses concerning the Formes and Effects of Divers Sorts of Weapons* (Lond. 1590).
Dialogue	Barnaby Rich, *A Right Exelent and Pleasaunt Dialogue, betwene Mercury and an English Souldier* (Lond. 1574).
Discourse	Antonie Wingfield, *A True Coppie of a Discourse written by a Gentleman employed in the late Voyage of Spaine and Portingale* (Lond. 1589).
Fruites	Barnaby Rich, *The Fruites of Long Experience* (Lond. 1581).
Lawes of Armes	Matthew Sutcliffe, *The Practice, Proceedings and Lawes of Armes* (Lond. 1593).

Martiall Discipline	Thomas Styward, *The Pathwaie to Martiall Discipline* (Lond. 1581).
Moderne Training	Sir Clement Edmondes, *The Maner of our Moderne Training* (Lond. 1600).
Moderne Warres	Robert Barret, *The Theorike and Practise of Moderne Warres* (Lond. 1598).
Military Discourse	Sir Thomas Wilford, *A Military Discourse whether it be better for England to give an invador present battle, or to temporize and defend the same* (printed 1734).
Orders Mylitarie	Sir John Smythe, *Instructions, Observations, and Orders Mylitarie* (Lond. 1595; written 1591).
Pathway	Barnaby Rich, *A Pathway to Military Practise, Containinge Offices, Lawes, Disciplines and Orders to be observed in an Army* (Lond. 1587).
Prooved Practice	William Clowes, *A Prooved Practice for all Young Chirurgians, concerning Burnings with Gunpowder, and Woundes made with Gunshot, Sword, Halbard, Pike, Launce, or such other* (Lond. 1591).
Stratioticos	Leonard and Thomas Digges, *An Arithmeticall Warlike Treatise named Stratioticos* (Lond. 1590).
Weapons of Fire	Humphrey Barwick, *A Breefe Discourse concerning the Force and Effect of all Manuall Weapons of Fire and the Disability of the Long Bowe or Archery* (Lond. 1594?).

MANUSCRIPT SOURCES

British Museum:

Add. MSS.	*Additional Manuscripts.*
B.M. Loan 23	*The Hulton Manuscripts: Papers of the 2nd Earl of Essex.*
Cott. MSS.	*Cottonian Manuscripts.*
Harl. MSS.	*Harleian Manuscripts.*
Lansd. MSS.	*Lansdowne Manuscripts.*

Public Record Office:

S.P. Dom.	*State Papers, Domestic, Elizabeth.*
S.P. France	,, ,, *France, Elizabeth.*
S.P. Holl.	,, ,, *Holland, Elizabeth.*
S.P. Ire.	,, ,, *Ireland, Elizabeth.*

Lambeth Palace:

Lambeth MSS.	*Lambeth Palace Library Manuscripts.*

I

CITIZEN VERSUS CROWN

ELIZABETH inherited from her predecessors little more than the withered remnant of a medieval military organization, which had to serve her in wars that were already becoming modern.

Elsewhere in Europe the foundations of the professional armies of the future had been laid. The pikemen of Switzerland had made a great and not very flattering name for themselves plying a lucrative export trade in mercenary warfare. The accent was on 'mercenary', and the contemporary saying 'No cash, no Swiss' had a firm basis in reality. They were succeeded by the Germans as efficient purveyors of military service. By the middle of the sixteenth century Spain had a highly disciplined army financed from the wealth of her colonial possessions. The French had founded *their* standing army a hundred years earlier. The English counterpart, however, was not to appear until a hundred years later. Neither the few score yeomen of the guard with whom Henry VII surrounded himself, nor the small permanent garrisons in key places like Berwick and Dover, nor the Honourable Artillery Company of Henry VIII were even the germ of a standing army.

Why then was England the odd man out? And what in fact were the military rights of the Crown and the duties of the citizen? How was Elizabeth equipped at the beginning of her reign to carry out the tasks of safeguarding her realm and succouring her allies?

The answer to the first of these questions is complex. England was physically separated from the rest of Europe and therefore insulated from military developments there. Her continental neighbours had a much stronger incentive to study what was happening across their land frontiers and to ensure by imitation and experiment that they did not lag behind in the arms race. The economy could not yet support a large permanent army. The natural development of the fyrd, the Anglo-Saxon militia, had been impeded by the establishment of the continental feudal array after the Norman conquest, and by the occasional employment of mercenaries. And perhaps the Anglo-Saxon's antipathy to change, and suspicion of the new-fangled, were material factors even a thousand years ago.

This insulation could work the other way round. The English long-bow was brought to perfection in a period when there was little military contact with the continent, so that when Edward III faced the French at Crécy in 1346 his men carried what was virtually a secret weapon. This made possible a remarkable victory in which 60,000 Frenchmen, caught in a daylong murderous crossfire of arrows to which they had no reply, lost at least 10,000 killed, against English casualties of two knights, an esquire, and perhaps 100 other ranks. But as a general rule her isolation hindered England's military development. In the middle of the sixteenth century she lagged behind the rest of Europe.

The rights of the Crown and the duties of the citizen were not fully defined in the statute book when Elizabeth came to the throne. To understand the constitutional position it is necessary to look briefly at the earlier legislation and practice.

The English version of the feudal army had come and gone. An unstable pyramid of conflicting loyalties erected by William the Conqueror after he had beaten the native militia at Hastings, it never had a firm foundation. Everything was against it. At home, the central authority was constantly threatened by the power which its loose structure left to the landowners, who could readily employ in their private squabbles the forces they owed the Crown. The short period for which it was legally required to serve abroad—forty days in the year—reduced its value as a fighting force outside the country at a time when movement of any kind, and particularly of an army, was painfully slow. The king could invite the barons to serve for a longer period, but they were under no obligation to accept his invitation. If they did, they had to be paid. Moreover, the very nature of the feudal army, an agglomeration of magnates often suspicious of each other, supported by fighting men whose practical loyalty was to their immediate superior rather than to the Crown, ruled out an effective chain of command, without which no army can function efficiently.

Successive kings deliberately undermined the system on which the feudal host was based by encouraging their vassals to pay their dues in cash rather than in military service. The development of a money economy, which this practice of commuting service reflected, enabled the Crown to enter into arrangements with others who contracted to supply a given number of men in case of need, in return for an annual payment. This produced something akin to a commodity market where military obligations were bought and sold by the central authority; and whereas in the basic feudal system the Crown had been dependent on the goodwill of the barons, under the system of 'money fiefs'—these contractual payments for the promise of troops—the vassal was now dependent on the goodwill of the Crown, which could stop payment whenever it pleased. Thus, while the same broad relationship was maintained between the king and those who supplied him with men, the centre of gravity in the matter of control was unobtrusively tipped in favour of the central authority.

The feudal army would in any case have died a natural death. Many of its ideas were alien to an age when war was a hard, efficient, and highly functional tool—the ransom of captives, to bring them back into the fight like pieces restored to a game of chess by the process of queening; the papal ban on the unsporting too democratic cross-bow, with which the merest villein could lay low the worthiest of knights; and so on. Even the system of money fiefs, which might have led to a modern army, was bedevilled by the curious feudal conception of warfare. It was used by the Crown to buy military service from the nobility of other countries as well as from the domestic nobility. This could be awkward. The vassal could sign contracts with two principals who might later wish to make war upon each other. It was therefore stipulated that his services were to be provided according to an agreed order of priority, much as the services of a jockey are retained by a number of employers. The Crown never knew how far it could rely on the troops in which it had invested.

The feudal game of chivalry, which passed for warfare, and in which it was bad form to hate the enemy (except perhaps the infidel), simply could not evolve, even if it had been given the chance, to meet the scientific requirements of the modern age.

Recruitment through money fiefs disappeared in the fifteenth century. The military tenures out of which the feudal army was built were not abolished in law until the seventeenth, but the feudal levy was little more than a name when Elizabeth succeeded Mary Tudor. It is clear enough in retrospect that it had less chance of survival than the least adaptable of the prehistoric monsters—even if intelligent monarchs had not made it their business to kill it.

There remained the older militia, the people's army, service in which had been part of the threefold duty of the Anglo-Saxon freeman—the others being maintenance of bridges and of fortifications. Although overshadowed by the feudal army immediately after the Conquest, it continued in being, ready to be called on as occasion arose. It was given statutory recognition by Henry II in 1181 in the edict known as the Assize of Arms, seven years after it had helped him to defeat his rebellious nobility. This recognition of the county levies was repeated in the statute book at long intervals between 1181 and the middle of the sixteenth century, notably in the Statute of Winchester of 1285, which re-enacted the provisions of the 'ancient assize'.

The earlier legislation was concerned only with the duties of the citizen, but in the fourteenth century parliament began to defend his rights against the Crown. A statute of Edward III, which stemmed from resentment of the dictatorial behaviour of his immediate predecessor, set down that men need provide arms only to the extent required by the earlier laws, and that none would be required to serve outside their county except to meet an invasion.[1] Another act referred to the king's failure to

---

[1] 1 Edward III, st. 2, c. 5. Some constitutional historians (e.g. F. W. Maitland) quote the relevant part of this act as follows: 'and that no man be compelled to go out of his shire, but where necessity requireth, and sudden coming of strange enemies into the realm'. This would mean that a man could be conscripted for service beyond the county boundary not only to meet invasion, but whenever the Crown considered it necessary. In fact, the act says that none will be compelled to leave his shire 'si noun pour cause de necessite de sodeyne venue des estraunges enemys en Roialme', i.e. a man could be taken from his county *only* to meet invasion and not, for example, to help to put down rebellion, even in a neighbouring county. In 1402, 4 Henry IV, c. 13 reaffirmed the earlier legislation. The English translation of this act in *Statutes of the Realm* reads: 'that none shall be constrained to go out of their counties, but only for cause of necessity of sudden coming of strange enemies into the realm'. Foreign service was of course still provided for, but only volunteers or those who owed military service could be asked to go abroad (and then they had to be paid) according to the strict letter of the statute.

provide wages for men raised by commission of array, so that the counties had to foot the bill, and undertook that this would be remedied.[1] Another specifically laid down that men chosen to serve abroad would be paid by the Crown from the time they left their county.[2] Yet another provided that forcing men to sign contracts to serve in the army would be stopped, and that any such contracts that were against all right and reason would be cancelled.[3] The last, however, was two-edged. It observed that these written contracts were out of order. Indeed, they were made to the dishonour of the king, as they cast doubt on his undeniable right to require military service of any man at any time. Nevertheless, in spite of this reservation, Edward III's legislation was a step forward in the citizen's struggle for the reasonable definition of his military duties.

There were three methods of raising troops outside the ordinary militia system—the employment of mercenaries, the enlistment of men by commission of array, and recruitment by indentures.[4] Mercenaries were common in Europe generally in the later middle ages. They formed part of William's victorious army at Hastings, and in England they were one of the answers to the unreliability of the feudal army. Stephen employed them in great numbers against the barons. Later kings continued to use them, especially in their foreign wars, for which the feudal levy was too clumsy and the militia was not intended. They were hated in England (for example, when they were used by John), but their use in limited numbers dragged on into the middle of the sixteenth century. The military experts in Elizabeth's reign were against them, not only on patriotic grounds. Matthew Sutcliffe gives two practical reasons for employing only 'the natural subjects of the realm'. The English soldier is content with less pay than any other, and he can be more easily disciplined than a mercenary, having a family and possessions at home to serve as a guarantee of his good behaviour.[5]

The Crown in practice succeeded in evading most of the restrictions imposed on it in the fourteenth century, taking its stand on the ground of national emergency, or the common law; but the fact remains that in those early days parliament's line

---

[1] 1 Edward III, st. 2, c. 7.   [2] 18 Edward III, st. 2, c. 7.
[3] 1 Edward III, st. 2, c. 15.   [4] See Chapter II.
[5] *The Practice, Proceedings and Lawes of Armes*, 70.

was singularly vigorous. It markedly contrasts with its apparently more docile role in Tudor times, when the only statutory provisions reflect an impairment of the citizen's constitutional exemption from service overseas. The preamble to Edward VI's army statute refers to the fact that the king's majesty's loving subjects had 'according to their bounden duties' sent soldiers overseas, to Scotland, and to other places. Later on the act provides penalties for offences committed by soldiers serving in the king's dominions, on the seas, beyond the seas, and in Scotland.[1]

Elizabeth's reign saw no great military statute, which may suggest that her parliaments, being well aware of the constant threat of invasion, accepted that a tough line on recruitment was needed: that they were content to let matters run on as before, whatever their innermost thoughts about the rights of the citizen. It may also suggest that members were conscious that individually they might land in trouble if they questioned the handling of military policy, and were therefore all the more willing to leave the management of the country's defences in the hands of the queen and the Privy Council. Parliament did, however, take a deep interest in the affairs of the army, and considered four major army bills in the reign. One, 'concerning captains and soldiers', had its first reading in the House of Lords on 10 February 1588, and was sent to the Commons on 22 February. It was given a second reading there by 131 votes to 96. At the committee stage it was compared with the existing legislation, when many imperfections were found in both the existing and the proposed law. It was, nevertheless, given its final reading, although it still raised 'sundry sharp and dangerous points'. These were referred to the Lords by a deputation which expounded the Lower House's opinion about the weaknesses in the bill. The Lords duly answered the objections, but alas, owing to the negligence of the clerk no record was made of their answers.[2] Nor is there any further mention of the bill. In the same year a bill 'for the having of horse armour and weapon' had its third reading in the Lords, but made no progress beyond this point.[3]

A bill for increase of people for the service (in some references

---

[1] 2 & 3 Edward VI, c. 2.
[2] Sir Simonds D'Ewes, *Journals*, 422–3, 448, 452.
[3] Ibid., 425; *Journals of the House of Lords*, ii. 161.

'strength') and defence of the realm, had its first reading in the Commons on 7 December 1597. There was a good deal of argument about it before it went to the Lords, who did not like it and suggested a conference with a 'competent number of chosen members of the lower house'. The Commons agreed and, after some procedural complications, replied to the Lords' objections on 20 January. The bill was then referred to a committee, which took the view that it could not proceed. A completely new bill was needed. A draft was prepared re-enacting the provisions of an act of Henry VII 'against the destruction of towns and houses of husbandry'; and this measure duly reached the statute book.[1]

Fourthly, in 1601 a bill 'concerning musters, soldiers and other things appertaining thereto' had its first reading in the Lords. There was much discussion at the committee stage and so many flaws were found that amendment was considered impracticable. The bill was accordingly redrawn and given the new title 'concerning captains, soldiers, and others in the queen's wars'. It had its third reading in the Lords on 12 December, but in the Commons it failed to get a second reading by 81 votes to 48.[2]

What was the substance of the proposed legislation? This cannot be answered fully, for all four bills were destroyed in the Palace of Westminster fire of 1834. It is possible, however, to guess roughly what parliament was trying to do, from surviving scraps of evidence.

The bill 'for horse armour and weapon' has the same title as the statute of Philip and Mary. It was almost certainly on the lines of a revision of that act, having regard to the newer ideas about arming the forces, and particularly the desirability of requiring those who supplied weapons to increase their contributions. Throughout the reign it had been clear that despite many protestations to the contrary the taxpayer was able to provide arms and equipment at a much higher rate than the statute required.[3] In the first general musters of the reign a voluntary additional contribution was in many cases several times the statutory minimum, and this was also true of later musters. It may well have been felt by parliament that it would

---

[1] H. Townshend, *Historical Collections*, 90, 113, 117; 39 Elizabeth I, c. 1.
[2] H. Townshend, *Historical Collections*, 142; Sir Simonds D'Ewes, *Journals*, 687.
[3] S.P. Dom. 58, no. 13.

be better to increase the statutory contribution rather than to continue to appeal to people to provide more than the law required.

But the other bills? The most interesting is that of 1597, the title of which suggests something much more far-reaching than the alternative that did reach the statute book, which was simply a law to mitigate the evils of the decay of husbandry—as do the strong objections voiced by the Lords to the proposals put up to them by the Commons. But it is idle to speculate.

No draft of the 1588 bill dealing with captains and soldiers has survived. There is, however, a draft of a proposed additional clause requiring commanders of forts, castles, bulwarks, and blockhouses (of which there were nearly a hundred) to make a return of soldiers and others in the queen's pay under their command.[1] This was to be submitted twice a year to the Exchequer Court, with a copy to either the Warden of the Cinque Ports or the Lord Admiral, depending on the location of the fort or castle. A list of weaknesses in the bill also survives.[2] One is that it is too much to expect commanders of castles to make a six-monthly return. Most of the others are related to provisions about the retention and maintenance of arms and equipment. If this list is in fact the speaking brief used by the Commons delegation in their discussion with the Lords, the points raised hardly seem 'sharp and dangerous', although there was of course always a good deal of anxiety about leaving fire-arms in the possession of the citizens in time of peace. It is possible that there were other 'dangerous points' of which no record has survived.

We do know that the 1601 bill was, apart from anything else, a consolidating measure. In a passing reference a speaker in the Commons said: 'there is a bill for the reducing of the two statutes for soldiers into one. It hath lain in the deck[3] this fortnight. If it had been read, it might have been committed.'[4] The two statutes must have been the military statutes of Mary Tudor; but how were they to be revised? One important proposal was that the minimum age for conscription should be raised from 16 to 18; but the draft still required that every man in between

---

[1] Lansd. MSS. 68, no. 58.   [2] Ibid., no. 60.
[3] 'A pile of things laid flat on each other' (*O.E.D.*).
[4] H. Townshend, *Historical Collections*, 308.

18 and 60 should come to the musters and hold himself liable to serve. This was too wide in the view of Sir Walter Raleigh and some other members. One of them said: 'In too much generality there never wanted error: and so in this bill, being too general, namely that all from the age of 18 to 60 must appear at the musters and may be pressed, no exception of any, and therefore no profession exempted. It is not unknown to you that by profession I am a lawyer and therefore unfit to be a professor of the art of war.' The speaker therefore proposed an amendment exempting all lawyers from military service. 'At which the house laughed heartily, it being done for mirth; and divers motions of the like nature were made.' The only other fact to be gleaned from the surviving records of the proceedings of the House is that the justices of the peace were to continue to play a part in the affairs of the army. One member, who had made a violent attack on the justices only a day or two before, had to have his say again. He demanded that the justices should be 'excepted out of the bill'. If they were, he would not only be ready to go (that is, vote for it) but 'to run forth, to have so good a law established'.[1]

The proposals reflected by these scanty references hardly seem to be revolutionary, despite the strong controversy they provoked. The fact that three of the four bills originated in the Lords, who were perhaps less likely to strike a blow for the freedom of the common man than the Lower House, suggests that the legislation may have been designed to improve organization rather than to increase constitutional rights—although the raising of the lower age of conscription to 18 was a step forward on the latter front. Whatever their content, these bills show that parliament did interest itself in the army.[2]

---

[1] H. Townshend, *Historical Collections*, 328–9; Add. MSS. 48041, f. 381.

[2] There were at least four other bills relating to the army which never became law, although they were discussed at length in both Houses of Parliament. They were: 'for training and exercising sundry of the Queen's Majesty's subjects in the use of handguns, arquebuses and calivers' (1571); 'for the true making, proving and marking of calivers' (1572); 'for furniture of armour and weapon' (1580); and 'to reform sundry abuses committed by soldiers and others used in her Majesty's service concerning the wars' (1597). Sir John Smythe, in his book *Instructions, Observations and Orders Military*, written in 1591, considered that new legislation was needed. Having given his views on mustering and enrolling, he says: 'I would wish they should be with great consideration and advice of counsel propounded, considered of, and established by Act of Parliament.'

The constitutional position of the forces was also discussed outside parliament. In 1590 the commissioners of musters in Somersetshire boldly wrote to the secretary of state saying that they had been advised by lawyers that their commission to levy men was invalid, except in time of rebellion or invasion.[1] There is no evidence that they suffered for their temerity, but Sir John Smythe was less fortunate. He appeared at the musters at Colchester in 1596 and made a speech to the effect that parliamentary sanction was needed before troops could be levied for service abroad. He then proclaimed the lord treasurer to be a traitor, and called on the assembled pikemen to follow him—whither it was not quite clear. He was arrested and brought before the Court of Star Chamber. After an inquiry which seems out of all proportion to his offence (and shows that the Privy Council were thoroughly alarmed by the line he had taken) he was committed to the Tower.

He pleaded in his defence that he had been drunk and had spoken without thinking. He had eaten heavily the previous evening, been 'distempered' all night, and had drunk 'white wine and claret wine' to settle his stomach the following morning. But the witnesses, who were no doubt reluctant to align themselves with a man who called the lord treasurer a traitor, drunk or sober, refused to confirm that he was drunk. Even the highly coloured account of the episode given by his servant to three cronies counted against him. The servant, Thomas Wendon, accosted some friends sitting outside their cottage just before sunset on the day in question. 'Had they been at Colchester that day?' They had not. 'Why, then,' said Wendon, 'you shall hear news, for my lord treasurer was this day proclaimed a traitor by my master.' He went on to say that there were so many men slain and lying in heaps about the court at Greenwich that men were over the ankles in blood. 'God save the Queen!' cried one of his audience. 'Nay,' said Wendon, 'I doubt it be too late.' It is perfectly clear that the servant was making the most of the morning's events, and that he would have chosen his words more carefully, had he known they would be used in evidence, to put his master in a sinister light.[2]

A letter from the Tower shows that however drunk Smythe was on that Saturday morning in June, he had thought a great

---

[1] S.P. Dom. 230, no. 26.   [2] Ibid. 259, no. 22.

deal about conscription for service overseas. He told the Council that he had discussed it with lawyers, when he pointed out that it was difficult for the King of Spain to levy troops to use against England, since by the law of Spain only those who came as volunteers at the sound of the drum could be enlisted. The lawyers agreed, adding that in England the Crown had been bound by a similar law. In former times the king could recruit only volunteers for foreign service. The use of the past tense is interesting. It suggests that the lawyers were either being typically careful not to express an opinion about the current position; or that they considered that the earlier limitation on the Crown's rights had lapsed. Smythe also referred to a talk with Sir Roger Manwood, who had said that the foreign expeditions of Edward III and other kings had consisted of volunteers and men hired out by the nobility.[1] A year later he was still claiming that his only fault was that he had been drunk. His 'raging speeches' towards the treasurer were not to be taken seriously; and so far as his attempt to lead the men at the musters was concerned, he was in no case to lead men, but rather goslings.[2]

In their anxiety to measure the feeling of the country on this matter the Council had scores of witnesses examined, and threw into prison anyone who might be remotely of Smythe's presumed frame of mind. One victim was one of the lawyers with whom he had discussed conscription in the first place, who bought his release from the Fleet prison with a letter which was a masterpiece of calculated grovelling, and at the same time an admirable statement of the legal position as the Privy Council wanted it to be. The wretched man told the Council that he most humbly acknowledged himself to be in great fault, and that he was heartily sorry for the same. He then went on to make it clear that he had never suggested that the queen had no right to send men overseas—thereby raising doubts as to what 'great fault' he was apologizing for. Finally, after promising to pray for the long and prosperous health of the Council, he gave a legal opinion which must have been music to their Lordships' ears:

> I do, my most honourable Lords, know it to be most true that the Queen's Majesty both by the common law and statute laws of this realm may lawfully compel and enforce her subjects to serve her beyond the seas in any parts where and wheresoever it shall please

[1] Ibid., f. 65.   [2] *Dom. Cal. 1595–7*, 422.

her Highness, and that the experience of all times hath been so. And I am of opinion that no learned lawyer will or can maintain the contrary for that there is neither common law nor statute law to maintain but that her Majesty may by her Highness' prerogative compel her subjects to serve beyond the seas.[1]

The author of this effusion was immediately released, but Smythe remained a prisoner for two years—a heavy sentence for being no more than drunk and disorderly.

There is no doubt that the Council were sensitive about the constitutional position. In 1579, for example, when issuing orders for general musters, they asked the lords lieutenant to ensure either by announcements in church or in some other way that the people did not get the idea that this was a preliminary to dispatching them on some expedition. There was no intention of sending either those who were to be mustered and trained, or the equipment which the counties had provided, out of the county, unless 'some great and necessary occasion of service of the realm' required it.[2]

The position then, in Elizabeth's reign, was this. The feudal army, which in its prime had been something of a menace at home and never of much use abroad, had virtually ceased to exist. Lip service was paid to it in occasional acts of parliament, but this was no more than a matter of form. The national militia had been reincarnated from time to time during the preceding four hundred years as the Crown's principal instrument to oppose invasion and to control internal disturbances; but it was, nevertheless, statutorily exempt from service overseas, and indeed even from leaving its county of origin to deal with rebellion. On paper it was less mobile than the feudal levy, which could be sent anywhere—within the forty-day limit.

In practice, however, the earlier limitations on the royal prerogative no longer applied. The Crown ignored the statutory restrictions on the movement of troops. Whatever the constitutional niceties, the militia was the only reserve of trained men with some rudimentary idea of the art of war. It might or might not be legal to lead them from their counties to put down rebellion or to send them to the wars overseas; but it had to be done if the State were to survive. Parliament had its own ideas about revising the law, but they never came to anything. The Privy

---

[1] *A.P.C.* xxvi. 4.   [2] Lambeth MSS. 247, pt. i, f. 31b.

Council must have been aware of the true constitutional position, but fought shy of changing it, as it might have brought all those who thought like Sir John Smythe into the open—indeed, the Council's excitement over the Smythe affair shows clearly that they considered that they were skating on thin ice.

Many may have thought as he did, but they were wise enough to keep their thoughts to themselves. It is unlikely, however, that the thinking minority troubled much about the constitutional position. They joined the army of their own free will to win first a fortune and then honour and glory. It was the voiceless majority, for whom the wars held only hardship and misery, that suffered; and they were powerless to alleviate their suffering.

So much for the constitutional framework inside which Elizabeth's forces were recruited. What was required of them in the forty-odd years of her reign?

At her accession, England was technically at war with France. She had had no army on the continent of Europe, however, since Calais had been recaptured by the French in January 1558, ten months before Elizabeth became queen. Hostilities were ended in 1559 by a treaty which gave Calais to the French for the next eight years, after which it was supposed to return to England. The first actual fighting of the reign came when a force invaded Scotland in the spring of 1560. John Knox and his followers had precipitated a civil war in which French intervention might ultimately lead to invasion of England from the north, and this had to be prevented. Lord Grey of Wilton led an army to join the Scottish rebels; and their combined forces besieged Leith until the garrison was starved into submission. Under the peace treaty the French evacuated Scotland and the threat of a pincer attack on England from north and south was for the moment withdrawn.

In October 1562 an expedition was sent to France under Ambrose Dudley, Earl of Warwick, to help the Huguenots and win back Calais. This army and its reinforcements occupied Le Havre until July 1563. It was then compelled to surrender after suffering terrible privations, including a devastating outbreak of plague.

In 1569 the Catholic north of England, which had not yet been fully integrated either politically or in the matter of religion, staged a rebellion aimed at removing the Protestant Elizabeth and replacing her with the Catholic Mary, Queen of Scots. Lord Clinton, and Robert Dudley, Earl of Leicester (the Earl of Warwick's younger brother), led an army from the south to join the forces assembled in York by the President of the Council of the North, the Earl of Sussex; and thanks largely to the incompetence of the rebel leaders, the Earls of Northumberland and Westmorland, order was restored with little difficulty, after a few anxious days. In 1570 a smaller rising, an echo of the rebellion of the previous year, was in its turn put down by a force commanded by Lord Hunsdon. In the same year the Earl of Sussex led into Scotland an expedition partly in support of the anti-French party there and partly to carry out reprisals against the borderers who had helped the rebellious northern earls.

Three hundred volunteers, including the redoubtable Sir Roger Williams (probably the prototype of Shakespeare's Fluellen), went to the Low Countries in 1572 to help the Dutch in their struggle against the Spanish army of occupation. They were supplemented by 1,200 men under Sir Humphrey Gilbert —again a volunteer force. English volunteers continued to serve in the Low Countries until 1585, which was a turning-point in the reign. It saw the final substitution of Spain for France as England's traditional enemy; and it marked the beginning of a period of war in which ever-increasing numbers of Englishmen served in expeditions overseas. The government agreed to send an expeditionary force to the Low Countries and, from this time to the end of the reign and beyond, English troops were committed there.

In 1588 the news that the Spanish Armada had sailed triggered off the whole military machine. The defences of the maritime counties were put in readiness and a vast swarm of men came to cluster round their queen at Tilbury, ostensibly to fight and die in their finest hour. Alas, they were never called upon to fire a shot in anger. What might have been the most glorious campaign in the history of British arms was condemned by fate to be little more than a typically haphazard general muster.

In the following year the government was compelled to send a defensive expeditionary force to France. There was the danger that Philip of Spain would take advantage of the religious troubles there to capture the ports in Normandy and Brittany, which he would then use as a base for a new attack on England. Peregrine Bertie, Lord Willoughby, went to Normandy in September 1589 to support Henry IV against the Catholic league. He fought an exceedingly trying three-months' campaign.

Throughout 1590 the French king asked Elizabeth to help him with another expedition, but she refused to move until one Spanish force entered France from the Low Countries and a second landed in the west. It seemed that the whole French coastline would fall into Spanish hands. Elizabeth was on the point of sending troops to prevent this when Brittany, which had thrown its lot in with Henry, appealed to her. As the French would now share the cost, the queen was all the more ready to help. In June 1591 Sir John Norreys took to Brittany an army consisting half of recruits from England and half of veterans from the Low Countries, which was reinforced from time to time. There was also a force commanded by the Earl of Essex in Normandy from August to September 1591. These expeditions to France, the last of which was withdrawn in 1597, must have numbered close on 20,000 men, of whom perhaps half died on active service.

There were three major combined naval and military expeditions. The first went to Portugal in 1589 under Sir Francis Drake and Sir John Norreys, who were later joined by the Earl of Essex, with the object of harassing Spain and possibly winning back Portugal for Don Antonio, the pretender to the throne which Philip of Spain had won ten years earlier. It landed first at Corunna and, while laying siege to the town, defeated a Spanish force sent against it; but it could not capture the town. Its efforts in Spain reduced the chance of success in Portugal, where in any case the people did not rally to Don Antonio's cause. About 20,000 soldiers were involved and, as before, some of them were seasoned troops from the Low Countries.[1]

A second expedition combining land and sea forces went to Cadiz in 1596 under the command of Essex and Lord Howard, the lord admiral, who had commanded the English fleet in the engagement with the Armada. Of its 6,000 soldiers about a

---

[1] Professor R. B. Wernham has provided a valuable account of this expedition ('Queen Elizabeth and the Portugal Expedition of 1589', *E.H.R.* lxvi (1951), 1–26, 194–218).

third came from the Low Countries. In the following year Spanish preparations for a new attack on England inspired another combined operation, the main purpose of which was to attack the Spanish ships in port. This idea was abandoned, however, when it was learned that the Armada would not sail that year; and instead an unsuccessful attempt was made to intercept the Spanish treasure fleet off the Azores.

From the beginning of the reign there was a garrison in Ireland which was increased from time to time to meet the rebellion of the day. Shane O'Neill's rebellion, which ended with his death in 1567, is reputed to have cost the lives of 3,500 English troops. That led by James Fitzmaurice, and the Desmond War of 1579–81, were more serious. All were dwarfed by Tyrone's rebellion, which broke out in 1595 and lasted until near the end of the reign. It was eventually suppressed by the largest expeditionary force to leave England in Elizabeth's time, commanded unsuccessfully at first by the Earl of Essex, and then with complete success by Lord Mountjoy, the queen's most distinguished general.

The war effort was steadily intensified as the reign progressed. At first there was comparative quiet; a little trouble in Scotland and France, rather more in Ireland, and then of course the domestic rebellions of 1569 and 1570. But after the official armed intervention in the Low Countries in 1585 the curve went rapidly up.

The government's main struggle, however, was not with the French, or the Spaniards, or the rebels in occupied Ireland. It was against its own citizens, whose enthusiasm for military service, never great, diminished in direct proportion to the demands made on them.

II

RECRUITMENT

THE statutory basis of the militia at Elizabeth's accession rested mainly on two acts of her predecessor and one of Edward VI; but all three were concerned with the mechanics of army management rather than with the constitutional aspects of military service.

Edward's act 'for the reformation of captains and soldiers serving in the wars' provided new penalties for desertion, the sale of equipment, the corrupt discharge of soldiers, pay offences, and so on. The act was to be proclaimed monthly in the field, quarterly in garrison; and successful informers were to be rewarded with an amount equal to one month's pay of the man informed against.[1]

Eight months before she died Mary gave her royal assent to two bills dealing with the militia: 'an act for the taking of musters'[2] and 'an act for the having of horse armour and weapon'.[3] The latter repealed the earlier legislation on this subject and set out afresh the provision of warlike equipment to be made by every citizen. The community was divided into ten income groups ranging from men worth five to ten pounds a year at one end of the scale to those worth a thousand pounds and over at the other. The former were required to keep a coat of plated armour, a bill (a simple spear) or a halberd (a combination of spear and axe), a long-bow with a sheaf of arrows, and an iron helmet. The latter had to provide 16 horses, 60 suits of light armour, 40 pikes (long wooden shafts with iron points), 20 bills or halberds, 20 arquebuses (guns fired from a rest), 50 iron helmets, and 30 long-bows with the requisite arrows.

Similar proportionate demands were made on citizens with worldly possessions valued at ten pounds and upwards. It was also laid down as a makeweight, perhaps at the behest of some early puritan in Mary's parliament, that anyone who was not

---

[1] 2 & 3 Edward VI, c. 2. [2] 4 & 5 Philip and Mary, c. 3.
[3] Ibid., c. 2.

already obliged by the act to maintain a horse must do so according to a formula of Henry VIII's time. If his wife's gown were adorned with velvet (except for the trimming) or if she wore a silk petticoat, then he would be assessed as if he were worth a hundred marks a year (just under seventy pounds), and would therefore have to provide one horse with the appropriate equipment. This liability ceased on divorce, however. We may perhaps be forgiven for speculating about the domestic strains that the clause imposed on the not-so-well-off couple in which the female partner had a highly developed dress sense, and the male was rather mean.

Those whose incomes were below the lowest limit specified in the act were also required to do their bit. The commissioners of musters assessed what equipment they could reasonably be expected to furnish and ensured through their inspections that it was actually provided. Rich and poor alike were subject to substantial penalties for failing to comply with the law. A missing bow cost a man a fine of ten shillings every three months, while a missing horse cost ten pounds.

The ultimate control of military affairs in peace and war was firmly in the hands of the queen and Privy Council, with parliament very much in the background. As a rule the whole Council was concerned with major decisions affecting the army, but there was some attempt at specialization. At the beginning of the reign a committee of six was set up to deal generally with 'things appertaining to the war by land and to the defence of the realm'.[1] Policies were given effect either through a royal proclamation, which in practice had virtually the same force as a statute, and was easier to produce, or by directions from the queen and Council. These arrangements worked smoothly and effectively, but they had one curious consequence. By their very efficiency they obscured the government's success, such as it was, in the field of military administration. There were many developments in the reign, but they were never consolidated in a single great military statute which would have left posterity in no doubt about the sum total of what was accomplished.

The county was the administrative unit for military affairs, as it was for general purposes. The Crown's representative there was the key figure in running the militia and in organizing

---

[1] S.P. Dom. 9, no. 3.

troops for foreign service. At the time of the Conquest the sheriffs had been responsible for summoning and commanding the units of the militia when they were required to back up the feudal array; but in the first half of the fourteenth century they became too powerful, and the Crown began to appoint justices —half a dozen or more for each county, there being safety in numbers—for the 'better keeping and maintaining of the peace'. These justices of the peace were gradually given the administrative control of the county, and then two hundred years later they were themselves superseded in their military capacity by the lord lieutenant. The offices of sheriff and justice continued, however, and in Elizabeth's time all three played a part in managing the militia, although the lord lieutenant was by far the dominant figure.

The office of lieutenant was not an original creation of Elizabeth's—like so many other English institutions it developed gradually over a period—but it was enlarged to such an extent during her reign that it may almost be regarded as Elizabethan. Earlier commissions of lieutenancy had been issued as the quickest means of assembling the forces in time of emergency, but as soon as the emergency passed the lieutenancy ceased to exist. The Crown feared that a permanent lieutenant might become too powerful and transfer the balance of power from the central to the local government. But as Elizabeth consolidated her position the lieutenancies tended to become permanent. She could afford to take chances that might have been unwise in her earlier years as queen.

The lord lieutenant had far-reaching powers. His commission gave him the right to call up the men of his county; to array, try them out, and arm each according to his capability; to lead them against the enemies of the Crown; and, still within the county limits, 'to repress, subdue, slay, kill and put to execution of death these enemies by all ways and means'. He was authorized to appoint muster masters to inspect the forces; and a provost marshal to administer martial law in time of rebellion or invasion. Finally, he had at his disposal the services of all the justices of the peace, sheriffs, constables, and other local officials.

The complementary instructions which accompanied the commission of lieutenancy show how the lieutenant was to operate. He had to summon the justices so that they might know of his commission, and undertake to obey his orders. He was at some convenient time to arrange for a muster to be taken, and to ensure that it was properly organized. Before the muster he was to let the people know that they were expected to provide weapons in accordance with the law, so that there would be no room for excuses when the appropriate punishments were meted out to the backsliders.

These powers were the least that were needed to make the lieutenant an effective arm of the Crown in the shires; but they were so wide and potentially dangerous that a number of safeguards were provided. The Crown took the obvious precaution of limiting the lieutenant's sphere of activity to the county, echoing the old provision that the militia was primarily concerned with local defence, and reminding the lieutenant of the geographical limits of his authority. He was empowered to appoint deputies, but they were nominated by the Crown; and the danger that he might become a petty despot was further lessened by the Crown's practice of moving the lieutenant's responsibility from one county to another at intervals.

There were other safeguards. At any given moment several members of the Privy Council were also lords lieutenant. This meant on the one hand that they had first-hand knowledge of the Council's thinking and policy, and on the other that the Council as a whole had a particularly close control of a large proportion of the lieutenants. In 1587, for example, of the sixteen active and eligible members of the Council, eight were also lords lieutenant; and during the latter part of the reign the number who were also members of the Council was seldom less than one-third of its membership. The link between the policy-making body and its executive arm was further strengthened by the fact that several members of the Council held offices connected in varying degree with the defence of the country. Lord Cobham was Warden of the Cinque Ports; Lord Howard, the high admiral; Sir Amyas Paulet, Governor of Jersey; and the Earl of Warwick, master of the ordnance. Finally, almost beneath the surface, were the sheriffs and justices of the peace who still played their part in the affairs of the militia, and were a potential counter-balance to the lieutenant, although Lord Cobham declared that he should not even have to associate with them. They were inferior officials and should have nothing to do with the levy of troops, except in a very minor capacity.

It was wise to minimize the part played by the minor local representatives, for they were guilty of a good deal of sharp practice. 'A justice of the peace is a living creature', said a speaker in the House of Commons in 1601, in a debate which caused a good deal of amusement, 'yet for half a dozen of chickens will dispense with a whole dozen of penal statutes. . . . So unless you offer sacrifices to the idol-justices, of sheep and oxen, they know you not. If a warrant come from the Lords of the Council to levy a hundred men, he will levy two hundred and what with chopping in and choosing out he'll gain a hundred pounds by the bargain.'[1] The Council pointed out to the lords lieutenant that the implementation of all their orders (and indeed almost all the queen's laws) was in the hands of the justice of the peace, who must be kept up to the mark. If any were found guilty of neglecting his duty, or refused to carry out the lieutenant's orders, then he must suffer the normal penalty laid down by the law. The proper punishment of a justice would do more good than the punishment of forty inferior persons.[2]

The performance of the justices came in for a great deal of criticism from both military men and the Council itself, which had a remarkably efficient intelligence system, and must often have surprised the justices with its intimate knowledge of what they were up to. Robert Barret complained that many captains were chosen by favour, friendship, or affection; the fawning flatterer, the audacious prater, the subtle makeshift, was preferred to the silent man and the plain-dealing fellow.[3] Speaking of the choice of captains, Barnaby Rich says that they 'are appointed more for favour than for knowledge, more for friendship than for experience, more for opinion than for desert'.[4] He might have had in mind an episode in Dorset which brought the wrath of the Council on the heads of the justices there. When they appointed two men to serve as captains who had not the slightest experience of war—moreover, one was too old, and the other given to books and study— they were promptly admonished

---

[1] Sir Simonds D'Ewes, *Journals*, 661.   [2] Lambeth MSS. 247, f. 4b.
[3] *The Theorike and Practise of Moderne Warres*, 7.
[4] *A Pathway to Military Practise*, sig. c. 2.

and told to make a better choice. It was very odd, said the Council, that people like these should be selected when there were so many able and experienced men in Dorset.[1] But even with its fine intelligence service the Council could not hope to uncover every shady appointment to the lucrative post of captain, and many unworthy men became officers.

One expert, not strictly a military writer, has left a vivid picture of a typical levy, in which the villain of the piece is clearly the recruiting captain and not the justices, who try, though not very hard, to see that the army gets a fair deal. The captain has come down from London with authority to recruit four soldiers in their parish. The local commissioners of musters, two doddering old justices, assemble five men for him to choose from, two young and able-bodied, and three miserable specimens of humanity. The two fit men and the least impossible of the others are selected, but when the captain is having a drink with the justices the two able-bodied recruits tackle his corporal. The first pleads: 'Be my friend. I'd rather be hanged than serve in the army. Maybe a couple of pounds—?' 'It's a deal', says the corporal. 'Be my friend,' says the other man, 'for my old woman's sake. Maybe forty shillings—?' 'It's a deal', says the corporal. One of the weaklings, a woman's tailor by trade, shows more spirit. He sees what is going on between the corporal and the others, but will have none of it for himself. 'I don't care!' he cries. 'A man can die but once, and no man's too good to serve his prince.'

When the captain returns the corporal takes him aside and explains that he has had *three* pounds from the two fit men for their release. 'Fair enough', replies the captain, and to the great surprise of the justices forthwith dismisses the able-bodied men. When they remonstrate with him he turns fiercely on them. What do they know about choosing soldiers? Size isn't everything. It's the spirit that counts. The first man he had selected— a fragile creature with legs like pins—would be able to load and fire his musket as quick as a pewterer worked his hammer; the second was so thin that the enemy might as well shoot at the edge of a penknife; and when it came to retreat, the third, who was as brave as an angry dove or a great-hearted mouse, would leave the rest of the army standing. 'Oh, give me the spare men,

[1] Harl. MSS. 4943, f. 34b.

and spare me the great ones!' And with that he marches the trio away.[1]

All able-bodied men between the ages of 16 and 60 were liable for service with the militia. They were recruited by county. The queen and Council decided which counties were to supply soldiers, in what numbers, and how they were to be armed. As a rule, the Council, and more rarely the queen, would write to the lord lieutenant, or, in those counties where there was no lieutenant, to the justices of the peace acting as commissioners of musters, requiring them to have so many recruits ready by a certain date. Sometimes, however, soldiers were levied by individuals holding a special commission from the queen. These commissions were less formal than the traditional commissions of array which first appeared in the reign of Edward I, and were used by Charles I, under which an individual was authorized by the sovereign to recruit a given number of men. Recruitment by commission was referred to in the legislation of both Edward VI and Mary Tudor, but with the growing importance of the lord lieutenant in Elizabeth's reign the need for raising troops in this way disappeared, and commissions were rarely used. A volunteer force of 1,500 was, however, recruited in this way in 1586 by six specially-commissioned captains.[2] Sir Matthew Morgan levied 200 musketeers for the siege of Rouen 'by the Queen's orders'.[3] Sir John Norreys and Sir Francis Drake were commissioned by the queen to 'levy, prest, muster, arm, transport, and command' soldiers for the Portugal expedition of 1589. But these are isolated examples. The great majority of Elizabeth's troops were found through the normal machinery of the county authority.

Another method of recruiting had fallen into disuse—the indenture system, under which the sovereign contracted to pay an individual for the provision of soldiers. It is still mentioned in an act of Henry VIII,[4] but it was not used at all by Elizabeth. It would have concentrated too much power in the hands of a single individual. Indentures are, however, frequently mentioned in connexion with recruitment in her time, but they were not contracts to find men. They were simply receipts given to

---

[1] W. Shakespeare, 2 Henry IV, III. ii.   [2] A.P.C. xiv. 55–56.
[3] H.M.C. Salisbury, iv. 183.   [4] 3 Henry VIII, c. 5.

the local authority by those appointed to lead the men to their port of embarkation, which were sent to the Privy Council as evidence that their orders had been carried out.

Although all men between 16 and 60 were liable to serve, special arrangements were made for certain groups. The 'Lords of Parliament' were exempt from having to appear at the musters, as were their servants, who were supposed to get their training as part of their master's retinue. Members of the Privy Council were also excused personal appearance at the musters, as were clergymen and justices of the peace, although they were financially liable like everyone else. Those who did not recognize the established church—the recusants—were considered to be a poor risk as soldiers, and they too had to contribute in cash rather than to serve in person.

For foreign service a distinction was occasionally made between the trained and the untrained men in a county. Although all fit men were supposed to serve in the militia, the idea of a whole nation in arms was a thing of the past. It was impossible to keep the entire male population fully armed and trained. Moreover, the training and exercising of every fit man was costly and unnecessary.[1] The development of the trained bands in Elizabeth's reign was a recognition that there must be specialization for war. The total number eligible for military service was probably between 200,000 and 250,000. The number in the field at any one time, however, was seldom more than a tenth of that figure. There was therefore plenty of room for specialization. The theory of the trained bands was spelled out in 1572 as follows: the queen wanted to

> have perfect knowledge of the numbers, qualities, abilities and sufficiencies of all her subjects from the age of 16 years upward that may be found able to bear armour or to use weapon on horseback or foot; and out of that total and universal number being viewed, mustered, and registered, to have a convenient and sufficient number of the most able to be chosen and collected to be by the reasonable charge of the inhabitants in every shire tried, armed and weaponed, and so consequently taught and trained for to use, handle and exercise their horses, armour, shot and other weapons both on horseback and on foot for the service and defence of her Majesty, her crown and realm, against all attempts, both inward and outward.[2]

[1] Lansd. MSS. 155, f. 340.   [2] Harl. MSS. 6844, f. 16.

In 1575, out of a total of 183,000 able men recorded in the national musters in thirty-seven counties, there were 12,000 selected for special training, and 63,000 equipped but untrained. The balance was made up of pioneers, able men who were neither trained nor provided with weapons; and about 3,000 cavalry.[1] The figures for the county of Suffolk two years earlier were: total number of males between the ages of 16 and 60, 19,000; able men, 9,000; selected for training, 2,600; carpenters, smiths, and labourers, 1,500; and just over 100 cavalry.[2] Clearly, the trained men were the best material for the army and it was for this reason considered unwise to send them out of the country. They were the backbone of national defence, and if possible they were exempted from service abroad.[3]

This had two unfortunate results. It was obviously bad for the forces sent overseas. Secondly, it meant that the trained bands became a refuge for men reluctant to go abroad with the army; and towards the end of the reign it was reported that they were full of worthless creatures trying to escape foreign service. They were intended to be recruited from gentlemen, farmers, and better-class yeomen and labourers, but in fact they were full of servants and other members of the poorer classes who had always been regarded as more suitable for service outside the country.[4] From time to time the urgent needs of the expeditionary forces made it necessary to enlist even the trained men, while on at least one occasion their recruitment was justified on the ground that it would save burdening a county with the provision of new equipment.

The trained men, however, were only a small part of the troops sent abroad in Elizabeth's reign. The great majority were untrained—ordinary volunteers and 'gentlemen volunteers' and men conscripted more or less against their will. The gentlemen volunteers were the smallest group. It is uncertain what was their precise position in the Company organization, but there is little doubt that they served in the hope of eventually becoming captains. Their numbers varied, but in the Low Countries in 1585 allowance was made for four in a company of 150.[5]

---

[1] Lambeth MSS. 247, f. 76.
[2] Harl. MSS. 309, f. 171.
[3] *H.M.C. Salisbury*, iv. 468.
[4] Ibid., xii. 181, 478.
[5] *A.P.C.* xvii. 442.

The ordinary volunteers were men who joined up as privates of their own free will by answering the call of the drum on a recruiting campaign. As might be expected, they made much better soldiers than the conscripts, and captains were advised to release pressed men and fill their places with volunteers whenever possible.

The conscripts were by far the largest group. There were two sorts. On the one hand, honest men taken away from steady employment; and on the other, the unemployed, rogues, and vagabonds who menaced the peace of the countryside and were a good riddance.

The former naturally made the better recruits, and had the efficiency of the army been the only consideration the levies would have been drawn exclusively from them. But the more this was done, the more serious the unemployment problem when the forces were disbanded and the soldiers tried to get back to their civilian jobs. Experience taught that those who returned from the wars little resembled the men who went away. Employers were reluctant to take them back, even if their jobs had not been filled in the meantime. This point was taken by the Privy Council when some men were levied for Ireland. It was known that their employers would be unwilling to have them back when their military service was over; and it was therefore decided to release them and substitute freeholders' sons. They would make excellent soldiers without creating an unemployment problem when they returned.[1]

The recruitment of rogues and vagabonds gave rise to one of the two great military controversies of the age—the other being the bitter argument for and against the use of the long-bow. The military writers naturally advocate the best type of recruit, and scathingly criticize the levying of rogues. 'In London, when they set forth soldiers,' writes Barnaby Rich, 'either they scour their prisons of thieves or their streets of rogues and vagabonds, for he that is bound to find a man will seek such a one as is better lost than found.'[2] Matthew Sutcliffe confirms this assessment. As a rule, the constable is ordered to take up rogues or masterless men, who if they had their deserts would go to the gallows rather than to the wars. If others are selected it is because of some

---

[1] *A.P.C.* xv. 99–100.
[2] *Allarme to England*, sig. K 3b.

grudge; and in any case those with friends or money can get off quite easily.¹

Sir John Smythe also wants a better type of recruit, but for rather different reasons. He is not so much concerned about the dangers of enlisting wastrels, for in his opinion they take good care to be out of the way when a levy is made; but he is strongly critical of some judges who let men off—even cattle thieves who by rights should have been hanged—simply so that they may be available for the forces. This is bad enough in itself, but it also encourages others to take to a life of crime, knowing that if they are brought to justice they may find a safe haven in the army. Smythe vouches for the truth of this from knowledge of affairs in his own County of Essex. If the army continued to be recruited from the dregs of the nation anything might happen. There were plenty of unpleasant precedents:

> I will only make mention of the *bellum servile* that gave the Romans so much to do in the time they flourished most, the Jacquerie of France, and the dangerous rebellion of the peasants of Hungary; and last of all the revolt of the disarmed Moors of Spain, very little more than twenty years past, that cost the lives of 40,000 Spaniards, and continued two years and more. Commonly, the beginnings are very small, and therefore lightly regarded, but once begun, they suddenly grow great, and then they turn all to fire and blood.²

The recruitment of the dregs of society had a long history and, despite its manifest drawbacks, it persisted throughout Elizabeth's reign. It was first seen in her time when prisoners in Newgate were set at liberty to reinforce the troops besieged in Le Havre, a desperate measure to meet a desperate situation;³ but cases where the contents of a prison were emptied into the army were rare. The levy of rogues and vagabonds, however—disreputable men who probably ought in any case to have been in prison—was quite common. They formed part of the first official expedition to the Low Countries in 1585. The Privy Council ordered the recruitment of all able-bodied unemployed in Surrey and Sussex, and, to ensure that the maximum number was roped in, the constables raided fairs and popular meeting places all on the same day. They escorted their catch to Rye, where they were embarked.⁴

[1] *Lawes of Armes*, 62–63.
[2] *H.M.C. Salisbury*, iv. 5.
[3] S.P. Dom. 28, no. 63.
[4] Harl. MSS. 703, f. 41b.

Military recruiting was not the only thing the Crown had in mind in taking up masterless men. Domestic peace was certainly as near Elizabeth's heart as an efficient army, and if she could achieve it at the expense of the troops she was quite prepared to make the sacrifice. The menace of vagrants in the neighbourhood of London was very great. Local authorities stressed the benefits that would accrue on their departure into the forces, especially towards the end of the reign. In 1597 the Council authorized the levy of vagabonds to reinforce the expedition then in Picardy. In and around London there were many who stole for a living, and 700 were rounded up, principally because the country would be well rid of them. About the same time the Council informed the lord mayor that conscription of vagabonds had considerable advantages and asked that 200 should be apprehended and offered the difficult choice, between statutory correction, and service with the forces at Ostend.[1]

Sir John Norreys, a very level-headed soldier whose advice commanded a good deal of respect, assured the queen that the enlistment of rogues reduced the efficiency of the troops. His views seem to have been accepted for, in 1596, instructions to raise a hundred men for Ireland insisted that they must not be rogues, who usually deserted. To encourage a better type to enlist it was made known that the recruits would be well looked after.[2] Two years later the order to exclude vagabonds was repeated, and about the same time the local authorities in Oxfordshire were reprimanded for levying vagrants with an eye to ridding the county of idle people rather than helping the queen's service.[3]

Radnorshire also incurred the Council's displeasure for recruiting men from prisons, but this was more because they were so 'naked and bare' that the queen was driven to extraordinary charges in fitting them out. The bill for their clothing was sent to the county for settlement, however.[4] The Council were coming round to the view that the advantages of recruiting masterless men, substantial though they might be, were outweighed by the disadvantages. But they continued, perhaps against their better judgement, to authorize the levy of rogues and vagabonds. There was in fact one law for the central

---

[1] *A.P.C.* xxvii. 290.   [2] Ibid. xxix. 585.
[3] Ibid. xxxi. 94–95.   [4] Ibid. xxix. 43–44.

government and another for the local authority. In July 1601 the justices of the peace in Surrey and Middlesex were instructed to 'make perfect searches in all alehouses, inns and such places as those loose persons do lodge', and also to set watches where the streets ran into the fields. The men rounded up were inspected by the lord mayor and the most suitable sent to Ostend.[1]

That the balance of advantage was very even is shown by a dialogue between Barnaby Rich's two engaging characters, Captain Skill and Captain Pill. Earlier in his military career Rich had seen only the army point of view, but later on he had to admit that there were two sides to the question. Captain Pill notices a band of townspeople, armed with rusty old bills, dragging someone, as he thinks, to the place of execution. When he asks what offence the fellow has committed he is told that he is simply an idle rogue being pressed for a soldier. He inquires of the constable in charge if his commission entitles him to levy rogues, whereupon that worthy grows very hot and angry. He is perfectly well aware how far his commission extends, and as for these rogues and vagabonds, it is a good riddance to purge the country of them, and keep honest men at home in their place. Pill is afraid to give the constable a piece of his mind, in case he is accused of interfering in the man's duties: so he asks, very politely, whether, if the constable's own town were being attacked, he would be happy to be defended by people like the vagrant he has just enlisted. 'No', replies the constable. 'Very well', says Pill. 'You clearly know what is good for you, yet you refuse to accept that it is good for the country as a whole.'

The argument is not over, however. The constable thinks for a bit; then says that he sees that Pill is on the side of the captains, and that he (Pill) would like to have honest householders enlisted—men that

> are of wealth and ability to live at home, such as your captains might chop and change, and make merchandise of, sometimes by retail, sometimes great (as men use to buy oxen at Smithfield) a whole company bought and sold together, not to him that was of best experience, but to him that would give most money? But God defend that any man of honest reputation should be levied just to be extorted! Besides the exactions of the victuallers they shall be infected with unwholesome and unseasonable provisions, oppressed

[1] Ibid. xxxii. 27–28.

by the provision master, cheated by so many scraping officers that it makes you mad to think of it. Let me tell you therefore that we learned long ago to seek out sleeveless [i.e. useless] men for sleeveless errands. When the wars shall be reformed and reduced to a more honourable course we will endeavour ourselves to find out men of better worth. In the meantime these may serve as befitting the discipline of this age.

In recounting this episode later to Skill, Pill admits that the eloquence of the constable left him speechless. He dearly wanted to continue the argument but simply couldn't think of anything to say. The best he could conjure up was 'Blurt! Master Constable!'[1]—'blurt' being a disparaging noise made with the lips, which the reader must himself supply if Pill's tale is to have its full value.

The clergy were not expected to attend the musters in person or to go on active service, but they did share in the burden of maintaining the national forces. They had their horses and their servants, so it was appropriate for them to equip cavalrymen, who put in an appearance at the musters along with everybody else, and from time to time were called up for active service. Sometimes the church put up money instead of men. In 1585 the Privy Council wanted a thousand horsemen for the Low Countries, and as they felt that they could not reasonably make any further calls on the lay population they asked the bishops to do their bit.[2] The cost of putting a cavalryman in the field was assessed at twenty-five pounds, and the clergy were therefore ordered to raise £25,000 between them.

As a rule they showed great reluctance to help, mainly on the ground that they could not afford it. In 1581 the Bishop of Coventry and Lichfield reported that he had been able to collect only half the sums levied on his diocese, which he considered to be the most stubborn in the whole country. His clergy were most unwilling to further the queen's service, especially if it affected their pockets.[3] As the reign wore on, and the pressure on all sections of the community to contribute to the war effort was intensified, the clergy became more difficult, and the Council more severe in their treatment of the backsliders, who were summoned to London to hear its displeasure. There were, however,

[1] *The Fruites of Long Experience*, 62–63.   [2] S.P. Dom. 183, no. 72.
[3] *Dom. Cal. 1581–90*, 18.

occasional exceptions to the rule of reluctant co-operation. In 1587 the Bishop of Winchester volunteered, on behalf of his diocese, to raise a company of infantry and one of cavalry. The queen was most grateful for the offer, which showed that the Church was alive to the dangers of the time and was not wanting in loyalty; but the bishop's public spirit must have earned him some odium in the other dioceses, for the queen and Council kept reminding them how generous Winchester had been, and hinting that they might with advantage go and do likewise.[1]

None took the hint. Two years later, when the Armada scare was building up and there was real need for a united effort, the Privy Council grumbled to the Archbishop of Canterbury that the clergy in most parts of the country were ignoring their liability to equip light cavalry and show them at the musters, despite the fact that they enjoyed good livings and could well afford to help. Instead of trying to escape the cost of providing men they should rather be setting a good example to the rest of the country. The archbishop was instructed to raise forthwith a force which was to become part of the queen's bodyguard at Tilbury. These instructions were passed on to the bishops in a circular letter in which the archbishop asked for their willing help, partly because of the dangerous international situation (which of course he knew all about as he was a member of the Privy Council); and partly because it would 'stop the mouths of such as do think those temporal blessings which God hath in mercy bestowed upon us to be too much, and therefore spare not in grudging manner to say that themselves are forced to their great charge and danger to fight for us, while we rest quietly at home without providing of any furniture or munition in these public perils'. In the end of the day the archbishop's appeal produced 560 cavalrymen.[2]

When the threat of invasion was renewed in 1599 the defence plan used at the time of the Armada was again adopted. Once more the clergy (who had been finding men and horses regularly for the overseas expeditions) were required to provide cavalry to protect the queen's person. On this occasion they found it more difficult to help. Their temporal blessings were insufficient to enable them to do what was required of them. Recent levies for Ireland had taken away many horses and men

[1] *A.P.C.* xv. 413; xvi. 89.   [2] Lambeth MSS. 2009, ff. 9, 11.

—they had made 'a clean sweepstake' in one diocese—and there had not been time to replace them. The Bishop of Winchester pointed out that it had been easy enough for his predecessor in 1588 to supply horses and men, for he had been in office many years and had had time to amass a reasonable fortune; he himself, however, had held his appointment for only two years, and he was not yet a rich man. Another complaint was that it had been very difficult to find riders for the horses and that when the county authorities had been asked for help it was not forthcoming. The net result of all these difficulties was that the Canterbury contingent was about 130 fewer than in 1588.

The archbishop's own contribution in the emergency was a new prayer directed against the latest Spanish enterprise. He sent it off to Sir Robert Cecil for submission to the queen. Cecil's own reaction was favourable enough (or so he said), but in fact the prayer was not submitted to the queen, who had herself composed two prayers at the time of the Cadiz expedition three years earlier. In a tactful reply to the author, Cecil agreed that the prayer was very proper—and, after all, prayer to God, the giver of all victories, was the country's best anchor; but as the archbishop well knew, the queen did not like this sort of thing to be sprung on her at short notice. In any case, the prayer would not be needed until the Spanish fleet was sighted off the English coast.[1]

No class escaped the liability to man the forces. The recusants, those who refused to attend the services of the reformed church, had also to play their part; thus the government raised troops through the faithful as a token of loyalty, and through the unfaithful as a punishment for their disloyalty. So long as the recusants paid up—on the same lines as the clergy—they were left in peace. The sheriffs and justices of the peace were told that the queen was graciously pleased because of the readiness with which the recusants had provided cavalry to grant them immunity from the pains and penalties to which they were liable, on condition that they continued to pay some reasonable compensation annually.[2] If necessary, sterner measures could be taken against them than against the clergy. The financial position of those who failed to comply with the Council's demands was

---

[1] Lambeth MSS. 2009, f. 102. [2] *Dom. Cal. 1581–90*, 307.

carefully investigated, and if they were able to pay they were summoned before the Council to explain their failure.[1]

Towards the end of the reign many members of the legal profession were invited to make contributions ranging from £10 to £30 for the provision of cavalry, while a number of gentlemen were required to supply horses. An appeal was made to the public spirit of the contributors, and the queen's favour was promised if they gave readily.[2]

There was no point in asking various sections of the community to provide horses for the army if there were none to be had; and throughout the sixteenth century the decline of the horse had caused the government almost as much misgiving as the disappearance of the bow. An act of Henry VII had made horses subject to export control and to an export duty, because so many had been shipped overseas.[3] Henry VIII followed this up with statutory provisions for breeding. Every owner of a park with a perimeter of a mile or more was to keep at least two mares 'of an altitude of thirteen handfuls'; and these were not to be mated with stallions of less than fourteen hands.[4] A further act of Henry VIII provided that stallions under fifteen hands were not to be allowed to run loose in the forests or commons where mares were accustomed to graze. Anyone finding such a stallion in a prohibited place was allowed to keep it for his own.[5] This provided a golden opportunity for those who lived in East Anglia, for there big horses could not be bred 'without danger and peril of the miring, drowning and perishing of the same' in the marshes and fen grounds. Quick-witted people realized that the new law gave them the right to take possession of virtually every horse wandering loose in the fen country, and they reaped a rich harvest under its cover. The act therefore had to be amended to put a stop to this legalized robbery in the marshlands, and the size below which horses must not run loose in the fens reduced to thirteen hands. At the same time, however, the queen issued a proclamation reminding the people of the earlier legislation about the breeding of horses, and this was followed up by others later in the reign. The queen took strong exception to the neglect of the breeding of horses, since it had

---

[1] *A.P.C.* xiv. 87. [2] Ibid. 125.
[3] 11 Henry VII, c. 13. [4] 27 Henry VIII, c. 6.
[5] 32 Henry VIII, c. 13.

serious implications for the safety of her person, the defence of the realm, and the welfare of every citizen.[1]

The composition of the forces in Ireland presented a special difficulty. Should Irishmen be recruited for them? It was dangerous to include too many, for if they outnumbered the English there was no guarantee of their good behaviour. On the other hand, it was worth while enlisting some, if only to prevent their serving with the rebels. This, however, was not why captains tried to fill their companies with Irishmen. They were a good investment, for they were content with even lower wages than the English[2]—despite Matthew Sutcliffe's assertion. In practice, the inclusion of Irishmen must have done more harm than good. One captain, who recommended that their number should be limited to six in a hundred, said that in his own company he had had eight, all of whom ran away, enticing some Englishmen with them. This was quite common, and not only did deserters to the enemy take their equipment, but also what they had learned of English drill and tactics.[3] In 1597 it was reported that in some companies the Irish outnumbered the English by three to one. The Privy Council said that to discharge these men would merely swell the ranks of the rebels and give them the benefit of the superior training of the English troops.[4] It was suggested that they should be drafted to the Netherlands or France and their places taken by levies from England; but the Privy Council finally decided that the Irish element should be allowed to decay through natural processes, and that the consequent gaps should be filled from England.[5]

In the earlier part of the reign there was no machinery for replacing men who had died, deserted, or been invalided out of the army. Companies were therefore almost always below

[1] 8 Elizabeth I, c. 8. Proclamations of 14 July 1565, 3 February 1568, 14 April 1580. Indentures recording cavalry levies provide information about the types of horse generally used in the army. For example, in a levy of 169 cavalry for Ireland in 1601 the horses were mostly 6- or 7-year-olds, although ages ranged from 5 to 10 years. Height ranged from 13 to 17 hands, but as a rule was 14 to 16 hands. The great majority of the horses were 'trotters', a few being recorded as 'trot and amble'. These particulars, together with descriptions of colour and markings (e.g. 'bay, two white blazes on the forehead', 'a fleabitten grey, a white stripe on the nose'), made it possible to identify individual horses with a reasonable degree of accuracy, both on active service and on the rare occasions when they returned to England and their owners. (Exchequer Accounts, Q.R., bundle 65, no. 5 (3).)

[2] *H.M.C. Salisbury*, iv. 567.   [3] *Irish Cal. 1599–1600*, 349.
[4] Ibid. *1596–7*, 450.   [5] Ibid. *1598–9*, 156.

establishment, and could be brought up to strength only when new levies arrived from England. Every new force was depleted as soon as it arrived at its destination overseas, and the Privy Council was left with a false idea of the strength of the troops abroad. This of course applied mainly to Ireland and the Netherlands where there were permanent garrisons, and not so much to the other theatres where the campaigns were relatively short. It was unsatisfactory from the captains' point of view, as well as from the Council's, as it meant that even if they were willing to keep their companies up to strength they could not do so without returning to England to find replacements.

This important question was raised before the Earl of Leicester led the first official expedition to the Netherlands. Sir John Norreys pointed out that the inevitable gaps in the forces could be filled by drawing on the English volunteers who were already in the service of the Dutch. Secretary of State Walsingham agreed that it might be possible to find as many as a thousand men in this way.[1] The captains' views were expressed in a petition which dwelt on the lack of machinery to fill up the companies from time to time and stressed how harmful this was.[2]

In 1594 the Privy Council ruled that the captain should be responsible for the immediate replacement of all who departed from the company, whatever the reason. For the expense of levying, transporting, and equipping a recruit he was allowed a man's pay for a month out of the fines collected for deficiencies in equipment, provided that the recruit was taken on within two months of the departure of his predecessor, and that his arrival was duly certified to the muster master. The captain was also given the uniform allowance of the departed soldier from the beginning of the season—summer or winter—to the day of his departure, to enable him to provide the replacement with arms and equipment. Every effort was made to ensure that the recruit was actually with the colours before these sums were paid.[3]

In Ireland the question of replacements was particularly troublesome, for there it was easy to keep the companies up to strength—so far as the records were concerned—by the simple device of inviting natives or resident English civilians to join the company on the muster day. The practice drew a remonstrance

---

[1] *For. Cal.* xx. 4, 8.   [2] Ibid. xxii. 163.
[3] Cott. MSS., Galba, D IX, ff. 309b–310.

from the Council, which pointed out that, as there had been no replacements from England, either the muster rolls (which showed the companies to be full) were false or large numbers of Irishmen had been enrolled. Henceforth, only men who had been sent from England for the express purpose of serving in the army were to be admitted to the companies.

Demobilization was almost as troublesome as recruitment. The end of a war, as Matthew Sutcliffe pointed out, meant the beginning of beggary and calamity for many a poor soldier.[1] The few domestic campaigns were too short to give rise to serious resettlement problems, but the men coming back from Ireland and the Continent had often been away for long periods. Their old jobs had gone and the government had, in equity, to do something about finding them new employment. This was hard enough, but it was even harder to cope with the very large number of deserters—many of them the worthless characters who had been conscripted in the first place to get them out of the country—whose army service had killed any taste for honest work. Thirdly, the vast company of rogues and vagabonds who escaped military service found that they could strengthen their precarious foothold in society by pretending that they were home from the wars; and the authorities found it almost impossible to separate the sheep from the goats.

Leonard and Thomas Digges held that as soon as a soldier was discharged he should return to his former occupation and not regard it as degrading to follow an honest trade again.[2] This was certainly the government's objective. In 1559 the men freed from military service by the peace with France were already a problem. Local authorities were asked to ensure that they were kept in employment. If they had to make a journey they were to put up only at inns and victualling houses, when the owner of the establishment would be responsible for their good behaviour; and in particular they were forbidden to carry guns on their travels so that the 'notable felonies and burglaries' of recent months might be stopped.[3] At first the returning soldier simply got a pass from the justices of the peace at the

---

[1] *Lawes of Armes*, 298.
[2] *An Arithmeticall Warlike Treatise named Stratioticos*, 82.
[3] S.P. Dom. 13, no. 24.

port where he landed, which gave him protection against the anti-vagrancy legislation;[1] but there was no guarantee that he would find a job when he got home. In 1589 the problem was suddenly aggravated by the return of the expeditions to France and Portugal. A proclamation in August of that year recites that the queen had learned that the soldiers returned from Portugal (many of them, to their credit, volunteers, for which she had been most grateful) were gathering in unlawful assemblies and had even presumed to bring their grievances to Court.[2] These gatherings must stop forthwith and the men return to the counties where they had been levied. The ordinary conscripts should give particulars of their services to the justices of the peace—their captain's name, their pay, and how much they reckoned was still due to them—which information would be forwarded to the Council so that a settlement might be made. Those levied by commission, who still maintained that they were owed something, could also make claims: and if they were substantiated, payment would be made in the counties out of the proceeds of the sale of goods seized on the expedition. The volunteers, however, were to return home at once, taking with them no more than the queen's gratitude, and any profits they had managed to pick up abroad.

Three months later there was another proclamation much stronger in substance and tone. The queen had appointed provost marshals in the counties—and also the Knight Marshal of the Household—to punish by martial law soldiers, and those pretending to be soldiers, who had not returned home. This might well have been done without further warning, but the queen was graciously pleased to give the offenders two more days to get their passes and make for home. Those who did not obey were to be executed by the provost marshals. The passes required the men to cover a minimum of twelve miles a day on the journey home, unless they were incapacitated, in which case the day's march was reduced. They also specified the route the man was to take. If any master refused to re-engage a man he was to be imprisoned and suitably punished. The seriously disabled were to have some financial assistance in the parish where they had been levied. If that parish were too poor, then the neighbouring parishes must help. Finally, if any mayor or

[1] 14 Elizabeth I, c. 5.   [2] Proclamation of 24 August 1589.

justice failed in his duty he was to answer for it before the Court of the Star Chamber.[1]

The provost marshals thus appointed were a mixture of poor law, peace, and military officer, and were quite distinct from those who were part of the army organization. They first appeared in 1570 when the Corporation of London appointed a number of 'marshals' to clear the city streets of rogues, vagrants, and maimed soldiers. 'In function, pay and retinue they were the prototype of the provosts the rest of England was to experience.'[2] Sometimes they were appointed by the government direct, and sometimes through the lord lieutenant—when the appointment was more military than anything else—and in the last decade of the reign they were one of the main instruments of law and order.

When the Earl of Essex left for France in 1591, plans were made to receive back the troops 'if Almighty God shall not dispose otherwise of their lives by sickness or casualty of war'. The port authorities were instructed to list the names and equipment of the men as they landed. They were then to be given enough money and passes to get them home; and if they loitered, they were to be dealt with as ordinary vagrants. When they reached their own parish they were to settle down again with their parents or masters; and if their jobs had gone, they were to be supported by the parish until work could be found for them.[3]

With every year that passed the problem became more acute. New proclamations expressed deep concern at the multitude of soldiers, and men passing themselves off as soldiers, in and around London. A commission, which included justices of the peace from London and Middlesex and the treasurer-at-war, was appointed to examine them and sort out the genuine soldiers from the impostors. Next year the Council arranged for the more detailed examination of discharged men. They were assembled and asked where they had served, under what captain, where they had been levied, what their job had been, if they had been wounded, and whether their wounds prejudiced their chance of earning a living again. Those who were incapacitated were recommended to one of the hospitals in London, able-bodied

---

[1] Proclamation of 13 November 1589.
[2] L. Boynton, 'The Tudor Provost Marshal', *E.H.R.* lxxvii. 443.
[3] *A.P.C.* xxi. 352.

men with satisfactory discharge papers were given a pass to take them home, and all others committed to prison.[1] But try as they might, the government could not stem the tide. Four years later a curfew had to be established, and all public gatherings declared illegal, except those held in church. A second commission was set up, this time including several men with experience of active service who were well qualified to weed out the imposters. Provost marshals were again appointed, and the sheriffs and justices of the peace were ordered to keep watch on the highways; men caught without passes were to be punished by martial law.[2]

In 1597 the proclamations were backed up by act of parliament. All unemployed soldiers and sailors were commanded to settle down 'in service, labour, or other course of life without wandering'. Anyone who did not have a pass from the justice of the peace at the port where he landed—which would give him time to get home, and a period of grace of fourteen days—or who had forged a pass, was liable to execution as a felon, provided he was brought to trial within a year of the offence. The justices of the peace would help the genuine cases to find work, if they could not get a job by their own efforts; and the parish would keep them in the meantime.[3]

The government did its best for the returning soldier, although perhaps that did not amount to very much. His fellow citizens, for whom he had been risking his life and limb, were less grateful. In 1578, long before the problem of demobilized men had reached threatening dimensions, Barnaby Rich wrote of the common soldier:

In the time of wars, they spare not in their country's behalf, to forsake their wife, children, father, mother, brother, sister, to leave their friends, and only betake themselves against their enemies: contented to yield themselves to continual watch, ward, fasting, hunger, thirst, cold, heat, travail, toil, over hills, woods, deserts, wading through rivers, where many sometimes lose their lives by the way, lying in the field, in rain, wind, frost and snow, adventuring against the enemy, the lack of limbs, the loss of life, making their bodies a fence and a bulwark against the shot of the cannon; but the wars being once finished, and that there is no need of them, how be they

---

[1] Proclamations of 28 February and 5 November 1591.
[2] S.P. Dom. 228, no. 23.   [3] 39 Elizabeth I, c. 17.

rewarded, how be they cherished, what account is there made of them, what other thing gain they than slander, misreport, false impositions, hatred and despite![1]

Rich was trying to alert England to the danger of her unpreparedness for war, as others have done since, and he no doubt allowed his pen to run away with him. But there was more than a grain of truth in what he wrote.

[1] *Allarme*, Sig. E. iv. b.

III

THE CHAIN OF COMMAND

MORTAL was never blessed with all the qualities that contemporary writers require in the supreme commander.

According to Leonard and Thomas Digges, he must be religious, temperate, sober, wise, valiant, liberal, courteous, eloquent, of good fame and reputation, and a man of great patience—to start with. He has also to be learned in history and mathematical science. In a year he can glean more from books about the military art than he will from a hundred years' experience in the field—an exaggeration for which Digges, father and son, may perhaps be forgiven, as they make the claim in their textbook designed to simplify the technicalities of war.[1]

Barnaby Rich adds to the catalogue of necessary virtues. The general must be magnanimous, easy to be spoken with, constant in his counsels, quick to make decisions, and able to keep his plans secret.[2] Robert Barret demands that he must be a pattern, light, and lantern to the whole army; but he accepts that it is hard to find one man with all the qualifications, and the army must therefore make do with someone endowed with a reasonable number of them.[3] This is echoed by Sir Philip Sidney: 'let us love him for his small virtues, for a number have none at all'.[4] William Blandy asks that he should not be 'miserably bent to filthy lucre'.[5]

Both Rich and Barret insist that the general must be of noble birth. How else can he win the respect of the men he commands? Matthew Sutcliffe takes a rather more democratic line. It is essential to appoint a first-rate general, but if he is chosen for favour, or kindred, or nobility, he may also be young in years, green in experience, and destitute of merit.[6]

How near did Elizabeth's generals come to this impossible

---

[1] *Stratioticos*, 307–9.   [2] *Pathway*, Sig. E 1.   [3] *Moderne Warres*, 169.
[4] Sir Roger Williams, *A Briefe Discourse of Warre*, 2.
[5] *The Castle of Policy*, f. 19.   [6] *Lawes of Armes*, 35, 46.

specification? Their quality varied greatly, but on the whole she was not well served by her chief commanders. This was partly her own fault, for she appointed them; but perhaps she could not have chosen any better. Her choice was limited to the nobility, partly for the reasons advanced by most of the military writers, partly because only the nobility had experience of command, and partly for domestic political considerations. In a sense the Crown was still living in the past. It had been quite unthinkable that a common man—however great his military genius—should ever be called to command the feudal levy. The king—however incompetent—must be the apex of the military pyramid, and the divine right of the upper classes to rule in the army inevitably continued when the king disappeared from the field.[1] This right persisted until the end of Elizabeth's reign. The Elizabethan general was as much the shadow of the sovereign and a political appointee as he was a military man; and as a rule there was no more than a presumption that he would understand and succeed in military affairs.

Lord Grey of Wilton, who was in command of the expedition to Scotland in 1560, was, in the eyes of the chronicler of the expedition (Sir John Hayward), fully qualified for high office. He was 'valorous in war, and in peace courteous; great both in birth and estate, but greater in courage; in counsel a commander, a soldier in arms'. He was in fact a singular failure. He missed his opportunities, allowed himself to be stampeded into assaulting Leith without adequate preparation, and then blamed others for the disastrous result. Elizabeth had realized that he would have to be nursed when she appointed him, but he turned out far worse than she expected.

The general had occasionally to be a statesman as well. This was true of some of the supreme commanders in the Netherlands, and the lord deputies in Ireland; and as a rule they demonstrated that the qualities of general and statesman do not mix very well. Leicester had one of these dual appointments, and did not make much of a success of it; but it is unlikely that anyone could have done justice to his terms of reference. He had, amongst other

[1] Divine right was assumed in other fields. Matters for consideration in parliament in 1599 included the following: 'That none study the laws, temporal or civil, except he be immediately descended from a nobleman or gentleman, for they are the entries to rule and government, and generation is the chiefest foundation of inclination'. (*H.M.C. Salisbury*, i. 163.)

things, to try to modify the constitution, and to stabilize the currency. Even his military instructions called for a superman. He was commanded by the queen 'to bend his course to make a defensive rather than offensive war', and to do everything in his power to avoid a battle or any other engagement where his forces would be at the slightest disadvantage—a strategic plan that would not have pleased Matthew Sutcliffe: 'he that entereth the enemy's country without purpose to fight and hazard, let him henceforth keep his head warm at home and entertain ladies'.[1]

Both Leicester and Essex sometimes gave their personal affairs priority over the affairs of the army. Essex was brave enough. He was quite prepared to risk his life in the field alongside the private soldier, or challenge the enemy leader to single combat, which does not necessarily make a successful commander. It is, however, difficult to sum him up. He was a brilliant and temperamental amateur. At one time he could be full of good sense and modern ideas;[2] and at another a dismal failure in the field. Had England been put to the test of full-scale invasion he might have become the saviour of the nation; but his immortality was to derive not from the field of battle but from the scaffold.

Willoughby showed some signs of ability in France in 1589, but he had charge only of an auxiliary force and the major strategic and tactical decisions were taken by his allies. He later became Governor of Berwick and the toughness of mind he displayed there suggests that he might have made a great commander had he ever been in charge of a major campaign.

By far the best of Elizabeth's generals was Lord Mountjoy, who was endowed with more of the desirable qualities than any other, and had the advantage of being given the biggest military job of the reign—the pacification of Ireland at the turn of the century. There was no room in his thinking for the inhibiting courtesy of the medieval approach. 'He became so deeply imbued with the principle of surprise and so determined in his pursuit of it that the word might have served as his motto.'[3]

---

[1] *Lawes of Armes*, 148.
[2] See L. W. Henry's admirable study 'The Earl of Essex as Strategist and Military Organiser, 1596–7', *E.H.R.* lxviii. 363–93.
[3] Cyril Falls, *Mountjoy, Elizabethan General*, 11.

The military situation was never desperate enough to compel the supremely selfish majority to put service to the community above their own comfort, safety, or profit. Equally, it could not bring into the open latent military genius. The raising of forces and the appointment of their commander was hand-to-mouth, and there was no opportunity for a military class to develop. The nearest were the few gentlemen who served almost continuously in the various theatres, and who by virtue of their experience and ability came to the notice of the government. They got to the top, or as near to it as men of their station could hope to get, on their merits. They had their reward in occasional commands, for example when the general was absent, or had been recalled to London; and while they milked their companies just as much as their less successful colleagues did, they gave better value for money. They made admirable leaders, and had circumstances demanded they could well have produced a supreme commander of great distinction. Had the Spaniards landed on English soil military success must for the first time have become the sole objective of government policy. The corruption which bedevilled the forces throughout the reign would have been ruthlessly swept away; and the pressure of events would have produced a leader of great stature, whatever his origin. In practice that pressure was avoided. The immortal commander may have been born, but he remained mute and inglorious.

The general's formal commission, which he had from the queen, was very wide, but his powers in the field were more directly controlled by the instructions from the queen or Privy Council, or both, which usually accompanied his formal commission, and were suited to the needs of the moment and the temperament of the general. The queen's contributions were devoted more to the political aspects of the campaign, while the Council tended to concentrate on the practical military points likely to arise. The military writers of the time all have strong views on the authority given to the supreme commander. Matthew Sutcliffe holds that the queen should give him greater or lesser freedom in his commission, depending on her assessment of his ability and the gravity of the emergency. Either he is to be given detailed instructions, or be left quite free to use his own judgement. It is scarcely possible for the queen and Council to foresee every contingency, however, and if the general is to make the most of his opportunities he must not be bridled and bound by his commission. Of course, he must be ready to forget it; he is to be completely trusted and given the freest possible hand.[1]

Barnaby Rich makes the same point. Tie your general's hands with a commission if you like; but then you must give him minute instructions on what to do in every conceivable circumstance. Yet how can those at home with no experience of the wars possibly tell the general what to do and what not to do?[2] This was recognized by the Privy Council. Buckhurst's instructions for the Low Countries were pretty comprehensive, but they nevertheless included the statement that 'it would be very hard or, rather, impossible to give particular direction in all things'; and he was therefore authorized to do anything likely to advance the service.[3] Sir Roger Williams considers the commission of secondary importance. 'It matters not how wide it is, if the holder be not a competent leader; and so it has been ever since the world began.'[4]

The Earl of Warwick's instructions when he was sent to command the English garrison in Le Havre in 1562 were spelled out in great detail. He was adjured to be 'of great foresight and circumspection, have his eyes open, look well about him, watch and be warned, and use all diligence to discover the practices, pretences, crafts and subtleties and warlike practices of his enemies as well by day and by night both within and without the town'—and so on, for twenty-four pages.[5]

Willoughby's commission did not give him the political powers which Leicester enjoyed in the Low Countries; and his instructions even contained a proviso that he was to do nothing without the blessing of his second-in-command.[6] He was highly displeased at this curtailment of power, especially as he was not allowed to appoint his own second-in-command, which he claimed was against all precedent. Nor had he the right to appoint captains. He said bitterly that he was hardly more important than a company clerk, and that he would rather serve as a private than bear a glorious but empty title.[7] When

---

[1] *Lawes of Armes*, 53–54, 56–57.   [2] *Fruites*, 16.
[3] Add. MSS. 40814, f. 431.   [4] *Brief Discourse*, 4.
[5] Cott. MSS. Caligula C V, f. 204.   [6] *For. Cal.* xxi, pt. 3, 414.
[7] Ibid. xxi, pt. 4, 524.

Sir Francis Vere succeeded him in 1589 the power of the supreme commander was still further limited. Vere was given command only of the troops in the field. The governors of the garrison towns of Flushing and Brill had full control of their own forces.¹

The limitation of the general's authority is illustrated by the position of Essex in France. Sir Thomas Heigham was sent out to advise the commander, and more particularly to prevent him from taking foolish risks. If Heigham found any captain tempting him to do something rash, he was to reprimand the offender in the queen's name. In this case the control was rather special. It was not so much that the Council wanted to limit the supreme commander's power as that the queen was anxious to keep her favourite out of trouble.² But the commission given to the same general in 1597 for the amphibious expedition to Spain and the Azores does show that a deliberate attempt was being made to make the commander more directly responsible to the government. It was accompanied by lengthy instructions about the movement of the fleet and the control of the forces on shore.³

On this occasion, too, the council of war, which had always been accustomed to advise the general, was put on a more formal basis. The Privy Council appointed the vice-admiral, the lieutenant of the infantry, the high marshal, the master of the ordnance, and the sergeant-major-general to act as a council to guide the commander. If they could not come to a unanimous decision on any point, the general was then allowed to use his own judgement, but he had to have the support of at least three members of the Council; and so that the Privy Council might be satisfied that their instructions had been carried out, minutes were to be made of all the Council of War's deliberations, and forwarded to London.⁴

The Crown also curtailed the leader's powers in other respects. His right to award knighthoods, a privilege which had its origin in times when the sovereign had been his own commander-in-chief, was progressively diminished. Leicester was warned to go slow in making knights, but he paid no attention and dubbed a batch of fourteen on a single day.⁵ The queen remembered this when Willoughby was being briefed for his expedition to

---

[1] F. Markham, *Epistles of War*, 144. [2] S.P. France, xxvi, f. 290.
[3] *Dom. Cal. 1595-7*, 434, 439-41. [4] Ibid. 434.
[5] Add. MSS. 48014, f. 163.

France in 1589. He was informed in a letter signed jointly by the lord treasurer and the secretary of state that, while his commission had the usual clause allowing him to honour deserving men with knighthoods, he must exercise the greatest discretion in making awards. It was the queen's express wish that none should be called to the degree of knighthood unless he had ample private means, or had given some extraordinary proof of bravery in action.[1] This was later emphasized in instructions to Lord Burgh, who was told to knight only those whose social position and income were satisfactory, or who had done something outstanding in the field.[2] In 1599 Essex was authorized to confer the title on the same conditions,[3] but at the end of the reign the general virtually lost the privilege. Mountjoy was ordered to refer all his proposed awards to the Privy Council in England for their approval.[4]

The ultimate control of the troops in time of battle belonged of course to the general. It was up to him to issue the orders to attack or withdraw, and for this purpose he must always have messengers by his side. Opinions differed as to where he should station himself, and whether or not he should be mounted. Should he be in the heart of the fight, near one of the ensigns, or should he be outside the main struggle on some point of vantage? Thomas Digges preferred that he should be mounted on a nag so that he could move quickly from one part of the battle to another and thus get a better picture of the whole.

Second-in-command was the high marshal. Apart from understudying the general, he had two main functions: the administration of justice, and the management of the camp. He had to ensure that the laws laid down by the general were known to all the troops, and that they were duly obeyed. He himself investigated the more serious breaches of discipline, in particular offences that carried the death penalty. He was generally responsible for the camp, having to select the site, arrange the disposition of the forces within it, and see that the watch by night and the ward by day were properly kept. He gave the order to strike camp when he was satisfied that it was safe to do so; and he controlled those officers whose functions were of

---

[1] *H.M.C. Ancaster*, 288.   [2] *Carew Cal. 1589–1600*, 295.
[3] R. Bagwell, *Ireland under the Tudors*, iii. 281.
[4] *Irish Cal. 1599–1600*, 446.

importance to camp organization—the trench-master, for example, whose duty it was to provide any necessary fortifications.[1]

In both his main spheres of activity his direct and most important subordinate was the provost marshal, who on the one hand investigated the less serious breaches of discipline, and looked after the executive side of disciplinary control; and on the other had management functions in the camp, some of which were indirectly related to the maintenance of good order. He imprisoned the convicted—not an easy job when the army was on the march—and hanged the condemned. He was therefore supposed to be well versed in military law. In his other capacity he acted as liaison officer with the victuallers supplying the forces, as there was always the danger that the greed of the suppliers and the attempts of the soldiers to get something for nothing would lead to trouble. He fixed food prices at a level which the men could afford to pay and yet was reasonably attractive to the victuallers. He had also to ensure that the latter did not come in for any rough handling from the troops that would scare them away. This was reckoned to be a particularly important part of the job. Finally, he was responsible for keeping the camp clean, which was very important at a time when it was almost impossible to stop an epidemic once it had started.

The office of provost marshal had existed long before Elizabeth's time, and indeed there must always have been someone whose duty it was to dispose of malefactors in the army; but like the office of lord lieutenant, with which it was closely associated, it developed considerably during the reign. The provost marshal, on active service both at home and abroad, was concerned primarily with the administration of military law, although this was sometimes erroneously described as martial law; but in England his activities 'impinged on soldiers and civilians alike'.[2] This did not mean, however, that the army provost marshal automatically had control over civilians. There were, in fact, essentially two sorts of provost. First, the army officer whose normal responsibility for the administration of military law might, if circumstances warranted it, be extended to martial law, and thus give him the right to arrest and punish civilians; for example, the wholesale hanging of civilians after

[1] Harl. MSS. 168, f. 119b.   [2] L. Boynton, art. cit.

the rebellion of 1569 was carried out by the provost marshal. Secondly, the purely peace officer, who appeared more and more frequently towards the end of the reign and whose job it was primarily to control the ever-increasing numbers of unemployed. Even these provosts had a slightly military flavour, partly because they were often associated with the lord lieutenant, who was the military commander of the county, and partly because the people they were appointed to control were either discharged soldiers or men passing themselves off as ex-servicemen. But their function was essentially civilian.

There was usually a general or lieutenant general of the infantry, with a status just below that of the high marshal; and if there were cavalry in the army, there would be a general of the horse, with comparable status.

The master of the ordnance had one of the most difficult and responsible jobs. On the one hand he had to manage all the ordnance stores, which was a big enough task in itself; and he also had to direct the artillery in battle. His men looked after not only the heavy guns, but also the stocks of calivers, muskets, and other weapons, and a wide range of ancillary equipment. He had to have technical skill to train and direct the gunners, and this could be acquired only by experience. The science of ballistics had not yet made much progress—although there were of course the inevitable textbooks. On the administrative side he was responsible for the issue of stores to the troops at large, which was carried out through the captains. He had his own company to guard the artillery train, and his own pioneers—the army service corps—to clear the way and entrench that part of the camp where the artillery was stationed. He also had charge of the armourers, smiths, carpenters, and wheelwrights, specialists who were becoming steadily more important as artillery developed. In action he had to place the guns and direct their fire, once the general had decided what part the artillery was to play. He had a free hand in managing his men, so long as he kept the general informed what his 'orders and policies' were.

There were a number of less important officers, including the quarter-master (sometimes known as the harbinger, at the beginning of the reign), the trench-master, the forage-master, the scout-master, and the carriage-master. The master of the victuals, the forage-master, and carriage-master were allowed to call on the services of the cavalry when they were in camp, but in action the sole command of the cavalry was naturally vested in the general of the horse. In the routine of camp life the trench-master took his orders from the high marshal, who was, responsible for the construction of the camp, but in action he was under the direct orders of the master of the ordnance. The treasurer-at-war was in rather a special position. He was a non-combatant, but was, nevertheless, usually a member of the council of war. The importance of his function gave considerable weight to his contribution to the Council's deliberations.

In the middle of the sixteenth century there was a vacuum between the higher command and the sum total of the companies comprising the rank and file. In technical language, the chain of command, on which the efficiency of an army depends, was weak. Command in the feudal levy had been exercised through the obligations which one stratum owed to the next. With the disappearance of the feudal links, the army became simply a collection of companies; and it was more difficult to convey orders and generally manage the forces. The general could not give his orders personally to each private; nor could he ensure by personal supervision that they were carried out. The gap between the higher command and the captains had to be filled somehow. The first step was the creation of the sergeant-major, sergeant-general, or sergeant-major-major—a variety of combinations was used. This officer was one of the public officers of the army—that is to say, his authority spread over the whole force. He had to have 'the most exquisite knowledge' of military affairs, especially the mechanics of putting the army into marching and battle formations.[1] To assist him in instructing the captains about the part their individual companies were required to play in the general arrangements, he had the services of four corporals of the field. They too had to be men of great experience, and had a status above captain.[2] When the army was drawn up in the traditional formation of 'vaward, battle, and rearward', one corporal of the field was assigned to each of the three elements, and the fourth was spare. The status of the sergeant-major-general was unusual. On one occasion he is

[1] B. Rich, *Pathway*, Sig. F i.   [2] Harl. MSS. 847, f. 54.

assigned the command of the army in the absence of the general and the marshal, although at the same time it is provided that for the purposes of precedence 'he is set down after divers officers of the army and divers colonels'. But it is again emphasized that he was a public officer, which the colonel, who was responsible for his regiment, was not.[1] The real measure of status is remuneration, and by this test the sergeant-major was well ahead of the colonel at the end of the reign. In 1588 he had only ten shillings a day, whereas the colonels had a pound if they were noblemen, and 12s. 4d. if they were not. In Essex's army in Ireland in 1598, however, the position was reversed. The sergeant-major had a pound a day, and the twenty colonels only ten shillings. The corporals of the field had 6s. 8d., compared with the captain's 4s., but the latter amount was increased at this time by an allowance of six dead pays, equal to 4s. a day.[2]

The creation of the sergeant-major gave the general a much better control over the rank and file; but it was not enough. As warfare became more complex so it was more necessary to keep a tight rein on the companies if they were to be used to best advantage. The sergeant-major and his corporals of the field helped, but they did not completely fill the gap between the apex and the base of the pyramid. They could no doubt carry out their primary function of 'ordering' the army in accordance with the wishes of the higher command, but that did not achieve the second objective—supervision of the execution of orders. The four corporals of the field might be able to transmit by word of mouth instructions for the day's march; but they could not be responsible for the actions of perhaps forty separate companies, simply because they could not be everywhere at the same time.

There was a ready-made solution; and this was adopted. Continental armies had for some time been organized on the basis of the regiment. Groups of companies were joined together in an easily managed microcosm of the whole army, with a colonel at their head. Regimental organization seems to have been assimilated unobtrusively about the middle of Elizabeth's reign. Although there are virtually no references to it before about 1580, the military writers after that year take it for granted. This may be surprising. It might have been expected

[1] Add. MSS. 48162, f. 316; Harl. MSS. 168, f. 120.
[2] F. Grose, *Military Antiquities*, i. 289.

that a major change in organization would have received as much public notice as the struggle for survival between the bow and the musket; but it was accepted by most writers as an accomplished fact.

One of the rare attempts to evaluate the new organization is made by Sir John Smythe, who grumbles at the size of the English regiment, largely because a small regiment sub-divided into small companies needs a very large number of officers. He bases his argument on the fact that the continental regiment had about 3,000 men, with companies of about 300; and suggests that anything smaller must reduce the effectiveness of the chain of command. The Essex regiment at Tilbury in 1588 had 4,000 men divided into companies of about 500, but there was pressure from captains returned from the Low Countries—who were, in Smythe's view, 'more hungry after charge, spoil and gain, than skilful to do any great service'—to make the companies much smaller, so that they would all have a command, and the perquisites that went with it.

Smythe is honest enough to set out the arguments in favour of the smaller regiment—it is more easily commanded, quartered, and guarded; and when the army is to be formed into the three large groups of 'vaward, battle, and rearward' it can be more readily done from a large number of small units. He further weakens his case by admitting that the continental regiment has been reduced, first from 5,000 to 4,000, and finally to 3,000, showing that experience suggested the smaller regiment was the more efficient.[1] Ralph Lane, who had served as muster-master, and was therefore an expert witness, considered that the 'regiment or colonelship' should not exceed 1,400 men. The companies should be about 150 to 200 strong, so that there would never be more than seven in a regiment.[2] But whatever the arguments for and against, the English regiment settled down to round about 1,000 men.

The regiment proper appeared about 1572. Forces had been called regiments long before this, but then the word was simply a synonym for army. Both the invasion force which went to Scotland in 1560 and the army sent to suppress the rebellion in the North in 1569 had their sergeant-major-general and four

[1] *Certain Discourses concerning the Formes and Effects of Divers Sorts of Weapons* ff. 6–9.   [2] Lansd. MSS. 24, no. 30.

corporals of the field, but the colonel had not yet made his appearance. According to Sir Roger Williams, the volunteers who went to the Low Countries in 1572 were the first 'regiment' of Englishmen to serve against the King of Spain; and although he may possibly have been using the word in the sense of 'force' rather than in its newer technical meaning, it did in fact have ten companies commanded by a colonel.[1] For Willoughby's expedition to France in 1589 the men were divided into regiments, each nominally of 1,000, with a colonel at its head, and each recruited from a different county. Two of the colonels were the general and the marshal and all four had their own companies—a sign that the new organization was not yet fully-fledged. The sergeant-major-general survived in this army, and indeed beyond the end of the reign.[2] He ranked above the ordinary colonels, but his status must have been impaired a little by the mere presence of colonels in the organization. Before, he had been dealing with captains: now, his immediate contact was with men who were ranked far above a captain. In the expedition to Portugal in the same year there were fourteen regiments whose colonels acted as a council of war. On one occasion nine of them proceeded against the enemy: the vanguard, the battle (the middle formation), and the rearguard had three each—an interesting conjunction of the classical, medieval, and modern forms of organization.[3]

The force carried to Cadiz had eight regiments of 750 to 1,000 men, with six or seven companies in each.[4] Essex drew up a code for his colonels on this occasion. They had to be in the vanguard in attack, and the rearguard in retreat; in camp to have their headquarters in the midst of their men; and once a week to preside at the provost marshal's court for their regiment. Each had a lieutenant to take over should the need arise.[5] By the end of the century the regiment was firmly established as a tactical unit. Robert Barret says, in 1598, that it should be drawn up with the colonel dismounted at the right-hand side of the front rank. If it is assigned an individual task the colonel is to lead it with the full authority of the general.[6]

---

[1] *The Actions of the Lowe Countries*, 69.   [2] Cott. MSS., Galba E VI, f. 413.
[3] A. Wingfield, *A True Coppie of a Discourse*, 492; 502–3.
[4] *Dom. Cal. 1595–7*, 222.   [5] Harl. MSS. 703, f. 25.
[6] *Moderne Warres*, 86–87.

The basic unit was the company. An infantry company varied in establishment from 100 to 200 men, with a tendency to become smaller as time went on. Squadrons of cavalry ranged from 60 to 100 men. A paper prepared for the Privy Council's consideration in 1589 recommended that infantry companies should have 150 men and cavalry 100, excluding 'colonels and, men of note'.[1] In practice, the establishment, especially of cavalry squadrons, was usually smaller; and the number physically present at any given moment was smaller again. It was of course in the captain's interest to have on paper the biggest possible company, and to keep it physically as small as he dared, so that he might pocket the pay of the missing ranks. In 1585, for example, it was reported from the Low Countries that although the companies there were nominally 150 strong each captain had on average no more than eighty men.[2]

The captain was the link between the higher command and the company. He

stood between the Queen's officials and his men, in some respects the exploiter of their labour, in others their representative and defender. He was to a certain extent responsible for arming, clothing and feeding them, all of which were expenses covered by their pay; and if provision was made by royal officials—which was not necessarily the case—the sums expended were charged against the company and settled between the treasurer-at-war and the captain when payment was made. He was also responsible, so far as the supply of men allowed, for maintaining his company at its proper strength: his clerk kept muster rolls to record changes in numbers and accounts to show how the company stood with the treasurer.[3]

The captains were thus in a powerful position and could swindle with comparative ease and impunity both the government and their men. In the Low Countries they were accused, no doubt with good reason, of dismissing their men (who were, of course, only too happy to go), so that they could pocket their pay; of taking the arms of the men thus discharged and selling them to new recruits; and of enrolling in their companies Dutch freebooters whose activities further enriched them.[4] This sort of thing continued and in 1592 the Council made a determined

---

[1] Lansd. MSS. 62, no. 8. [2] *For. Cal. 1585–6*, 246.
[3] Sir J. E. Neale, 'Elizabeth and the Netherlands, 1586–7', *E.H.R.* xlv. (1930), 373–96. [4] S.P. Holl. xxx, f. 189.

effort to stop it. Allegations that the captains had been selling or pawning uniforms were investigated, and the regulations for distributing uniform were tightened up. At the same time, an attack was made on the practice of keeping companies under establishment and drawing pay for a full company. If the strength of a company of 150 infantry fell below 110, or a company of 100 cavalry below 60, the captain was to be dismissed. Until the Council had appointed a successor, and he had had the chance of building the company up to its proper level, it was to be paid in proportion to its actual strength. If the captain was not to blame for gaps in the company's ranks—if they had been brought about by losses in battle, or the ravages of disease—he was not to be dismissed, but the facts were to be reported to the Privy Council for further consideration.[1]

The captains' crimes in Ireland, which included enticing men from other companies to fill up the gaps in their own on muster days, hiring 'churls' for the same purpose, and being frequently absent from their duties, gave rise to the suggestion that each should be compelled to keep a full record of the activities of his company. This was to be sent each month to the chief of the province, who was in turn to send copies to the lord deputy and the Privy Council; by this means the queen would have a monthly statement how every captain had been employed. The arrangements would at least have helped to control absenteeism; but it seems that they were not acted on.[2]

Sir John Smythe makes a sweeping indictment of the English captains' behaviour. As soon as they learn that money has arrived for the army's pay day, they send their men off on dangerous and hopeless missions, knowing that for every man killed there will be an extra 'dead pay' for their own pocket. They do not hesitate to order their men to assault a fortress before the walls are sufficiently breached, while they themselves remain in safety, 'feasting, banquetting and carousing with their dames'. So that they may 'hit two marks at one shot' they will order subordinates whom they hate to lead these desperate enterprises, knowing that there is a good chance that they will not return. They allow their men to go badly armed, in tattered uniforms, bare-legged and bare-footed, like rogues. They commandeer their rations for their own use, leaving the men to

[1] Cott. MSS., Galba D IX, ff. 294–5.   [2] *Irish Cal. 1599–1600*, 277–8.

forage for themselves. In fact, they are more like merchants than military men, selling their companies when it suits them, or letting them for a yearly rent to their lieutenant, as if the men were flocks of milch cows. It would take a huge volume to record all their malpractice. Smythe is never guilty of under-statement, but his criticisms are fully supported by all the evidence.[1]

The Privy Council reserved the right to appoint captains, which was usually done through the agency of the commissioners of musters, although on one occasion Willoughby claimed that it was the general's prerogative. The Council did not always exercise their rights, however, and in practice it was easier for appointments to be made by the general when the forces were overseas. The first official expedition to the Low Countries turned up without any captains in the pioneer companies, and the omission had to be remedied locally. In 1588 there was a move to promote men on the spot without first obtaining the approval of the Council in England. The Governor of Flushing, for example, claimed that six of the companies in the garrison were at his gift. On this occasion Willoughby said that neither the general nor the commanders of the garrisons should have the right to make captains, which shows that his views had radically changed. The proper procedure, he maintained, was for the general and his advisers to send recommendations to the Council, the final choice being left to the queen.[2]

In 1590 the Council issued specific instructions about promotion. In future, when a captaincy fell vacant, they were to be informed immediately. The local commander was to send in the name of the lieutenant, and was not to appoint a successor until he had been approved by the Council.[3] Presumably this meant that in general the Council would promote the lieutenant unless there was something against him. In Ireland, however, the appointment of captains was left to the commander-in-chief.[4] At one stage Mountjoy was accused of appointing captains for his own gain rather than for the good of the service. In his defence he said that he had appointed only men of known ability and that some of them in any case had the approval of the Council.[5] The appointment by the Council of captains in the forces overseas meant that the best men were not always chosen.

[1] *Certain Discourses*, Sig. 3 i–iii.   [2] *For. Cal.* xxii. 9, 30.
[3] S.P. Holl. xxxii, f. 260.   [4] *Irish Cal. 1596–7*, 59.   [5] *Irish Cal. 1600*, 503.

The Privy Council did not know the relative merits of the various candidates, and sometimes made the mistake of appointing inexperienced men.[1]

The subordinate company officers were selected by the captain. In the normal company of 150 infantry there were a lieutenant, an ensign-bearer, two sergeants, two drummers, a preacher, a cannoneer, a surgeon, and about six corporals.

The lieutenant was the captain's understudy in everything. If the captain fell in battle, or was absent from the army, the lieutenant took over all his duties. He occasionally handled the administrative side of the company's affairs, for example the collection of the company's pay; but this was exceptional, as no captain could afford to let anyone see just what happened to money drawn for wages. The lieutenant had to be generous with advice to the captain—but only when consulted; and he must be careful not to assume too great authority in the presence of the captain. He also had to act as friendly mediator between captain and men in disputes about pay and kindred matters.

The ensign-bearer had much in common with the second lieutenant of a later age. He had to be of gentle birth, for if both captain and lieutenant fell the command of the company devolved on him. He carried the colours and, in time of action, was the inspiration of his comrades. The ensign pole was fitted with a metal point, which could be used for thrusting, if the enemy ever got through the group of billmen told off to defend the colours, but it was to be used in this way only as a last resort. On the march he carried the ensign pole upright, and was on no account to make flourishes with it as the ensign-bearers of London did on midsummer night—that was a mockery of all true discipline. He had also to be careful not to let the ensign trail on the ground, for example, when he was marching downhill with the pole sloping on his shoulder. When passing the general he must incline the pole forward, and bow his head.[2] The ensign-bearer's post was recognized to be of great importance. This was acknowledged in the regulations. Cowardice in any man carried the death penalty, but cowardice in the ensign-bearer was singled out for special mention.[3]

[1] Ibid. *1596–7*, 59.
[2] Sir John Smythe, *Instructions, Observations, and Orders Mylitarie*, 129–30.
[3] Add. MSS. 48162.

The sergeants were responsible for drilling the men and for supervising the issue of rations and equipment. They had to see that the company marched properly, and for this purpose the elder of the two stationed himself on the right of the column abreast the ensign to keep an eye on the front half of the company. The younger was at the rear on the left hand side to watch the other half. The sergeants also fetched the watchword from the sergeant-major of the regiment and conveyed it to the captain and the corporal of the watch. Their place in the organization of the army was broadly similar to that of the company sergeant in the modern army.

The corporals had about twenty men in their sections. They had to see that their men were adequately equipped with powder, match, bullets, and other equipment, and that they kept their arms in good order. They had to ensure that their men knew and obeyed the regulations, and in particular that they did not spend their time gambling. According to one authority, the corporal had to discourage his men from eating and drinking to excess. If they dissipated all their pay in riotous living there would be nothing left to buy the equipment they needed for battle. The corporal also saw that the watch was properly kept. As he was one degree in dignity above the private, so must he surmount his inferiors in wit, discretion, and diligence. When he was alone with his section he commanded it with the authority of the captain.[1]

The two drummers were employed to beat time on the march —which they did in turns—make inquiries about prisoners, summon the company to assembly, and sound commands on the field of battle. They were supposed to be privileged in their dealings with the enemy, but they did not always get their due. One who was sent to ask for a parley before the battering of a town on the Portugal expedition was shot at from the ramparts. The man who had fired the shot was immediately hanged from the wall. When the parley was eventually held the commander of the garrison apologized for the incident and said that he wanted to stick to the rules of war.[2]

Two members of the company, the preacher and the cannoneer, are always grouped together—perhaps because they were both odd man out. In Ireland, a special deduction was made from

[1] R. Barret, *Moderne Warres*, 16–17.   [2] A. Wingfield, *Discourse*, 488.

the company's pay for them. The cannoneers duly received their pay, but according to the commissary for musters there was not a single preacher in the forces in Munster.[1] At this time it was decided that preachers and cannoneers should not be included in the ordinary pay sheet, but should depend on dead pays for their living.[2] In 1600 there were supposed to be fourteen preachers attached to the troops in Ireland—considerably fewer than one a company. Of these, three were absent in England and the rest were said to be useless. One was drawing a salary as Dean of Cork, and it was reported that he was never with the forces. Another was the Dean of Christ Church in Dublin, who never stirred from the city.[3] It was now laid down that the cannoneers should be dispensed with as there was little need for their services in Ireland.[4]

The cannoneer was the first important specialist in the modern army. Cyprian Lucar's compilation on the 'properties, office, and duty' of a gunner lays down a difficult specification. The cannoneer, like the general, must be something of a superman—'sober, wakeful, lusty, hardy, patient, prudent, and quick-spirited'. He must have a good eye for country to enable him to plant his guns where they will be well protected and inflict most damage on the enemy; and he must also be skilled in arithmetic and geometry, eat in moderation, and not be a great or sluggish sleeper.[5]

As a rule the preacher was attached to a single company, but occasionally he held a more important appointment. In the 1589 expedition to France each regiment had a preacher drawn from the same county as the troops. The Archbishop of Canterbury was asked to find some learned and discreet person for the London regiment, who was to be paid a pound a day by the clergy of the diocese. On this occasion the general's instructions referred at length to the importance of caring for the spiritual needs of the men. Prayers were to be said twice daily, unless the needs of the service made it impossible.

What of the private soldier, on whose back everyone else in the army marched and prospered? The military writers provided a specification which was no easier to comply with than the

---

[1] *Irish Cal. 1599–1600*, 383.
[2] Ibid. 397.
[3] S.P. Ireland, 207, pt. i, f. 459.
[4] *Irish Cal. 1600*, 275.
[5] Printed in *Journal of the Royal Artillery*, lxxi. 211.

general's, or the cannoneer's. He must have 'the eyes, quick, lively and piercing; the head and countenance upright; the breast broad and strong; the shoulders large; the arms long; the fingers strong and sinewy; the belly thin; the ribs large; the thigh big; the leg full; and the foot lean'.[1] In practice the army used a much rougher measure. If the private were tall and strong, he should be a pikeman; if he were small and nimble, he was given a gun. If he were of medium build he carried a black bill, or a halberd.

There was genuine sympathy for the private among the Privy Council, although they found that there was little they could do to ameliorate his position. Secretary of State Robert Cecil made a speech in the House of Commons in 1601 which seems to come from the heart. The House was debating the continuation of the military pensions act, and, in supporting the measure, Cecil said: 'War is a curse to all people, and especially the poor creatures that come from the wars poor, friendless, and unhappy. I am glad you are resolved that this statute shall be kept alive, whereby in some measure those poor maimed souls shall be provided for. . . . there is never a soldier relieved with such contribution as his misery requireth and his service hath deserved.'[2]

This, alas, was only too true. Neither the disabled soldiers, nor those who returned to England fit men, had their just deserts.

[1] R. Barret, *Moderne Warres*, 33.
[2] Add. MSS. 48041, f. 365b; W. Townshend, *Historical Collections*, 307.

IV

MOVEMENT AND COMMUNICATIONS

THE sixteenth-century army moved slowly. Vehicles were reserved for the transport of stores and equipment, and for carrying the wounded; but even if they had been available in unlimited numbers, the condition of the roads, where they existed, prevented carts from going faster than a walking pace. The cavalry would of course move faster, and as a rule more safely because of their extra mobility, but the army as a whole had to proceed at the rate of its slowest component part. Sir Roger Williams says that few captains would force their men to march more than fifteen miles without a rest,[1] and, in practice, a day's march was about ten or twelve miles.

It was essential that levies should be marched away from their point of origin the moment they were complete. If they were not, the ill-assorted mass of recruits—unwilling conscripts dragged from honest employment or from a life of more or less profitable lawlessness, leavened with a few yeomen volunteers thirsting for adventure, and gentlemen volunteers with a stronger thirst for money—simply melted away.

At the beginning of the reign there were virtually no ready-made arrangements for moving troops. The only institution was the payment known as 'coat and conduct money', in which 'coat money' was the recruit's uniform allowance and 'conduct money' the sum provided for the expenses of the march from the assembly-point in the county to the port of embarkation. The latter sum was paid at the daily rate of eightpence a head,[2] and was supposed to be enough to feed the men on the day's march (which was usually expected to be from twelve to fifteen miles)[3] and provide them with a night's lodging at the end of it.

The time taken by the levies on their journey naturally varied with the remoteness of their county from the coast. Men levied in Montgomery were given three days' conduct money to get

---
[1] *Briefe Discourse*, 42.   [2] Add. MSS. 37,999, f. 27.
[3] F. Grose, *Military Antiquities*, i. 342.

them to Chester, the main port of embarkation for Ireland, while Londoners were allowed a fortnight for their march to the same town. Other times authorized for the journey to Chester were: five days from Derby; seven from Warwick and Worcester; eleven from Buckingham; and eighteen from Norfolk.[1] Levies going to Bristol were allowed nine days from Warwick, six from Oxford, and five from Wiltshire.[2] Both the allowance of eightpence a day and the distance the levies were asked to cover were quite reasonable, and if men took longer than the authorized time to reach the seaport, and consequently had to go on short rations for the latter stages of the journey, they had only themselves to blame.

Conduct money was advanced by the authority in charge of a levy and in due course recovered from public funds. The method of recovery varied. The physical movement of money, especially to remote areas—Devon and Cornwall, and the northern shires—was not easy (it was also risky), and the transfer of funds from London had therefore little to commend it. In many cases, nevertheless, conduct money was repaid in London to someone sent by the local authority.[3] A safer and more satisfactory method adopted from time to time was to make payment from government funds already in existence in the area, in the hands, for example, of the Receiver of Taxes, or the Collector of Customs;[4] but the practice of sending to London for the money persisted to the end of the reign. No doubt the local authority often considered that it was the only certain way (subject to highway robbery) to get their hands on what was due to them.

If the troops had been gathered by an officer holding a commission from the queen, they usually marched to the coast in his charge. But most of the levies were found by lords lieutenant or sheriffs and justices of the peace acting as commissioners of musters. It was hardly practicable for them to escort men to the coast, even if they were qualified for such an arduous task, and an individual was appointed for the purpose, either locally or by the Privy Council.[5] His job was to lead the men, to see that they covered each day the dozen or so miles expected of them, and to ensure that none deserted on the way or sold their arms or equipment. The journey money for the whole levy was

---

[1] *A.P.C., passim.*   [2] Ibid. xxix, 315.   [3] Ibid. xxix. 643–4.
[4] Ibid. xxvi, 59, 242.   [5] Ibid. xxiv, 15; xxxi, 21.

handed over to the leader so that he could buy food and pay for lodgings, an arrangement which gave him the chance of lining his pockets at the expense of the comfort of the troops.

If a man claimed to have gone sick or fallen lame (no doubt a fairly frequent occurrence), he was committed to the charge of the mayor or justice of the peace in the next town through which the levy passed. If his claim turned out to be genuine, he was looked after until he was well enough to return home. He was then given a pass with full particulars of his affliction, which enabled him to reach without molestation the place where he had been levied.[1]

The Privy Council fully appreciated the importance of getting the troops quickly to their destination and contrived to minimize the distances to be covered by raising recruits in the counties nearest the theatre where they were to serve. If an unusually large force were required at short notice it might be necessary to levy part of it in a comparatively remote shire, but the records show that as a general rule the regions nearest the theatre of war supplied the men. For example, the Welsh counties were usually called on to send men to Ireland. Of the troops raised there after 1585 nearly 9,000 were sent to Ireland, while only 300 went to France and 200 to the Netherlands. On the other hand, 1,400 Hampshire men went to France, and only some 600 to Ireland and 500 to the Netherlands. Again, Hertfordshire was nearly equidistant from the three main theatres, and sent troops to them in almost equal numbers.[2]

But even when their journey had thus been shortened, the levies seldom reached the coast intact. Leaders were usually anxious to supplement what they pocketed out of the conduct money by conniving at desertion in return for bribes. Once a levy had been broken up in this way it was a hopeless task to reassemble it. Sir John Norreys complained to the Privy Council on one occasion that more than a hundred men had escaped. Although he had written several times to the justices asking them to have the deserters arrested, so careless of their duty were the constables and other officials responsible for pursuing the runaways that not a single one had been recaptured. Villagers had given the escaped men sanctuary in their homes, and had helped to smuggle away both them and their equipment.

[1] Ibid. xxx. 794–8. [2] See Appendix No. 2, and No. 3.

Norreys blamed the Hampshire authorities for this sorry state of affairs, and suggested that as a punishment they should be compelled to levy a hundred recruits to take the place of those missing. He added that Hampshire was a well-populated county and could easily spare the men.[1]

In 1600 a leader chosen by the Earl of Shrewsbury to take a levy from Derbyshire to Chester was accused of releasing seven of the men entrusted to him and replacing them with others, no doubt at a handsome profit,[2] and a captain reported from Barnstaple that, of a hundred men levied in Hampshire, the leader had allowed seven to run away.[3] At Chester large numbers of soldiers escaped, and few were recaptured by the constables.[4] In the following year the men responsible for getting the levies to the ports were still being blamed for their inefficiency and corruption. A force from Lancashire and Lincolnshire was twenty-two short when it reached Chester. The Council sent the names of the escaped men to the commissioners of musters in these counties, and instructed them to have the offenders arrested and initiate proceedings against the ringleaders. It was pointed out that the man in charge had probably gained through the desertions. The commissioners were therefore instructed to question closely all who were apprehended to find out how much they had paid for their freedom.[5]

Clearly it was vital that the forces should not be thus depleted before they even reached the port of embarkation. The levies were, however, usually drawn in comparatively small numbers from several counties, which meant that many leaders were needed, at least before the confluence of the smaller levies on the highway to the seaport. It was probably before this confluence that most desertions took place, for it was more difficult for the Privy Council to police effectively the activities of the leaders on the earlier stages of the journey.

As soon as the number of troops required from each village or hundred was complete the whole body was transferred to the charge of the appointed leaders. Two lists of the recruits' names were written on the same paper or parchment, and then separated by an irregular cut, from which the documents took their name of 'indenture'. One list was signed by the individual

---

[1] *A.P.C.* xxx. 794–8.   [2] *H.M.C. Rutland*, i. 358–9.
[3] *H.M.C. Salisbury*, xi. 431.   [4] Ibid. 473.   [5] *A.P.C.* xxxii. 359–60.

receiving the men and sent to London, so that the Privy Council would know that the desired number had been found and were actually on their way to the coast. The other was signed by the sheriff or justice of the peace and taken by the leader to the port. It is likely that even when the leader was comparatively honest a large proportion of the levy slipped away without his connivance while they were still in a friendly neighbourhood where they knew the lie of the land; and it is even more likely that when the leader was corrupt he would be willing to sell their release to men whom he had probably known since childhood.

Indentures at first recorded only the name of each recruit, his armour and weapons, and the parish in which he had been levied. Towards the end of the century, however, the Privy Council extended their scope in an attempt to achieve a better control over the levies on the earlier stages of the march.[1] They now contained, in addition to the man's name and a note of his equipment, details of his personal appearance, which would make identification easier should the leader be accused of changing men. Indentures recording cavalry levies showed the colour, height, age, markings, pace, and equipment of the horse, as well as the names of the owner and rider.[2]

Widening the scope of indentures gave little better guarantee that the levies would be efficiently led to the coast. What was really wanted was an improvement in the type of men appointed as leaders, and this the Council strove to achieve. Instead of leaving the arrangements entirely to its regional representatives, it took an increasing interest in the appointment of leaders, in the hope that if honest men were appointed recruits would find it impossible to buy their way out of the army. It seems that the Council's solution of the problem was to choose the leaders more from established captains than from local men, no doubt on the ground that the former were less likely to be influenced by local ties. In 1601 a captain who was commissioned to find a hundred men in Gloucestershire was also made responsible for leading a hundred from Wiltshire and fifty from Pembrokeshire. Another, who had raised a hundred in Monmouthshire for his own company, was ordered by the council to lead twenty-five men from

---

[1] *H.M.C. Salisbury*, xi. 5.
[2] See p. 34 n. above. A typical indenture for an infantry levy is printed in Appendix No. 4.

each of the shires of Radnor and Cardigan to Bristol, where they were to embark for Ireland.¹

But despite the Council's efforts the abuses in leading the recruits persisted throughout the reign. In 1600 a number of small levies were handed over at Chester to a single captain who was responsible for taking them on the second stage of their journey to Ireland. In its instructions for raising this force the Privy Council referred pointedly to the prevailing abuses, and said that as there had recently been a great deal of changing of recruits the captain was to be particularly careful to satisfy himself that he received the men actually specified in the indentures. If it turned out that there had in fact been substitution the offenders were to suffer the extreme penalty of the law.²

The second stage of the troops' journey was usually done in privately owned vessels hired for the occasion by the Crown, although the royal navy was also used, for example, to carry some of the troops to Scotland in 1560. The masters of merchant vessels were seldom eager to give their services, for government work of this sort seriously interfered with their private trading activities. Men were at best unprofitable cargo, and at the worst they left disease behind.

Even when the masters were graciously pleased to carry troops they might make some condition about their destination, to enable them to reach the most favourable port abroad from the point of view of subsequent trading. In 1592 a number of ships were detailed to go from Poole to Brittany, but on the pretext that the Brittany coast was too dangerous the masters proposed to land the men in Normandy, whither they would have been taking their ships in any event. The Council tried to win them over by offering the services of pilots well acquainted with the coast of Brittany, but without much effect. Some masters persisted in their refusal to make ready for sea, and the Council accordingly instructed the Mayor of Poole to send the chief offenders to London to receive the punishment they deserved, and serve as an example to their fellows.³

Perhaps there was some justification for the masters' reluctance on this occasion, for the Council had forbidden Sir John Norreys, who was commanding the troops, to use the navy for their transport, because the dangers of the crossing were

[1] *A.P.C.* xxxii. 452.   [2] Ibid. xxxi. 21–22.   [3] Ibid. xxiii. 252.

increasing with the approach of winter. But, as a general rule, it was necessary to use persuasion before the merchants would agree to substitute soldiers for more profitable merchandise.

Unwilling masters were not the only problem. Though a fair wind might waft the levies well on their way almost as soon as they embarked, it more often happened that they were held up day after day by adverse weather, while their food bill mounted, and the men themselves became more and more discontented.[1] Or it might be that after the force had embarked and left port the wind would change, and what should have been a short voyage would take many days.

Important enough in themselves, these delays were generally far-reaching in their consequences. The longer the men remained inactive on English soil the lower fell their morale. There was opportunity for wholesale desertion, the unaccustomed demand for food tended to cause a serious rise in local prices, and the concentration of large numbers of men in small areas rendered them easy victims of disease. Moreover, if the troops were unable to leave within a reasonable time of their arrival at the seaport, money would run short. On one occasion a force made three attempts to put out of harbour and each time was driven back. So long was its departure held up that the treasure chest was completely emptied, except for some French currency which was intended for use when the men reached France.

While weeks of waiting at the coast did much to dispirit and disorganize the forces, the hardships of the actual crossing could be no less serious in their effects. Edward Norreys had a gloomy tale to tell in 1585. He set out with five companies in good order, but a ten-day crossing in foul weather, scarcity of food, and eight days spent in a draughty church at Middelburg so undermined the health of his men that most went sick and many died.[2]

Costs of carrying the troops overseas depended largely on the bargaining power and greed of the shipowners; and if the ships were held up for weeks by bad weather, as often happened, the normal costs would be greatly increased. The minimum price varied from about 2s. a head for the trip from England to France to 8s. for the journey to Ireland—rates which covered only the hire of vessels, and did not include feeding the soldiers.

[1] Ibid. xxx. 283.   [2] *For. Cal.* xx. 103.

It was left to the queen's representative in the port of embarkation to make the best bargain with the masters for the hire of their vessels. His efforts did not always meet with the approval of the Privy Council. When the Mayor of Bristol contracted with the shipowners to carry troops to Ireland for 10s. a head, the Council protested. Instead of agreeing to the high rate, it instructed the mayor to reopen negotiations with the owners and get better terms.[1] It was, however, quite prepared to be generous in its dealings with the shipowners. On one occasion the Mayor of Chester was foolish enough to requisition some vessels without first making a bargain with the masters, who took advantage of the strong position in which his carelessness had placed them, and stuck out for an unusually high price. The Council agreed that the mayor's proposed offer of 6s. was satisfactory, but authorized him to raise it to 8s., as the ship had been detained for some time in Chester awaiting the arrival of the levies.[2]

The Council sought to control the shipowners, and at the same time help the local authorities, by appointing an official charged with the general supervision of the arrangements at the seaport. Nicholas Erington was appointed on the occasion of a levy of 1,500 men to replace veterans transferred from the Netherlands to France. He was required to arrange the embarkation of the men sailing from London, and also to see that contingents from Harwich and Sandwich were safely shipped. He was responsible under Sir John Norreys for the provision of vessels and food for the crossing. The ships from the three ports met at sea and proceeded in convoy to Flushing. On their arrival Erington had to distribute the force in such a way that the gaps left by the withdrawal of the troops for France were satisfactorily filled.[3]

Five years later Maurice Kyffin, who had experience of other branches of organization,[4] was given a similar appointment with greater responsibilities. He had complete control of troops at Chester. He was their paymaster while they remained in England; if they were detained longer than four weeks for lack of a favourable wind he was authorized to start paying them as if they were on active service. He co-operated with the mayor and the Crown officers in the port in requisitioning sufficient shipping to carry the men to Dublin, mustered the contingents from

---

[1] A.P.C. xxvi. 339.
[2] Ibid. xxx. 243-4.
[3] Ibid. xxi. 23.
[4] See Chapter VIII.

the various counties as they came in, recorded their strength, and made a detailed inventory of their equipment for comparison with the indentures brought by the leaders. All changes in personnel and shortage of weapons thus disclosed were submitted to the Privy Council. Kyffin was also expected to keep a benevolent eye on food supplies.

The Privy Council was favourably impressed by the success of these experiments, and in 1595 appointed two officials for the sole purpose of finding and requisitioning transports. John Goite was given charge of Bristol, Milford, Padstow, and Barnstaple, and Robert Davies of Chester and Liverpool. They were instructed to visit the ports allocated to them and to hire ships as they were required. If the shipping available in the ports was insufficient for the needs of the moment the agents were empowered to requisition any vessel that came in, unless it was a foreigner with cargo or an English ship bound on an important voyage. Goite and Davies spent thirty days finding ships for Ireland. They were reappointed in the same year, Goite now having to control all the ports from Bristol to Land's End, and Davies to control Chester and Liverpool and the ports and creeks in their neighbourhood. If one of them found a surplus in his region he was to inform his colleague, so that if necessary a transfer could be made. Apparently there was a surplus in the south, for the Council asked that seventeen vessels should be sent from Barnstaple to Chester, whence they were to proceed to Dublin.[1]

These new appointments relieved the local authorities of some of their responsibilities, and at the same time materially improved the efficiency of transport. It was now possible for the central government to exercise much greater control over the movement of troops by sea. Much of the work still fell on the shoulders of the authorities in the coast towns, however, especially in the west. The corporation accounts afford a glimpse of the work involved in shipping a levy. The men had to be fed and billeted during their stay in the town, which might be indefinitely prolonged through lack of a favourable wind. The town officers had to co-operate with the official transport supervisor in finding ships, and occasionally finding crews. Victuals had to be found for the voyage and packed in casks able to withstand

---

[1] *A.P.C.* xxix. 511.

the effects of salt water. Straw for bedding on board ship, and rowing-boats to embark the soldiers and tow the vessels into the fairway had to be supplied. Pilots had to be engaged, and also a large staff of watchmen to be found to prevent the men from deserting before they embarked.[1] The civic authorities were at all times expected to enlist the aid of the Crown officers in the port. In 1600 the Mayor of Bristol was reprimanded by the Privy Council for ignoring these officials when embarking troops.[2]

The efficient movement of troops, especially to an overseas destination, was virtually impossible. The Privy Council might improve its control over the levies while they remained in England by widening the scope of indentures, and by selecting competent leaders, but after the recruits were safely brought to the coast it was still necessary to contend with the shipowners and the vagaries of wind and weather. One of the reasons why Leicester was ordered to avoid any engagement in the Low Countries in which there was the slightest risk of defeat was the difficulty of sending him reinforcements quickly. The queen pointed out that however anxious she was to send reinforcements 'the uncertain passage of the sea' might prove a stumbling block. The shipowners could be disciplined, but against the elements the government was no more powerful than Philip of Spain when the Almighty blew to destruction the remnants of his Armada.

The factors that made it difficult to move an army quickly and efficiently also affected communications. Signals could be transmitted over long distances at nearly the speed of light by means of the beacon system; but it was not a very flexible method of communication, despite the ingenuity that went into it. The early warning system based on the Isle of Wight, for example, was so devised that it could send three different messages. There were groups of three beacons at each end of the island, commanding the English Channel to the east and to the west. The firing of a single beacon in either group of three was simply a warning to the coastal defences to get ready for action. This signal was not repeated by any other station in the chain.

[1] Exchequer of Receipt, Army, Navy, and Ordnance Accounts, box 12, no.2.
[2] A.P.C. xxx. 166.

But if two of the three were fired simultaneously, it was a signal for all the beacon stations in Hampshire, Wiltshire, Dorsetshire, and Sussex to fire one of their two beacons, which alerted the troops in these counties. If all three beacons at one of the Isle of Wight stations were fired, all the two-beacon stations in the above four counties fired both beacons. This signal was picked up by the beacons in Oxfordshire, Berkshire, Gloucestershire, and Somersetshire, and their fires would in turn be seen by the stations in the counties further inland.[1] Thus, in a very short time a vast area could be alerted—if the weather was right and the men on watch kept a good lookout.

The beacons were maintained by the local authorities. The Privy Council decided when they should be manned. The initial firing could not take place without the authority of a justice of the peace; but in spite of this precaution the chain reaction was occasionally set off accidentally or maliciously. The system was as a rule suspended in the winter.

The beacons were of use only to bring out the militia quickly in times of great crisis. In ordinary circumstances riding was the quickest method of carrying instructions to recruit men, orders for the army in the field, and so on. This worked well enough inside England, but as most of the Elizabethan army's active service was overseas the dispatch riders were often at the mercy of wind and weather for part of their journey.

The arrangements made by the Archbishop of Canterbury (John Whitgift) in 1599 to raise cavalry from the clergy show clearly the problems posed by slow communications. The Privy Council set the machinery in motion when they wrote to him from Wimbledon on 29 July. The news had come in that the King of Spain was fitting out another great expedition against England, and it had been decided to provide both infantry and cavalry as a bodyguard for the queen. The archbishop was therefore to instruct his bishops to make the same provision as their dioceses had done eleven years before at the time of the great Armada.

The Council's letter was delivered to the archbishop in his palace at Croydon in the afternoon of the same day. He at once got down to the job of drafting letters to the bishops, and managed to get them off later in the evening—a better performance

[1] S.P. Dom. 12, no. 22.

than in 1588, when the dispatch of the letters had taken two days. They were imbued with a sense of great urgency. The enemy was expected to reach England within forty days and in this grave emergency all excuses from the reluctant clergy must be swept aside. Each bishop was to find out what his diocese had done in 1588, and arrange for the same, or something more, to be done now. The warning had been so short that the archbishop had not himself had time to look up the records to discover what happened last time; but he suggested that the bishops should get their registrars to turn up the details.

On 4 August the Council sent a further communication. They instructed the archbishop to arrange for the cavalry to assemble at Lambeth and Southwark not later than 12 August. The only exception was the contingent from Kent, which, owing to a misunderstanding of their instructions by the commissioners of musters in that county, had been enrolled in the ordinary county muster book. For the sake of simplicity it was decided that they should serve for the duration with the troops from Kent. This letter from the Council reached the archbishop late in the evening after dinner; but once again he passed the gist of it on to the bishops without delay.

On the following day, however, the Council had second thoughts. It had occurred to them that there would hardly be time to bring up the forces from Wales, Devon, and Cornwall. The archbishop should therefore cancel his orders for these areas and arrange instead for the men to be mustered and kept in readiness in their own counties. The Council also observed that they had omitted to say anything about clothing in their earlier instructions. Would the archbishop choose some suitable colour for the men's uniforms and arrange for the bishops to provide it? Once again, Whitgift wrote off immediately, asking that the levies should be held back in the distant counties, and that all should be clad in blue or tawny.

Although the levies were originally due in London on 12 August, this time-table proved to be quite impossible, and they were given an extension to 15 August. They stood by in the capital for four days after that, and then the Council decided that the emergency had passed. The queen expressed her gratitude for the clergy's help and authorized the archbishop to send the men home. She made it clear that ideally they would have remained longer in London, as there was still an outside chance that they would be needed, but it was too costly to keep them. They must, however, stand by when they got home, ready for a further emergency.

It was not long in coming. On 26 August, only four days after the levies had been dismissed, and probably before a good many of them had found their way home, the Council told the archbishop that the Spanish fleet had been sighted off the coast of France. The cavalry must be recalled. The archbishop went into action with his usual speed. The bishops were to send the men back to London at once; and to see that they had enough money in their purses to get them there. Later in the same day, after the letters had gone, the archbishop received yet another communication from the Council. The emergency had again passed. It had been a false alarm. He should therefore reinstate the earlier instructions that the men were to stand by in their counties. So once again the archbishop summoned his secretaries and dictated instructions to the bishops that they should ignore his immediately preceding letter, and now simply keep the men on call.

This levy gives a clear picture of the amount of paper work incurred by a relatively small (although admittedly unusually complicated) levy. On a single day the archbishop got off about forty letters to his bishops, all of which had to be carried by hand; and the whole transaction took between one and two hundred letters. When it was all over the archbishop collected a list of the 'defects and inconveniences' in the arrangements, with a view to improving them on the next occasion. The most common complaint from the bishops was that they had not been given enough time to summon and equip the men.[1]

The fact that all messages had to be carried by hand meant that security was a constant problem. Ciphers were essential to protect information which would prove of value to the enemy if a messenger fell into their hands. They were primarily used to guard political secrets, but they were, nevertheless, of importance to the army. The art of cryptography was well established. There were many kinds of ciphers, according to Sir Francis Bacon—wheel ciphers, key ciphers, doubles, &c.—but there were three essentials in the perfect cipher. It must be easy to

[1] Lambeth MSS. 2009, ff. 98–134b; *H.M.C. Foljambe*, 73, 87, 99.

read and write. It should be impossible to decipher it. And ideally it should not appear to be a cipher.[1] The ciphers used for general purposes in Elizabeth's reign were less elaborate. They were as a rule what Bacon describes as 'simple ciphers and changes, and intermixes of nulles and non-significants'. That is to say they were a combination of a pre-arranged transposed alphabet, of which one copy was kept by the person enciphering the message, and a second by the person to whom the communication was addressed, and other devices to confuse third parties. These included the use of pre-arranged code words for places (London for Antwerp, Rochester Castle for Flushing, Dover Castle for Calais, Shooter's Hill for Bruges), and for people (*virgo* for Sir Thomas Bodley, *amphora* for Sir Francis Vere). There were also symbols, often very complex, invented to represent letters of the alphabet, or complete words; or geometrical figures (for example a square for peace, and a rectangle for war). Finally, there were usually half a dozen or so of Bacon's 'non-significants'—symbols to which was attributed no meaning at all, but which made it more difficult to decipher a message by methods based on the frequency with which letters occur in the ordinary course of writing.[2]

Invisible writing was also used occasionally, lemon juice as a rule taking the place of ink. It was not a very safe medium, however, if used on its own, for everyone knew (as every schoolboy knows) that if the paper is warmed the writing will show up quite plainly; and anyone finding a blank sheet on the person of a captured messenger would immediately heat it. But, properly used, it could save a great deal of time spent on enciphering and deciphering. It could, for example, be used to write between the lines of an ordinary letter. This was done on one occasion in 1589, the juice of an onion being the medium used.[3] Or a combination of invisible writing and cipher could be used. Sir Thomas Smith, the English ambassador in Paris, in writing to the Earl of Warwick when he was besieged in Le Havre, devoted the first part of his letter to general matters. He then added a cipher postscript which said 'Warm this well and you shall see more'. When Warwick did as he was bid the rest

---

[1] *Of the Advancement of Learning* (1605 edn.), 60–61.
[2] Cott. MSS., Galba, D VI, f. 332.
[3] S.P. France, 20, f. 18.

of the letter (written in lemon juice), which dealt with military affairs of significance for the beleaguered garrison, appeared.[1]

There were frequent complaints by the Privy Council about the paucity of reports from the field. In particular, when Willoughby was in France in 1589 he was being pressed constantly to send more frequent dispatches. He admitted that the Council might think that it was easier to hear from Venice than it was from him, but defended himself on the ground that there was little to report—which was all too true—and that the messengers' journey was very dangerous.[2] The problem of communications was aggravated, when the English army was besieging Leith in 1560, by the insertion of an unusual link in the chain of command, in the person of the Duke of Norfolk, who, although supreme commander, had his headquarters in Berwick. The fact that every dispatch and order had to go through him made the efficient conduct of the campaign almost impossible. It took anything from three to six days to get a letter from London to Berwick, where in practice it would be delayed at least another day before being passed on to the camp at Leith. If the general with the army asked for directions, it might be a fortnight before the Privy Council could get a reply through to him—by which time the whole situation would probably have changed.

This, of course, was a problem common to all sixteenth-century armies; but it was aggravated for the English forces by the fact that most of the time communications between the Privy Council and the higher command were hindered by the English Channel and the Irish Sea.

[1] *For. Cal.* v. 449.   [2] S.P. France, 20, f. 269.

V

RATIONS

ONE of the hardest tasks, and one of the most important, was feeding the army. Valiant minds, declaimed Barnaby Rich, looking back on a lifetime of service, will oppose themselves against the pike, will adventure upon the musket shot, or run upon the cannon; but never had he known the man who would willingly encounter famine. A hungry man can neither observe discipline, nor perform any great enterprise.[1] The provision of food was relatively easy in the Netherlands, where the fertility of the land impressed the English soldiers,[2] and in France, where on one occasion they found bread, milk, and cider set out for them in almost every house on their route.[3] But in the third main theatre of war, Ireland, the barren soil hardly satisfied the simple needs of the native population.

Sir John Perrot, when lord deputy in Ireland, frequently expressed alarm at the difficulty of keeping the garrison fed. He confessed that it was beyond his power to better the lot of the soldiers; either they had to suffer the pangs of hunger, or the queen had to take the expensive course of sending food from England.[4] As the garrison increased, so did the difficulty of victualling. Towards the end of the century Sir William Russell warned the Privy Council that food shortage might compel him to withdraw his troops from the field.[5]

It did not follow that there were no problems at all in the comparative plenty of France and the Netherlands. The additional demands for produce inevitably forced prices up. Soon after Leicester arrived in the Netherlands he arranged for the shipment of food from England, partly to provide a reserve in case the enemy cut off local supplies, and partly to keep prices (which were admitted to be reasonable enough) from getting out of hand. He feared that the uncertainty of the weather,

---

[1] *Fruites*, 9. [2] *For. Cal.* xx. 244.
[3] T. Coningsby, *Journal of the Siege of Rouen*, 14.
[4] Perrot MSS. i, ff. 98, 241b. [5] *Irish Cal. 1596-7*, 165-6.

which might delay ships, and the distance from England, would make it difficult to send food from there at short notice.[1] In Dieppe a few years later Sir Roger Williams found food so expensive that the men were hardly able to support life.[2] Nor was Williams's experience unique. Periodic complaints about the poor quality of food and the extreme difficulty of buying it at reasonable prices suggest that the French and the Dutch did not take very seriously their moral responsibility for helping to feed their allies.

In the early part of the reign the supply of food was mainly in the hands of merchants working on their own account. They followed the army as civilians, bought provisions locally, or carried them from England, and retailed them to the troops. Traces of 'purveyance' (which was to become a matter of controversy in the next century) still remained, however. Purveyance—the requisition of goods and services by the Crown for its own use—had been seriously abused in the thirteenth century, particularly by royal officials and servants, and many acts of parliament had been passed to limit it to the genuine requirements of the king, which included those of the armed forces. A new attempt to control purveyance was made by Edward VI in a statute which for the next three years forbade purveyors and others acting under a commission from the sovereign to take any victuals without the consent of the owner —although post horses could still be freely taken at a charge of 1d. a mile;[3] but at the beginning of Elizabeth's reign purveyance was still being used both for the ordinary purposes of the royal household and for the army.[4] It was not a very satisfactory device for keeping the forces supplied over a long period, however. Edward Baeshe, the navy victualler, suggested to the secretary of state in 1562 that it would be far better and cheaper to enter into agreements with butchers, bakers, and brewers for the supply of victuals—prices to be adjusted according to current supply and demand—than to have them purveyed through commissions. It might seem at first sight that purveyance was cheaper, but when all the extra costs that it involved were added in, it was just as costly as direct contracts.[5] Baeshe was thinking

---

[1] *For. Cal.* xx. 358.
[2] S.P. France, xxiv, f. 55.
[3] 2 & 3 Edward VI, c. 3.
[4] *For. Cal. 1559–1600*, 422.
[5] *H.M.C. Salisbury*, i. 293.

in terms of supplies to the royal household and to the navy, but what he said was just as true of the army; and in practice the Privy Council followed his advice. They relied progressively more on the services of private merchants.

At first the Crown's help was limited to giving the merchants a small advance to enable them to lay in their first supplies.[1] It also helped by relaxing the restrictions placed from time to time on the export of foodstuffs. On one occasion, when there was a general revocation of licences to export beer, because of the scarcity of corn, an exception was made in favour of merchants supplying the principal officers in the Netherlands.[2]

As the troops had to buy their rations out of their wages, which were constantly in arrear, it is hardly surprising that the existence of the victualler was precarious. The loan he received from the Crown was soon spent, and as often as not never recovered. When the army was fortunate enough to have arrears of pay made up, the merchant naturally tried to make good his losses by charging high prices; and the troops had either to pay up or go hungry. If the army was not paid, the victualler had to live on credit, or go out of business. The difficulties of the private merchant are dwelt on in a letter from one of them to the secretary of state in 1585. He was making no profit on the beef, butter, and cheese which he supplied, and he had lost heavily on the beer. It had been brewed in August, the worst possible month, and much of it had leaked away. On top of all this there had been heavy charges for freight from England, unloading in the Netherlands, and the staff he employed to distribute the food. His labour had been great, but he had made no profit. Unless he got a bigger advance from the Crown he simply could not carry on.[3]

There were frequent complaints about the private merchants. The captains in the Netherlands said on one occasion that they were charging 30 per cent. more to the army than prices on the open market, although the food was so bad that it was undermining the health of the men.[4] Leicester himself was well aware of the disadvantages of the rather haphazard system of freelance victualling: he urged that the number of operators should be kept to a minimum, pointing out that if more were appointed

---

[1] *For. Cal.* xx. 198.   [2] *A.P.C.* xiv. 384–5.
[3] *For. Cal.* xx. 198.   [4] Ibid. xxi, pt. 2, 180–1.

those already doing the work would give it up.¹ Competition between the private merchants for supplies did in fact cause a lot of trouble, and various attempts were made to regulate it. In the expedition to Normandy in 1589 private victuallers were ordered to provide only for the troops drawn from their own county, to prevent competition among them for the custom of the entire force. This was a step in the right direction, but it did not eliminate the competitive element. It was still open to the native suppliers in the invaded country to play off the private merchants against each other.

Poor victuals at high prices gave rise to much discontent. They partly caused the serious mutiny at Ostend in 1588.² Yet in this case there may have been something to be said for the victualler, whom the soldiers threw in the harbour in the hope that he would give better value in the future. He claimed that a man who was dissatisfied with his rations could have them replaced; and furthermore that the prices were not unreasonable when the original cost of the food, and transport, storage, and customs dues were taken into account.³ One of the victualler's accusers made a comparison between the prices of the goods he supplied to the troops and those ruling in England. The discrepancy between the two sets is considerable, but the English prices may have been pitched too low. For example, butter was supplied in Ostend at just over $4d.$ a pound, whereas it was claimed that in England it cost only $3d.$ But in fact in England the price of butter was ranging from $3d.$ to a fraction over $4d.$ a pound, and it may well have been that instead of making a profit of $5s.$ a firkin (or something over 30 per cent.) the victualler was making rather less than a shilling, or about 6 per cent., which was hardly excessive. Indeed, when transport and other charges (the cost of which the hungry soldiers were not in a position to assess accurately) were brought into the account, the profit may have been much smaller.

But profiteering did happen, and it was not the merchants' only crime. They were quite prepared to sell food to the enemy if the price were right. The illicit dealings of smugglers who carried goods to the enemy from the garrison towns in the Netherlands were bad enough, but far worse were the activities of those who shipped whole cargoes to the enemy. Merchants

---

[1] Ibid. xx. 205.   [2] Ibid. xxii. 166, 202, 341.   [3] Ibid. 168–9.

caught doing this were executed from time to time, but the traffic continued. Leicester reported that large quantities of food were being carried to Calais, whence they found their way to the enemy.[1]

There was nothing to be said for private victualling. It was clearly intolerable. If only because of the irregularity with which the army was paid, the burden of financing the purchase of food was too much for private individuals. Even had the army been paid regularly and the victuallers been able to recover their money at reasonable intervals, the dangers of competition between them for the available supplies and of smuggling food to the enemy remained. The Privy Council tackled the problem by associating itself more and more closely with the victuallers. It entered into agreements with merchants which made them progressively more responsible to the Crown. This enabled the Council to keep track of the movement of supplies abroad, and it also transferred a greater part of the financial burden to the broader shoulders of the government.

This shift of responsibility for feeding the troops was beginning round about 1570. In that year the Privy Council arranged that a merchant should supply food to the forces in Ireland, and that for this service he should be paid half-yearly from the revenues of that country. This did not work, however. The money which should have gone to the merchant was allocated to other purposes, and the food supply broke down. The Council had to come to the rescue and advance £2,000 to the merchant so that he might have some working capital.[2]

Ten years later the Council went a step further. They entered into a contract with a Liverpool merchant to carry food to the troops in Ireland under which he was paid half the value of the supplies contracted for when the agreement was signed, and the balance when the food reached Ireland. The Crown still did not take over full responsibility, however, for the goods were carried at the merchant's risk. If, for example, the contract was for £2,000 worth of food, the Council made a down payment of £1,000. The merchant, working, for the sake of argument, to a profit margin of 10 per cent., would lay out £1,800 in purchasing and shipping the victuals, so that if the whole cargo

---

[1] *For. Cal.* xx. 321, 359; xxi, pt. 2, 148; pt. 3, 76.
[2] *A.P.C.* vii. 395–6.

were taken by the enemy he would sustain a loss of only £800, the balance of £1,000 going to the Crown account. There was thus every incentive for the merchant to ship short weight, or poor quality food, trusting in the inefficiency, or more likely the corruptibility, of the official inspectors in Ireland to let him get away with a handsome profit on the cargoes that reached their destination, which they would offset against the losses on any that did not.[1]

There was a similar development in the Netherlands a few years later, when a 'victualling commissary' (George Leicester) was appointed for the garrison towns; but this time the Council gave even more authority to the merchant. He was empowered to buy food at reasonable prices and to requisition wagons and ships to transport it. He was told exactly what he might buy in England. He was, for example, given a licence to export 4,000 quarters of wheat in specified amounts from particular counties, and he had to give a bond to the commissioners of grain, which was redeemable when he proved that the wheat had arrived safely.[2] Shortly after this type of contract was introduced the Crown took a further step towards the complete underwriting of the victualling arrangements. The queen, at George Leicester's request, agreed to make good losses sustained by enemy action up to the value of £2,000.[3]

The illegal export of foodstuffs was a constant problem. It often helped to sustain the enemy forces. It had damaging effects at home, where it aggravated shortages and increased prices, which in any case were being steadily driven up by the general inflation of the period. In an attempt to discourage these exports—and also the export of munitions—royal proclamations were issued in 1588, 1591, and 1597.[4] In 1591 the Council, understanding that great quantitities of grain had been exported to the Netherlands without licence and were being freely sold in the garrison towns there, authorized the victuallers to seize any such grain that they could lay their hands on, and sell it. Half the proceeds of the sales were to go to the Crown, and a quarter each to the commander of the town where the grain was discovered and the victualler himself.[5]

---

[1] Ibid. xii. 228–9.   [2] Ibid. xvi. 398, 411–12.   [3] Ibid. xvii. 171–2.
[4] Proclamations of 9 November 1588, 10 September 1591, and 27 September 1597.   [5] *Dom. Cal. 1591–4*, 4.

The domestic supply position was always in the mind of the government, and later victualling contracts were related to it. A contract entered into in 1588, for 400 quarters of wheat and 4,000 tuns of beer annually for the Netherlands, was modified three years later. If these commodities became scarce in England the amount of beer allowed for export was reduced. The merchants were authorized to export the full quantities under the contract only so long as the prices of wheat and malt did not exceed 23s. 4d. and 13s. 4d. per quarter respectively. If prices rose above these limits only 2,000 tuns of beer a year could be sent to the Netherlands, although there was no reduction in the quantity of wheat.[1]

The most elaborate attempt to control prices was made at the time of the Armada. A royal proclamation laid down prices for all 'grain, victuals, horsemeat, and lodgings' within a radius of twenty miles of the army at Tilbury. The schedule to the proclamation contains nearly fifty items, including many foodstuffs. For example: 'a quarter of the best wheat, clean and sweet—20s. 0d.'; 'a fat pig, the best in the market—14d.'; 'a couple of chickens—8d.'; 'a dozen pigeons—18d.'; 'a full quart of good single ale or beer—$\frac{1}{2}d$.' There were also controlled prices for lodgings and the meals provided in them. Soldiers in the queen's pay were to be charged no more than 3d. for their supper; and to prevent landlords from serving an inadequate meal the minimum menu was laid down. It was to include 'good wheaten bread, and drink; boiled beef, mutton, veal, or lamb; and roast pork, beef, mutton, veal or lamb'. On fish days, salt fish or ling, eggs, butter, buttered peas, or beans were substituted for the meat dishes. Each man was to have food 'competent and sufficient for the sustentation of his body'. A single night's lodging on a feather bed cost a man 1d.; a week, 6d. A double feather bed cost 8d. a week; but a double flock bed could be had for only 4d.[2]

The contracting system was further developed at the end of the reign when the war effort reached its climax in the suppression of Tyrone's rebellion in Ireland. There were many contracts, mostly on the following lines. The Council struck a bargain with merchants who agreed to provide a given quantity of food (usually enough for one or three periods of twenty-eight

[1] *Dom. Cal. 1591–4*, 40.   [2] Proclamation of 7 August 1588.

days) by a certain date. The Crown paid for this service in two instalments: one when the bargain was made, so that the merchants would have something in hand to buy supplies, and the other when it was proved that the goods had been shipped or had safely reached their destination.

In a typical contract (of November 1598) a merchant undertook to provide, ship, and deliver about sixty tons of bread or biscuit, ten tons of butter, eight tons of cheese, and a quantity of oatmeal, all of 'good, wholesome, and serviceable quality'. These provisions were to be dispatched from Chester and Bristol to Cork and Youghal in Munster, and handed over to the army authorities there. Under the terms of the contract the merchant was paid £2,000, half on signature; and he had to give the Council a bond for £3,000 as a guarantee that he would fulfil his part of the bargain. The balance of the payment due to him was made within six days of the Council's receiving a certificate from the Mayors of Bristol and Chester that the food had been duly shipped in good condition; and his bond was redeemable when he submitted the receipts which his agents in Ireland got from the army authorities when the victuals were handed over.[1]

Subsequent contracts were broadly on the same lines. There were, however, minor modifications intended to give the system greater flexibility, and also to transfer rather more of the responsibility to the Crown. If the contractors found that they could not buy the stipulated quantities of one foodstuff they were allowed to use their own discretion in making good the deficit with a suitable substitute.[2] The risk of shipwreck was clarified. In the earlier contracts the merchants carried it, to the extent that if a cargo was lost at sea they were out of pocket—although, of course, shipwreck did not vitiate the whole contract and make them liable to forfeit the bonds they had put up. Now the risks both of capture by the enemy and loss by shipwreck ('which God forbid!' says the contract) were placed firmly on the shoulders of the Crown.[3] Again, the Council promised that the authorities in Ireland would unload the food ships as soon as they docked, to avoid extra expense through delays in discharging. If delays were inevitable, the additional cost was to be borne by the government.[4]

[1] *A.P.C.* xxix. 273.
[2] Ibid. 623.
[3] Ibid. 458–60.
[4] Ibid 624–5.

The merchant's job was to buy food in England and get it into the hands of the queen's representative in Ireland. Thereafter it was the army's responsibility. Distribution was anything but satisfactory, however, and, as the build-up of the forces in Ireland accelerated, the need for better arrangements quickly manifested itself. At the beginning of 1599 the Privy Council appointed four 'commissaries of victuals' with very wide powers. They were to take possession of the food as soon as it was discharged at the Irish ports, and see to its efficient distribution. They were authorized to fit out and operate the bakehouses, brewhouses, mills, granaries, and stores which the queen already owned in Ireland; and to requisition others. The authorities were to help them to acquire all the many things which the distribution system needed—casks for beer and butter, canvas for packing the meat; salt; ships; lighters; horses and carts; and also the necessary staff, including bakers, brewers, and coopers. At least two of the commissaries now appointed had previous experience of victualling in Ireland. Robert Newcomen had been 'victualler for Ireland'; and another, John Travis, had been clerk of victuals attached to one of the contingents of the army. But now that 'the great army' was coming to Ireland the functions and status of the commissariat had to be enhanced.[1]

The new system soon broke down. There were many complaints that rations failed to reach the troops, and that when they did their quality was unsatisfactory. It was suspected that at some point in the chain of distribution the wholesome food was sold on the black market, and inferior provisions substituted. When the Privy Council taxed the merchants with this, they pointed out that under the terms of their contracts they were responsible only for delivering the food in satisfactory condition to the authorities in Ireland. What happened after that had nothing whatsoever to do with them. If distribution was unsatisfactory, it was the fault of the victualling commissaries. The latter, for their part, blamed the merchants. The Privy Council decided that a thorough investigation would take too long, and in the meantime the army had to be fed. Something must be done to conserve the food sent at great expense from England, and to stop the issue of sub-standard rations, which took the heart out of the private soldier. They therefore decided to make the

[1] *A.P.C.* xxix. 518.

contractors responsible for the whole of the supply and distribution arrangements 'from the beginning to the ending'. This would mean that from now on if there were any shortcomings in the provision, keeping, or issuing of victuals, they need do no more than call the merchants to account—unless of course the trouble arose from something beyond the merchants' control.

The Council must have had great faith in the merchants to arrive at this decision. Even so, they deemed it necessary to send their own instructions to the new employees. These left them in no doubt that they *were* the employees of the merchants and not of the Crown; but they also stressed the Crown's interest in their new duties. Having rehearsed the reasons that moved them to make the merchants solely responsible for the distribution of rations, they proceeded to authorize the agents to take over the balance of the supplies remaining in the hands of the official commissaries and to receive from time to time further quantities sent from England. The latter were to be examined simultaneously by the agents and by commissioners appointed by the army; and they were to be accepted only if in good condition and likely to remain so for five months from the date of loading in England. If they were not acceptable, they were to be retained by the merchant, who would dispose of them as he saw fit and replace them with better quality at his own expense.

The local agents were to have copies of the victualling contracts so that they might know the total quantities being supplied, and what the standard ration was to be. They were to do what they could to keep the provisions in their charge in good condition by regularly turning them and salting them; and, as far as possible, they were to issue the more perishable stores first. They were also to study the soldiers' likes and dislikes so that future supplies could be varied according to their preferences—provided that it did not cost any more. At least every two months they were to make up a statement showing how much each captain had had for his company 'five score to the hundred and sixteen ounces to the pound' to enable the treasurer-at-war to make the appropriate deductions from the captain's pay. Finally, they were to work closely with the army authorities, and in particular to enlist their support if they found themselves the target of attacks or abuse from dissatisfied soldiers.[1]

[1] *A.P.C.* xxx. 623–33.

At first, provisioning, like everything else, was done hand to mouth. This was dangerous. It was an age when the success of an army depended to a marked degree on the fitness of the rank and file. Great physical effort was needed to carry a pike on the march and wield it in action. Although the long-bow weighed little, only a strong man could get the best out of it. The troops therefore had to be kept well-fed, or be at a permanent disadvantage. But it was also an age when the methods of food preservation were relatively primitive. How then to maintain adequate reserves of wholesome rations through a long winter, or a siege?

The problem was solved in the Netherlands by the establishment of permanent food stores for wheat, cheese, butter, and beer. It was hopeless to try to keep these commodities indefinitely, so arrangements were made for their systematic use and replacement. Any surplus remaining when the stores were due to be replaced was sold to private citizens. It was thus possible to make provision for a greater reserve than the minimum needed for the army's normal use, which was kept in the best possible condition by frequent replacement; and by systematically disposing of any surpluses to the civilian population the Crown avoided waste of money by having to throw out food that had gone bad. These arrangements were continued in the Netherlands to the end of the reign; and they were also introduced into France for a time.[1] Another measure in the Netherlands required the householders in the garrison towns to keep enough food in their homes to last for a year. This spread the burden effectively. It provided a generous safety margin, and relieved the army victuallers in time of scarcity.[2]

It was particularly difficult to keep food in the damp climate of Ireland. The Council there told the Privy Council that although the weather had affected the health of many of the soldiers, much more damage had been done by the food. It had got damp on the voyage from England, and had further deteriorated by being kept too long in store. It was therefore suggested that the storage of food locally should be abandoned. Instead, provisions could be bought in Ireland as they were required.[3] This proposal was supported by one of the muster officials, who pointed out that if the English army were supplied from Ireland

---

[1] *Dom. Cal. 1591–4*, 4, 574–5.   [2] *Irish Cal. 1599–1600*, 379.
[3] Ibid. 289.

there would be less food available for the rebels. Moreover, the inconvenience of carrying the food from England would be avoided. The mobility of the troops would be increased as they would no longer have to keep open a line of communication to the storehouses.[1] A point which these suggestions overlooked was that there was no guarantee that the scarcity induced by cutting off supplies from England would be limited to the rebel forces. It was probable that the English army would suffer more than the enemy. One captain maintained that discontent and disease were the inevitable consequences of victualling from government stores, and proposed that men should have their ration money in cash. They would then be able to buy the sort of food they liked best.[2] This again presupposed that the food would be there waiting to be bought, which was hardly likely; but the captain's real objective was probably a system of provisioning which would give him and his colleagues more direct control of the army's victualling money. At the end of the century the plan which had been adopted in the Netherlands was introduced in Ireland. Householders in the fortified towns were required to lay in a year's stock of corn, and, if they could afford it, also of butter, cheese, and salt beef.[3] Sometimes plain carelessness was responsible for damage to foodstuffs. In Ireland a consignment of oatmeal was stored at low tide in the cellars of a ruined castle by the sea, and most of it was 'utterly spoiled' when the tide came in.[4]

The transport of food overseas was organized in much the same way as the transport of the levies. Ships were requisitioned and sailors pressed into service as occasion demanded, the greater part of the work falling on the shoulders of the civic authorities of the ports from which the food transports sailed. The Privy Council used its influence to facilitate the purchase of provisions and their carriage to the coast. Public officers were instructed to help the merchants buy provisions, and to see that they or their representatives were allowed to ship them without hindrance.[5] If the civic authorities failed to give full and intelligent co-operation, the Council quickly showed its displeasure. When the Mayor of Bristol did not provide a ship to take a cargo of food to Cork, on the ground that all the available ships were

[1] Ibid. 484. [2] Ibid. 289. [3] Ibid. 379.
[4] Ibid. *1600*, 111. [5] *A.P.C.* xxix. 258–9.

being held in reserve to transport a new levy of 1,000 men, he was severely reprimanded and ordered to provide a vessel at once. In a postscript to their letter the Council added that they marvelled at the mayor's indiscretion in a matter of such great importance.[1]

The staple diet of the forces was loaf bread, or biscuit, butter, cheese, and beer. This was leavened by a variety of other foods: oatmeal, peas, beans, pork, bacon, fresh and salt beef; dried cod (stockfish), ling, and herring. The quantities of food provided for in the victualling contracts were directly related to the official daily ration of the private soldier. In a typical example (of 1598) the daily allowance was a pound of bread, or biscuit (costing $1\frac{1}{2}d.$), three ounces of butter ($\frac{3}{4}d.$), six ounces of cheese ($1d.$), and three-quarters of a pint of oatmeal ($\frac{3}{4}d.$). Transport and other expenses were reckoned at $\frac{1}{2}d.$ per man, raising the cost of a single day's ration to $4\frac{1}{2}d.$[2] This amount was deducted from the private's daily wage of $8d.$; but he still had to pay for what he drank. The victualling allowance for soldiers waiting to embark was usually $8d.$ a day, which seems generous when compared with the active service rate, even when the beer and lodging which it covered are taken into account. Perhaps the rate was deliberately pitched high in the interests of morale, and to minimize the danger of mutiny before embarkation.[3]

The daily ration varied from time to time. Another version in 1598 was a pound of biscuit, or a pound and a half of bread. Half a pound of butter was served three days a week, and a pound of cheese on the other three days. On the seventh day the bread ration was accompanied by two pounds of salt beef, or two and a half pounds of fresh beef. On this occasion the merchants were authorized to provide fish if they could not lay their hands on enough beef. The stipulated equivalents of one man's beef ration were: a quarter of a Dutch ling; eight herrings; one large cod; or one and a half small cod.[4] Fish, however, was not always a popular substitute for meat. It did not keep well, and, as Essex and the Council in Ireland complained on one occasion, aroused a thirst that was not easily quenched.[5] This objection did not apply in the same degree to fresh fish, although in Mountjoy's view all fish was less nourishing than bread,

---

[1] *A.P.C.* xxix. 353.   [2] Ibid. 272.   [3] Ibid. xxx. 496.
[4] Ibid. xxix. 383.   [5] *Irish Cal. 1599–1600*, 31.

butter, and cheese, and had the further disadvantage that kettles and fuel were needed to cook it.[1] Other variants of the meat ration were a pound of pork with a pint of peas, or a pound of bacon with a pint of 'great oatmeal called clees'.[2]

Lord Buckhurst suggested that food supplies in Ireland should be augmented by subsidizing the fishing industry. His idea was that the river Bann, Lough Foyle, and Lough Swilly, where there was an abundance of salmon, herring, eels, and cod, should be intensively fished. Fishermen, if they could give satisfactory guarantees, were to have their tackle provided by the government and repay their debt in fish. In the Netherlands fish was, at least on one occasion, more popular than bread and cheese. The men sold their bread and cheese rations, which were becoming monotonous, for half their value, and replaced them with fish or meat.[3] Some of the English soldiers at the siege of Leith were lucky enough to get salmon. Thomas Randolph saw two of them buy a piece of fresh salmon 'two spans long within an inch' for 3*d*. They thoroughly enjoyed it, and Randolph said that it did his heart good to see the men so merry.[4]

Bread and cheese had the great advantage, as Mountjoy pointed out, that they did not have to be cooked. They were also easily carried around, and were the obvious rations to take when the forces had to march some distance from their base. In camp, however, provision was made for relatively elaborate meals. The forces that went to Lough Foyle and Ballyshannon at the beginning of 1599 carried with them equipment to set up camp kitchens. The Lough Foyle contingent, which consisted of 3,000 infantry and 200 cavalry, took 20,000 bricks and a quantity of lime to make ovens. They also had 100 frying-pans, two pairs of weighing scales, and a variety of measures used in cooking. So that the kitchen might go into action as soon as the men landed, they carried ten loads of firewood. All this equipment—and also a signal bell for calling the men to supper, and a number of fishing nets—was paid for by the Crown. Things which were used by the individual soldier, however, or even by the company as a whole, came out of the private's pay. These included kettles, which would no doubt be used to cook the whole company's ration of oatmeal (one being allowed for every

[1] Ibid. *1600*, 491.
[2] *A.P.C.* xxx. 186.
[3] *For. Cal.* xxi, pt. 2, 180.
[4] Ibid. *1559–60*, 543.

100 men), and other common user items—brass mortars and iron pestles for 'bruising aniseed and liquorice', large platters, cans, and candlesticks (all made of wood), lanterns (one per company), candles, funnels, taps, and tap-borers for dispensing beer. The utensils for personal use were 'deep dishes, or porringers', which cost 1$d.$ each, and wooden spoons ($\frac{1}{4}d.$).[1]

Beer was an essential item in the soldier's diet. If he drank water he was more likely to fall a victim to disease.[2] In the Netherlands at one time the allowance was half a gallon daily.[3] In Ireland at the end of the reign the ration was half a pint of sack every day, plus a quart of beer and a quarter of a pint of aquavitae every second day—a generous allowance by any standard.[4] A drink made from aniseed and liquorice was also provided.[5]

The Privy Council tackled the problems of long-term victualling with intelligence. The reign saw a gradual change from a mixture of purveyance and freelance victualling by private merchants, at a time when there was relatively little military activity, to a highly organized contracting system in which the activities of established merchants were underwritten by the Crown at a time when the whole military machine was under great pressure. One of the Council's most interesting decisions was to elect to be served by private enterprise when faced in Ireland with the alternative of bringing the whole victualling system into direct government control, or throwing it completely over to the private merchants. It was a bold decision, and it paid. It was impossible, however, for anyone to reach a very high standard of efficiency, given the primitive methods of food preservation then available. Vegetables and fish could be dried, beef salted, but all the time the sixteenth-century victualler was up against difficulties undreamed of in a later age—difficulties that were intensified by the fact that most of the campaigns were fought overseas.

---

[1] *A.P.C.* xxx. 11. [2] *Treaty Papers*, xxxiv, f. 103.
[3] S.P. Holland, 51, no. 5. [4] *A.P.C.* xxix. 70. [5] Ibid. 272.

VI

UNIFORM

UNIFORM is a misnomer. There was only partial uniformity in clothing the troops. The levies were provided with their initial equipment—both arms and clothing—when they were called up. The men from one county would, as a rule, all be fitted out in much the same way, but there was no real national standard, nor did one county necessarily work to the same standard for successive levies. When the army was finally assembled the men were clothed in a variety of outfits.

Under the earlier Tudors, soldiers wore white coats, but in Elizabeth's time colours—nearly all the colours of the rainbow—were introduced. In 1560 the garrison of Berwick were clad in jackets 'of the queen's colours of white and green'.[1] Archers levied for Ireland in 1566 were dressed in blue cassocks with white borders, and in 1574 infantry coats were blue, and cut in the style of Gascony.[2] The clothing of the levies depended partly on the ideas of the lord lieutenant. The Earl of Rutland laid down that men levied in his lieutenancy for Leicester's expedition to the Netherlands in 1585 should have a cassock and red cloth hose.[3] Infantry for service in Ireland were clad in motley, or russet, which it has been suggested may have been for camouflage.[4] In 1599, when the Archbishop of Canterbury was ordered to raise cavalry from among the clergy the choice of colour was left to him by the Privy Council; and he decided on tawny or blue 'as had been the custom'.[5] On another occasion it was stipulated that each company should have its own colour.[6] As the reign progressed, however, there seems to have been an increasing preference for red.

The provision of coats was the responsibility of the county, and was usually made without specific instructions from the

---

[1] *For. Cal. 1560–1*, 328. [2] Harl. MSS. 1926, ff. 28b, 29.
[3] *Dom. Cal. 1581–90*, 285.
[4] Sir Charles Oman, *The Art of War in the Sixteenth Century*, 385.
[5] Lambeth MSS. 247, f. 118. [6] Harl. MSS. 168, f. 118.

Privy Council. The Crown did, however, contribute 4s. towards the cost of each coat, which was round about 15s. or 16s. It was clearly the intention that its own liability for coat money should be limited. When Lord Chandos suggested that, as the central government gave only 4s. per coat, it was hardly fair to require the county to pay more than an equal sum, and in fact provided only 4s. for coats in his lieutenancy of Gloucestershire, there was a strong reaction from the Council. They found the lord lieutenant's action very strange, considering that the practice in his county and everywhere else had always been to put up most of the coat money—which he knew well. It was quite wrong to be so niggardly in fitting out men who were to fight in a foreign country. Some counties had found 12s. or 15s. for the men's coats, and on top of this had given both officers and men something for their own purses. Chandos was therefore ordered to make a collection in the county so that his lieutenancy would not be singled out for its 'strait and sparing dealings' in matters that touched the honour of the queen and the realm, and pay up the balance due—which amounted to 10s. 10d. a coat.[1]

As a rule infantrymen were given only a coat when they were levied, but the Privy Council encouraged the local authorities to fit them out more generously. It admitted that the counties had been willing enough to supply coats in the past, but pointed out that many recruits had perished because they were so badly provided with other garments.[2] Perhaps as a result, the accoutrement of men from Anglesey in 1601 showed a great improvement. They had caps, cassocks, doublets, breeches, netherstocks, shoes, and shirts, and their clothing aroused considerable envy among the men from other counties.[3] The general intention, however, seems to have been to issue at the time of levy the minimum needed to last the troops until the first deliveries of uniform were made overseas.

Clothing for the army abroad was supplied twice a year, as in the Spanish forces. The regulation winter outfit for a private in the Netherlands was a cassock, a doublet, a pair of venetians (breeches of cloth first made in Venice and imitated in England), a hat, two shirts and collars, three pairs of stockings, and three pairs of shoes. When it was suggested that this outfit should be

---

[1] *A.P.C.* xxi. 306–7. [2] Ibid. xxix. 238. [3] *H.M.C. Salisbury*, xi. 474.

varied by the issue of extra shoes, stockings, and shirts instead of the doublet, the Privy Council thought a change unnecessary. It promised, however, to discuss the matter with the suppliers and to make any modification that seemed desirable.[1]

The private's summer clothing in the Netherlands consisted of a canvas doublet lined with white linen; a pair of venetians of Kentish broadcloth, also linen-lined; two shirts and collars of Holland cloth; two pairs of leather shoes; two pairs of kersey (coarse woollen cloth) stockings; and a hat.

Officers were more elaborately fitted out. In summer they had a doublet of Milan fustian, faced with taffeta; a pair of broadcloth venetians, trimmed with silk and lined with cotton and linen; and a pair of worsted stockings. In winter they had in addition a broadcloth cassock, lined with baize and faced with taffeta.[2] In Buckhurst's opinion officers' clothing was too elaborate. He proposed that only officers from colonels upwards should be allowed to wear silk and lace. Captains were to be content with fustian, cloth, and canvas, and were to spend on arms the money saved on clothing.[3] Thomas Digges also deprecated the captains' love of dressing up in silks, gold lace, and adorning themselves with jewels; and, writing from Leith in 1560, Cecil commented unfavourably to the queen on the extravagance of the captains' dress.[4]

There was a controversy about the clothing most suitable for the troops in Ireland. Sir Henry Wallop, the treasurer-at-war, suggested that it should be provided locally. Not only would the men be better equipped, but their outfits would cost thirty shillings a head less. He advocated the provision of Irish linen shirts and frieze cassocks, and in particular of a mantle which would keep the soldier dry by day and give him good shelter at night in a country where decent billets were few and far between.[5] Wallop's proposals were unsympathetically received by the Privy Council, whose spokesman said that there was no doubt that English clothing was best for Englishmen, although he admitted he had never been to Ireland and therefore had no first-hand knowledge of conditions there. He found it difficult to believe that a soldier could carry an unwieldy mantle and

---

[1] *A.P.C.* xx. 337. [2] Add. MSS. 5753, ff. 229b–230.
[3] *Irish Cal. 1599–1600*, 379. [4] *Scot. Cal.* i. 427.
[5] *Irish Cal. 1599–1600*, 359.

still be able to fight. It was his opinion that only long practice had made the Irish expert in manipulating it, and that Englishmen would abandon the garment in the heat of battle.[1]

This might seem to be a straightforward argument between a civilian and a man with practical experience of military affairs, but there was more in it than meets the eye. Wallop's proposal was sound enough, but it was inspired by an ulterior motive. If the Privy Council substituted Irish clothing for English—frieze for cloth, calfskin or sheepskin brogues for shoes, and mantles for cassocks—it would mean that considerable sums would be sent to Ireland to make purchases there. Wallop, who was allowed a percentage of the money carried by him to Ireland, would benefit accordingly, although it was said that he was already making more than he should.[2]

Another objection to the purchase of clothing in Ireland was that, although it might be supplied to the army by men loyal to the government, the chances were that it would in the first place have come from rebels; and they would use the English currency received in payment to buy munitions in Scotland and Denmark. Burgh therefore warned the Privy Council to weigh very carefully any scheme for buying uniform in Ireland. On the whole, he thought it preferable that enough money should be set aside in England to clothe the troops from there.[3]

The question came up again in 1599, when it was proposed to substitute for part of the outfit then issued two pairs of Irish frieze stockings and three pairs of brogues, which were in the opinion of the men who knew the country much more suitable than the English equivalent. If this change were made the money saved could be used to provide a mantle, and it was urged that the proposal should be considered before winter set in, as it was then that the mantle was most needed. It was of the greatest use both in sickness and in health, for however wet it got a little shaking and wringing made it perfectly dry. At night it was the soldier's bed, and without it men fell easy victims to dysentery, especially when they had to sleep in the open or do night guard duty.[4]

Essex favoured the adoption of Irish-made clothing. English uniforms shrank when they got wet, which often happened when

[1] *Irish Cal. 1596–7*, 381. [2] Ibid. 413.
[3] Ibid. 383. [4] *Carew Cal. 1589–1600*, 334.

the troops had to wade across rivers. In winter the short English cassocks gave little protection against the cold. He was convinced that if they were replaced by mantles, and that if brogues were substituted for English shoes, the troops would keep their health much longer. He had, however, to be tactful. He was well aware that the Privy Council had given the whole question careful thought, and therefore said he would not presume to thrust forward his own views.[1] In reply, the Council told him that the order had already been given to issue the types asked for,[2] and in 1600 men were issued with either a mantle or a specially long broadcloth cassock.[3] In the same year the use of brogues was recommended by the Council.[4]

The supply of clothing to the troops abroad towards the end of the reign was mainly in the hands of merchants working under contract. In 1588, however, the treasurer-at-war was still sharing in it. It had been proposed to buy clothing abroad for issue to the garrison of Ostend, but it was subsequently decided that it would be more satisfactory if the goods were procured in England. A better quality would be obtained, and the transaction would be in keeping with the best mercantilist principles of the age. Sir Thomas Sherley was accordingly instructed to buy clothing in England and have it dispatched immediately.[5]

It was natural that the cloth merchants, whose activities bulked so largely in the commerce of the country, should be deeply interested in the supply of uniform. In 1588 some merchants offered to make themselves responsible for the provision of clothing for the troops in the Netherlands, and stressed the benefits which would accrue from this step. Not only would English workmen turn out better goods, but the cost would be reduced by about one-tenth. Moreover, it was the Spanish practice to send uniform from home to the forces abroad, and it was suggested that what was good enough for the Spanish army should certainly be good enough for Englishmen.[6] Soon afterwards the Privy Council announced that certain merchants had been commissioned to provide doublets, hose, stockings, and hats at reasonable rates, and that deductions to pay for them were to be made from the soldiers' wages. The general

---

[1] *Irish Cal. 1599–1600*, 93. [2] Ibid. 112.
[3] *H.M.C. Rutland*, i. 357. [4] *Irish Cal. 1599–1600*, 310.
[5] *A.P.C.* xv. 352. [6] *For. Cal.* xxi, pt. iv, 34.

(Willoughby) was ordered to see that the captains made no profit when distributing supplies to their companies.[1]

Apparently this scheme was a success, for in the same year an agreement on similar lines was drawn up between the government and four merchants. Clothing was to be supplied to the value of £12,000 for the winter season, and to the value of £8,000 for the summer season. The whole winter issue had to be delivered by 1 November, and the summer issue by 1 June.[2] A year later Uriah Babington and Robert Bromley (who continued their operations into the next reign) were supplying clothing for the Netherlands. They complained that the customs authorities there were charging the usual import duties on ready-made outfits intended for the use of the English troops. The Privy Council sent a strong note of protest to the burgomaster of Flushing, and apparently succeeded in redressing the merchants' grievances, for the matter was not raised again.[3]

Several captains in the Netherlands complained that the arrangements were far from satisfactory. They said that clothing actually supplied was not as good as the standard outfits kept in the wardrobe office; that it was made of inferior material which wore out quickly, and shrank into the bargain; that the stockings were too short; and the shoes badly made. To remedy this they suggested that cloth should be sent from England and made to each soldier's measure on the spot.[4] Sherley, however, asserted that the merchants were operating quite satisfactorily, and added that the captains had no right to meddle in the supply of clothing. All they wanted was to get their hands on the troops' uniform allowance.[5]

Negotiations with the merchants in 1595 show how the contract system worked. The Privy Council had arrived at the conclusion that existing arrangements were inadequate. The contractors were not doing an honest job, and other merchants were asked to submit tenders. John Jolles, a London merchant, offered to 'arm, apparel, victual, and pay the forces in the Low Countries and Brittany'; to employ the agents of the previous contractors, provided an assurance was given that no attempt would be made to entice them away; and to give a bond for the due performance of his part of the bargain. This offer was

---

[1] *A.P.C.* xv. 412.   [2] *For. Cal.* xxii. 327.   [3] *A.P.C.* xviii. 351.
[4] *Dom. Cal. 1591–4*, 331.   [5] Ibid. 332.

deemed too ambitious and was not accepted.¹ Nor was an offer by George Leicester and William Beecher, two merchants whose activities had been singled out for criticism by the Privy Council, but who claimed that the allegations against them were quite without foundation.²

The successful merchants were John and Thomas Bolton and Richard Catcher, drapers and merchant tailors of London, who agreed to supply clothing for officers and privates at a fixed rate per head. They undertook to manufacture up to £1,000 worth every fifteen days, until the whole amount was provided, it being a condition that the goods should be paid for by the Crown at the time of delivery. They did not contract themselves to carry the uniforms abroad, but a separate agreement was entered into with Thomas Catcher, Richard's brother, who was paid £1,000 a year to see the goods safely to their destination overseas, deliveries having to be completed by the end of May for the summer period and by the middle of October for the winter. When it was suggested by the Council that the contractors should put down £10,000 as evidence of their good faith, they objected, and said it would be more reasonable for the Crown to give them some security for the due payment for supplies delivered. Later they agreed to put up a bond for £1,000, and brought forward three reputable citizens to vouch for them.³

The Boltons' and Catcher's offer was gladly accepted by the Privy Council, for it represented a substantial saving on the rates charged by the previous merchants.⁴ Indeed, when the new suppliers learned just how much the Crown was saving they regretfully informed the Council that they had not realized how low their offer was compared with earlier prices, but that they were, nevertheless, prepared to abide by it.⁵

Some idea of the incompetence of the government officials of the time may be gathered from the contractors' dealings with the wardrobe office, which was responsible for keeping the standard outfits and displaying them to would-be suppliers. The overseer of the office was unable to tell the difference between

---

¹ Ibid. *1595-7*, 22–23.   ² Ibid. 25.   ³ *Dom. Cal. 1595-7*, 22.
⁴ Ibid. 27. The actual prices were: private's outfit: Boltons and Catcher, £3. 5s. 3d., Beecher and Leicester, £4. 2s. 6d.; officer's outfit: Boltons and Catcher, £4. 0s. 10d., Beecher and Leicester, £5. 12s. 6d.
⁵ Ibid. 29.

officer's and private's suits, and passed off as a private's cassock one made of very good cloth, lined with baize and faced with taffeta, which was much more costly than the standard garment. He also showed samples of Devonshire kersey stockings, which were worth half a crown a pair, although the official allowance for stockings at this time was about half that amount.[1]

In practice, delays in payment by the Crown handicapped the merchants. At first no payment was made until it had been established that the goods had safely reached their destination abroad, which meant that the suppliers might have to wait for their money for many months. It was eventually arranged, however, that instead of having to wait until the goods had arrived overseas the contractors could be paid after supplies had passed inspection by the officers of the wardrobe office. The clothing was then packed, sealed, and dispatched. This not only relieved the merchants of a considerable financial burden, but also ensured that only satisfactory uniforms were sent abroad.[2]

The actual distribution of uniforms to the troops was far from efficient, and as usual the captains were largely to blame. Private soldiers in the Netherlands sent the Privy Council many complaints that the captains were retaining uniforms which they ought to have handed out, and thus were lining their own pockets at the expense of the soldiers' comfort. It was therefore decreed that the captains should cease to take part in distribution. Instead, clothing was to be issued jointly by the agents of the merchants and an official chosen by the Crown.

At the same time other changes were made in the arrangements for distribution. As it was difficult for men to carry their spare clothing about with them, and as experience had shown that privates generally sold everything not immediately needed by them, it was laid down that shoes and stockings were to be doled out at intervals instead of all at the beginning of the season. No soldier who was not a full member of a company—who did not keep watch and ward—was eligible for an outfit, which meant that enlisted men who were doing part-time civilian jobs in the garrison towns did not qualify. Men disposing of their uniforms were to be severely dealt with and have their pay stopped until the value of the clothing sold had been

[1] *Dom. Cal. 1595–7*, 22.   [2] Ibid. 29.

recovered. The official in charge of deliveries was instructed to keep a separate register for each company, which was to be submitted for the Privy Council's inspection every six months; and to make it more difficult for captains to introduce outsiders into the company for the express purpose of collecting a uniform he was expected to familiarize himself with the muster-master's records.[1]

These precautions suggest that there must have been a good deal of fraud in this branch of organization in the Netherlands. In Ireland, however, matters were much worse. The principal merchants, Babington and Bromley, and their accomplices, pocketed vast sums of public money. The frauds were not brought to light until 1616, when the Crown sued the merchants' executors for the recovery of money which it was alleged they had misappropriated, and, although the case against them was eventually dismissed in 1630, it is quite clear that the contractors, Sir George Carey (the treasurer-at-war), and most of the captains were guilty of large-scale fraud.[2]

Even if the Crown's case against the merchants was not strong enough to convince the court (and there were probably special reasons for this), there is little doubt about their guilt. Another merchant complained that although he had devised the method of supplying the troops in Ireland, and had sold it to Babington and Bromley for a third of their profits, he had never had a penny from them. He took proceedings against them in 1599, but six years later, when he had found his way into the Fleet prison, he had got no satisfaction.[3] James Quarles also accused Babington and Bromley of underhand dealing. They had asked him to engineer a break between himself and the Privy Council (he had himself been supplying clothing), but he had refused, despite their warnings about his fate if he persisted in working on his own. Instead he told Babington and Bromley that if they continued in their disorderly course he would lay the facts before the queen and Council.[4]

William Holliday was a third merchant who accused Babington and Bromley. He alleged that they had defrauded the Crown of £27,000 between 1597 and 1600. They had supplied

---

[1] Cott. MSS., Galba D IX, ff. 303b-6.
[2] H. Hall, *Society in the Elizabethan Age*, 125 ff.
[3] *H.M.C. Salisbury*, xvii. 241.   [4] Ibid. vii. 202-3.

only two-thirds of the uniforms contracted for, and had also given captains money in lieu of clothing at the rate of twenty-four shillings for the winter outfit, for which the Crown was paying the merchants forty-nine shillings, and proportionately less for the cheaper summer outfit.

Holliday quoted figures to prove that out of about 1,000 men only some 600 received a uniform, and that the money which should have clothed the other 400 had been shared between the merchants and the captains. He suggested that there should be an official inquiry, but none was held, and a year later he raised the question again. He said that as the treasurer and the lord chief justice had decided against an inquiry, despite the fact that the merchants had broken the terms of their agreement by supplying money instead of uniform, he perhaps should not take the matter any further.[1] He had, however, taken counsel's opinion and had been advised that the contractors' action was quite inexcusable.[2]

These accusations made by rival merchants are strongly supported from independent sources. There were innumerable complaints from Ireland about short deliveries of clothing. For example, in the winter of 1598–9 the merchants reported that they had supplied enough for all the forces, although in fact they had delivered only 2,500 suits. The Council in Ireland made the best of matters by sharing out the available supplies so that every man would get something, but the companies resented this and were reluctant to accept anything less than complete outfits.[3] The Privy Council said it was very ready to believe that the contractors were profiteering, and suspected that as the captains and muster-master made no complaint their mouths must have been stopped by bribes. Mountjoy was therefore ordered to investigate the whole position.[4]

Again, one John Byrde submitted that the Council had been hoodwinked by the contractors in various ways. He said they had supplied uniforms which were so rotten that the men had been eager enough to sell them back for seventeen or eighteen shillings a suit; and by disposing of the same suit over and over again the merchants had made as much as twenty pounds on a single outfit. Byrde also hinted at the implication of higher

[1] *H.M.C. Salisbury*, xi. 535–6.   [2] Ibid. xii. 704–6.
[3] *Irish Cal. 1598–9*, 464.   [4] Ibid. *1599–1600*, 442.

officials, whose names he dared not commit to paper (probably Sir George Carey was among them), and said that Babington and Bromley had sent him to Bristol to persuade the mayor and Crown officers to certify the shipment of a much larger number of uniforms than had actually left the port. He offered to justify his accusations by an investigation of the merchants' accounts, and of the books of the port officers of London, Bristol, and Chester.[1]

The one certain fact that emerges from the welter of accusation and counter-accusation—the merchants' criticisms of each other, the treasurer-at-war's allegations against them, and theirs against him, the doubts and suspicions of the Privy Council—is that there was deep and universal corruption in this branch of organization. In the very last months of the reign the Irish captains succeeded where their brothers in the Netherlands had failed. They won the right to handle the supply and distribution of uniform, perhaps because it was felt that they could hardly make a worse job of it than the merchants had done. If this is what the Privy Council thought, they could not have made a greater mistake. The wretched soldiers now found themselves infinitely worse off than they had been before, and the supply of uniform was quickly transferred back to the merchants—the lesser of the two evils.[2] The captains had much to answer for: but there is no greater indictment of them than this evidence that they were able to beat the clothing merchants at their sordid game.

[1] *H.M.C. Salisbury*, xvi. 75–77.
[2] H. Hall, *Society in the Elizabethan Age*, 126.

VII

ARMS AND EQUIPMENT

By far the most important military development in Elizabeth's reign was the victory of fire-arms over the older missile weapon, the long-bow. It was by no means an easy victory. It was achieved slowly, in the face of considerable technical and financial difficulty and bitter opposition from some professional soldiers.

The long-bow was still common enough at Elizabeth's accession; but more and more its use had been fostered by legislation—a sure sign that its days were numbered. It had had a long and glorious history, and, with the great triumphs it had won for England at Crécy and Agincourt in mind, parliament tried hard to keep it going. Their motives were complex, however. National defence was important and the bow was the country's traditional weapon. Therefore it must not decay. But archery had also been the main recreation of a great number of the people: it had kept them amused and physically fit. Now town life and pastoral farming impaired the physical condition of the nation as a whole. There were fewer strong men to master the bow. Further, the country was swept by a gambling craze, and it seemed to the legislators that if only archery could be brought back to its former glory the astonishing addiction to gambling, with all its attendant evils, would be abated.

The price of bows was going up, and the ordinary man could no longer easily afford one: something must be done about this. Again, the disappearance of the bow had encouraged, and been encouraged by, the introduction of guns. It was easier to provide game for the pot with a gun, especially if hail shot were used, than with a bow and arrow. The latter might make less noise and not attract the attention of the gamekeeper, but it was also for this purpose less efficient. A royal proclamation referred to the widespread illegal use of fowling and birding pieces which was despoiling all parts of the country of pheasant, partridge, and other sorts of game which should serve for the delight of her majesty, the nobility, and other men of quality.[1] The campaign for the bow was therefore partly a campaign against the non-military use of the new weapons, which were a godsend to the poacher, the robber, and the murderer. Finally, and not the least important, a large number of people made their living from archery—bowyers, fletchers, stringers, and arrowhead makers; and they could not change from one craft to another overnight. Something had to be done to keep them in work.

The relative importance of these different aspects of the decline of the bow changed with the passage of time. In the last quarter of the fifteenth century the main concern was with the efficiency of the country's archers and the steadily increasing cost of bows, which discouraged people from buying them. Attempts were made to increase the supply of bowstaves in the hope that prices would fall. The obligation on foreign merchants, trading from Venice and other places where England bought her bowstaves, to bring in four for every ton of cargo they imported was increased to ten staves for every cask of wine imported.[2] This obligation still existed in the middle of Elizabeth's reign, and although it had not proved very fruitful, it was extended to all foreign merchants trading from the east and from the seventy-two Hanseatic towns.[3]

The efficiency of the country's archers was a matter of concern at the beginning of Henry VIII's reign. An early act required every able-bodied man under the age of 60 to keep a bow and practise with it. When boys reached the age of 7 they had to be given a bow and two arrows; and so that there would be a plentiful supply at reasonable prices, especially for the children, bowyers were ordered to make two bows of elm or other cheap wood for every one of yew. Archery butts were to be set up, and the people were to practise shooting on holidays and at other convenient times.[4]

Although two years later this act was made perpetual[5] ('to stand and be in full strength for ever more'), it had little effect. Later in the reign its general provisions had to be re-enacted.[6] Now, bowyers were to manufacture four cheap bows for every one of yew. Bows for boys up to the age of 14 were to be sold

---

[1] Proclamation of 21 December 1600.   [2] 1 Richard III, c. 11.
[3] 13 Elizabeth I, c. 14.   [4] 3 Henry VIII, c. 3.
[5] 6 Henry VIII, c. 2.   [6] 33 Henry VIII, c. 9.

at no more than a shilling; and others at reasonable prices. The demand continued to fall, however, despite price control, and the bowyers accumulated stocks of the cheaper bows that nobody wanted. In 1566 parliament came to their rescue by reducing the proportion of cheap bows to be made outside London, where stocks were particularly heavy. London bowyers, however, still had to keep a minimum stock of fifty poorer quality bows. Finally, higher prices were allowed. The cost of imported bowstaves had risen in the last hundred years from £2 to £12 a hundred, and the bowyers' profit margin had dwindled away to nothing. The new controlled prices for bows were 6s. 8d. each for best foreign yew; 3s. 4d. for second quality; and 2s. for English yew.[1]

These higher prices reflect a change in the government's attitude. They were becoming more concerned with the welfare of the bowyers. The importance of archery was still piously stressed—'the use of archery not only has ever been but also yet is, by God's special gift to the English nation, a singular defence of the realm'[2]—but it was now widely accepted that the bow had had its day. Indeed Henry VIII's last act on this subject stemmed more from the representations of the bowyers, who were having a thin time, than from genuine concern about the future of archery. Bowyers who could not get enough work were leaving England, to the detriment of the realm and the benefit of the countries to which they emigrated. Worse, they were coming to London in large numbers, although they were not freemen of the city, to the disadvantage of those who were. This deprived the rest of the country of their services and it also raised serious problems in London, where their competition was unwelcome to the established bowyers, already in difficulty. It was therefore decreed that those who had come into London were to be removed; and any who remained were subject to heavy penalties.[3]

The change in the government's attitude to archery, which it now regarded as a social rather than a military problem, is further reflected by the legislation on gambling, and the civilian use of fire-arms. The connexion between archery and gambling may seem remote, but in fact it was very real, at least in the

---

[1] 8 Elizabeth I, c. 10.   [2] 13 Elizabeth I, c. 14.
[3] 33 Henry VIII, c. 9.

mind of the government and others who interested themselves in social problems. It was certainly very real to the bowyers themselves. Along with the fletchers, stringers, and arrowhead makers, they asked that some leading men in their companies should have authority to carry out the suppression of unlawful games.[1] In 1596 they commissioned a treatise addressed to the noblemen and gentlemen of England, making a strong plea for the bow, and nobly concluding with the sentiment that if the reader were not persuaded of the justice of their cause they would rather sink in their own misery than become a burden to the community.[2] Men who should be practising with the long-bow were tempted into gaming houses where new and crafty games were all the rage—bowls, quoits, ninepins, tennis, dice, and cards, to name a few. These games were declared illegal, and common houses or alleys where they were played were closed. Gambling was banned in the interests of archery, and archery was made compulsory to attract men from gambling; but it proved difficult to change human nature by act of parliament.

Roger Ascham has the last word about gambling and the decline of the bow. In *Toxophilus* he makes Philologus point out that cards and dice can be every bit as honest as archery. A man can play at cards for small stakes—after all, a pack costs only 2*d*., far less than a bow—and no harm done. Equally, in an archery contest he may shoot away all that he ever had. All very well, replies Toxophilus. Gaming may provide a vain present pleasure, but it leads to the loss of reputation, loss of goods, and the winning of a hundred gouty, dropsy diseases, as everyone knows. On the other hand shooting may be a painful pleasure, but it leads to bodily health, quickness of wit, and the ability to contribute to the defence of the country. But even Ascham has to admit the futility of trying to keep up the bow through acts of parliament. Men were playing with the king's statutes just like the man who, when householders were ordered to hang a lantern outside their door to illuminate the street at night, dutifully hung out the lantern, but positively refused to light the candle. So men bought their bows to give some appearance of obeying the law, but never loosed an arrow from them.

[1] Lansd. MSS. 22, f. 108.
[2] S.R., *A Brief Treatise*.

Parliament's efforts to keep the obsolete weapon in use (for reasons, be it repeated, that were not purely military) were backed by experts outside. Sir John Smythe was the most outspoken. In his book on the war in the Netherlands, published in 1590, he made a vitriolic attack on the misguided young men who thought that fire-arms were the weapon of the future. By seeking to abolish the bow, which was better than any weapon that ever existed, or would be invented, they were accomplishing the downfall of the realm.[1]

The disadvantages of the fire-arm were impressive even when set down by a dispassionate authority like Robert Barret. In addition to the gun itself, which was carried on the left shoulder, there was all the ancillary equipment: a flask of ordinary 'corned' powder carried at the waist, which provided the main charge; a box of finer touchpowder, suspended on a piece of string long enough to reach the gun for priming; a canvas or leather bag for bullets; three or four yards of slow match, also hanging from the waist; a further yard of match lighted at both ends and looped on the third finger of the left hand; paper or tow for wadding; and finally a flint and steel to rekindle the match if it went out.

The gun was loaded by pouring the right amount of powder into the barrel: too little would produce a feeble shot; too much would burst the barrel in the marksman's face. It was then primed with touchpowder. Finally, the bullet was rammed down the barrel with the scouring stick, followed ideally by a tow or paper wadding, although it was quicker to wedge the bullet with a few grains of powder dropped down the barrel. The weapon was now ready to fire.[2]

Smythe found the disadvantages of the fire-arm almost too numerous to record. It had to be accurately aimed. If the marksman erred by the length of a wheatcorn in the height of his point and blank he could miss even a big target. Seven or eight shots would overheat the weapon and make it dangerous to use. It was heavy to carry, and easily broken. The match, touchpowder, and main charge all had to be perfectly dry. Loading and firing were slow processes. If the wadding were forgotten, the bullets would roll from the barrel before the gun

---

[1] *Certain Discourses.*
[2] *Moderne Warres*, 34.

was fired. Those carrying fire-arms could not stand up to a cavalry charge.

Compare this miserable weapon with the long-bow. It was just conceivable that the stave might break, or the string snap; but not if the bow were regularly waxed, and the string treated with water-repellant glue. Think of the clouds of arrows flying together, thick as hail, terrifying the ears and eyes and hearts of horses and men, leaving not a single man or horse unscathed. Smythe might have been giving an eyewitness account of the battle of Crécy. He was, however, aware that the standards of archery had fallen. He would not employ those who shot in the new fashion, using only two fingers to pull the bow-string, instead of the customary three, as they lost a great deal of power. Nor would he have anyone in the army who had not practised archery all his life.[1]

Sir Thomas Wilford, who served as high marshal on Willoughby's expedition to Normandy in 1589, considered that there was still a place for both weapons. He accepted that the arquebus and the musket were more powerful than the bow, but held that the latter was still a serviceable and warlike weapon:

> First in the field against horsemen, though it be shot at the highest random, only with the weight of the fall it galleth both horse and man, and though the wound be not mortal, yet both horse and man are made unserviceable then and long after, if so be they escape death. Secondly, in rainy weather and when men come near together, it is a very good weapon. Thirdly, in the night it is both a ready and secret shot, and doth not discover itself as doth the arquebusier both with his fire and blow; and the use of it is good when it be in forcing the enemy's trenches, in sallying out of town, or otherwise. Fourthly, at an assault, when all the defences of a town are taken away, you deliver your arrows over the wall and rampires (i.e. ramparts) with its fall only. The like use we have of them out of the town, when an assault is given, in delivering them into the enemy's trenches, and among men at their approach to an assault, though they be shot over the wall by chance. Fifthly, to shoot arrows with wildfire, to burn a gate or drawbridge, to fire thatched or shingled houses. In France when we were before Paris and divers other towns that we besieged, bows would have stood us in good stead and I did then wish that we had brought some bowmen with us. Surely we have no reason to give over the bow as we have done, for I hold that the

---

[1] *Certain Discourses*, ff. 19b, 28.

worst bowman that can draw but his bow to be far better than a bad fire-shot.[1]

The majority of the military experts, however, favoured the new weapons. Writing fifteen years earlier than Smythe, Barnaby Rich came down heavily against the bow. This, the burning topic of the day, is left to the very last in his dialogue between Mercury and an English soldier, perhaps to keep the reader in suspense. Indeed, Mercury has proposed that the discussion should end, and that they should adjourn to the court of Venus, when the soldier begs leave to ask just one more question—does Mercury think that the caliver is better than the long-bow? He has often heard this debated, and his own opinion, for what it is worth, is that the bow is the superior weapon.

Mercury has little difficulty in disposing of this. Warfare has changed recently, and therefore there is no point in quoting biblical and classical precedents (a truth which few Elizabethan military writers accepted). It is true that the earlier fire-arms were not of much use, but the new caliver and musket are quite different propositions. Powder is better made. Men are more skilful in using fire-arms, and even if a man is not strong enough to use a bow, he can do quite well with a caliver. The archer needs a lot of elbow room, but the caliverman can operate easily from behind a bush, or a tree, almost from behind a molehill.

The soldier obediently changes his ground, and agrees that Mercury must be right. The caliver is the better weapon. The English long-bow may now finally be hung upon the wall; but it will be difficult to make others believe this. Mercury, however, says that archers still have their uses. They must not yet be dispensed with altogether. But he does wish that people would adopt a more sensible attitude to fire-arms, and also that those who use them would become as expert as possible. Having delivered his judgement he hastens to lead the soldier off to the court of Venus.[2] Two years after writing this Rich claimed that the bow had now been set aside in England.[3] Sir Roger Williams was satisfied that 500 musketeers were far better than 1,500

---

[1] *A Military Discourse whether it be better for England to give an invador present battle, or to temporize and defend the same*, 21–22.
[2] *A Right Exelent and Pleasaunt Dialogue*, Sig. H iib–vii.
[3] *Pathway*, Sig. K 3b.

archers, and also that, all things considered, the musket was better than the caliver. It was true that it fired only about a dozen shots with a pound of powder, compared with twenty or thirty from the caliver; but its range and effect were so much greater that there was no doubt that it was the superior weapon.[1]

While parliament was doing its best for the long-bow, the Privy Council was applying its mind to the development of fire-arms. In 1569 they sent a circular to the local authorities throughout the country with comprehensive proposals for 'the increase of arquebusiers' and asking for comments. This document is remarkable enough for its ideas, but it is even more so for the administrative technique it reveals. Whereas the long-bow legislation was simply fired hopefully at the heads of the people, and steadfastly ignored by them, the groundwork for the wider introduction of fire-arms was prepared with infinite care. It was accepted that there was little point in legislating for the greater use of fire-arms unless they had the support of those concerned with military affairs in the shires; and it was also accepted that the county authorities might make some helpful contribution to any scheme the Privy Council devised. Even if they did not, the mere process of consultation, and the good relations established by it, must ease the eventual introduction of an expensive and highly controversial change in military organization—which the counties had to pay for. There was never a clearer case of a government's striving to carry the people with it.

First, the commissioners of musters were required to invite those liable for arms under Mary Tudor's act to provide an arquebus, or better still a caliver, above their legal liability, if they could afford it. Some counties were able to tell the Council proudly that they had already taken it upon themselves to exact a higher rate.[2] The extra weapons had been readily forthcoming and were now available for the queen's use should the occasion arise. Not every county was able to report such willing co-operation—some had to plead poverty—but over the whole country substantial extra provision of fire-arms was made. In London, for example, the assessments under the statute produced only 150 guns, whereas the voluntary scheme raised an

---

[1] *Briefe Discourse*, 40, 46.
[2] S.P. Dom. 54, no. 16.

additional 450.[1] Some other counties were responsible for equally big increases.

The rest of the circular sounded out the county authorities about the future of fire-arms generally. How could men be trained to use them without abuses creeping in? How was the provision of powder, shot, and storehouses for the guns to be financed? Would it be reasonable to require holders of office under the Crown, certain clergymen, and justices of the peace to supply one arquebus more than they were now required to by law?

The Privy Council offered their own ideas on these points. They suggested that any justice of the peace who was not liable to provide a gun under the statute should now do so, or be dismissed from office. This was manifestly unfair. It carried the clear implication that the justice, who was unpaid, must be making something on the side; and it evoked an emotional response from the justices in some shires. Those of Kent said that they deprecated being lumped together with men who occupied paid offices: the Council must think that they, the justices, were making a profit out of their duties. What happened, or was imagined to happen, in other parts of the country was not their business, but if it were not for their service to the queen and their anxiety to see the peace kept in Kent, they would be glad to be rid of their office, which was becoming heavier day by day. Feeling that they might have gone too far, they humbly besought the Council to take all this in good part. They had been asked for their opinion, and had given it honestly.[2] Other counties did not take this point. The justices of Warwick, for example, said they would all be delighted to supply an extra gun, without thinking of the implications that had occurred to Kent.[3]

To popularize the new weapons in the militia, without at the same time facilitating their illegal use, posed a delicate administrative problem throughout the reign. A proclamation of 1579, for example, referred to the carrying of 'great pieces'—arquebuses, calivers, and the like—on the pretence of using them for military training. The use of these weapons was to be encouraged at the musters, or at the city practice grounds, but nowhere else. Even the gun-makers had to test their products at the

[1] S.P. Dom. 58, no. 13.   [2] Ibid. 59, no. 1.   [3] Ibid. 61, f. 22.

training grounds.¹ The Council's proposed solution in 1569 was that gun stores should be established at strategic points in the county. Their management would be in the hands of a corporation set up by those liable to provide fire-arms under the act, who would see that suitable managers were appointed. The corporations would also provide practice grounds, and have power to license men to shoot on practice days. There would be training once a fortnight, always under the supervision of a justice of the peace.

The reaction to this proposition was almost unanimous. It simply would not work. The commissioners of musters in Hertfordshire summed up national opinion when they said that the county could not afford such an elaborate scheme.² Moreover, the scheme had no hope of success unless the individual providing the gun were allowed to keep it in his possession and use it when he felt like it. There were other objections. The county of Essex feared that the concentration of many weapons in one place was asking for trouble. In towns where there were 'shoemakers, tailors and weavers and other light persons' they might band together to seize the armoury; and if they did, honest citizens would have no fire-arms to deal with them. Moreover, weapons were more likely to rust and become unserviceable in a public store than in the hands of the owner.³ This, in fact, was a real difficulty. A survey of the ordnance office in Ireland in 1578 showed that weapons stored for two years had suffered very badly. The whole stock of arquebuses was found to be unserviceable. Many calivers were 'no better than scrap iron'. Muskets had rusted, and leather powder flasks had perished. Most of the bows broke when they were tested, and the bowstrings and arrows had been affected by damp.⁴

There was also the problem of financing the stores, providing gunpowder and bullets, and prizes for the best marksmen. (One scheme envisaged five prizes every practice day, ranging from 1s. 8d. to 6s. 8d.)⁵ The Privy Council's idea was that these charges should be borne by those who owned parks and rabbit warrens, or went in for hawking. They would find that their game was better preserved if the county's fire-arms were

---

[1] Proclamation of 26 July 1579.   [2] S.P. Dom. 54, no. 16.
[3] Ibid. 58, no. 19.   [4] Harl. MSS. 4943, ff. 407–13b.
[5] S.P. Dom. 59, no. 1.

kept under lock and key, and only brought out under supervision. But the commissioners of musters paid little attention to these proposals, as virtually all considered the whole scheme to be impracticable.

The Council, however, was not content to leave the matter here. It was wise to try to carry the local authorities with it in any new scheme, but if they were unwilling to co-operate they could always be compelled to toe the line. In 1570 Kent, Essex, and Hampshire were required to make special arrangements for equipping and training arquebusiers—without prejudice to their obligation to equip and train able-bodied men in general; and the deputy lieutenants were urged to ensure that neither captains nor men took advantage of their possession of guns to go after game, or people on the highways.[1] Lord Burghley's instructions to his Deputies in 1589 show how the county system worked ideally. Each muster day those responsible under the statute to provide equipment were to have it 'well-dressed and scoured' and to hand it over to the soldiers appointed to carry it. The company sergeants kept lists of the names and addresses of those who provided the equipment. They examined it every six weeks, and ensured that the owner made good any deficiencies. The fire-arms, however, were kept together under the sergeant's care in the home of a 'substantial inhabitant', or otherwise, ast he deputy lieutenants might decide,[2]—a half-way house to a formal county store.

It was accepted by the Council that the new 'weapons of fire' had come to stay and, on balance, they felt that it was safer to keep them centrally. As time went on and the volume of military activity increased, stores were set up generally, although not on the elaborate scale originally planned. They were intended primarily for equipping the trained bands, but in practice were drawn on to equip men levied for service abroad. As more and more soldiers left the county it became difficult to keep the stores replenished. On one occasion the Council had to remind Buckhurst that his lieutenant's commission gave him authority to compel those liable for arms to make their contributions.[3] Again, Lord Cobham, when he had to equip a body going to France, said that his lieutenancy was unwilling to pay for it,

---

[1] *Dom. Cal. Addenda, 1566–79*, 305–6. [2] *H.M.C. Salisbury*, iv. 16–17.
[3] *A.P.C.* xvi. 218.

and asked how, in these circumstances, he was expected to replenish the store.[1]

In fact, the development of the stores tended to confuse the legal position. The statute required certain citizens to 'find and keep' weapons and to make them available when called upon. But if the weapons were turned over to a common store, and in due course issued for use abroad, what was the position? It was difficult to determine whose weapons had gone, but even if this were done the owner could claim that he had fulfilled his statutory obligation by finding a weapon, and that he was not liable to provide a replacement. In practice, however, statutory niceties were forgotten. The need for arms became so urgent that the county authorities had to bypass both the statute and the store system and take arms from individual citizens where they could find them. In Oxford, for example, men levied for service in Ireland were equipped with weapons commandeered from citizens selected by the corporation. But before they were issued the weapons were valued so that in the event of their being lost or damaged the owner would receive compensation from a fund raised from all the townspeople.[2]

It was, of course, intended that arms should be returned to the county store when the men came home, but the safe return of weapons was most exceptional. After the expedition to France in 1589, Willoughby remarked on the fact that the troops had restored the bulk of their equipment to the proper authorities— the like of which had never happened before in his experience.[3] A levy raised in the city of London in 1593 followed the more usual pattern. Seven companies were recruited and fitted out with weapons and armour. It was decided, however, to disband them before they had left the city. When their equipment was returned to store, 55 fire-arms were missing, 49 corselets, 32 pikes, 14 halberds, and 495 swords—which suggests that the sword was the most useful weapon for civilian life, and that the troops regarded it as a perquisite.[4]

The change-over from bows to fire-arms took place gradually through the reign. There were still a good many archers in the army at the siege of Leith in 1560. Humphrey Barwick, who

---

[1] *Dom. Cal. 1581–90*, 647.
[2] H. E. Salter, *Oxford Council Acts, 1583–1626*, 127.
[3] *H.M.C. Ancaster*, 312.   [4] Lansd. MSS. 73, no. 55.

served in this campaign, made a point of asking one of the French captains, after the capitulation, what success the English archers had had. The answer was simple. They had accomplished virtually nothing. None of the besieged had been killed by an arrow, and only one wounded. Moreover, the principal harm to this unfortunate came not from the arrow but from the efforts of the surgeon who treated him for his wound. Even so, he recovered.[1]

The force sent to suppress the northern rebellion in 1569 included bowmen. In the 1570's the shires were still fostering archery as the law required.[2] Leicester took a company of bowmen with him to the Netherlands in 1585.[3] In 1589, however, the Council decided that there was no longer any need to make provision for archers in the standard company organization. The bow was 'a natural weapon of the realm' and bowmen could be organized in their own separate companies—a tactful way of saying that the bow had had its day as a front-line weapon.[4] This was confirmed in 1595. When the commissioners of musters in Buckinghamshire reported that they had begun to convert some of the bowmen in their trained bands to caliver-men and musketeers, the Council said that they heartily approved. Calivers and muskets were of more use than bows. Moreover, in no other county were archers now regarded as trained men. They were simply 'able men untrained'. Buckinghamshire was therefore instructed to have all the bowmen in the trained bands converted to muskets or calivers.[5] The bow was now firmly hung on the wall.

As the bow went out, the weapons of fire came in. When the Council reviewed, in 1589, 'how the footbands shall be sorted with weapons to make them most serviceable', they concluded that the ideal company of 100 would contain 60 fire-arms, 30 pikes, and 10 halberds or bills.[6] There was, however, no guarantee that the men would be forthcoming in the prescribed proportions. It was one thing to theorize about the most effective balance of weapons, and quite another to equip the troops accordingly. The orders for Willoughby's expedition to

---

[1] *A Briefe Discourse concerning the Force and Effect of all Manuall Weapons of Fire*, ff. 15b–16.
[2] Harl. MSS. 309, f. 206.
[3] Add. MSS. 5753, f. 233.
[4] Lansd. MSS. 62, no. 8.
[5] *A.P.C.* xxv. 27–28.
[6] Lansd. MSS. 62, no. 8.

Normandy in the same year were for 46 guns, 54 pikemen, plus 10 dead pays in a company nominally of 100.¹ Two years later, when Essex went to France, the number of guns increased to 54.² It dropped to 47 in a levy devised personally by Lord Burghley in 1596—plus 47 pikes and the 6 dead pays allowed for service in Ireland,³ and in the same year the queen ordered that a levy for France should have two-thirds pikemen and one-third shot;⁴ but by 1601 the balance had swung definitely in favour of fire-arms. Companies of 100 now contained 64 fire-arms to 36 other weapons. Although the counties, as a rule, found it difficult to supply just what the Council wanted—the 900 men levied in Hampshire for Normandy in 1589 had only a handful of guns between them—practice did occasionally conform to theory. In Essex's force in France, in 1591, a company 135 strong was supposed to have 75 men armed with fire-arms, and 60 with other weapons. A muster taken in France shows that, on average, the companies had 73 fire-arms and 62 other weapons—almost exactly what the current regulations required.⁵

An odd missile that never really caught on was the musket arrow. This was a metal arrow eight or ten inches long. The rear end was screwed into a plug which was rammed against the powder charge in the musket. It is tempting to believe that it was a device designed to combine the efficiency of the fire-arm with the nostalgic attraction of the arrow—that it was the gunsmith's answer to Sir John Smythe. It is more likely, however, that this clumsy and unnatural weapon was used for special purposes, for example to carry incendiary material into the rigging of ships. There is a solitary example in the armouries of the Tower of London.

The introduction of fire-arms greatly raised the cost of equipping the forces. The long-bow had been an economical as well as an effective weapon, but the new weapons were expensive. Calivers ranged from 12*s.* 0*d.* to 30*s.* 0*d.*, compared with 6*s.* 8*d.* for a first-quality bow. Muskets were 18*s.* 0*d.* to 40*s.* 0*d.* Pikes and bills cost from 2*s.* 0*d.* to 3*s.* 0*d.* If we take 30*s.* 0*d.* as the average cost of fire-arms, 3*s.* 0*d.* for the other weapons, and the

---

¹ *A.P.C.* xviii. 88. (For 'dead pays' see pp. 151–8 below).
² Ibid. xxi. 222.　　　　　　　　　　³ Ibid. xxvi. 164.
⁴ *Dom. Cal. 1595–7*, 219.　　　⁵ S.P. France, xxvi, f. 174.

statutory price for bows, and apply them to the early and late companies described above, it appears that the cost of a company's weapons went up by about 50 per cent.

The change in weapons also affected the pockets of the individual soldiers. All had the same wage of 8*d*. a day; but whereas the running costs of a pike were virtually nil, the man who was allocated a musket had to pay for his gunpowder out of his wages. This seems manifestly unfair, yet there were no complaints on this score. There was no difficulty in finding men to carry fire-arms. Why? Partly because the musket had a prestige value, and partly because it could earn its keep in non-military activities—poaching, or worse. And in due course it could be sold for a handsome sum. There was no doubt about the popularity of the fire-arm with the ordinary man. The commissioners of musters in Kent told the Privy Council that if they wanted to increase the number of guns available for the forces it could be done very easily: simply repeal the legislation controlling the use of fire-arms, and let every man shoot when he wanted to, at anything he pleased, so long as no other had an interest in the thing shot at. It might be feared that this would reduce the country's stock of wildfowl, but the commissioners thought that this was not a serious risk.[1]

The archer's equipment, in addition to his six-foot long-bow and sheaf of arrows, consisted of a skull (a steel cap); a jack (a coat made of small overlapping metal plates, and covered with fabric); a shooting-glove of buckskin; and a bracer (a leather cuff protecting the arm holding the bow). Beneath the jack he wore a doublet, which, ideally, was made from fustian (cloth with a nap) or chamois leather, to prevent the metal of the jack from chafing, but more often was of canvas. An alternative to the doublet and jack favoured by Sir John Smythe was an 'eyelet holed doublet' that would withstand a sword-thrust. It should be covered with 'some trim and gallant kind of coloured cloth to the liking of the captain'. The archer also carried a sword—no more than three feet long—and a ten to twelve-inch dagger, so that he would not be defenceless when his arrows were spent, or when he was engaged in hand-to-hand fighting and had no elbowroom to use his bow. He had a stout leather belt to carry the sword, which, according to Smythe, must hang

[1] S.P. Dom. 59, no. 1.

elegantly by his side and not bump on his rear as did those of the drummers when they marched.

The functions of the musketeer and caliverman corresponded to those of the archer, and their arming was similar to his. They, too, wore fustian doublets and jacks of mail—although sometimes they might have corselets—and steel caps. If they wear morions, says Smythe, let them be of the upright or sharp model. Barwick advises against black morions. The white (i.e. the natural colour of the metal) 'doth beautify the soldier more and is of greater terror in the sight and eye of the enemy'. The musketeer also carried a sword and a dagger.

The pikeman, who was as a rule a much more heavily built man than the musketeer or archer, was also much more heavily armed. He had of course to do all his fighting at close quarters, unlike those who carried missile weapons, and he therefore needed much greater bodily protection. In addition to his pike —a pole, usually of ash, about eighteen feet long, and tipped with metal—he, too, carried a sword and dagger for use when 'the push of the pike' gave way to hand-to-hand fighting. Ideally, all the pikes should be of the same length. This increased the solidity of the wall of wood and metal presented to the enemy, and it also looked better. According to Smythe, if the pikes vary in height, like organ pipes, they are less likely to terrify the opposing army.

The pikeman's body armour at the beginning of the reign included a corselet (a metal shell that gave all-round protection to the torso and conformed more or less to the shape of the body), pouldrons, vambraces, tasses (metal plates protecting the shoulders, arms, and thighs respectively), and gauntlets. His headpiece was a burgonet—'well-stuffed for comfort'—which was tied with a scarf under the chin; or he might wear a morion. As the reign progressed there was a tendency to lighten the armour of the pikeman in the interests of increased mobility. One of the captains on Willoughby's expedition to France in 1589 took the law into his own hands and ordered his men to throw away their pouldrons, vambraces, and tasses—to the horror of the lord lieutenant, who had gone to a great deal of trouble and expense to provide them.[1] This practice also upset Sir John Smythe, who records that, contrary to all true discipline, many

[1] S.P. Dom. 226, no. 73.

captains both in France and the Low Countries made fully equipped levies from England give or throw away their pouldrons, vambraces, and tasses, leaving them with a cuirass (breast and back-plate fastened together) as their main body protection. It was said that this was done because these days there were no longer any pitched battles—only skirmishes which needed the maximum of mobility.[1] Eventually the Privy Council agreed with this line, despite the objections of the old school. In 1596 they adopted a suggestion put up by London that 'entire corselets' were not needed for a levy for France. Cuirasses would suffice. The Council also accepted that tasses and vambraces might be dispensed with.[2]

Fire-arms also hastened the obsolescence of heavily armed cavalry. They needed powerful horses, which became more difficult to find as time went on (although the lack of suitable horses was probably a symptom rather than a cause of the disappearance of the heavy cavalry); and they were impossibly slow in a period when speed was becoming more and more important. Men-at-arms, the heaviest of all, had virtually disappeared by the beginning of Elizabeth's reign. They were almost completely encased in heavy armour, with bullet-proof cuirasses. Their horses also had metal protection. Some of the nobility continued to own and occasionally wear this type of equipment, but the outfits of the men-at-arms were now showpieces, or all-metal command posts from which operations were directed, rather than fighting suits.

The demilances, the medium-heavy cavalry, persisted throughout the reign, but in diminishing numbers. There were 600 of them at the siege of Leith, but they had little more than prestige value. According to Robert Barret, their armour should consist of a good pair of cuirasses, the fore-part to be pistol-proof; but the rest of their equipment was as light as may be, and their horses were unarmed. The riders should wear cassocks under their armour, of the same colour as the ensign.[3] The conservative Sir John Smythe wanted to keep the demilances as heavily armed as they ever were. Indeed, his specification reads more like a description of the men-at-arms. Even the light cavalry should be in heavy armour, according to him. Their 'red and pied

---

[1] Sir J. Smythe, *Orders Mylitarie*, 196. [2] *A.P.C.* xxvi. 200.
[3] *Moderne Warres*, 141–2.

caps, and steel skulls within them', and their jacks, simply were not enough. They should be armed almost as heavily as the pikeman, and they should carry an eighteen-foot spear. They should also use Morocco saddles, which were much larger than the 'Scottish' saddles currently in use. In short, he wanted to see the light cavalry heavily protected at the expense of their mobility.[1] Had he had his way they would have followed the men-at-arms and the demilances into oblivion. As it was, they survived Elizabeth's reign, although they did not play a great part in it, and lived on for more than three hundred years. The national musters showed only 270 demilances in 1575, compared with 2,500 light cavalry.[2]

Although the liability to provide weapons and equipment rested clearly on the county authorities, the central government was, nevertheless, deeply concerned. It had to ensure that the counties made the right sort of provision, having regard to the current theories of warfare; and it also had to ensure that the country's stock of weapons and armour was equal to the demands made on it. The national supply was controlled through import and export policies, and by direct government purchase. The export of artillery and gunmetal was regulated, partly to deny supplies to enemies abroad, and partly to keep adequate quantities available for emergencies at home. As we have just seen, imports of bowstaves were encouraged by act of parliament. At the beginning of the reign, when the international situation was particularly threatening, England was badly off for arms. Sir Thomas Gresham, the government's financial agent in the Low Countries, arranged for large-scale shipments of equipment of every sort from the Spanish-controlled arsenals, by the extensive use of bribery and corruption—a truly remarkable feat. He reported to Cecil on one occasion that he had 'by trickery' drawn 2,000 corselets from the royal arsenal at Malines, and that their disappearance had caused 'no small stir among the officers'. The supplies thus acquired from abroad, and those available from home production, were pooled in the armoury and ordnance offices, ready to be drawn on as occasion demanded; and from time to time the county authorities were notified that if they were short of equipment, it could be had from London.

[1] *Orders Mylitarie*, 198–203. [2] Lambeth MSS. 247, f. 76.

The lack of central control of the types of armour and weapons used in the forces came in for criticism from time to time. Before Willoughby's expedition left for Normandy in 1589 Lord Buckhurst, who as lord lieutenant was responsible for equipping the Sussex regiment, suggested to Burghley that the Privy Council should supply standard patterns which the counties could copy when fitting out levies, so that the whims of individual captains need not be taken into account.[1] Sir Thomas Wilford, Willoughby's high marshal in Normandy, touches more vigorously on the same point in his *Military Discourse*. Although in his opinion the bow still has its uses, he accepts that fire-arms have come to stay. He considers, however, that so many 'Fire-shot' are being recruited these days that in a serious emergency there will only be enough gunpowder for a tenth of them. Further, the government must give more positive guidance about the design of equipment. It is a great pity that

upon some few men's private fancies we do alter and change arms and weapons as we do, putting the country to great charge therewith and oftentimes their furniture spoiled and marred thereby; for one man upon view of the country's furniture will break all the stocks of their pieces and cause them to make crooked. Another man cometh after and will break the crooked and force them to make straight stocks again. Then cometh the third and will make them to cut the barrels of their pieces shorter and bore them bigger. And another cometh with a smith's sledge and he will break both the pieces and batter armours and will have all men furnished according to his fancy. It is to be wished that there should not be any suffered to make an alteration of arms and weapons of himself, but rather the same to be done by an order established for the same, and by those that are of judgement and in authority.[2]

The armoury office was more concerned with the supply of fine armour for the nobility than provision of equipment for the rank and file, but it did provide at least swords to troops going overseas. In the last twenty years of the century it issued more than 11,000 swords to the forces in Ireland.[3] But apart from supplying these, and more rarely corselets,[4] morions, and targets,[5] the office contributed little to the equipment of the army.

---

[1] S.P. Dom. 226, no. 73.   [2] *Military Discourse*, 22–23.
[3] Exchequer accounts, army, navy and ordnance, bundle 64, no. 11.
[4] *A.P.C.* xxx. 375.   [5] Ibid. xxxii. 298; *H.M.C. Salisbury*, iii. 409.

The ordnance office was a larger establishment, and much more important for the army. In addition to its administrative staff, which included six clerks to keep the books, it had about a dozen craftsmen. There were a bowyer and a fletcher, who continued to be employed far into the seventeenth century, long after the bow had disappeared from the army, and whose jobs must have been sinecures even in Elizabeth's reign; a cooper to make barrels for ammunition and tallow; a carpenter and wheelwright to provide the wooden parts of heavy artillery; a smith for metal work generally; a plumber, who was not concerned with drains, but with the provision of lead shot; and two furbishers for burnishing the bright metal parts of armour and equipment. Lastly came two proof-masters, who tested the efficiency of armour by the simple method of firing bullets at it, thereby materially weakening the area where the bullet struck, without providing a very reliable guarantee that the rest of the armour was bullet-proof. Two men were employed testing gunpowder and saltpetre, and there were about twenty labourers, a carter, and a messenger. The craftsmen were paid a wage for their day-to-day services in maintaining and making equipment; and they were also commissioned to lay in stores in their own particular line from outside suppliers. The muskets and calivers held in the ordnance office were examined periodically, and defective weapons were sent out to gunsmiths for repair.[1]

The office was responsible for the provision of heavy guns, small arms, match, shot, and a whole host of ancillary supplies, including bandoliers, moulds for making bullets, melting ladles, musket rests, powder flasks, touchboxes, shovels, spades, crowbars, pickaxes, felling-axes, hedging bills, scythes, reaping hooks, tarred and white rope, canvas for binding halberds, chests for muskets and calivers, nails, tallow, and wood in all forms.

The master gunner was included in the establishment of the ordnance office. He had under him the keeper of the small arms and shot, and the keeper of the rich weapons; and for the greater part of the reign he was also in charge of the work of proving armour. Part of his job was to 'exercise scholars in the Artillery Garden'.

The ordnance office did not manufacture artillery, but bought from the gun-founders, and from abroad. Heavy guns had been

[1] Exchequer of Receipt, Miscellaneous Books and Papers, no. 13.

used in warfare for more than two centuries before Elizabeth's time; and by the middle of the sixteenth century there was a wide variety ranging from the tiny robinet, which fired a one-inch ball, to the cannon, with a calibre of about eight inches, and a shot weighing (in bronze) upwards of sixty pounds. Between these extremes were the falconet, the falcon, the minion, the saker, the demi-culverin, the culverin, and the demi-cannon. Although artillery was occasionally used on the battlefield, the main use was in battering fortifications; and as a rule an enormous amount of effort was expended in achieving very slender results. Projectiles were of iron or bronze for the smaller calibres, but for the larger, stone balls were preferred. Being lighter than iron they required a smaller charge to propel them the same distance; and the loss in battering power was assumed to be compensated for by the greater safety which the smaller charge afforded the gunner. The price ratio of bronze to stone was about 100 to 1, which provided a further incentive to use stone as far as possible for the larger calibres.[1]

The science of gunnery was only just beginning; and much of the advice in the textbooks was based on the fancy of the author rather than scientific fact. Cyprian Lucar, for example, recommends that the gunner should drink, and eat a little meat before discharging any piece of artillery. If he does not, the fumes of sulphur and saltpetre will be hurtful to his brains. But he must take care never to fire any gun while his stomach is full. Most of his advice is practical, however. The gunner must consider whether the air be thin and clear, or close and thick, because the 'pellet' will pass more easily through the thinner air. The gun carriage must be properly maintained. If one wheel is greased more than the other, if the wheels are not exactly the same size, or if one wheel hub is bigger than the other, then there must be an uneven recoil, and the piece cannot shoot straight. The wadding and the shot must be well rammed home: if they are not, there is the danger that the gun will explode.[2] The gunner's quadrant was an instrument designed to make it easier to get the angle of elevation right, but in

---

[1] O. F. G. Hogg, 'Elizabethan Artillery', *Journal of the Royal Artillery*, lxv. 130-42; A. W. Wilson, 'The Story of the Gun', ibid. lxxi. 227-40.

[2] Cyprian Lucar, 'The Properties, Office, and Duty of a Gunner', *Journal of the Royal Artillery*, lxxi. 211-16.

ARMS AND EQUIPMENT

Elizabeth's time gunnery was more an art than a science. The man with the right knack was more likely to get good results than the man who relied on textbooks and instruments.

New regulations for the administration of the ordnance office were drawn up by the master (the Earl of Warwick) in 1584. Two sets of records were kept, one for the information of the Council and the other for the use of the office itself. All contracts for the purchase of munitions had to be signed by the master and two other officers before they were valid. Records of the receipt and issue of stores were preserved in the 'great standard chest' to which the master, lieutenant, and surveyor held keys, and were examined once a year. The private purchase of munitions was strictly forbidden, unless on a warrant from the queen or the Privy Council. Five years later Warwick introduced new regulations. It was now laid down that all the chief officers should meet twice a week, on Tuesdays and Fridays. Four journals of the proceedings were to be kept—one each by the surveyor, the clerk of deliveries, the keeper, and the master's clerk. Books were made up every two months, and no application for the issue of powder was considered unless it was addressed to the master.[1]

It was revealed, when Warwick died, that he had been misappropriating official funds. He was entitled by the terms of his appointment to claim certain fees, but a commission set up to investigate his accounts reported that he had been pocketing sums considerably in excess of his allowance. The new master, the Earl of Essex, was exhorted by the Privy Council not to follow in his predecessor's misguided footsteps. At the same time the Council tightened up the regulations. A more elaborate system of accounting and book-keeping was introduced. The Council stressed the importance of keeping exact records of receipts and deliveries of munitions, and instructed the clerks of receipt and delivery to compare their books on the first Monday of every month to reveal discrepancies. If one of the clerks was found to be at fault, he was fined a month's pay. If he continued in error, he was dismissed. All transactions were summarized each quarter and the records preserved for future reference. The master was made responsible for getting quarterly returns from the royal arsenals at Woolwich, Rochester, and Chatham, so

[1] S.P. Dom. 228, no. 20; Harl. MSS. 309, f. 72.

that an up-to-date statement of the country's stock of munitions would be readily available.[1]

Normally the ordnance office was able to do what was required of it—which was to keep reserves of those types of weapons and equipment which the counties had to provide, and also to have adequate supplies of the munitions which were the direct responsibility of the government. Occasionally emergency measures were necessary. At the beginning of the reign Sir Thomas Gresham was commissioned to buy arms in the Netherlands, and Sir John Norreys had a similar commission before the Portugal expedition left.[2] Once or twice private individuals offered to supply arms by contract, but at first their offers were not accepted. In 1588 the master smith of the ordnance office in Ireland offered to provide there all kinds of munitions at the price at which they were issued from the ordnance office in London, so that the Crown would save the cost of transport and avoid the risk of loss at sea. The Council was tempted by the offer and instructed the lord deputy to accept it if he could be certain that the arms thus manufactured in Ireland could not possibly find their way into the hands of the rebels, and that the merchants who were accustomed to carry munitions to Ireland at their own risk would not be discouraged from doing so in future.[3] Apparently, there was no assurance that the conditions would be met, for nothing more was heard of the proposal.

A few years later a manufacturer asked for a ten-years contract to supply annually a thousand muskets and a thousand calivers. He said that if his offer were accepted he would be able to keep in employment craftsmen whom he had assembled from all over the country, and suggested that in time of national emergency his establishment would be of great benefit to the state. He proposed to deliver the arms free on board at Chester for shipment to Ireland, but again nothing further was heard of the offer.[4]

The growing needs of the army at the end of the reign compelled the Council to enlist the aid of private suppliers. In 1601 Edmund Nicholson offered to supply both cavalry and infantry weapons at prices lower than those current, and a commission

---

[1] *Dom. Cal.* 1595–7, 381–3.
[2] Ibid. 1547–80, 121, 128; S.P. Dom. 219, no. 16.   [3] *A.P.C.* xvi. 186.
[4] *Irish Cal.* 1588–92, 377.

was set up to consider the offer and examine samples. The project was opposed by some of the armourers in London, who feared that their business would be hit. On the other hand, a number of other armourers, cutlers, and gunmakers—no doubt those likely to be employed by the contractor—were strongly in favour of the scheme. The commission heard evidence from the rival groups and eventually decided to accept the offer. Nicholson supplied corselets, pikes, pouldrons, calivers, muskets, bastard muskets, bandoliers, morions, and Turkey swords for a levy of 2,000. His agents delivered the supplies to the companies as they embarked at Southampton, Bristol, and Chester, in the presence of the officials supervising embarkation, and received from the captains receipts which were in due course used as authorities for payment.[1]

Far more weapons were lost through dishonesty than by enemy action. So many of the men disbanded from the army at Tilbury sold their weapons on their way home after the destruction of the Armada that a royal proclamation had to be issued warning offenders that they were liable to arrest. They would also be fined, half the fine to go to the informer, and half to the county where the informer lived, to buy gunpowder for the shire musters.[2] There was a further proclamation the following year, drawing the attention of soldiers to the fact that selling or pawning of their arms now carried the death penalty. The man who bought the arms had to hand them back to the authorities and suffer imprisonment. So that arms which were sold might be traced, all were to be marked with a sign which was recorded in the muster rolls.[3] The proclamations were backed up by an act of parliament introduced at the queen's special request.[4] Anyone who disposed of any armour, ordnance, munition, shot, powder, or habiliments of war belonging to the Crown worth more than 20s. 0d., was to be dealt with as a felon. But these measures made little difference. Things went on as before, with the captains playing their part as usual. In 1591 eleven men were found guilty of buying their discharge partly by a cash payment, and partly by handing over their equipment, which the captain sold to a London merchant.[5] A few years later

---
[1] *A.P.C.* xxx. 381; xxxii. 472–3.   [2] Proclamation of 25 August 1588.
[3] Proclamation of 23 January 1589.   [4] 31 Elizabeth I, c. 4.
[5] *Dom. Cal. 1591–4*, 89.

captains in France were selling their men's arms and even the clothing off their backs.[1] Another money-making device they used was to sell a soldier his discharge, and then when a replacement turned up, to sell to him the equipment which had belonged to the discharged man. This earned the captains two to three pounds for every men they got rid of, and it also kept their companies permanently 'raw and green'.[2]

The replacement of equipment issued to the levies and never returned was a heavy charge on the county funds. In 1596 the Council tried to ease the burden by decreeing that the captain or lieutenant receiving the troops should give the county authorities a bond for double the value of the equipment supplied. The bond was redeemable when the arms were returned to store, or, if they had been lost in battle, then a statement by one of the principal officers was produced describing exactly how the weapons had been lost.[3] But the captains could not possibly have taken such a proposal seriously.

In 1598 the Council in Ireland appealed for fresh supplies of arms from England. Not only were weapons broken and lost in the ordinary course of service, but they invariably disappeared when a man died or deserted. It was also common for the men to sell their arms to the Irish, including the rebels.[4] About the same time some of the captains in Ireland admitted that their men were selling their arms, but excused them on the ground that it was the only way they could get money for food.[5] Lord Buckhurst tried to solve the problem by proposing that an indenture should be made between the captain and the treasurer-at-war recording the weapons carried by every man in the company. The captain would provide a monthly certificate of lost equipment, and if it appeared at the muster day that any had been sold the captain would have to replace it from his own pocket.[6] This also was much too drastic to be countenanced by the captains.

Before 1588 the country had been largely dependent on imported gunpowder, despite the fact that in 1561 the government bought from a German inventor a method of making the principal ingredient: potassium nitrate, or saltpetre. The dangers of having to depend on foreign supplies of such a vital material

[1] *Dom. Cal. 1595–7*, 495.   [2] *For. Cal.* xxiii. 82.   [3] *A.P.C.* xxvi. 163.
[4] *Irish Cal. 1598–9*, 138.   [5] Ibid. 148.   [6] *Dom. Cal. 1591–4*, 200.

were emphasized by the heavy expenditure of powder in the sea-fight with the Armada, and induced the Council to encourage home production. Chemistry was not yet sufficiently advanced to enable powder manufacturers to dispense with imported sulphur, but charcoal was readily available from indigenous sources. Saltpetre (of which there were no natural deposits in England) could be made artificially from lime, ashes, and earth treated with animal excrement.

The Council entered into a contract with certain manufacturers, authorizing them to acquire earth for saltpetre anywhere in the country, except London and two miles around, and the five northernmost counties. They were licensed to dig in dovecotes, barns, stables, stalls, and outhouses, provided that they re-erected any buildings that collapsed as a result of their activities, and replaced with fresh supplies the earth which they removed. The local authorities were instructed to give them every assistance. They must have been called in frequently, for the removal of earth which weakened the foundations of their houses was naturally unpopular with property-owners.

In 1599 the northern counties which had been exempt were also required to make earth available. It was recorded at this time that the requisitioning of wagons to carry earth to the factories had been an unwelcome burden to the people, who had also suffered through the massive destruction of forests for charcoal manufacture. The powder makers now agreed to supply the Council with a hundred lasts of gunpowder a year (something over 100 tons) at 7*d*. the pound. If they were able to produce more than this they were authorized to sell it to merchants at the controlled price of 10*d*. a pound. As it turned out there was a considerable surplus, and in 1601 over 30 tons were exported to the Netherlands, which had been England's main source of supply in the early days of the reign.[1] But despite the great increase in domestic production, powder was still imported from time to time.

The main powder store was in the ordnance office, but private merchants also held substantial stocks. In 1586 the lieutenant of the Tower complained that one was holding a stock of over forty tons in a store on Tower Hill. He said that it was in great danger, as vagrants were accustomed to light fires

[1] S.P. Dom. 195, no. 112; 224. no. 28.

near it at night.¹ But even in the ordnance office no great precautions were taken with powder. Large quantities were left lying about in the open, although it was supposed to be stored carefully in the vaults.² Throughout the country there were smaller powder stores, which the lord lieutenant was expected to keep stocked with purchases from the ordnance office. In practice many counties made no attempt to keep their stores full. They were reprimanded by the Privy Council and ordered to make immediate purchases from London.³

Although the county was responsible for supplying the gunpowder used in training at the shire musters, on active service the cost of powder, both for training and for battle, was deducted from the soldier's wages. The free issue of powder had been authorized by Mary Tudor, who allowed two pounds of corn powder monthly to every arquebusier in the garrison of Berwick 'so that by the exercise of their pieces they might learn to be the more perfect in the feat'. This continued after the queen's warrant had expired on her death, and there was trouble when the captains suddenly had the cost of the powder deducted from their companies' pay. They pointed out that if the men had known that they were paying for their powder again they would never have used so much in practising. The Privy Council was asked to give covering authority for the powder issued without warrant, and to confirm that free issue should be discontinued.⁴

The usual arrangement for issuing powder was for the captain to apply to the master of the ordnance for the company's requirements. He gave a receipt which was passed to the treasurer-at-war, so that the appropriate amount might be deducted from the company's next pay.⁵ That deductions were still being made for powder in 1589 is shown by a recommendation that the private should be given a special allowance for fire, light, and laundry. Otherwise these expenses, added to the levy for the surgeon, clerk, muster-master, priest, and for gunpowder, would leave him with nothing at all.⁶ The naturally slow rate of fire of the new weapons must have been further decelerated by the private's knowledge that every time he pulled the trigger he was knocking something off his next week's

---

[1] *Dom. Cal. 1581–90*, 311.   [2] Ibid. *1595–7*, 81.   [3] *A.P.C.* xxiii. 273.
[4] *For. Cal.* ii. 7.   [5] L. and T. Digges, *Stratioticos*, 255.
[6] Treaty Papers, xxxiv, f. 103.

pay. Essex had the good sense to urge that powder should be issued free, but others objected strongly. Such a practice would be against all reason, equity, good order, and justice.[1]

The captains in Ireland also objected to the soldiers' having to supply their own powder. It was a constant source of worry to the men, who knew that the more powder they used the less would they have in food and clothing. It made the men unwilling to fire, and turned brave men into cowards.[2] In 1598 it was alleged that this method of issuing powder was the only reason why an English force was defeated by the rebels.[3] Frequent engagements towards the end of the reign imposed a much greater strain on the already over-taxed resources of the private, and Lord Buckhurst at last conceded that the men should have free powder for use in action.[4] The logical step was taken shortly afterwards when Mountjoy was authorized to issue powder from time to time for training purposes as well as for battle.[5] This decision was confirmed in 1601 when it was ruled that neither the cost of powder, nor the loss of arms on the battlefield, was to be borne by the private soldier.[6]

[1] *Irish Cal. 1599–1600*, 380.
[2] Ibid. *1598–9*, 148.
[3] Ibid. 252–3.
[4] Ibid. *1599–1600*, 380.
[5] Ibid. 448.
[6] *A.P.C.* xxxii. 337.

VIII

MUSTERS

THE whole Elizabethan military organization depended on the efficiency of musters in peace and war. There was a fundamental difference, however, between the peacetime shire musters, and those taken on active service. The latter were the key to the success of a campaign. The former were vital to the future of the army.

Musters on active service recorded the numbers of men with the colours and their absences on leave and sick leave. They provided a basis for the distribution of rations and uniform. They gave the treasurer-at-war the information he needed to calculate pay. They revealed the quantities of arms and equipment and were therefore a mirror through which the commander-in-chief and the Privy Council viewed the fighting state of the forces. Without accurate musters in the field the Crown could not get value for money invested in the army; and the general might find himself leading into battle troops that existed only on paper.

The shire musters added training to the function of counting, and it was this difference that gave them their broader significance. It was unnecessary to make special provision for training on active service. The men trained on the job. Equally, counting was in the short run less important in the shire musters. Even if the captains contrived to pocket the pay of some absentees it was only for a few days at a time. But if those who did turn up were not given their training, and the shire muster was no more than a glorified picnic, it was not just a campaign that was put at risk. The effectiveness of the national force was prejudiced, and with it the safety of the realm.

The authority for mustering the militia lay in Mary Tudor's act 'for the taking of musters' of 1557.[1] The preamble recited that many able-bodied men had refused to come to the musters to train. Others had been exempted in return for bribes, or for

[1] 4 & 5 Philip and Mary, c. 3.

friendship's sake. Men quite unfitted for active service had been called up simply to give captains the chance of selling them their release. All this had greatly impoverished the people and endangered the realm. Now, all who did not attend the musters on the due days, or who appeared with inadequate equipment, were made liable to a fine of 40s. or ten days' imprisonment. Muster-masters convicted of taking bribes paid ten times the amount of the bribe. A captain who allowed men to buy their way out of the forces was fined ten times what the men paid. If he withheld pay for more than ten days after he had received it for distribution to the troops, he was again liable to a fine of ten times the amount retained. He had also to pay the aggrieved soldiers three times their due. The fines were split equally between the Crown and the informer who brought the offender to court.

Ideally, general musters would have been held annually. By training together regularly under the same captain men would have become more efficient, and an *esprit de corps* would have developed—or at least the way would have been opened to these desirable ends. Annual general musters were hardly practicable, however. For one thing, the work of the nation had to stop for the duration of the musters. They put a heavy administrative burden on the shoulders of the already over-worked justices of the peace. They entailed a vast amount of clerical work in the compilation of returns, of which at least two copies were required—one for the information of the Privy Council, which was to be kept by the surveyor-general of the muster rolls; and one to be kept by the county as a check list for the next musters. The compilation of the rolls was left to the constables, but as it was recognized that they entailed 'much writing' the commissioners of musters were empowered to call in the clerk of the peace to help out.

The government therefore planned to hold a universal muster every four years or so; and in the intervening period the county was supposed to keep the training programme going as best it could. There was, however, nothing sacrosanct about the four-year cycle, and in time of crisis general musters were held more frequently. There was one in 1587 because of the threat from Spain.[1] The international situation was still dangerous in 1589

[1] *Dom. Cal. 1581–90*, 400.

and the queen instructed the lieutenants to carry out a new muster on the same lines as the previous one. The opportunity was to be taken to remedy any shortcomings revealed last time, and to fill any vacancies; but because it was a costly business to keep men away from their jobs for too long the lieutenants were to cut out elaborate training. It would be enough to see that those attending had their weapons and equipment in good order.[1]

The government could hardly wait longer than four years between the national reviews. The muster rolls went out of date as men died or left the county, or reached the age of sixty and no longer had to bear arms. Also, unless they were revised at short intervals they did not contain the names of youths who had just become liable for military service. The four-year period made good administrative sense, and it was retained for the greater part of the reign.

Elizabeth called for a national muster a few months after her accession, although one had been held the year before. Danger threatened from abroad and it was natural that the new sovereign should wish to be reassured about the nation's defences. The arrangements made on this occasion were broadly followed throughout the reign.

The first step was to instruct the lords lieutenant to set the machinery in motion; and in those counties where there was no lieutenant, to appoint commissioners of musters. The latter were selected with great care from the justices of the peace and other leading gentlemen of the county. The Privy Council paid particular attention to getting just the right number for the job. If there were too few in any shire the load would be heavy and there would be inefficiency. If there were too many there was a greater likelihood that some of them would be corruptible, and that unwilling trainees would use them to escape their obligations.[2]

The men selected were formally commissioned by the queen; and their commissions were accompanied by detailed instructions that left little to chance or to their imagination. When the date for the county muster had been set the lieutenant or commissioners of musters explained to the constables what they wanted done, and the constables passed the word round the hundred. The county was divided into a convenient number of

[1] *H.M.C. Foljambe*, 62–63. [2] S.P. Dom. 61, f. 14.

smaller areas. If all were mustered at one central point the men in the outlying districts would have a long journey to the place of assembly. Moreover, the Privy Council was always terrified of very large assemblies. In 1559 the number to be mustered in one place was limited to 300, unless the lord lieutenant himself were present; and because of the danger of riotous behaviour the muster was not to continue after sunset. When it was finally concluded the men were to go straight back to their villages and resist any temptation to visit strange towns; and at all times one or two justices or other 'grave and discreet persons' were to be present to keep order.

So that there might be some measure of continuity in the militia, captains were as far as possible given charge of the same companies at successive musters. It was recognized that the better the captain knew his men the easier it would be to control and train them. In 1559 the importance of training was specially emphasized. The queen said that she was well aware that men did not know how to use their weapons, wear their armour, or even march in good order. All this was to be changed. There was little point in providing equipment for the militia if nobody knew how to use it. Moreover, the better the men could handle their weapons, the easier it would be for them to be brave in time of action. If any county needed additional instructors the government would be glad to send experienced captains from London.

The cost of training was borne by the county. Individual assessments were left to the discretion of the commissioners of musters on the ground that they knew best who could afford to contribute. They were, however, advised not to trouble the poorer classes, especially the cottagers. Later in the reign the commissioners were enjoined to show a good example by taxing themselves; and they were again advised to avoid the poor. They were rather to exact contributions from keepers of alehouses and taverns who made their money out of people seeking pleasure.[1] Trustworthy men were appointed to distribute the money, which was paid out at the rate of 8*d.* per day per man. This was considered a generous figure, having regard to the fact that the muster would often be held on a holiday, when the man would in any case be earning nothing. It compared very favourably

[1] Lambeth MSS. 247, pt. i, f. 29b.

with the 8*d*. a day which the private had on active service, and out of which he had to feed and clothe himself and buy his gunpowder.

There was no set form for the muster returns, nor were the musters uniformly efficient. Everything depended on the energies and abilities of the commissioners in each county. Some made it easier for the Privy Council to assess the national position by providing neat totals showing separately the able-bodied men in the county, the number required by statute to provide equipment, how much equipment they were liable for, and so on. In the general musters of 1569, when the Council asked that people should be urged to supply equipment over and above the minimum laid down by law, the more conscientious authorities set out the extra quantities provided side by side with the minimum provision; and when the increasing degree of specialization made it desirable to record craftsmen separately the more helpful counties suitably modified their returns. Others, however, tried to get by with a minimum of effort. They simply recorded names and weapons hundred by hundred and left it to the Council to have the figures totalled and any necessary analysis made.[1]

If the shire musters fell short of the ideal, it was because few took them seriously. Musters on active service, however, were much less efficient, because it paid the captains and often the higher command to make them so. The muster-masters themselves were seldom any good at the job, and were often dishonest into the bargain. The price which captains could afford to pay for false certificates, which would enable them to claim more pay, more clothing, and more food than was justified by the number of men actually in their company, was too tempting. Not only did the muster returns on active service seldom give an accurate picture of the strength and equipment of the forces; they were a device that enabled unscrupulous senior officers to feather their nests without any real fear of detection.

When in the field troops were supposed to be inspected at least once a month. The inspections were made at irregular intervals and at very short notice, to make it more difficult for captains to anticipate them and fill up their depleted companies for the occasion by hiring anyone willing to masquerade as a

[1] S.P. Dom. 93, f. 92.

soldier for a day—in return for a suitable reward. Usually only two hours' notice was given; and the muster took place in the early morning. It was more difficult to smuggle strangers into the ranks before the bustle of the day's routine had begun.

Even the commanding officer was informed only the night before. He was required to set a special watch at dawn if the troops were in camp, and to post extra sentries if they were in garrison. This done, he ordered the captains to lead their companies to the scene of the muster, which was normally near a church or some other building big enough to hold the men. They were marched into the building and the captains then handed the muster-master lists of those absent because of sickness or wounds, who were thereupon inspected in their billets or where they were lying in camp. The absentees were supposed to be identified with particular care, for it was presumed to be easier to deceive the muster-master from an alleged sick bed than on the parade ground. The other members of the force who could not pass muster with the main body of the troops—those on guard or engaged on special duties—were also inspected at this stage, although they were sometimes mustered before they went to their posts.

In the meantime the rest of the force had been waiting patiently behind locked doors, which were now thrown open. The men came out one by one as their names were called from an earlier company list. These lists, or rolls, varied in the amount of detail they contained. Some recorded only the man's name and his equipment. Others included his age, height, complexion, colour of hair and beard, and any distinguishing marks on face or body. Names were called at random in an attempt to make it more difficult for a man to answer successfully any name but his own.

The test of a man's right to pass muster was his regular presence at watch and ward. That is to say, he had to be taking part in all the activities of the company. All others who were brought before the muster-master and passed off as soldiers—labourers, victuallers, pedlars, vagrants, and the like—ran the risk of hanging; and the officers who presented them were liable to be cashiered. The corporals had to stand beside the table where the muster-master officiated to identify any interlopers; but in practice it was just as easy for the captain to buy the corporals as it was to corrupt the muster-master, and this provision was not much of a safeguard.

If a private claimed that he had not received his due from the captain (who was, of course, responsible for doling out pay), the muster-master had to tell the man what he was entitled to, and how much he was still owed over and above the weekly part payments which he had already received. If he were still dissatisfied the matter was referred to a superior officer for further investigation. If it were proved that a captain was trying to get round the regulations he was liable to forfeit his pay and be dismissed the service. If the muster-master himself were convicted of accepting bribes the penalty was hanging.[1]

All this was the theory, evolved in Whitehall, and promulgated to the army with admirable clarity. Indeed, the regulations governing the muster office could not have been better drafted. Had no more than one of the links in the chain of responsibilities which they embraced been dishonest, it would have been glaringly revealed. The Privy Council could have dealt with the offender in isolation. But when the whole of the chain was corrupt—the muster officials, the treasurer-at-war, the captains, the company clerk, the auditor, as well as those on the fringe, the clothing and food contractors—it was quite impossible to run the machine efficiently.

The main obstacle in the path of the muster-master was the uncompromising attitude of the captains, who were in the army to make money, and knew that their worst enemy was the muster office. The muster-master who wanted an easy and affluent existence did what the captains told him. Any who tried to protect the interests of the Crown or the private found himself fighting a losing battle. Thomas Digges, the first muster-master in the Netherlands, was one of the few who tried to do an honest job. His description of the good and bad muster-master reveals some of the difficulties and temptations facing the muster office.

The good muster-master insists on reasonable pay both for himself and his assistants and is careful in his spending. He urges the general to establish strict rules for musters, and

---

[1] This description of the muster regulations is based on S.P. Holl. xiv, ff. 245 et seq.; S.P. Dom. 234, no. 36; Cott. MSS. Galba D IV, ff. 298b–301b; and A.P.C. xvii. 438–46.

ensures that his subordinates know them. He deducts nothing from a captain's pay without being absolutely certain about the rights of the matter; and if he is in doubt on any point he puts it to the general or the council of war for a ruling. If a captain claims to be entitled to a refund in respect of weapons lost in battle he submits the facts to the general for approval. If his assistants become too friendly with the captains he reads them a lecture. If they are found guilty of conniving at the captains' frauds they are dismissed. If they are cleared of suspicion they are, nevertheless, moved to another post in the interest of public relations. He cheats neither captains nor queen of a penny, nor does he accept a penny in bribes.

The bad is the exact antithesis of all this. He cares not how small his salary is, knowing that he can make a fortune out of corrupt practices. He spends money freely by playing the good fellow in the company of those who join him in deceiving the queen. He hates strict musters as much as the captains do, for they give him less room for corrupt manœuvre. He insists on making some deductions from pay for the sake of appearances, but keeps them so small that the captains do not mind. He accepts anything—money or goods—and strains his elastic conscience in any direction to please the general and those in authority. He is so liberal with the queen's purse that he is extolled for a brave man, an honourable officer, and the queen (whom he deceives horribly) is persuaded that the jackdaw is an eagle, and the cuckoo a nightingale. The more he robs the queen the more friends he makes, and the more do captains and colonels sing his praises.[1]

Both Thomas Digges and his brother James tried to follow the precepts laid down for the good muster-master, and both had for their reward the cordial hatred of the captains. It was axiomatic that the honest and efficient muster-master should be unpopular. Some accused Thomas of doing his job carelessly—for example, certifying that companies were properly equipped when they were no better off than pioneers, and failing to examine the horses and equipment of sick or wounded cavalry-men[2]—in the hope that the Privy Council would dismiss him. Others complained that he was doing his job too well, and that

---

[1] Printed at the end of his *Proceedings of the Earl of Leicester* (1590).
[2] S.P. Holl. xv, f. 153.

he was forcing the captains into bankruptcy.[1] Digges himself claimed that by exacting the last penny in stoppages and deductions he had saved record sums for the Crown.[2] In his campaign against the captains he even invited soldiers with grievances to come forward and lay information against their leaders. Many joyfully accepted the invitation. Some, however, regarded it as an excuse for flouting the authority of their superior officers, and a serious mutiny was narrowly averted.[3]

Captain Thomas Morgan took up the cudgels on behalf of his fellow officers and demanded that Digges should be made to mend his ways. The captains, he said, resented so much interference by a civilian. They were soldiers, and would give their last penny to keep their companies efficient. Later, Digges's administration of the muster office was the subject of a report to the secretary of state. It was admitted that he was doing no more than carry out his instructions, but it was suggested that it might be better for everybody if he were to temper his enthusiasm for saving public funds.[4] Digges himself claimed that even if he had earned the enmity of the captains he had at least forced them to keep their companies up to establishment.[5]

James Digges had much the same experience. He crossed swords with Sir John Norreys and the treasurer-at-war, Sir Thomas Sherley, and found himself 'prosecuted by strange and extraordinary means'. He swore to the Privy Council that Norreys's uncontrollable malice was such that even if he had ten lives he would lose them all if he did not do precisely what the general wanted. Rather than follow the example of his immediate predecessor (not his brother), who had not dared to stop a penny from the companies' pay, he would ask leave to quit the service.[6]

In the Netherlands, however, it was not only the captains who made life difficult for the muster-master. He had to contend also with the Dutch muster officials who were supposed to co-operate, but were in fact singularly obstructive. Further, the garrisons were widely scattered, which meant that the muster-master had to be constantly travelling about the country.

It had originally been agreed that the troops should be

[1] *For. Cal.* xxi, pt. ii, 390.　　[2] Ibid. xx. 438–9.
[3] Ibid. xxi, pt. ii, 431–2.　　[4] Ibid. 3.
[5] Ibid. 440–1.　　[6] Lansd. MSS. 62, no. 46.

mustered by the English and Dutch officials working together, but in the summer of 1586 the Dutch authorities protested to the Earl of Leicester that this had not been done since the first general muster when the English troops arrived in the Low Countries.[1] Yet when, only three months later, Digges asked for a joint muster, the Dutch objected, on the ground that to muster the men without money to pay them would inevitably lead to mutiny. They refused to allow their own muster-master to take part, although Digges made no secret of his suspicion that their real motive was to allow the accounts to fall into confusion. It seems, in fact, that the proposal to hold joint musters, instead of promoting greater efficiency, had made inefficiency just as welcome to the Dutch as it was to the English captains. If no reliable muster records were available, they might contrive to escape some part of their financial obligation to the English government.[2]

The other problem in the Netherlands—the wide separation of the garrisons—was overcome by the appointment of resident muster officials. Thomas Digges proposed that someone should be appointed in every important garrison to record the death, discharge, or other departure of soldiers, so that the drain of public funds in paying wages for men who did not exist should be halted. If half a dozen new appointments were made, either the Crown would save vast sums, or companies would be kept up to establishment.[3]

The queen agreed that the task of mustering the troops in the Netherlands was too much for one man, and Digges was authorized to appoint deputies, who were to have as their wages 2 or 3 per cent. of the stoppages they effected.[4] The difficulties persisted, however. Digges told Burghley that even with the new arrangements the muster office could not function effectively. His staff made little or no effort to ensure the accuracy of their returns, although with goodwill this should have been quite easy.[5]

As the garrison in Ireland increased, so it was necessary to augment the muster office there. But the muster officials never succeeded in defeating the captains, who raised the arts of

---

[1] *For. Cal.* xxi, pt. ii, 90–91.   [2] Ibid. 198.   [3] Ibid. xx. 285.
[4] Ibid. xxi, pt. ii, 41; Stowe MSS. 163, ff. 21, 25; *H.M.C. Salisbury*, v. 240.
[5] S.P. Holl. xxv, f. 153.

deception and corruption to a level of efficiency that has perhaps never been attained in any sphere since. Whereas in the Netherlands and elsewhere it was usual to draw pay and allowances for large numbers of men who were no more than names on a muster roll, in the Irish service the 'invisibles' in the company sometimes reached 100 per cent. This was made possible by a thriving industry that grew up in the town of Chester, one of the main assembly points for troops destined for Ireland. The procedure for a captain who wanted to get a perfect score in deceiving his sovereign, lining his pocket, and undermining the army, was as follows. He would receive a group of new recruits in the county where they were levied, a muster roll specifying their names, descriptions, and arms, and enough conduct money to take them to Chester. He would then lead them off on the first stage of their journey; but as soon as they were clear of the place where they had been levied, he would sell their freedom to the whole company, exacting from each man whatever he could afford to pay. It was physically impossible to take over their arms and equipment. They were left in the men's possession, but the captain no doubt exacted some further payment for them.

So far so good. The captain was now in pocket to the extent of the conduct money provided by the local authority (which was no longer needed for its original purpose, as there was no-one left to conduct, but was available for the second stage of the enterprise) plus whatever the recruits had paid for their freedom and for their equipment. He also had in his pocket a considerable liability—the muster roll, copies of which had been circulated among members of the Privy Council in London as evidence that he had taken over the men and their equipment. It was to help him to cope with this liability that the new industry grew up in Chester—a 'robber's cave' in the view of one official who saw what was going on in the town, but was powerless to stop it. The captain, having arrived with his piece of paper, had to find enough men and equipment, and even horses, if the fictitious band he was leading happened to be a cavalry troop, to enable the officials in the port to confirm that all recorded in the muster roll were present and correct. He simply let it be known in the appropriate quarters how many men he needed, what sorts of arms they must carry, how many should be mounted, and on the due date the perfect reflection of the company he had taken into his charge a few days earlier would be ready for inspection. It was solemnly reviewed and the muster roll was certified correct. The agents of the stand-ins were paid off. The men who had passed muster pocketed their fee and went back to their normal occupations, to await the next summons to be soldiers for an hour. The horses and equipment were returned to their rightful owners.

The captain was now free to proceed to Ireland with a hundred men in his pocket, for whom he might later try to exact passage money from the treasurer-at-war. The muster roll would have to be made good on muster days in Ireland by borrowing from companies with real men in them, and perhaps by hiring natives, but the game could be played indefinitely. In the opinion of one observer the queen would have been far better off to pay these captains a thousand pounds to keep them out of the army.[1]

It was difficult to deal with crime organized on this scale, and the position was not made any easier by wrangling between the muster officials, two of whom hated each other and were constantly complaining, each about the other's activities. These were Sir Ralph Lane, who had been muster-master on the Portugal expedition in 1589, and Maurice Kyffin. The only thing that the two agreed about was that the muster arrangements in Ireland were in a shocking state, and that the best way to improve matters was to increase the number of muster officials, and also their quality. Kyffin told Burghley that he found the difficulties and confusions in the muster office quite unbelievable. Shameful corruption among the muster officials, and the infinite and inveterate art of falsehood practised by captains had 'irrecuperably damnified the state'. Not a single company was mustered either in camp or garrison without including an incredible number of hired or suborned *passevolants*. When, in the course of his duties, he had warned these people that their offence was punishable by death, they simply laughed at him. They had been assured by the captains that they would come to no harm. The soldiers themselves were not much help. If they tried to expose their captain they feared that he would hang them as mutineers the moment the muster-master's back was turned.[2]

[1] *Irish Cal. 1596–7*, 172. [2] Ibid. 231.

Lane was also loud in his complaints to the Privy Council. He was constantly putting up schemes for the reformation of the muster office, which had little chance of working successfully. One of these was designed to make fraud quite impossible. He pointed out that, as things were, the muster-master was completely at the mercy of the company clerk, who was, of course, hand in glove with the captain. The clerk alone could know accurately the strength of a company. In Lane's view this was not good enough, and he proposed that information about 'alterations, entries, and vacancies' should be more widely circulated. He suggested that in an infantry company of 100, eight men (perhaps the non-commissioned officers) plus the heads of the 'camaradas' (the smallest units in the company), of whom there would be about twenty, should have access to the muster records. Before there could be fraud under this arrangement many members of the company would have to lay their heads together, which was unlikely, as the rewards of fraud would be spread much too thin. But nothing seems to have come of this scheme, which would have been administratively much too cumbersome.[1]

The muster office was the key to the efficient management of the army. If it had been allowed to function properly it would have given the government an accurate assessment of the state of the forces. For example, had the Privy Council been aware of the actual strength of the troops besieging Leith in 1560, which was probably much less than even the higher command suspected, they might well have ordered the general not to attempt the assault on the town, which turned out to be one of the most disastrous enterprises of the reign. Accurate muster returns would have paved the way for immense savings through stoppages on the pay of absentees and corresponding savings in the supply of food and clothing. They would have compelled men to keep their arms and equipment in a satisfactory condition. Above all, they would have exposed the magnitude of the captains' deceptions, and perhaps forced the Council to do something about them once and for all. But a corrupt and inefficient muster office was the captains' passport to wealth; and they were clever enough to ensure that it remained so.

[1] *Irish Cal. 1592–6*, 187.

IX

PAY

THE arrangements for paying the troops played right into the eager hands of the captains, who took full advantage of the generous opportunities afforded them.

The theory was that the companies should receive only a proportion of their wages week by week, and that the balance due to them should be made up at six-monthly intervals. Each week the treasurer-at-war was supposed to issue to the captain the weekly sum to which his company was entitled. The captain, assisted by the company clerk, then paid the individual soldiers. Every six months a further sum was issued to the captain to enable him to bring each man's reckoning up to date. The weekly payments were known as 'imprests' or 'lendings'. The six-monthly payment was a 'full pay'.

There were two fundamental weaknesses in the system. That the captain should be responsible for the financial affairs of his men was an atrocious arrangement. Matthew Sutcliffe says that to give the pay of the common soldier to the captain is a 'notorious abuse'. It was never done by the Romans, nor by any other nations until the Italians introduced it in their 'scambling' rapacious wars in the fourteenth century, which were largely fought by mercenaries. But now that mercenaries were a thing of the past in the English forces there was no reason to continue this method of pay.[1] This was generally accepted by everybody except the captains, who fought desperately, and with almost complete success, to retain all the more profitable elements in the system.

Secondly, the soldier's wage was intended merely to be a subsistence payment. It was supposed to be just enough to cover his food and drink, clothing, gunpowder, match, and so on. There was certainly no provision for saving. This meant that if he were cheated out of a single penny his standard of living

[1] *Lawes of Armes*, 78.

immediately went below the subsistence level; and the more he was cheated the more difficult it became to support life.

The men concerned with pay were the treasurer-at-war, the muster-master, the auditor, the clerk of the check, the captain, and the company clerk. The auditor and the clerk of the check, however, did not appear in the establishment of every force. In the background in London were commissioners who examined the accounts of the treasurer-at-war annually, but in practice they added little to the control of the public funds expended on the army. The damage had been done before the accounts reached them; and even if they detected fraud it was usually too late to do much about it. If all the men in the field had been honest, the system of pay would have worked admirably. The theory could hardly be improved. If only one were corrupt, he would very quickly have been found out by the others. But if all were corrupt, which was usually the case, the whole system ceased to safeguard the taxpayer, and simply facilitated the end-result that the Privy Council was striving to avoid—the enriching of the captains at the expense of the exchequer and the private soldier.

The clerk of the company was a non-combatant—'a penman rather than a swordsman'—whose position gave him great influence, and without whose co-operation the captain could not bleed his company to the full. His duties are described by the military writers, and they are elaborated in a number of manuals, which are early textbooks on organization and method. They show the clerk how he can simplify his task by arranging the names of the company in corporalships, for ease of reference, and suggest that he should prevail upon the victualler to arrange his lists in the same way, so that when the two are working together they will find it easier to compare notes. He should equip himself with a pound measure, to speed up the issue of gunpowder from the bulk supply obtained from the master of the ordnance; and it will also save time if he weighs out pound lots of match in advance. Otherwise the men will have to wait in an impatient queue for their issue.[1]

The clerk's company list recorded the names of the men's villages, so that if any ran away the authorities would know where to look for them first. The list also showed how much

[1] Sloane MSS. 292, f. 48b.

equipment the men received from the county when they were levied, the quantities of powder, match, bullets, food, and so on issued from time to time, so that the clerk would know how much was to be deducted from each man's wages. He visited all sick men weekly, and compiled a list of their names and where they were billeted, for the use of the muster-master: if he were found guilty of including fictitious names he forfeited a week's pay.[1] When the half-yearly issue of uniform was made he presented each member of the company to the official in charge of the distribution, and made a note of the articles supplied against each man's name. If he presented the same man twice he went to prison for a month.[2]

The company clerk was well placed to expose the captain's malpractices; but he had neither the status nor the incentive to do this. In practice he worked hand in glove with his captain and between them they defrauded both soldier and government at will. There was a general complaint about the corruption of clerks in the Netherlands, and Willoughby was urged to see that their books were better kept in future,[3] but it was not until 1600 that there was any real attempt to get at the root of the trouble. It was proposed that the clerks should cease to be the captains' employees, and become the agents of the Crown with a wage of 2s. a day. Had this been done at the beginning of the reign it might have made a difference, although it seems likely that whatever the Crown saw fit to pay the clerk the captain would have been able to make a higher bid for his services.

The job of the clerk of the check—when there was one—was to satisfy himself that the appropriate deductions had been made for absences without leave, defects in equipment, and offences against the regulations for which the penalty was loss of pay—swearing, or failure to attend divine service, for example. He had, of course, to co-operate closely with the muster-master and treasurer-at-war. He made his books up twice a year—one copy for the Privy Council and one for the treasurer-at-war. In the Netherlands a third copy was required for the Dutch authorities, who were responsible for contributing towards the cost of the English forces, and naturally wanted to be satisfied that they were getting value for their money.

[1] Cott. MSS., Galba D IX, f. 300b.   [2] Ibid. 305b.
[3] Ibid., Galba D I, f. 24.

Efficient checking could save substantial sums. For example, in the year ended October 1588, the stoppages in the Netherlands totalled over £9,000.[1] But, like everything else, the work of checking was seldom efficient. In Ireland, at the end of the reign, the checks on many companies amounted to no more than a shilling or two for a period of six months, and this can hardly have been because there was no occasion for them.[2]

The activities of the clerk of the check, the muster-master, and the treasurer-at-war were reported on by the auditor. There is not much evidence about the functions of this official, but they may be deduced from descriptions of the good and bad auditor compiled by the indefatigable Thomas Digges. The good will maintain a diligent watch on the treasurer and his assistants; keep an accurate record of the army's outstanding debts, and encourage the treasurer to pay off the older first; ensure that the stoppages ordered by the clerk of the check are just and that they are regularly paid over to the Crown; and require the treasurer and the captains to keep proper accounts, which he will examine periodically. He will demand to be reasonably paid, so that the incentive to take bribes will be reduced, and he will shun the treasurer as the good muster-master shuns the captains. He will use his best endeavours to have the soldiers and the honest creditors of the company paid, whereas the corrupt auditor (who knows that the honest creditors cannot afford to give the treasurer 10 per cent. to have their money) will allow the treasurer to pay off the captains' bills for silks and gold and silver lace, knowing that those who have supplied these luxuries can afford to give the treasurer 30, 40, or 50 per cent. when he pays them.

Digges also describes the good and bad treasurer. The bad—no doubt drawn from life—will refuse to show up his accounts for as long as possible, but 'rather seek all devices to huddle things up in confusion, knowing it is good fishing in puddled water, according to the old proverb'. He will see that the bills and receipts are safely locked up in a chest with two locks and keys (one each for the treasurer and the auditor), so that no aggrieved party can see the accounts until he brings the treasurer and the auditor together—'a matter as easy as to catch a hare with a tabor'. The good treasurer, on the other hand, will

---

[1] S.P. Holl. xxxii, f. 130. [2] *A.P.C.* xxxi. 130.

make up his quarterly accounts regularly, and have them ready for inspection at any time. He will supply copies of any part of the account to anyone who is prepared to pay the appropriate fee; and he will always be ready to give a captain a bill setting down in detail how much he has paid him, and how much has been deducted from the company pay—'for what, to whom, and how much particularly, taking a double thereof signed by the captain, and this particular double he will leave in the auditor's hand to be examined'. He will live modestly, and will avoid cultivating people by giving presents and holding lavish banquets.[1]

A paper written in 1588 reveals the sorry state of the army's financial affairs in the Netherlands. Despite the fact that huge sums of money had been sent there by the queen, neither the army's creditors nor the soldiers had had their due. The treasurer-at-war's pay and allowances came to £2,000 a year (more than either the Lord Chancellor or the Lord Treasurer of England had). He was also able to make substantial sums on the side, and he found it easy to use this money to make friends, so that the queen would never know how she was robbed. The two chief bridles to a corrupt treasurer were the muster-master and the auditor. The latter, however, had been removed, and now every possible device was being employed to get rid of the muster-master as well, or at least to discredit him. A commission with the treasurer at the head of it had been set up to examine the affairs of the muster-office, so that the treasurer was made judge of the only man who could uncover his own misdeeds; and the others who were sitting on the commission were all men who had been accused by the muster-master. It was therefore essential that there should be an impartial inquiry into the affairs of the office of the treasurer-at-war. The practice of auditing the books from London was ridiculous. The treasurer might have £50,000 of the queen's money in hand, yet he could easily contrive to make it appear that she was in his debt—unless there was an auditor on the spot.[2]

There was no machinery to enable widows or dependent relatives to claim that part of his wage which a soldier who died on active service would have collected at the next full pay, had he lived; but as the wage was really no more than a subsistence

[1] Cott. MSS., Galba C VIII, ff. 238b–9b.   [2] *H.M.C. Ancaster*, 76–77.

payment there was no need for it. It is true that there was a very small element at the soldier's own disposal which he could, in theory, save, if, for example, he never bought a drink; but it was no more than a few pence a week. When a man died, the Crown would save any part of what was still due; but economies of this sort (on which the government can hardly be congratulated) were more than offset by losses through corruption in the muster office. For every penny saved on the wages of dead men, the Crown paid out pounds for men who never were—who existed only on the pages of the muster records.

The principal treasurers-at-war in the 'war period' after 1585 were: Sir Henry Wallop, who acted in Ireland for twenty years until his retirement in 1599; Sir George Carey, who succeeded Wallop and held office until 1606; Richard Huddilston, the first treasurer-at-war in the Netherlands; Sir Thomas Sherley, who replaced him and was a dominating figure in military finance for ten years in Brittany, Normandy, and Picardy, as well as the Netherlands; Sir Thomas Fludde, who followed Sherley, and was himself followed by William Meredith; and Sir Moyle Finch, who was treasurer-at-war in the army in England in 1588.

The treasurer-at-war's post was the most lucrative in the army, not because his basic salary was high, but because of the value of the perquisites which, in Sir Thomas Sherley's case, were reckoned to be worth £2,000 a year.[1] Huddilston was paid about £500 a year, plus 1 per cent. of the money passing through his hands.[2] There was a tendency to reduce the treasurer-at-war's remuneration. In 1594 the daily wage came down to a pound, and in 1597, when Meredith was appointed, it was further reduced to 10s.[3] Moreover, after arrangements had been made to pay the army in the Netherlands through the merchant adventurers, the percentage allowance on the money passing through the treasurer-at-war's hands was stopped, as he was no longer responsible for transferring the money from England.[4] But there was a good deal of flexibility in the arrangements. It was relatively easy for the treasurer to increase his illegal earnings at least at the same rate that his official salary was reduced.

[1] S.P. Holl. xxxii, f. 80.
[2] Ibid. xxxiii, f. 106.
[3] Dom. Cal. 1595–7, 415.
[4] H.M.C. Salisbury, iv. 579.

Under both Huddilston and Sherley the establishment of the treasurer-at-war's office in the Netherlands was an under-treasurer and three paymasters. In addition, thirty men were employed to guard bullion as it was moved about the country.[1] Sherley, however, complained that he could not supervise payments at the scattered garrisons without more assistance.[2] Fludde had a bigger staff: two deputy paymasters, two clerks in England, and four in the Netherlands.[3]

Of the seven officials at least three served the Crown badly. The evidence against them is not all reliable: much was invented by associates who hoped to gain through their downfall. Huddilston may have been a victim of unscrupulous rivals when the queen got to hear reports that he was pocketing the soldiers' wages. She said that if the allegations turned out to be justified, the men were to be told of it openly. It troubled her not a little that poor deserving soldiers who hourly ventured their lives in her service should want their due: if the treasurer had been corrupt or negligent he would get what he deserved—but she added that it was well known that she disliked discharging a man whose guilt had not been proved beyond all doubt.

Apparently the verdict was 'not proven'. The queen was informed that Huddilston had tried hard to save her money and it was hoped that he would not be condemned without a fair hearing. The treasurer was not dismissed, but the Privy Council recorded a vote of no confidence in him by appointing Sir Thomas Sherley to act as joint treasurer. Huddilston was forbidden to receive or pay any money without Sherley's knowledge, while the treasure chest was given a double lock to which Sherley and Huddilston both held keys, and which could be opened only when both were present.[4]

Inefficiency was probably Huddilston's only crime, but of his successor's guilt there can be little doubt. Indeed, in promoting Sherley to be sole treasurer the Privy Council could hardly have jumped more resolutely into the fire. During his first four years in office his books were thrice subject to a special examination. The third investigation was made at his own request, which suggests that he was complete master of the situation. He complained that the queen was listening to tales carried by men

---

[1] Cott. MSS., Galba D IX, f. 327. [2] *For. Cal.* xxi, pt. ii. 142.
[3] *H.M.C. Salisbury*, vii. 92. [4] *For. Cal.* xxi, pt. ii. 82, 345.

whose only grievance was that his handling of public funds was leaving them no richer than they were entitled to be. A commission duly examined the accounts, but as before nothing untoward was revealed, and Sherley continued in office.

It seems fairly clear that he had pulled the wool over the examiners' eyes on this occasion, but in 1596 the crash came and he was dismissed. During his term of office he must have squandered immense sums, for he was deeply in debt when he lost his job.[1] In 1589 he was reported to be making £16,000 a year on top of his salary, by advancing money to officers at a discount before a full pay was due, selling concessions to victuallers, taking over soldiers' debts when it was believed that there was no prospect of a full pay, and using the queen's money to carry on the business of general money-lender.[2]

The evidence against Sir George Carey came to light several years after his death. He was charged in an Exchequer Court case against his executors with extensive fraud in Ireland. It was said that he had paid Irish troops nothing, and the English troops much less than their due; that he had retained quantities of the debased coinage after it had been recalled, used it to make official purchases, and repaid himself in the new currency; that he had offered debased currency as new in paying the forces; and that he had connived at the frauds of the clothing suppliers in Ireland. It was estimated that over £150,000 had found its way irregularly into his pocket. A decision was not given until 1630, when the case was dismissed, probably because the Carey family now had great influence and because a conviction would have implicated many who had used Carey's ill-gotten gains to rise to high positions. But whatever the reasons for the acquittal, there can be little doubt of Carey's guilt.[3]

At first the treasurer-at-war was personally responsible for carrying the army's pay overseas. Huddilston was instructed to carry money to Middelburg, or any other town selected by the general, there to be issued as occasion demanded. He was to pay the troops in local currency at the best rate of exchange available.[4] It was hardly surprising, however, that the Council should abandon this somewhat primitive arrangement and

---

[1] *For. Cal.* xxii. 357; *Dom. Cal. 1591–4*, 54, 77, 373, 536; *1595–7*, 44.
[2] S.P. Holl. xxxii, f. 80.   [3] H. Hall, *Society in the Elizabethan Age*, 128–32.
[4] *For. Cal.* xx. 163; xxi, pt. ii. 83–84.

enlist the services of the merchants, who had long experience of the machinery of exchange.[1]

This scheme, which first applied to the garrisons of Flushing and Brill, seems to have met with success, for it was later arranged that all money for the troops' wages should be paid to the merchants in London and repaid by them in the Netherlands. The only loser was the treasurer-at-war, who no longer was given an allowance for carrying money overseas. This advantage was, of course, offset by the fact that the merchants had to be paid for their services, but there is no doubt that the change was justified. The irregular arrival of money in the Netherlands had made it impossible for even the weekly imprests to be paid. To encourage the merchants, who did not wholeheartedly approve of the proposed arrangements, the Council pointed out that their co-operation would greatly benefit the service and help to save the life of many a poor soldier.[2]

Payment through the agency of the merchants became the regular procedure, although it did not prove entirely satisfactory. There were occasional complaints that units were not being properly paid, but despite these shortcomings it was recommended that the assistance of the merchants should be enlisted for paying the army in France in 1592. This was done, and the merchants, whose headquarters were at Caen, asked that a definite limit should be placed on the sums they might be required to find, and that they should receive payment in England six weeks in advance.[3]

There were three special institutions in the system of payment: payment by concordatum, payment by poll, and dead pays. The first existed only in Ireland. The concordatum fund was intended to cover expenses which it was difficult to provide for in advance, including the payment of messengers and spies, hiring of packet-boats, rewarding men for services rendered, and the keeping of prisoners.[4] There was every opportunity for abuse, for the treasurer-at-war was not required to render detailed accounts of sums expended by concordatum. As early as 1578 Sir Henry Sidney was reprimanded for gathering unnecessary servants around him, and having them paid from the concordatum fund.[5] Again, in 1600 Sir George Carey was accused of paying by

---

[1] Ibid. xx. 114. [2] Ibid. xxi, pt. ii. 316. [3] *Dom. Cal. 1591–4*, 213.
[4] Exchequer of Receipt, Q.R., box 3, roll 1. [5] *Carew Cal. 1575–88*, 150.

concordatum sums which should properly have been detailed in the ordinary accounts.[1]

Payment by poll was a device intended to cut down wastage of public money, and at the same time improve the lot of the private soldier. The treasurer was no longer to pay the captain a lump sum according to the muster returns, which were not regarded as satisfactory evidence of the numbers present in the company, but only to issue enough money to pay the men he had himself counted by the 'poll' or head. Moreover, their wages were handed direct to the men, without passing through the captain's hands. The system was used in 1563 during the siege of Le Havre, although it was at this time applied only to the pioneers. Sir Maurice Denys, the treasurer-at-war, told Cecil that Mr. Pelham, who was in charge of the pioneers (as he had been at the siege of Leith three years earlier) refused to have them paid by the poll, but 'stood so much upon his reputation that he would have them paid as every captain there paid his soldiers'.[2]

The payment of the men strictly according to their numbers was not enforced at Le Havre, but instructions issued to Leicester again made provision for this method of payment. He was to have the troops carefully mustered on his arrival in the Netherlands, and see that they were paid by the head.[3] Apparently this did no more than upset the captains. Thomas Digges, the muster-master, complained to Walsingham that they had been enraged by the new method of payment, which made it impossible for them to gain through the death or absence of men under their command. They held Digges responsible for it, though he claimed that he had never interfered with their interests except when the queen's interest came first.[4] His complaint bore fruit in instructions from the Privy Council to Buckhurst, who was told to punish captains who suggested that Digges was responsible for orders about payment, and who disobeyed them for that or any other reason. Only their strict enforcement would keep the companies up to full strength.

The captains claimed that if payment by poll were insisted on, they would become bankrupt, as they had advanced a great deal of money for their men, many of whom had died or

[1] *A.P.C.* xxx. 585.
[2] *For. Cal. 1563*, 303.
[3] J. Bruce, *Leycester Correspondence*, 13.
[4] *For. Cal.* xxi, pt. iii. 21.

deserted. The Council, however, maintained that there would be no difficulty if the clerks listed the men who had departed, and produced receipts from those merchants and victuallers to whom the captains had advanced money. Buckhurst was told to call together the senior captains and inform them of the queen's desire that henceforth payment should be made in accordance with the numbers actually in service.[1] The constant opposition to this method of payment suggests that if it could have been enforced the service would have greatly benefited. But, as usual, the captains were too powerful and by various means prevented the system from becoming effective.

Thirdly, there was the institution known as 'dead pays'. According to the *Oxford English Dictionary*, the expression 'dead pays' had two meanings in the sixteenth century. It meant 'pay continued to a soldier no longer in active service', in other words a pension for old or disabled soldiers; and it meant 'pay continued in the name of a soldier or sailor actually dead or discharged, and appropriated by the officer'.

This second meaning indicates an abuse which flourished in the Elizabethan forces. Sir J. W. Fortescue comments on this abuse in the financing of the English troops at the siege of Leith in 1560 in these words: 'Thus, though the muster-rolls of the army in Scotland showed eight thousand men for whom the queen paid wages, only five thousand were actually with the colours, and the pay of the remaining three thousand went of course into the captains' pockets.'[2] And again, speaking of the forces in the Netherlands in 1585–7: 'The companies fell into the hands of unscrupulous swindlers, who sent their men out to plunder and did not omit to take their own share, rejoicing over every soldier who died or deserted for the money that would pass into their pockets when the long-deferred pay-day should come.'[3] Fortescue, commenting that the prevalence of this dead-pay abuse proves the Elizabethan government guilty of neglecting the interests of the rank and file, concludes thus: 'There have been many sovereigns and many ministers in England who have neglected and betrayed their soldiers, but none more wantonly, wilfully and scandalously then Elizabeth.'[3]

[1] Cott. MSS., Galba D I, f. 24; *For. Cal.* xxi, pt. iii. 56.
[2] Sir J. W. Fortescue, *History of the British Army*, i. 128.
[3] Ibid. i. 146.

The expression 'dead pay', however, seems to have had a third meaning, neither mentioned by the *Oxford English Dictionary* nor touched upon by Fortescue. The earliest reference to this type of dead pay is in 1560,[1] when the Duke of Norfolk complained to Cecil about the mercenary nature of the captains in Berwick, most of whom put personal gain before service. He suggested that the queen would be better served if she were to allow the captains twenty or more dead pays in a hundred.[2] In 1562 the same thing is mentioned by the Earl of Warwick, who was in command of the English garrison at Le Havre, and asked the Privy Council's permission to modify the pay sheet in favour of certain deserving captains 'as well for their encouragement and relief as for the help of such gentlemen and expert soldiers as they are forced to consider above the queen's allowance'.[3]

The plan outlined was that the captains in question should be sent a hundred men's pay for every ninety-five men under their command. Part of this extra sum, which was called dead pays, was to go to increase the captain's own pay, and the rest was to be disbursed by him to the gentlemen volunteers attached to his company. The Privy Council eventually sanctioned the scheme, but stipulated that the number of dead pays awarded should never exceed 8 per cent. of the pay roll, that no part of the fund should be disbursed except in cases of obvious need, and that a full account of disbursements should be given monthly.[4]

After England's open intervention in the Continental struggle in 1585 this dead-pay system became properly established. In the interval it had been used in the payment of the English volunteers in the service of the Dutch; but in 1585 it was definitely included in the arrangements for the troops in the Netherlands, when the treasurer-at-war was instructed to award as many dead pays as had been allowed in the volunteer companies.[5] This was ten in every hundred pays issued to the captains (which meant that, when the muster rolls showed a hundred men, the actual strength of the company was only ninety), and until the close of the century this rate was maintained for the forces on foreign service.

[1] The earliest reference to the other types in the *O.E.D.* is in 1565.
[2] S. Haynes, *State Papers*, 239.
[3] S.P. For. 46, no. 918.
[4] Ibid. no. 933.
[5] S.P. Holl. iv, no. 11.

This extra fund, however, was too small to satisfy the captains, who continued to appropriate illegal dead pays. So flagrant was the abuse that the Earl of Leicester devised a new scheme (probably early in 1586), which transferred the dead-pay fund from the captain to other members of the company. The customary ten dead pays in the hundred were to be allocated as follows: one was to be divided between two corporals to increase their pay to a shilling a day; two between four gentlemen volunteers, making their pay likewise a shilling; three between twelve of the musketeers, increasing their wage to 10d. a day; three were to be bestowed on the officers at the captain's discretion; and the tenth was to be given to the captain's servant. This plan was not, however, adopted at this time. But in 1589 the Privy Council, when reviewing the whole question of pay and musters, ordered that Leicester's method of distributing the dead-pay fund should be adhered to in the future.[1]

In 1591, in answer to proposals from the garrison of Bergen-op-Zoom, the Council said that while dead pays were officially allowed to the captains it had been stipulated that some of them would be given to deserving soldiers, showing that even then Leicester's scheme had not yet been accepted to any great extent.[2] In 1593 the captains in the Netherlands asked that full control of the dead-pay fund should be restored to them, on the pretext that the ranks nominated by Leicester were often unworthy of extra pay.[3] On this occasion Sir Thomas Sherley advised the Privy Council to ignore their request, pointing out that in practice they were pocketing half the dead-pay fund, in defiance of all orders to the contrary.[4]

Such was the system in the Netherlands. It was never applied to the forces serving in England, as is shown by a ruling given in 1596 in answer to a request by Lord Hunsdon for a dead-pay fund in the garrison of the Isle of Wight. In their refusal the Privy Council stated: 'We have not heard of any such allowance to be made to those forces that are to be employed within the land.'[5] Presumably this was because the captain's expenses at home were much less than on active service abroad, and because

---

[1] Ibid. xxxiii, f. 165; *A.P.C.* xvii. 442.
[2] *A.P.C.* xx. 343.
[3] *Dom. Cal. 1591–4*, 331.
[4] Ibid. *1591*, 332.
[5] *A.P.C.* xxvi. 337.

the close proximity of the Privy Council and the Star Chamber inspired honesty in them without the use of bribes.

In Ireland, however, the situation was more akin to that in the Netherlands, especially after the outbreak of Tyrone's rebellion, and in 1596 the English captains were allowed dead pays in Ireland at the special rate of six in a hundred.[1] This did not satisfy them, and in May 1598 they petitioned that the same percentage of dead pays should be allowed them as was usual in the Netherlands. They backed up their claim by pointing out that the Irish wars were the hardest on the soldier, and brought forward the regular excuse that the dead-pay fund was essential if the gentlemen volunteers, who were 'a great aid and assistance upon any occasion of service', were to be kept in the forces.[2] But no action was taken by the Council, and the Irish rate remained unchanged until 1600, when the matter came up again for investigation. Buckhurst, the lord treasurer, voiced the opinion of the Privy Council when he advocated that the dead-pay system as it existed should be abolished. He suggested instead that a shilling a day should be paid to five gentlemen volunteers per company, the captain having no extra benefit. He also emphasized the gravity of the offence when captains pocketed illegal dead pays, and urged that the death penalty should be inflicted on any captain so doing, and on those who aided and abetted him.[3]

On the other hand, Mountjoy took the side of the captains and recommended that the customary six dead pays should be increased to ten, the increase being justified on the grounds that, as the musters were to be tightened up, fraud on the part of the captains would become practically impossible, and if any such fraud did take place severe punishment was to be meted out to the offender. But Mountjoy as spokesman of the captains was not content with urging an increase in the number of dead pays awarded, for he wanted their value increased as well. In the past they had been reckoned at 3*s*. 4*d*. each per week, the proportion of the private soldier's full pay which he was technically entitled to draw every week. Mountjoy now suggested that they should be paid at the full-pay rate of 4*s*. 8*d*. per week.[4] Buckhurst's plan won the day, and by the middle of 1600 the

---

[1] *A.P.C.* xxvi. 277.   [2] S.P. Ireland, 202, pt. ii, no. 38.
[3] Ibid. 207, pt. i, no. 7.   [4] Ibid., no. 76.

financial arrangements for the troops in Ireland made no allowance for dead pays.[1] But the system was not forgotten by the captains, for a memorandum of the following year suggests dead pays at the full-pay rate of 8d. a day, the rate which Mountjoy had tried to establish.[2]

The Privy Council had hoped that the greater amount of money available for distribution to the troops would increase the honesty of the captains' dealings and make possible the more adequate payment of the gentlemen volunteers, who, although not officially recognized, played an important part in the company. But the system depended for its success on sating the captains' greed, which proved to be impossible, and they continued to appropriate dead pays over and above their legal allowance. Thus an experiment to promote the efficiency of the forces and the welfare of the company simply magnified the evil it was intended to diminish.

These official dead pays were quite distinct from the others noted above. They were not pay continued to a soldier no longer in active service; and they were not pay appropriated by an officer. They were a legitimate bonus to the captains, part of which was to be passed on to deserving cases. This bonus may have had its origin in the appropriation of illegal dead pays, but it was in fact perfectly legal, and had the full blessing of the queen and Council. In Matthew Sutcliffe's view, however, it was an unsatisfactory half-measure. It would have been much more sensible to increase the captain's own pay and to stop his handling that of the company. There was no prospect of putting the army's financial house in order until those who had an interest in the game ceased to be controllers of it. To give the captain dead pays was just like allowing him to defraud the queen a little. It would be better to pay every man by the poll—better for the queen, for if the soldiers' receipts for the stores issued to them, the muster book, the treasurer-at-war's and the auditor's books all tallied, the queen could not easily be defrauded either of her money or her numbers in the army; better for the common soldier, for then he would have his due; it would even be better for the captains, for then they would no longer be condemned by the country in general and the soldiers in particular—often very unjustly. Who would for so small gain

[1] *A.P.C.* xxx. 415.   [2] S.P. Ireland, 208, pt. ii, no. 84.

incur the loss of his honour and reputation? Alas, the answer to this rhetorical question was 'virtually every captain', which Sutcliffe, who had practical experience of the wars, must have known quite well—just as he must have known that their gain would be anything but small.[1]

[1] *Lawes of Armes*, 78–79.

X

DISCIPLINE

THE military forces of the sixteenth century were not remarkable for the excellence of their discipline. Even the Spanish army, in many respects the best in Europe, sometimes went on strike. When the troops were dissatisfied with their treatment the whole force might agree to refuse to obey orders. They would appoint a representative to discuss their grievances with the higher command. While these talks were in progress they would carry out no more than the minimum guard duties needed to afford them protection from sudden attack by the enemy; and only when their grievances were redressed would they submit themselves again to the authority of their leaders. Their spokesman was then given money and an escort to take him beyond the reach of the law.[1] This sort of organized indiscipline was not found among Elizabeth's troops. They showed their opposition to authority in a less orderly fashion.

A body of military law had grown up in the centuries before Elizabeth. When the king led an army overseas he usually promulgated a disciplinary code to govern it. The army's own laws had to be 'set down and decreed'. It was not enough to rely on the laws of the land where they were fighting, which in any case would not have met the special needs of an armed force. The earliest complete code is the 'statutes, ordinances, and customs' issued by Richard II on the occasion of his war with France in 1385. This provided a model for later codes—for example, the statutes of Henry V for his troops during his invasion of France, and the orders devised for use in England by Henry VII. The Elizabethan codes were developed from these earlier regulations.

There is no record of a special code for the expedition to Scotland in 1560. The army used the garrison town of Berwick as a springboard for the invasion, and the standard disciplinary rules of the town were probably carried into the field. Two years later the Earl of Warwick, and his deputy Sir Adrian Poynings,

---

[1] Sir Roger Williams, *Actions*, 101.

issued their own regulations for the troops besieged in Le Havre. These were devised with the needs of a hard siege particularly in mind. The death penalty was prescribed for taking victuals by violence from the French in the town, for stealing weapons to the value of 6*d*., and for absence without permission from guard duty on the walls. Leaving the watch within the town' was punished by the loss of both ears, and banishment from the town—when the man would of course find himself alone in a hostile country. Quarrelling and fighting with the citizens or other members of the garrison force were strictly forbidden. Offenders against this rule had their hands cut off. Imprisonment (which was much easier to organize in a garrison town than when the army was on the march) was the penalty for 'swearing any horrible or detestable oath'; and the guilty party had to pay a day's wages to the man who informed against him. Other offences punishable by imprisonment were drunkenness, playing at dice and cards, and leaving one's quarters without sword and dagger. These regulations were set down by Poynings. They were supplemented by Warwick when he joined the garrison. Muster offences, which had been covered in the earlier code, were made more serious; and elaborate provision was made for the spiritual welfare of the troops, daily attendance at church (twice on Sundays) being made obligatory. Soldiers had to get the chaplain's permission before they could marry. Adulterers were imprisoned for six days, and then banished from the town. If a man passed muster in two places, or answered a name other than his own, he was liable to lose both ears and be dismissed from the garrison.[1]

Sir William Drury's code for his force at the siege of Edinburgh castle ten years later was short and sweet—again perhaps because the expedition was based on Berwick. It had only eight articles and therefore gives some idea as to what the general thought were the essential points. The first dealt with public relations—always an important aspect of Elizabeth's foreign expeditions. No English person was to misuse a Scottish person in 'word, deed, or countenance'. There were four capital offences: taking goods from the victualler; stealing arms; desertion; and leaving the watch and ward. Quarrelling with another soldier and leaving quarters without permission were both

[1] *For. Cal.* v. 326, 448.

punished with ten days' imprisonment, plus such other penalties as the commander thought fit. The eighth offence was keeping servants who were not on the army's strength, no doubt because such extra men would come in handy when a muster was held. If any were detected in this offence both master and servant were to be punished at the discretion of the higher command.[1]

The disciplinary code approved by the Earl of Leicester for the use of the troops serving under him in the Netherlands in 1585 is one of the most comprehensive of the reign. It opens with a resounding preamble lauding the value of justice duly administered and discipline orderly observed. 'No man can be so ignorant as not to know that honour, fame, and prosperity are bestowed upon the nation that enjoys good laws. Since martial discipline above all things is at this time to be followed, both for the glory of God and the orderly government of the army, and lest the evilly-inclined should seek to excuse their offences on the ground of ignorance of the law, these martial laws and ordinances are established and published.'

The first article requires everyone in the queen's pay to swear to obey the regulations. The code then goes on to deal with spiritual matters. Destruction awaits those who blaspheme, so there will be no blasphemy or taking of God's name in vain. No good outcome of any action can be expected unless God is first principally honoured and served. Therefore all men will proceed to divine service when summoned by the sound of trumpet or drum, unless they are sick or on special duty.

The day-to-day life of the private is then legislated for. None shall waste his time playing cards or dice, or other unlawful games, which breed contention or quarrels; or bring into the army any woman other than his lawful wedded wife. Women may, however, properly tend the sick, or serve as laundresses. Soldiers are also forbidden to lay violent hands on any woman with child, or lying in childbed, old persons, widows, young virgins, or babes—a collection which is interesting for its omissions, which may or may not have resulted from careless drafting. Habitual drunkenness and riotous behaviour are forbidden.

The rest of the code is devoted to purely military discipline. No-one is to have dealings with the enemy without the knowledge of the general. None may break rank without permission

[1] Cott. MSS., Calig. C IV, no. 41.

or leave the post assigned to him in the defence of any breach or trench. It is forbidden to linger behind with the wagons in the hope of getting a lift. Only those who are wounded or otherwise incapacitated, and who have permission, may ride. On the march there must be no outcry if a hare or other animal is put up, as it may lead the rest of the troops to think that they are being attacked. (There was a practical example of this in the expedition to Normandy in 1589 when 'a hot alarm' was caused by the excitement and noise of some men hunting a hare.)[1]

There are several articles governing the victualling arrangements. No man will steal his companion's rations, nor will he take victuals from the people of the country without due payment. The robbing of shops, or of victuallers following the army, is strictly forbidden; as is the taking of rations for a longer period than that authorized from time to time. Animals must be slaughtered only in the appointed place, and the waste must be buried. The waters of any river or stream adjoining the camp may not be troubled or defiled except some distance downstream. None are allowed to go foraging unless the forage-master has authorized it, and provided a sufficient bodyguard for the purpose.

A captain may not take into his company a soldier from any other band without the permission of the other captain concerned. Nor will he seek to entice men from other companies. No man will enroll under two captains, muster in several companies at the same time, or try to pass himself off as another man on the muster day.

Lending arms to others to enable them to pass muster as fully equipped is forbidden. Nor will any 'embezzle or diminish' the equipment issued to him by his captain. In particular, equipment must not be gambled away in unlawful games. Armour and weapons must at all times be kept clean and ready for immediate use.

Other subjects covered are communication with the enemy, leaving watch or ward without permission, sleeping on duty, revealing the watchword to the enemy, mutiny, striking a superior officer, resisting arrest, and the treatment of prisoners. The final article gives the general the right to punish at discretion any offence not covered by the regulations; and even

[1] Add. MSS. 4155, f. 59.

if a man has not taken the oath (for example, because he enrolled after the general swearing-in ceremony) he is deemed to be subject to the regulations as if he had done.

Punishments are graded according to the gravity of the offence, and whether or not it is a first offence. Swearing and blasphemy are punishable on a first conviction by a fine of 5s., on a second by five days' imprisonment, and on a third by loss of rank and the balance of pay due. Other offences punishable by fines are the illegal disposal of armour, and absence from divine service without reasonable excuse. Imprisonment is the punishment for killing cattle in the camp or garrison outside the place appointed for the purpose, for stealing provisions, and causing a disturbance in billets. Imprisonment with loss of pay awaits anyone found guilty of loitering with the wagons on the march, and refusing to obey orders. Discharge is the reward of soldiers caught gambling away their equipment. The same fate and a whipping is prescribed for those who introduce women other than those permitted by the regulations. The death penalty is imposed for many offences, including molesting women, striking a superior officer, and foraging without permission. The most serious offence of all, betrayal of the watchword, is punishable with death by torture.

The twenty-nine articles issued by Willoughby before his force left for France in 1589 are little more than a condensation of Leicester's code.[1] Fines are inflicted for failure to appear at divine service and abusing the chaplain. Marching with the baggage, straggling, and pilfering on the march are punished with imprisonment and the bastinado. Willoughby did, however, increase the number of offences punishable by death with torture, although the only offence punishable in this way in Leicester's code carries only the simple death penalty in Willoughby's.

Essex did not devise a new code for his expedition to France in 1591. He was content to use Leicester's, with such additions as his advisers deemed necessary.[2] Mountjoy, however, issued his own regulations in Ireland in 1600. They begin with the usual clauses about blasphemy and religious services, and proceed to enumerate the offences punishable by death. They make a formidable list. Harbouring rebels, molesting women, stealing

---

[1] *H.M.C. Ancaster*, 289.   [2] S.P. France, xxv, f. 103.

victuals or munitions worth more than a shilling, abandoning the ensign, sleeping on sentry duty, leaving a post without permission, threatening a superior officer, burning any house, corn, ship, or wagon intended for military use, departing more than a mile from the forces, breaking rank, exceeding the time limit, in a pass, unless it can be proved that the hand of God is responsible for the delay, taking two pays, and selling equipment.

It is also laid down that the troops are to cover ten miles a day when on the march and be content with supper and breakfast in the place where they spend the night. Horsemen who lose their mounts are to be degraded to the pioneer corps. No soldier is to be admitted to a company if he cannot produce satisfactory discharge papers. Magistrates and town officers are forbidden to detain a soldier more than twenty-four hours. Then they must hand him over to the provost marshal for trial 'by the speedy course of martial (i.e. military) law'. Wills made by men who have died on the battlefield are deemed to be valid, while the goods of men who die intestate are to be distributed among the wounded or given to the hospitals. Drunkenness is punishable on the first offence by imprisonment, on a second by the loss of two months' pay, and on a third by 'such far greater punishment' as the marshal's-court shall decide. Lastly, it is decreed that no woman is to follow the troops.[1]

The regulations were read over by the general to the captains at the beginning of a campaign, and by them in turn to their companies. Thereafter the oath was administered. The men raised their right hand and repeated after the captain: 'All these articles which have been openly read unto us we hold and allow as sacred and good, and those will we truly and stoutly confirm, fulfil, maintain, and keep, so help us God and His divine word, amen.'[2]

The officers principally responsible for the maintenance of discipline were the high marshal and the provost marshal. When a man was tried for a serious offence in the marshal's court, his captain and such members of the company as were considered necessary were present. At one court martial in the Netherlands, when four men were tried for inciting the troops to mutiny, all

---

[1] *Carew Cal. 1589–1600*, 502–5.
[2] T. Styward, *The Pathwaie to Martiall Discipline*, 64. (Another form of oath is given in Appendix 6.)

the principal officers were present. Each of the accused was heard separately, a unanimous verdict was given against all four, and sentence of death was pronounced.[1]

Military law operated only after the forces had left England. This was a pity in the opinion of the commissioners of musters of Bristol. They pointed out to the Privy Council that, as the city was a rendezvous for large numbers of troops on their way to Ireland, it would be a great help if the mayor were empowered to deal with offenders—deserters and mutineers, for example—by military law.[2] In Ireland, the troops were sometimes subjected to the law of the land, despite the exemption provided for in Mountjoy's regulations. Not only were English soldiers repeatedly attacked by the citizens of Limerick, they were even committed to the town gaol by the mayor, who refused to hand them over to the military authorities. This, it was said, was most irregular, as only the court martial was supposed to try soldiers on active service.[3]

Desertion was by far the commonest offence. As soon as a levy was complete, men began to disappear and they continued to do so when the force reached its destination. At the siege of Leith in 1560 men deserted 'by heaps'. The Earl of Warwick was reduced to despair by desertion when he was besieged in Le Havre in 1562. Despite elaborate precautions his troops kept melting away.[4] In 1585 Sir John Norreys complained that many men had vanished in the Netherlands. Few had perished at the hands of the enemy or for want of food. Desertion and sickness rather were to be blamed for the gaps in the ranks. Next year the Earl of Leicester had much the same tale to tell. Of 1,100 recruits, 300 ran away, but most of them were recaptured.[5] Several were executed as a warning to others, and Leicester begged the Privy Council to deal severely with any who contrived to get back to England. The only signatures to be accepted on passes were his own and those of the governors of the garrison towns.

This failed to check the offence. Soon afterwards Leicester reported that men were deserting in large numbers to the enemy, who gave them safe-conducts to the ports from which they could

[1] *A.P.C.* xxxiii. 262.
[2] *H.M.C. Salisbury*, xii. 170.
[3] *Irish Cal. 1599–1600*, 402.
[4] *For. Cal.* xx. 219.
[5] Ibid. xxi, pt. 2. 25.

most easily find their way back to England. He asked the Council to see that these men were arrested, have a few of them executed, and send the rest back to their units.[1] Willoughby, who succeeded Leicester as commander-in-chief in the Netherlands, attempted to stem the tide of desertion by forbidding captains to issue leave passes without the authority of the commander of the garrison where they were stationed. In addition to the signature of the commander and the captain, that of the muster-master was now required, unless the holder was engaged on secret service work, when the signature of the garrison commander alone was sufficient.[2]

Desertion was often encouraged by officials escorting the troops. Of a levy of 200 for Ostend in 1590, less than half reached their destination. The Privy Council investigated the disappearance of the others and concluded that their leaders had allowed them to escape, either through sheer carelessnesss or, more likely, in return for payment. This sort of transaction could be most profitable. In 1588 one official (helped by his wife) was getting about £2 a head for the men he allowed to escape. Some paid him as much as £8.[3]

The captain and the company clerk played the same game. In 1591 a number of deserters carrying passes issued by a clerk were arrested at Cambridge. The passes had been sold for sums ranging from a few shillings to £4, the proceeds being shared by the clerk and the captain.[4] In the following year captains of companies levied for France were making large sums by giving men permission to leave the service. The Council ordered an inquiry and asked that severe punishment should be meted out to any found guilty.[5] The expedition to Portugal fared no better. According to one estimate nearly 3,000 deserted from it.[6]

The Privy Council was fully alive to the importance of stamping out desertion. It issued instructions to the Crown officers and civic authorities in the ports where men were most likely to land, to scrutinize most carefully the papers of all who arrived from abroad. Any suspected of being deserters were to be put in prison to await further examination.[7]

In Ireland, where conditions of service were more rigorous

---

[1] *H.M.C. Ancaster*, 187.   [2] *A.P.C.* xix. 189.   [3] Ibid. xvii. 387.
[4] S.P. Dom. 239, no. 141.   [5] *A.P.C.* xxiii. 309.
[6] A. Wingfield, *Discourse*, 479.   [7] *A.P.C.* xiv. 73.

than elsewhere, desertion was particularly common. Often whole companies melted away as soon as they reached the country.[1] Many soldiers escaped to the Pale, where they hoped to find ships to take them back to England. Lord Burgh asked the Council that an example should be made of the ringleaders, and the rest sent back to Ireland. Men were often tempted to desert by offers of higher pay and better food from the rebels. Whenever there was a shortage of rations, or wages were not paid, there was wholesale desertion into the rebel forces.[2] Towards the end of the century the Council in Ireland said that desertion was still far too common. It confessed that it could not cope with the problem, and blamed the corruption of the captains.[3]

Absence without leave on the part of officers was almost as troublesome as desertion among the privates. If a captain wanted to return home to attend to his affairs he required a pass signed by the general or the commander of his garrison. In normal circumstances he could get this easily enough, but if he wanted to get back to England without reasonable excuse it was not unusual for him to take the law into his own hands and make the trip without official sanction. In 1592 the queen was forced to order that all captains absent from their companies in Ireland should return immediately, as their absence was proving a great hindrance to the service.[4]

A few years later the treasurer-at-war bemoaned the fact that most of the captains were still in England.[5] When some of them were brought before the Privy Council they swore that they had no company in Ireland, but all who admitted that they had ever served there were ordered back.[6] Few obeyed, however, and sterner measures were proposed.[7] The queen had learned that the absence of the captains was encouraging the soldiers to plunder the country and lower the English forces in the eyes of the native population. It was also allowing them to leave the colours and return to England, or follow some trade locally. Henceforth any captain who left his company without proper authority was to be discharged, unless he was sick. But this had little effect, and the captains continued to behave more or less

---

[1] *Irish Cal. 1596–7*, 179.   [2] Ibid. *1598–9*, 31.   [3] Ibid. 274.
[4] *A.P.C.* xxii. 480.   [5] *Irish Cal. 1599–1600*, 192–3.   [6] Ibid. 255.
[7] Ibid. 424.

as they pleased. So long as the profits of their company were secured for them by their subordinates in Ireland there was no need for their physical presence with the troops.[1]

The second most common offence was mutiny. It was usually caused by lack of pay. In 1560 the Duke of Norfolk stressed the importance of keeping the troops paid. It was well known that Englishmen became mutinous if they could not afford to buy the ordinary necessaries of life. Sometimes, however, recruits mutinied even before they left England. In 1587 a company levied for service in the Netherlands mutinied in London. The lord mayor was instructed to see that the offenders were punished 'with some severe and extraordinary correction', which included flogging through Cheapside to Tower Hill, the loss of an ear, and a spell in the pillory.[2] In 1602 a company from Gloucestershire mutinied at Bristol. The commissioners of musters had the ringleader seized, whereupon the whole company swore they would set him free, even if it cost their lives. They made a show of returning to their quarters, but instead suddenly fell upon the officers guarding the prisoner. The rescue attempt failed and another of the leading spirits was arrested. The commissioners of musters pretended that they had the right to execute offenders, and set up a gallows. A preacher was sent to prepare the prisoners for death, and at dawn they were brought forth with ropes round their necks in the presence of all the troops. It was only when they had said their prayers and were resigned to their fate that they were set free.[3]

Right from the beginning of the campaign in the Netherlands lack of regular pay was a constant source of unrest. A private accosted Leicester one evening as the general was on his way to dinner, and on behalf of his company demanded that they should have arrears of pay. Leicester discussed the request with Sir John Norreys, who ordered the provost marshal to arrest the fellow and have him hanged. This aroused the rest of the soldiers, who rescued their spokesman and threatened to shoot the provost and his men if they interfered. Fortunately, two companies came in from another garrison at this point, and with their help the offender was recaptured and imprisoned along with nine others.[4]

[1] *Irish Cal. 1600*, 272, 322, 442, 505. [2] S.P. Dom. 202, no. 8.
[3] *H.M.C. Salisbury*, xii. 170. [4] *For. Cal.* xx. 495.

More serious was the mutiny in Ostend in 1588. Again, the root cause was delay of pay, but atrocious victualling and the natural discomforts of the town played their part. The soldiers, including the gentlemen volunteers, sent a petition to the queen, which was boldly carried by one of their own number, in which they complained bitterly about the service they had had from the victualler. They also asked that they should have six months' back pay to alleviate their distress. To increase their bargaining power they took prisoner Sir John Conway, the governor of the town, and some of the captains; and they also had the satisfaction of throwing the victualler's assistant into the harbour. The queen took a moderate line with them, on the ground that their behaviour must be due to a few mutinous spirits, and did not stem from disloyalty. She told the mutineers that she had already taken steps against the victualler, on the advice of Conway—whom they had thus misjudged; but whatever the shortcomings of the victualler, it was no justification for what they had done. She had, nevertheless, ordered Willoughby, the commander-in-chief, to make a thorough inquiry. He would call before him one man from each company; and he would also be prepared to listen to complaints about the behaviour of captains and inferior officers. She added in the instructions to her envoy that if the men could not be talked into freeing Conway, force would have to be used.[1]

Sir Edward Norreys was chosen to smooth things over, but the men objected to him. He was a captain in the Ostend garrison, and therefore could not be impartial. It was known, for example, that he had said that if he had been there when the trouble started he would have ensured that it was a bloody day, and that authority was enforced. In a second petition to the queen the mutineers pointed out that they had done no harm to the governor when they seized him, and added that their lives were dedicated to her service. (They omitted to mention that the governor had been unharmed only because of the incompetence of their marksmen, ten or a dozen of whom missed him at six yards' range—if Conway himself is to be believed. But perhaps they deliberately fired in the air.)

The men listed their grievances. They claimed that they had not received a month's pay in the whole of the last two years.

[1] *For. Cal.* xxii. 166–7.

They could prove that seven months' pay had come into the garrison at one time, but not a penny of it had found its way into their pockets. Rations were neither 'wholesome, savoury, nor man's meat'. Companies were so depleted that the strain of watching and warding with insufficient numbers was quite intolerable.[1]

The queen, who had learned from bitter experience how she was served by her captains, continued to urge that the men should be given a fair hearing. Conway, however, thought that conditions were not as bad as they had made out; but as their commanding officer and principal victim he must have been biased against them. His experience must have been disconcerting. Company after company marched upon him, with drums sounding as if they were on their way to battle. Pikes, and muskets with lighted matches, were trained on him in ever-increasing numbers, and he and the small number of officers he had with him had no chance of putting up a fight. When the muskets started firing, they must have thought that their last hour had come; but they were simply seized and carried off to the common gaol.

Conway, who was released after a short imprisonment, reported that the victuals had not in fact been too bad, although it was true that the beer had gone sour through poor brewing, and that most of the cheese was 'very ill'. In his opinion, however, the men were not really to blame. They had been incited to mutiny by some 'needy and riotous officers'. Whatever the real cause of the trouble it continued for some weeks. The garrison remained in a state of uneasy calm until the treasurer's assistant arrived with a supply of weekly lendings. There was a dispute as to which companies should be paid first, and the situation got out of hand again. It was only by playing for time until new companies could be drafted into the town that Conway was able to save the day. When the new troops arrived he held a meeting of the loyal officers. They decided to arrest the leaders of each company in their billets and commit them to prison. This was done, and on the following day all the troops were drawn up in a square at the place of execution, with the new companies carefully interspersed among the old and disaffected. One man from each of the nine mutinous companies

[1] *For. Cal.* xxii. 188–9.

was executed. Later another four were put to death, and the other principal offenders were banished from the town.[1]

Conditions of service in Ireland had the troops on the brink of mutiny most of the time; and occasionally they were driven to take the law into their own hands as their brothers in the Netherlands did. In 1590 Sir George Carew reported to London that the seasoned companies in Dublin, who had long gone without wages, were aggrieved by the fact that recently arrived troops were being paid 'to the uttermost farthing'. Unknown to their captains and officers, Sir Thomas Norreys's company marched to Dublin Castle, with a drummer and a trumpeter at their head, to petition the lord deputy, Sir William Fitzwilliam, for their back pay and victualling money. They were met by his secretary, who pacified them, and they went off quietly to their billets. Next day, however, they came back to the castle and massed on the drawbridge. Fitzwilliam ordered Carew (who was master of the ordnance) to load the cannon with hail or chain shot, and fire on the mob. Carew agreed, with some reluctance, but before his guns could be trained on the bridge, the lord deputy had second thoughts. He decided to offer the men two months' victualling money, and to pardon them for their mutinous behaviour. To which the men replied that nothing but a full pay would satisfy them.

It was now time for church. Fitzwilliam thought that a show of firmness might calm the men down, so he mounted his horse and made for the drawbridge as if he were going to church. He had no idea what would happen, and asked Carew to stay close to his side, keeping his sword handy. The soldiers barred the way across the drawbridge, and begged with moderation that their requests should be granted. The lord deputy replied that he would think about their difficulties, and was about to move on when one of them—a musketeer—said something that enraged him. In a violent fit of temper he tried to ride the man down. The musketeer put up his hands to save himself, and Fitzwilliam, seeing the musket raised, thought he was about to be shot at—although in fact the man had no lighted match to fire his gun. He drew his dagger, which was the signal for a general affray in which the mutineers were quickly overcome. Of the original seventy-seven, sixty-one were seized, bound 'by

[1] Ibid. 322.

couples arm to arm' and taken to prison. The other sixteen made good their escape in the general turmoil. Many of the arms thrown down by the mutineers were snapped up by quick-witted bystanders, who helped themselves liberally before Carew's men could fight their way through the crowds to pick them up.[1]

Only the major offences were reported to the Privy Council, and therefore information about the day-to-day misbehaviour of the soldiers is relatively scarce. In 1585 Sir Roger Williams complained that the troops were so scattered that it was impossible to detect all disorders, although his impression was that there had been very little trouble. A sergeant had got drunk and had been well beaten and reduced to private. Three freebooters had been 'trussed up'. Two soldiers had been strangled in their billets for causing a disturbance.[2] In 1586 three men were executed in Utrecht for trying to rescue a prisoner from the custody of the provost marshal.[3] On the march across the Peninsula during the expedition to Portugal a man was hanged for disobeying the order that there was to be no violation of private property. The culprit, who had broken into a house, was put to death at the scene of his crime. A card was hung round his neck explaining what he had done.[4] At the siege of Rouen, Essex sentenced a member of his company of cavalry to be disarmed for striking a woman, and also presided over a court martial at which some men were condemned to death for attempting to return to England without passes, and some for other offences.[5]

The poor discipline of the Elizabethan forces did not stem from defects in the machinery controlling them. As usual, the theory was perfectly sound. The military law was well drawn, and just what the times needed. The administration of justice was in the hands of the high marshal, usually a man of integrity and ability; and he had his provost marshal and staff to back him up. Nor were the appalling conditions under which the men lived and fought solely responsible. There was a deeper cause. The fundamental difficulty lay in a change in the nature of the service which the ordinary citizen was called upon to render. In

[1] *Carew Cal. 1589–1600*, 31–33; 36–37. [2] *For. Cal.* xx. 105.
[3] Ibid. 557. [4] A. Wingfield, *Discourse*, 497.
[5] T. Coningsby, *Journal of the Siege of Rouen*, 29.

earlier times Englishmen had found their allegiance to an overlord a strong motive for loyal service, whatever the cause they were fighting for. The ties binding them to their superiors were close enough to make them good soldiers; and they had an added incentive in the knowledge that if their service proved unsatisfactory they would regret it on their return to civilian life when their lord's displeasure would make itself felt.

Some remnants of the feudal ties still existed in the sixteenth century, but they were beginning to be replaced by allegiance to the state. The idea of the state, however, was as yet too abstract for the average soldier to understand it and to fight for it with enthusiasm. The professional soldier might speak bravely enough about the privilege of shedding his blood for his sacred sovereign and dear country (as did Sir Roger Williams), and sometimes might even mean it. Not so the ordinary recruit. For him the fireside had more attraction than the firing line. If he went to the wars it was only because he had not enough money to buy his escape from them. The moment he saw a chance of escape he was off like a shot, and no oath dedicating his life to the state would stop him.

XI

THE MEDICAL SERVICE

BEFORE the fifteenth century the slender army medical service was reserved for the principal officers. Edward III's troops at the siege of Calais in 1346 had only one surgeon, in the retinue of the Prince of Wales.[1] More adequate provision was made by Henry V. In France, in 1415, he had a physician and surgeon, who were required to engage twelve assistants between them. In the following year he authorized the recruitment of an unspecified number of surgeons and makers of surgical instruments.[2] In 1474 Edward IV took to France twelve surgeons, in addition to two senior officers with the titles 'king's physician' and 'physician and surgeon of the king's body'.[3] At the battle of St. Quentin in 1557 there were fifty-seven surgeons in a force of between 5,000 and 6,000 men. Two were allocated to the general, and one each to the lieutenant general, the marshal, the generals of the cavalry and infantry, and the master of the ordnance. The rest were deputed to look after the rank and file, except the pioneer corps, for whom there was no special provision. Each had to look after about 100 men, which remained the normal quota until 1594.[4] Thus, in the two centuries before Elizabeth, the medical service had grown from virtually nothing into a recognized branch of organization.

Most Elizabethan army surgeons came from the Company of Barber-Surgeons of London, which, in return for the privileges of its charter, was required to keep the forces supplied with a medical officer and an assistant for every company. The barber-surgeons were, however, occasionally required to serve as ordinary soldiers, and in 1556 the master had to ask the Corporation of London that, so long as they provided qualified surgeons, members should not be conscripted as privates. The lord mayor agreed, and authorized the barber-surgeons to

---

[1] F. Grose, *Military Antiquities*, i. 274.
[2] T. Rymer, *Foedera*, ix. 363.
[3] Grose, i. 276.   [4] Harl. MSS. 6844, f. 67.

record his decision in their minutes.[1] Six years later the Privy Council confirmed that qualified surgeons should not have to serve as privates. In view of their obligation to act in their professional capacity in the army and navy they were not to be levied as common soldiers in the forces being assembled for the Earl of Warwick's expedition to Le Havre.[2] It was suggested in 1581 that the barber-surgeons should be given statutory exemption from ordinary service in the army, but this proposal came to nothing.[3]

Although surgeons were exempt from conscription as private soldiers, they were just as liable for military service as anyone else, provided they were required in their professional capacity. The lord mayor was constantly being instructed to 'take up and imprest' surgeons for service overseas. Recruiting warrants almost invariably coupled them with drummers, perhaps because like the preacher and cannoneer they were both odd men out.

The surgeons were probably better off than their fellow officers below the rank of captain. It was manifestly in the interest of the company as a whole to see that they were well looked after. One never knew when their services would become of vital importance. Even so, they had no greater love of the army than the ordinary recruit. In 1598, when half a dozen were conscripted for service in Ireland, at least one did not remain long with the forces. He appeared before the master of the company soon after he had been levied and confessed that he had bought his discharge for six pounds, half of which had found its way into the captain's pocket. Occasionally, an unwilling surgeon would escape military service by providing a substitute. In 1599 a sailor complained that because of such a substitution he had had an arm so unskilfully amputated that he had almost lost his life.[4] On active service the surgeon was a privileged member of the company, in that he was allowed to go through the watch without giving the password—so long as he was wearing his baldric (the special belt which was his badge of office) and was engaged in professional duties.[5]

In the earlier part of the reign warrants for levying surgeons

---

[1] S. Young, *Annals of the Barber-Surgeons of London*, 99–100.
[2] *A.P.C.* vii. 119.   [3] S. Young, op. cit. 320.
[4] Ibid. 321.   [5] B. Rich, *Pathway*, Sig. G 2b.

were sent by the Privy Council to the lord mayor, who passed them to the Master of the Company of Barber-Surgeons. Later, when the needs of the troops became greater, it was more usual for the Council to authorize captains to find their own surgeons without making formal application to the Company. In 1589, before the expedition to Portugal, the lord mayor was instructed to help Norreys and Drake to recruit trumpeters, drummers, fifers, surgeons, and armourers;[1] and the four regiments sent to France in the same year were authorized to recruit twenty-four surgeons between them. Similar arrangements were made two years later for Essex's expedition to France. Twenty captains were given warrants to enlist a surgeon and two drummers each, and the lord mayor was ordered to give them all possible help.[2]

The captain was responsible for seeing that the medical officer attached to his company carried out his duties satisfactorily. Answering an accusation that the Portugal expedition was inadequately provided with surgeons, a writer says that, if in fact there were too few, it was the captains who were to blame. It was up to them to provide capable surgeons, rather than the principal officers, who could hardly be expected to deal with matters of detail. The writer goes on to observe that English surgeons had seen little active service and were in consequence not very expert in treating gunshot wounds.[3]

Contemporary theory on the medical service (as on most branches of organization) was well ahead of practice. According to one authority, the surgeon had to be 'honest, sober, and of good counsel, skilful in that science, able to heal and cure all kinds of sores, wounds and griefs, to take a pellet out of the flesh and bone and to slake the fire of the same'. His equipment was expected to include a full set of instruments, and oils, balms, salves, splints, and bandages.[4]

It is easy to imagine how far short of this standard the average surgeon fell. It was said that those who attended Sir Philip Sidney after he had received his immortal wound at Zutphen were there 'some mercenarily out of gain, others out of honour of their art, but most of them with a true zeal (compounded of love and reverence) to do him good, and (as they thought) many

---

[1] *A.P.C.* xviii. 27.
[2] Ibid. 122; xxi. 22, 243.
[3] A. Wingfield, *Discourse*, 480–1.
[4] T. Styward, *Martiall Discipline*, 40.

nations in him'.[1] But Sidney was an exceptional patient and the wounded ranker can hardly have had the same attention. Moreover, medicine and surgery were still far from exact sciences, and the unlucky private more often than not found himself in the hands of a medical officer who would have learned something from a witch-doctor. Most surgeons used curious ointments made up by themselves. One (admittedly French) specialized in a balm, the ingredients of which included two whelps boiled alive and two pounds of earthworms purified in white wine. In some cases the popular treatment was probably more deadly than the ailment it sought to cure—for example, gunshot wounds might be cauterized with boiling oil.[2]

The most enlightened army surgeon was William Clowes. He went with the Earl of Warwick to Le Havre and later served with the navy. In 1585 he was ordered by the queen to accompany Leicester to the Netherlands. In his book *A Prooved Practice for All Young Chirurgians*,[3] he says that while incompetent surgeons were responsible for more deaths than the enemy, he himself did not lose a single patient who had the slightest chance of recovery. His book contains detailed case-histories of a wide variety of casualties, chiefly among the men in the Netherlands campaign, which he had treated successfully; and even if he does draw a veil over his failures, it is clear that he was well ahead of his times.

The fact remains that his times were not far advanced. His instructions for the amputation of a leg provide a grim picture of sixteenth-century surgery. One glimpse is perhaps more than enough:

You shall have in a readiness a good strong form and a steady, and set the patient at the very end of it. Then shall there bestride the form behind him a man that is able to hold him fast by both his arms. Which done, if the leg be to be taken off beneath the knee, let there be also another strong man appointed to bestride the leg that is to be taken off, and he must hold fast the member above the place where the incision is to be made, very steadily without shaking, and he that doth so hold should have a large hand and a good grip, whose hand may the better stay the bleeding. . . . In like manner there must be another skilful man that hath good experience and knowledge to

---

[1] F. Grevill, *Sir Philip Sidney*, 130.
[2] F. Grose, *Military Antiquities*, i. 273 n.
[3] London, 1591.

hold the leg below, for the member must not be held too high, for staying and choking of the saw, neither must he hold down his hand too low for fear of fracturing the bones in the time it is a-sawing off. And he that doth cut off the member must be sure to have a sharp saw, a very good catlin,[1] and an incision knife, and then boldly with a steady and quick hand cut the flesh round about to the bones without staying . . . then set your saw as near the sound flesh as easily you may, not touching it, and with a light hand speedily saw it off.

Clowes concludes this stage of the long operation by observing that the surgeon must have a good eye, a strong arm—and a stout heart.[2]

In the Netherlands the officers were often dissatisfied with the services provided by the surgeons. They were so lacking in skill that they failed to cure even slightly wounded men, who would have recovered with proper treatment. The Privy Council was asked that, instead of one surgeon for each company at a wage of a shilling a day, they should provide two for each regiment of ten companies, these to be paid at a much higher rate, to enable them to employ several assistants. After careful consideration this proposal was accepted. The general was authorized to appoint 'two able, expert and skilful surgeons', each with a salary of 5s. a day, part of which they were to set aside for their subordinates; and only one of them was to have leave of absence at a time.[3]

The new system had many advantages. It was now possible for the skill and experience of the better surgeons to be systematically passed on to their less expert colleagues, who found it more difficult to try out their random personal theories on unfortunate patients. At the end of the century a similar system was introduced for the forces in Ireland. The captains there protested against the deduction of one man's pay from the company funds for a surgeon who was never seen. They added that the absence of a surgeon had a bad effect on morale. The men knew that if they were wounded they would have no skilled attention, and they were therefore careful not to take the slightest risk. It was suggested that the surgeon's allowances for

---

[1] A long, narrow, double-edged, sharp-pointed, straight knife. (*O.E.D.*).
[2] *A Prooved Practice for All Young Chirurgians*, 25–27.
[3] Cott. MSS., Galba D IX, f. 311b.

THE MEDICAL SERVICE

each company should be collected together, and paid to a highly skilled man, who would appoint subordinates, as had been done in the Netherlands.[1] These recommendations bore fruit. Orders for the garrisons at Lough Foyle and Ballyshannon made provision for two surgeons in both places with a salary of 10s. a day each, out of which they were bound to keep three assistants.[2]

Women were occasionally employed to look after the wounded. Evidence on this point is scanty, but in the disciplinary code devised by Leicester for his forces in the Netherlands it was stipulated that while, as a general rule, no woman was to be allowed among the troops, an exception was made in favour of nurses.[3] And in the military hospitals 'old women' were appointed to look after the inmates.

There was a marked improvement in the treatment of sick and wounded men during the reign. In 1591 an official was sent to France to arrange the discharge of sick men who seemed unlikely to make a speedy recovery.[4] In the Netherlands sick leave was authorized in 1594, when the captains had agitated for it after disputes with the muster-master about the inclusion of sick men in the muster rolls. The Privy Council gave the captains a sympathetic hearing and decreed that all sick men were to have their usual weekly wages. Further, they should have a month's pay in advance. If a man survived, the money that had been advanced to him was deducted from his future pay at a rate which would enable him to exist comfortably (or, rather, no more uncomfortably than usual) until the full amount had been recovered. If he died, the loss to the captain was to be made good by the treasurer-at-war.

Secondly, if a man fell sick and had to return to England for treatment, he was now retained on the muster roll. Provided that he returned to his unit within three months, and brought with him a certificate from the hospital where he had been treated, or from a justice or high constable, he was paid for his absence at the ordinary rate for his rank.[5]

In 1601 a captain from the Flushing garrison who had been sick was allowed to return to England to recover his health.

---

[1] *Irish Cal. 1599–1600*, 383.   [2] Ibid. 396.
[3] See Appendix No. 12, article 5.   [4] S.P. France, xxvi, f. 290.
[5] Cott. MSS., Galba D IX, ff. 310b–311.

He was accompanied by two servants, and the Council authorized all three to draw their regular pay.[1] Sick leave with pay was allowed in Ireland also. The lord deputy was warned by the Privy Council that a captain who had returned to England to recover from a wound in his leg should not have his pay stopped.[2]

The establishment of military hospitals was a comparatively late development. The so-called 'guest-houses' in the Netherlands, private houses in which invalids were quartered, were the forerunners of the hospitals proper. The owners had been made responsible for looking after a number of sick men and reporting on their condition at regular intervals to the treasurer-at-war and the muster-master. This worked quite well in the Netherlands or France, where the country was thickly populated, provided with good houses, and comparatively healthy; but in Ireland the position was reversed in every particular and only regular hospitals could cope with the large numbers of sick.

In 1598 some of the leading citizens of Dublin were attracted by the possibility of doing a good work at a reasonable profit. They offered to provide in the city or the outskirts a hospital with fifty beds capable of accommodating twice that number of patients. The beds, bedding, a surgeon, and six nurses were also to be provided—all for £1,000 a year. It was argued that an institution of this sort would greatly encourage and comfort the poor soldiers, who were dying in the streets for want of proper medical attention. If they were better looked after many would be restored to health, which would not only enable them to fight another day, but would encourage their fellows to risk their lives more willingly.[3]

Nothing was done at this time, but in the following year the same proposal was made again. If the queen intended to continue fighting in Ireland, improved provision would have to be made for the sick and wounded there. There were two important points in favour of the extension of the medical services in Ireland. First, most of the men who died from dysentery—'the Irish ague'—would have had a good chance of recovery had they had prompt medical attention. Secondly, if the men could be given treatment locally the number of malingerers who contrived to find their way back to England in the company of the

[1] *A.P.C.* xxxii. 22. [2] Ibid. 194. [3] *Irish Cal. 1598–9*, 296–7.

genuine cases would be reduced. In any event, so many recruits were falling ill through lack of decent food and lodging that even if only genuine cases were allowed to return to England the facilities there would be over-taxed.[1] Men could not be expected to serve with enthusiasm if they were accustomed to see their wounded comrades lying in the streets. But if they knew that warm beds and competent surgery (even for the slightest wound) awaited them on their return from the battlefield every man would put forward his best foot, and show himself most valiant.[2] Another captain made the same point when he suggested that churches and abbeys should be converted into military hospitals. He had been horrified by the sight of sick and wounded soldiers dying in the streets. He pointed out that men who survived their first attack of dysentery were worth three raw recruits, and that for this reason alone hospitals would be a good investment.[3]

The attitude of the native population made the need of adequate provision for invalids all the more pressing. Irish folk were well disposed towards each other, but their natural hatred for the English prevented them from giving the slightest help to ailing soldiers.[3]

In 1600 Lord Buckhurst recommended that hospitals should be provided in every province in Ireland, and that officers should be appointed to have charge of them.[4] Soon afterwards the idea was developed by him, some members of the Privy Council, and the senior captains in Ireland. It was proposed that the government should hire suitable buildings and have them converted. This and the provision of bedding were to be the direct responsibility of the government, but the running expenses were to be met from a levy of one man's pay on each company. The hospitals were to be supervised by two worthy householders in each town. In addition, they would have a master, who would be either a physician or a surgeon, a servant, and four nurses. The two householders were to give their services free, and the master was to have 5s. a day. It is not clear if this plan was put into operation, but a hospital had been erected in the outskirts of Dublin by the middle of 1600.[5]

---

[1] Ibid. *1599–1600*, 334.
[2] Ibid. *1598–9*, 386.
[3] Ibid. *1599–1600*, 350, 377.
[4] Ibid. 395–6, 448.
[5] Ibid. *1600*, 209.

Sir Henry Docwra was responsible for building a hospital at Lough Foyle in the same year. He started on it before any of the other buildings, on the assumption that the men would be more willing to work on something which was intended for their own good. But he was mistaken. The troops had to be driven to complete the place. Eventually a ruined church was renovated and fitted out with twenty-eight beds, far too few to take 'the incredible seas of sick and wounded men' who flooded into it.[1] Its inadequacy was confirmed later; but it was agreed that all the hospitals in London could not have coped with the demands made on it. It was at the same time suggested that it would be sensible to exclude men suffering from infectious diseases. Less than one in ten of them survived, whereas men who were only wounded had an infinitely better rate of recovery. The point was also made—not unreasonably—that the use of the hospital as an ammunition dump, because of shortage of storage space, was undesirable.[2]

At least one hospital was founded in England specially for disabled soldiers—in Buckinghamshire in 1599. It was intended to house thirty-six 'maimed unmarried soldiers'. It differed from the institutions in Ireland and the Netherlands in that it provided a permanent home for the men.[3]

The climate of the countries where they served was responsible for much of the sickness among Elizabeth's soldiers. France and Portugal could be too warm for Englishmen, Ireland too wet, the Netherlands too cold, and Scotland both too wet and too cold. When it was suggested in some quarters that proper precautions had not been taken against disease in Portugal in 1589, one of the men who had been there indignantly refuted the allegations. Strange climates had always taken a heavy toll of the English forces. The cold, raw air in the Netherlands had been too much for them, and had caused many deaths even when the men had been in billets. The warmth of France, aided by the abundance of fruit and wine to which Englishmen were unaccustomed, had always undermined their health. Even the Spaniards had heavy losses through illness when they campaigned in the summer months. Finally, the critics of the arrangements in Portugal were reminded that the plague had

---

[1] *Irish Cal. 1600–1*, 113; Sir H. Docwra, *Narration*, 288–9.
[2] *Irish Cal. 1600–1*, 113.   [3] *Dom. Cal. 1598–9*, 13.

killed in London in six months more than twice the strength of the whole expeditionary force. Why, then, should it be expected that the troops should escape illness, especially when they had to drink wine rather than the beer to which they were accustomed?[1]

France was probably the least severe on the English soldier. Although sickness there was usually widespread it had fatal consequences less often than elsewhere. In both Ireland and the Netherlands bad food was often to blame for illness. In 1587 the governor of the garrison in Ostend asked for special rations for his invalids, who, in nearly every case, were victims of bad feeding. Men could not make a good recovery from sickness or dangerous wounds with nothing to eat but stale cheese and unwholesome bread.[2] In Ireland doubtful food, coupled with the climate and poor lodging, caused much sickness. One soldier told Burghley that his health had not stood up to the sudden change of diet. He had suffered from sea-sickness on the voyage, and had fallen a speedy victim to dysentery as a result of having nothing but the hard ground to sleep on, and scant medical attention.[3]

The question of relief for disabled soldiers is thus dismissed by the historian of the British army:

Elizabeth was not friendly to soldiers, and hated to be troubled with obligations towards men who had faithfully served her. An Act had been passed in 1593 throwing the relief of crippled or destitute soldiers on their parishes, and she could not see what more they could want. Bloody Mary had shown them compassion;[4] not so would Good Queen Bess; she would not be pestered with the sight of the 'miserable creatures'.[5]

The facts hardly justify this criticism. Indeed, they suggest that for humanitarian reasons as well as from motives of policy the queen, the Privy Council, and parliament were deeply interested in the welfare of old and disabled soldiers.

Provision was sometimes made for men with long or distinguished service, perhaps in the form of an appointment to a

---

[1] A. Wingfield, *Discourse*, 479.   [2] *For. Cal.* xxi, pt. ii. 385.
[3] S.P. Ireland, 44, no. 49.
[4] This refers to the increase in the private's daily pay from 6*d.* to 8*d.* in 1557, and to the home that Mary established in London 'for the relief and help of poor, impotent, and aged soldiers'.
[5] Sir J. W. Fortescue, *History of the British Army*, i. 157.

sinecure. In 1594 a private was given the post of gunner in the Tower of London, as a reward for his services overseas.[1] On other occasions a pecuniary reward was given;[2] and at least once a soldier's widow was awarded a pension—lands to the annual value of £20 in consideration of the long and faithful service of her husband.

It is of course true that there was a large element of self-defence in the government's attitude towards maimed soldiers, especially at first. A proclamation gave due credit to the queen's subjects who had 'truly and valiantly' served at Le Havre in 1562. But they had brought the plague back with them, and the principal ecclesiastical and civil authorities were commanded to provide remote places where those infected could be cared for by the richer members of the community. Christian charity required that the less fortunate citizens should be looked after, but the proclamation made no bones about the fact that it was in the best interests of the more fortunate to segregate and care for the returned soldiers. The rich must do this for their own preservation. Otherwise they might feel the sharp hand of God over them for their unmercifulness.[3] A later proclamation (in 1591) provided that returned soldiers should be looked after by the parishes where they were levied until they had recovered from their illness or wounds.[4]

Three years earlier the relief of 'maimed and impotent soldiers' had been listed as a possible subject for legislation,[5] but it was not until 1593 that parliament passed the first of three acts to help disabled soldiers and sailors—and in so doing to reduce the tension which their presence in and around London occasioned. The others followed in 1597 and 1601.[6]

The legislation was a noble attempt to deal with the problem, and embodied the essential provisions of the earlier proclamations. The first act proudly declaims that pensions were now to be provided:

Forasmuch as it is agreeable with Christian charity, policy, and the honour of our nation that such as have since the twenty-fifth day of March 1588 adventured their lives and lost their limbs or disabled

[1] Docquet Book, 1594–6 (30 May 1594).
[2] Ibid. (7 September 1594); Patent Roll, 19 Elizabeth I, no. 15.
[3] Proclamation of 1 August 1562.
[4] Proclamation of 5 November 1591.   [5] S.P. Dom. 218, no. 55.
[6] 35 Elizabeth I, c. 4; 39 Elizabeth I, c. 21; 43 Elizabeth I, c. 3.

their bodies, or shall hereafter adventure their lives, lose their limbs or disable their bodies in the defence and service of her majesty and the state, should at their return be relieved and rewarded to the end they may reap the fruit of their good deserving, and others may be encouraged to perform the like endeavours.

At the committee stage it had been recommended that the money to pay the pensions should be raised by an annual levy of 4*s.* on innkeepers and retail wine merchants, and 2*s.* on alehouse keepers and others,[1] but the final arrangement provided for a weekly parish rate. At first it was reckoned that a levy of between 1*d.* and 6*d.* per week per parish (compared with the poor relief rate of ½*d.* to 6*d.*) would produce enough money; but the number of disabled men kept increasing, and the rate had to be raised to a maximum of 8*d.* in 1597 and 10*d.* in 1601. There was a special rate for London, which had more than its fair share of disabled men, and was also better able to find money than most places. The Corporation was empowered to charge a parish as much as 2*s.* a week, so long as the average did not exceed 8*d.* per parish (twice the maximum of the average rate elsewhere); and this differential was maintained in 1601 when the London maximum was raised to 3*s.* a week, with an average of 1*s.*

The money was to be collected quarterly by the churchwardens, who were the logical choice for the job, as they already collected the poor relief tax. They remitted the money to the high constable, who in turn passed it on to a treasurer—a justice of the peace selected by his fellow justices—who paid out the pensions. To help the system work, heavy penalties were provided. The churchwarden who failed in his duty was fined 10*s.*, the high constable 40*s.*, and the treasurer at the discretion of the other justices of the peace. It was found by experience that the churchwardens and the petty constables who helped them (although they were not at first required by law to do so) were negligent both in collecting and handing over the tax; and in the 1597 act the constable was formally associated with the churchwarden and both were made liable, should they prove careless, to an increased fine of £1, which was to be paid into the pension fund.

The annual value of the pensions was: £10 for a private; £15

---

[1] *H.M.C. Salisbury*, iv. 298.

for officers below the rank of lieutenant; and £20 for a lieutenant—generous enough when it is considered that the private's full pay on active service was a mere £12 a year, out of which he had to keep himself and pay for his arms and ammunition.

To qualify for his pension the disabled soldier brought a certificate from abroad signed by the general or high marshal, and by the captain or lieutenant of his company. This was endorsed by the muster officials in England, who, having copies of the muster rolls in their possession, were well placed to detect fraud. Pensions were payable in the parish where the man had been conscripted, or, if he were a volunteer, in his native parish, or the place where he had mainly resided in the last three years.

The statutes created much new paper work, especially for the heavily loaded justices. They were to keep a record of all the sums collected, a register of the persons getting relief, and the certificates of eligibility. The surveyor-general of the muster-rolls, who endorsed applications for pensions, kept a record of the certificates he issued. Although all applicants were supposed to get the approval of the surveyor-general before they returned to their homes, it was arranged that manifestly genuine cases should be approved at the point where the men landed, so that they did not have to journey to London, where the surveyor-general was usually found. The men were given enough money in the county where they landed to get them on to the next county; and so they were handed from one to another until they finally reached home. If they were too ill to travel, they were looked after in the town where they disembarked until they got better.

It has already been suggested that the pensions legislation was, up to a point, defensive; but it is also true that there were many who genuinely sympathized with the lot of the wounded soldier. Surely Sir Robert Cecil was one of those. Hear him addressing the House of Commons in 1601, when the pensions act came up for review:

> I do not this out of popularity, because I have been oftentimes taxed by the men of war, and more than any gentleman of England. For when I have seen soldiers deceived by their captains, I have taxed them for it, and that makes me odious unto them.
>
> A captain is a man of note, and able to keep himself; but a soldier

is not. I wish not any to think that I do speak of all captains, for I make a difference between the wheat and the chaff.

The statute is, that the poor soldier must be relieved, either by the county where he was born, or out of which he was pressed. But if that were amended, and only to be relieved in the county where he was born, this would certainly yield a more certainty and greater relief. For in a man's county either charity, kindred, or commiseration will breed pity. But out of the county where he was pressed that cannot be expected. For the multitude pressed out of some little shire grows to be greater and the charge more than in some other three shires. As in London, where there be many parishes, infinite households and numbers pressed, and the division so small that it is a mere trifle. As in Lancashire, in respect of the vicinity to Ireland, where the disease of the war is. If it may please you that a commitment may be had,[1] I shall be ready to attend it; at which time I will speak further.[2]

Although from the very outset it was obviously going to be difficult to pay pensions at the statutory rate, the government steadfastly resisted any temptation to reduce them. They remained unchanged to the end of the reign. But it was one thing to prescribe pensions by act of parliament, and quite another for the counties to collect enough money to pay them, especially towards the end of the reign when the number of casualties went steadily up.

In several counties the authorities tried to satisfy all claimants for relief by reducing the amount of the pension paid to each. This earned a severe rebuke from the Privy Council, which ordered them to stick to the rates laid down.[3] Even after the county tax was increased the amount brought in remained inadequate, and the treasurers struggled to evade their liabilities. Norfolk put forward the plea that, as a man was a volunteer, he was ineligible for relief; but the Council ordered that he should be paid at the usual rates.[4] On another occasion a native of Hertfordshire, who had been levied in Middlesex, was sent from one county to the other without receiving any benefit until the Council intervened. It ruled that Middlesex could not support all the men levied there who had been maimed, and instructed the Hertfordshire treasurers to make provision for the man.[5]

---

[1] i.e. that the bill should go to committee.
[2] H. Townshend, *Historical Collections*, 307–8.
[3] *A.P.C.* xxv, *passim*.
[4] Ibid. xxviii. 393.
[5] Ibid. xxix. 235.

It is difficult to see what more could have been done for the disbanded levies, whether fit or disabled. There is ample justification for the Privy Council's claim that the queen devoted as much attention to the welfare of her discharged soldiers as to any matter of state. It was no doubt difficult to sort out the geniune cases in the vast throng of miscreants seeking to cash in on the kudos which the genuine honest soldier brought back from the wars, and many deserving cases must have suffered in consequence. But the central government can hardly be blamed for this. The time was not ripe for a national scheme. The parochial system was forced on the government as a simple method of ensuring that claimants were treated with justice, and separating the genuine cases from the rogues and vagabonds. As Cecil said in parliament, the best way to do this was to put the men in the hands of their own kith and kin in the parish where they had been born.

XII

DRILL, TRAINING, TACTICS, AND STRATEGY

A. DRILL

AN army cannot be managed without drill, even if it never fires a shot in anger; yet no system of drill was laid down by the government. It was left to the officers in the field, and at the periodical shire musters, to teach the men to understand their own interpretation of the traditional commands and the corresponding evolutions. Some notes on this subject, written in 1598, say that it matters little what commands are used, so long as they are used consistently, and throughout the whole army. Otherwise it will breed confusion.[1] In practice, however, there must have been substantial differences between one captain's version and the next. Several drill books were compiled during Elizabeth's reign, but they were the work of private individuals and did not carry the authority of the Privy Council. They simply set down the author's idea of the existing system, with a few glosses derived from his own experience or prejudices. They, nevertheless, give a clear enough picture of the theory, whatever the practice may have been.

The fullest is Sir John Smythe's *Instructions and Orders Mylitarie*, written in 1591, but not published until four years later. In 1591 the author was still under a cloud because of his controversial *Certain Discourses*, published on 1 May 1590 and suppressed by the government exactly a fortnight later; and probably both author and publisher thought it prudent to defer publication of his new book until the unpleasantness caused by the earlier work had been forgotten. Although the *Instructions* is very much a drill manual, Smythe cannot resist using it to disseminate the ideas about the virtues of the long-bow that had featured prominently in *Certain Discourses*. He himself says that the book contains 'all such instructions and advertisements

[1] S.P. Dom. 266, no. 100.

military as have at this time fallen into my remembrance that do concern the ordering, forming, and exercising of single bands and companies as well of horsemen as of footmen, as also of reducing and forming of squadrons into all the chief forms of battles that are requisite for armies to march or fight withal in the open fields'.

In the Dedication he points out that armour and weapons are purposeless if people do not know how to use them. He has set down what he learned from serving in the wars of foreign princes; and also from the opinions of many great captains—not the usual military stuff, which has been written up well enough already, but the 'reducing of single bands of horsemen and footmen into their simple and single order of ranks from point to point, and how to draw out many troops and societies of shot to enter into skirmish, and to continue the same; as also divers different ways how to reduce many bands and troops into squadrons and battles formed, as well to march in the field— all of which is very important'.

The commands and corresponding movements are described in detail. They cover elementary marching formations, the handling of the various weapons both on the march and in action, and the location of the ensign-bearer, drummers, and fifers in different situations. Orders, although called 'brief speeches', have not yet been reduced to the brevity of a later age. Some, it is true, are short enough: 'Advance your pikes', or 'Double your ranks by right line'.[1] But to achieve more complicated formations it is necessary to fall back on less brief speeches. For example: 'March up with your company upon the right flank, and you with your company by the left flank of yonder compartment (i.e. section) and incorporate your compartments in front, flanks, and back, with that company or compartment.'[2]

If the words of command are complex, even more so are the explanations of what they are intended to accomplish. This is hardly surprising. It is easy enough to teach a military evolution by demonstration, not so easy to reduce it to words which are few and readily understandable. The brief speech 'Shoulder your pikes and march' is simple enough, but there is more to it than meets the eye. The shouldering of the pike has to be done with a comely and soldierly grace,

[1] *Orders Mylitarie*, 9, 13.   [2] Ibid. 37.

all the pikers of the front rank falling back with their right feet almost a foot behind their left, that the pikes may the more leisurely and comely fall to their shoulders, and then, raising up their left feet about a handful from the ground and letting them fall again, they must all in an instant advance forward, and so fall into their march, first with their right feet. And so in like manner the second, third, and fourth ranks, and so subsequently all the rest of the ranks must in all points perform the like, and shoulder their pikes one after the other and carry the butt ends of their pikes three foot or more from the ground, straight in descent towards the right hams of the soldiers pikers marching before them, every rank being so even in front that the butt end of no piker's pike may precede the one the other in the same rank; and so even and straight by flanks that the butt end of every piker's pike may be just point and blank towards the right ham of the piker preceding in the rank before him; and so they must all with great silence and with a grave and soldierlike grace, march.[1]

The pikeman must have been alert both mentally and physically to get the movements just right.

The command 'Triple your ranks by both flanks' is another fair sample of the complexity of the sixteenth-century order. Smythe's exposition, in precise language that is reminiscent of the more absurd modern statutory instruments, runs as follows:

Upon which brief speeches pronounced either by the captain, lieutenant, or sergeants, the second and third ranks are presently to march up to the flanks of the first rank, that is to be understood, that the second rank shall march to the right flank of the first rank, and the third rank to the left flank of the said first rank, until they be all of one equal front, and in like and equal distances; at which time likewise the fifth and sixth ranks shall in the very same order and sort march up to both flanks of the fourth rank, and the eighth and ninth ranks shall march up to both the flanks of the seventh rank, and so subsequently all the rest of the ranks that are of any sort of weapon shall march up to both the flanks of the ranks of the like sort of weapon before them: so as of five that every rank did at the first consist in their simple and single order they are now by this tripling of the ranks by both flanks as aforesaid reduced to be fifteen in every rank throughout.[2]

A later book, of a different stamp, is *The Maner of our Moderne Training*, by Sir Clement Edmondes. This first appeared in 1600, and is a more workmanlike production than Smythe's.

[1] Ibid. 5-6. [2] Ibid. 14-15.

It is short—a mere ten pages, compared with nearly 200 in the earlier work. It starts very much from first principles by defining a file ('a certain number of men following singly one leader'); a rank; open order, where there is a distance of 12 feet between the follower and the leader, and between the files; order, where there is 6 feet between the follower and the leader, and 3 feet between the files—this being the formation to be used when the enemy are close at hand; and close order, to be used when attacking or being attacked, when the files stand shoulder to shoulder and the follower is only 3 feet behind the leader.

Ranks may be strengthened by doubling. This is done in two ways, either by inserting the second into the first to the right hand or the left hand, or else (the enemy being at hand) by joining whole troops together. Edmondes has not much faith in the former and more complicated method. It is simpler in emergency to join the two groups of soldiers together, otherwise there will be confusion. This was probably true of many of the more complex manœuvres. Elaborate theory must often have been thrown to the winds in the heat of battle.

Orders are delivered in a variety of ways. They can be sent by visible signs, by word of mouth, or by the sound of drum or fife. Directions by word of mouth, says Edmondes, are infinite. But they must be short, and without ambiguity. Some of the orders he mentions are: 'To your arms'; 'Follow your leader'; 'Faces to your right hand'; 'Double your ranks'; and 'As you were'. Barnaby Rich considers, however, that they may be misunderstood in the excitement and noise of battle. He prefers that the captain should use a series of hand signals and movements of his body (for example, right turn) which the men will imitate.[1] Visible signs can also be dangerous, as they may be obscured by snow, rain, mist, or dust. Again, hilly country may make them impracticable, or the watchers may be dazzled by bright sunlight. They do have the advantage that they can be seen over long distances in favourable conditions, but it is difficult to devise signs to cover every situation, especially as they have to be simple enough for the common soldier (who quite often can hardly understand plain words plainly spoken) to grasp them immediately and do exactly what the sign requires of him. Mountjoy's disciplinary code in Ireland provides that

[1] *Dialogue*, Sig. E 3.

soldiers must keep silent, on pain of imprisonment, when the army is on the march, or being arrayed for battle, so that the officers' commands may be clearly heard.[1]

The drum and fife are still used, but because it is possible for the men to distinguish only a few sounds without the danger of confusion, 'inarticulate' orders are limited to five: to arm, to march, to troop, to charge, and to retreat: and the common soldier must memorize them so well that he will carry them out as spontaneously as if his captain had issued the order.[2] The drum and trumpet could be used as weapons in their own right. Sir Francis Vere was once caught in a narrow valley in the Low Countries when he heard the sort of shouting the Spaniards were accustomed to indulge in before they launched an attack—which the terrain in this particular case would have made highly dangerous to Vere's force. They were still out of sight of the enemy, so Vere had his drums and trumpets sound a charge, whereupon the Spaniards, thinking that *they* were about to be attacked, promptly withdrew.

B. TRAINING

It was one thing to devise a system of drill, and quite another to put it into practice. The queen's instructions to the commissioners of musters often stressed the importance of training, both at the ordinary shire musters and when a batch of recruits was ear-marked for active service; but everything depended on the ability and inclination of the captain in charge. No-one took the county musters very seriously; and even when the levies were bound for the wars, and both the instructor and instructed had a strong incentive to make the army efficient, training left much to be desired. Barnaby Rich considers that a private can be well trained and made 'fit for the wars' in a month. If he cannot master his weapons and learn to march in that time, he never will. But even the best of captains finds it difficult to make anything of the material recruited into the English forces.[3] Matthew Sutcliffe asks that adequate time should be allowed for training. There is nothing more precious than time, which once passed cannot be recalled. It is dangerous to bring young soldiers face

---

[1] *Carew Cal.* 1589–1600, 503.   [2] *The Maner of our Moderne Training*, 137.
[3] *Allarme*, Sig. G iv.

to face with the enemy before they have been fashioned by training. Ideally, they will also be fleshed and hardened in light skirmishes before they are thrown into a full-scale battle.[1]

The military writers are staunch advocates of physical fitness. The soldiers should have plenty of running, leaping, throwing, and wrestling; and they must practise with their weapons both singly and in companies, so that they may have a chance of seeing where their own particular group of weapons fits into the general picture. Sutcliffe, who writes from experience, says that none of these things is done. Men are not encouraged to keep fit, nor are they given proper instruction in the handling of their weapons. They are simply marched up and down. Quite often all that happens at a training session is the useless expenditure of gunpowder.[2]

There was an attempt to provide periodic training in addition to the sessions that accompanied the shire musters. The Privy Council pointed out that unless training were regularly kept up 'the pains and charges' in the counties would be wasted. Therefore there was to be a two-day instruction period in Whit week, and another at a time to be selected by the county between then and Michaelmas. The costs were to be spread equitably among men of substance so that none would have cause for complaint.[3]

As soon as the men were assembled the captain appointed his subordinate officers and, with their help, subdivided the company into corporalships—sections of about twenty men— which might be further divided into fellowships, or camaradas. These were smaller groups led by the corporal's deputy, sometimes known as the 'lancepresado'. With the help of his sergeants and corporals the captain saw that each private was equipped with the weapon for which his physique best suited him. Then training proper could begin. There were three branches: the carrying and use of arms; marching; and the study of commands and drum signals.

Weapons must be carried 'comely and ready for use'. The pike is used either to give or receive a charge. The men must therefore be taught when and how to give the push of pike—the secret lies in the perfect timing of every man and every rank. In the case of fire-arms, the man is shown how to present his piece,

[1] *Lawes of Armes*, 82.   [2] Ibid. 84–86.   [3] Harl. MSS. 309, f. 214.

how to take his level, and how to give his volley at the same time as his comrades. This job belongs particularly to the sergeants. The old practice has been for all the musketeers to fire together, but by the end of the reign this is condemned. There is the danger that the rear ranks will shoot those in front in the back of their heads, or that to avoid this they will raise their sights so high that they miss the enemy as well. The new procedure is for the whole of the front rank to fire simultaneously, and then for the second rank to pass through the first, and deliver their volley in turn, and so on until all the ranks have passed through and fired, by which time the original front rank will have reloaded and be ready to fire again.

The introduction of fire-arms greatly increased the problems and cost of training. The manipulation of the pike or bill could be readily explained even to the poorest type of recruit. If he failed to master it right away he could, by imitating his more expert fellows, get a rough idea of the movements; and he would no doubt remember them from one muster to the next. Guns, however, demanded quite a different technique. Although infinitely less efficient than the modern fire-arm, they were infinitely more complicated; and if they were to be used to best advantage the soldier had to keep in regular training. This was costly and difficult to arrange in peacetime. The cost could be reduced if the marksman used only 'false fires', i.e. if he simply primed his gun without putting in the main charge and the bullet. He could in this way go through most of the motions of shooting. In particular, he could practise keeping the target in his sights as he pulled the trigger, which, according to Thomas Digges, was more than half the battle.[1] When the Privy Council asked for ideas as to how the shot might be trained with the least cost to the county, the reply came that training must always be a costly business. The expense must be met either by the queen, or the shires; and it was tactfully left to the judgement of the lords of the Council to decide which was the best way.[2]

In marching, the first objective was to train every man to 'observe his file and rank'—to keep directly behind the man in front, and directly abreast of his comrades on either side. There were, however, a number of fancy evolutions that 'were no

[1] *Stratioticos*, 104.   [2] Lansd. MSS. 62, no. 8.

marches at all'. These were to be shunned by the captain who took his job seriously. The men were to become accustomed to marching in time with the beat of the drum, and to familiarize themselves with the basic commands transmitted by drumbeat; and they had of course to learn and understand the particular set of verbal orders which their own captain was in the habit of using.[1] One of the marching showpieces was 'casting the men in a ring'. This was to form them into a compact audience so that they might hear without difficulty any general instruction which the captain wanted to convey. It was, however, a dangerous formation in time of action, as it left the ensign-bearer unprotected on the perimeter of the ring. Battle formations had always to ensure the maximum possible protection for him. Other special formations were the S or snail, and the D, which, according to Thomas Styward, all young soldiers ought to know.[2] It was dangerous to rely on a captain who was not himself fully trained. 'The inexpert captain, and the unlearned physician, do buy their experience at too dear a rate, for it is still purchased with the price of men's lives.'[3]

Training was not limited to the captain and his company. Textbooks were written for the benefit of the higher command. The best is Leonard and Thomas Digges's *Stratioticos*. This 'arithmetical military treatise' considers that the time has come when mathematicians must play an important part in warfare, and is designed to help the general and other field officers to solve quickly, by mathematics, some of the problems confronting the modern army. The first part of the book is devoted to algebra and arithmetic, and the rules and methods of working described in it are later applied to practical military problems. The sergeant-major is shown mathematically how to arrive at various battle and marching formations, given the number of men available, the distance required between the ranks, and so on. For example, how to draw up a field force of 8,500 in a square, with the files three feet apart, and the ranks seven feet behind each other. The high marshal is shown how to calculate the space which various infantry and cavalry forces will take up in camp, the master of the ordnance how to calculate what charges different sizes of field gun need, and the

---

[1] S.P. Dom. 266, no. 100. [2] *Martiall Discipline*, 67–70.
[3] B. Rich, *Pathway*, Sig. C 3.

DRILL, TRAINING, TACTICS, AND STRATEGY

victualler how to arrive at the quantity of food required by the army over long periods.

It is doubtful if, in the particular circumstances of the Elizabethan army, this book could have been much more than a curiosity. Few senior officers had either the intellectual ability or the time to profit from the system of ready reckoning provided by the Digges. It is much more likely that they worked on the basis of rule of thumb and their experience in the field. The Digges thought that book learning was worth many years' experience of active service. The senior officers, for their part, must have considered that a year in the field was worth a cartload of textbooks.

The propositions set down in *Stratioticos* are cumbersome, but at least they are the beginning of a new science. A typical example:

If 500 pioneers can, in ten hours, cast up 400 rods of trench, I demand how many labourers will be able with a like trench in three hours to entrench a camp of 2,300 rods compass? [The solution is given as follows]: First I say if 400 rods of trench require 500 soldiers, what shall 2,300 rods? Here, according to the plain rule of three I multiply the third by the second, so I have 1,150,000, which divided by the first delivereth in the quotient 2,825 soldiers. Then must I say for the second operation, if in ten hours 2,825 soldiers be able to discharge it, how many shall perform the same in three hours? Now, if you should work by the rule of proportion direct, you should find a less number of soldiers because three hours is less than ten hours; but because reason teacheth me that the lesser is the time wherein the trench must be made, the more labourers I ought to have, I must inverse the operation, multiplying 10 (the first number) by 2,825 (the second), and divide by 3 the third number,[1] so have I in the quotient 9,416⅔. So many pioneers must I have to entrench that camp in three hours.

No doubt the professionals who bought *Stratioticos* had some fun at the author's expense in disposing of the one-third of a pioneer left on their hands at the end of the calculation.[2]

Robert Barret has something to say about the use of textbooks for military training.[3] There are, in his opinion, three sorts of military author: learned men, including politicians,

---
[1] i.e. the product of 10 and 2,825.   [2] *Stratioticos*, 68–69.
[3] *Moderne Warres*, 5–6.

geometricians, and mathematicians, who have never seen the wars; men of small learning, who have had long experience of military affairs; and a few who are both learned and have followed the wars. There are also three sorts of reading captain: those who do not comprehend either the method or the meaning of the writer; those who understand the method, but not the meaning; and those who understand both, but are without practical experience of war.

If the first sort of reader is brought on to the field with a hundred men, he will never rank them right without help; and God knows what puzzling and toil it takes, even with help. That is as much as he can ever do, and, even so, he thinks afterwards that he has done a good job. The second sort will make some progress in training his company, but every now and then he will get into deep water and call out 'Hola, sirrah! Where is my book?' Then, after refreshing his memory, he will carry out some marching, nothing at all like a real soldier's march. Finally, he essays the most difficult manœuvre of the day—forming his men into a ring. He marches them round in a series of ever-decreasing circles until things get quite out of hand, and he finds himself trapped in the centre of a mass of humanity. He shouts from the depths of the chaos 'Hold! Stand still until I have looked in my book!'

Not even the third will do the job to Barret's satisfaction. He ranks them correctly by three or five or seven: pikes, half in front, half behind; colours and brown bills in the middle; divides his shot, half in vaward, half in rearward; and marches on in some pretty good sort. He can even make his ring, and happily come out again. But in the end he breaks down. Two to one he makes a mess of the counter-ring.

C. TACTICS AND STRATEGY

There is precious little to record about tactics and strategy, which in the sixteenth century were at a low ebb. Professor Michael Roberts has summed up this barren period in these words:

> The huge size of infantry units forbade the practice of minor tactics. The refusal of cavalry to behave as cavalry deprived commanders of their aid in attack. The strength of fortresses encouraged

blockade rather than assault. The steady increase in the proportion of musketeers to pikemen strengthened that element in the infantry which was least apt to the offensive. Contemporary theorists, rationalising their own impotence, extolled the superior science of the war of manœuvre and condemned battle as the last resort of the inept or unfortunate commander. Strategic thinking withered away; war eternalised itself.[1]

What was true of Europe as a whole was true of the English army, although its units could not be described as huge. The queen did what she could to stifle the initiative without which a leader cannot be a great strategist; and in any case the opportunities for strategy on the grand scale were really non-existent, if we set aside the plan to fight England's battles on foreign soil. Only in Ireland was there scope for tactical and strategic genius to flourish, and there only Mountjoy grasped the opportunities offered. Elsewhere, Elizabeth's forces were largely engaged in sieges—sometimes in attack, sometimes defence—or minor skirmishes where there was no planning of any kind.

It is necessary, therefore, again to fall back on the theorists to get some idea of the thinking of the age. The more ambitious drill books impinge on tactics and, indeed, the earliest book of this kind is more of a manual of tactical formations than a simple drill book. This is a compilation by Peter Whitehorne, published in 1560, as an appendix to his translation of Machiavelli's *Art of War*. The title gives a comprehensive description of the contents of this remarkable work: *Certain ways for the ordering of soldiers in battelry and setting of battles, after divers fashions, with their manner of marching: and also figures of certain new plans for fortifications of towns: and moreover how to make saltpetre, gunpowder, and divers sorts of fireworks or wildfire, with other things appertaining to the wars*. Formulae are provided for a variety of battles—squares, wedges, the shears, and the saw, for example. The sub-title of the book might well be 'First Steps in Tactical Formations'. But as a rule it was the safe and solid square that was used. The fancy formations were much too complicated for practical purposes—even if there had been reason to suppose that they might be more effective than the standard arrangement.

A treatise written by Sir Robert Constable in 1576 shows that

[1] *Military Revolution, 1560–1660*, 6–7.

the rules of chivalry were by no means dead, and therefore that the idea of tactics and strategy could hardly have been born.[1] As soon as the general has decided to lay siege to a town, and has made a careful study of the lie of the land, a herald is sent before the walls, where he sounds his trumpet thrice in the customary fashion. The commander of the garrison appears on the ramparts, greets the herald with much honour, and asks what he can do for him. The herald demands the surrender of the town. The commander thanks him for his honourable request, but regrets that he must refuse. He then bestows an honourable reward on the herald, and suggests that he depart in peace.

The herald conveys the reply to the general, who orders all the artillery in the camp to be 'shot off in triumph' and all the ensigns to be raised on high as a token of defiance. When this has been done, the commander of the town in turn fires all his guns, and displays *his* ensigns. The attacking force then hold a council of war at which the general explains his plan of campaign: how the trenches are to be made, which part of the wall will be selected for the assault, how the scaling ladders are to be taken forward, where the artillery will be planted. Then the detailed orders are passed throughout the army. Things are now being taken rather more seriously. The cavalry are ordered to roam the countryside to create a diversion, and minimize the danger of a surprise attack on the besiegers. Expert captains make skirmishes in the neighbourhood of the town to force the enemy to reveal their gun positions. When the mine is ready under the wall, and the train has been laid to it, a herald is again sent to the town for a parley. If the commander still refuses to surrender, the order to attack is given. The game is exchanged for a more serious encounter.

Matthew Sutcliffe's approach is much more modern. He describes with approval how the town of Nîmes was captured on a dark and blustery night 'when a man would think that none would look abroad' by a combination of secrecy, enterprise, and careful co-ordination of the units of the attacking forces. Sutcliffe is a strong advocate of surprise and swift movement. A town may be taken by soldiers wearing women's clothes, or dressed as clowns, or hidden in carts under straw.

[1] Harl. MSS. 847, f. 59b.

Spies must be used to find out where the walls are the weakest and most likely to succumb quickly to the battery. Before going into battle the general must satisfy himself that the enemy has no avoidable advantage. He should try to have the wind and the sun at his back—or the moon if the engagement takes place at night. A favourable wind will carry the arrows further, and it will blow dust into the eyes of the enemy soldiers. The opportunity should be taken to strike suddenly when the opposing forces are disorganized—for example, when they are passing through a narrow valley, or crossing a river. If the enemy are beaten in the field in an evenly matched contest, the praise must go to the soldier; but if they are trapped by tactical skill, that is the general's honour. Above all, cries Sutcliffe, spend no time vainly. 'Opportunity to do great matters seldom offereth itself the second time.' Nothing in the wars is more advantageous than expedition. Nor is anything more hurtful than delays.[1] Words of great wisdom, which were heeded by few of Elizabeth's leaders.

The nearest approach to strategic planning on a big scale came in 1588, when the invasion threat was at its height. The Privy Council invited a group of the leading military men to try to read the mind of the Spanish higher command, and devise plans to meet the presumed Spanish line of attack. The group, which included Sir Francis Knollys, Sir John Norreys, and Sir Roger Williams, concluded that the fleet from Spain would not venture too far up the Channel until they had gained control of some good harbour; and therefore the threat was greatest in the west. Milford might be chosen as the landing place, but it was less likely because of the barrenness of the country inland from the port, which an invading army would find tough going. But Milford had a very good harbour, and could not be entirely ruled out. A token force of 500 cavalry and 200 infantry should be kept in readiness there. Plymouth seemed a much more likely target. It was difficult to defend, and well placed to receive the enemy's reinforcements from France or Spain. Nor could Portland be ruled out. It had a great harbour, provided a good landing place, and the neighbouring countryside was easy to march through, and if the Spaniards established themselves on the island of Portland they would be in a very

[1] *Lawes of Armes*, 159.

strong position. The other element in the Spanish threat—the Spanish army in the Netherlands—had a wide choice of landing places. They might sail up the Thames, or choose the Downs, or Margate. If they decided to attack through Scotland, there was nothing that could be done about it—at least in the initial stages.

The group had little to suggest about strategy. This was something that they preferred to leave to the general. They did, however, have it in mind that the maximum degree of flexibility should be provided, so that troops could be moved quickly to any area that was threatened. They also recommended that all cattle should be driven from the area invaded, so that the only food the enemy would have was what they carried on their backs; and they should be harried with constant alarms. In no case should a major engagement be risked until an adequate number of English troops had been brought together in one place.[1]

Thomas Digges, who was at the time acting as muster-master in the Netherlands, and who had been recalled to England along with many of the more experienced captains there, put up a paper to Leicester covering the same ground. His reasoning and conclusion are worthy of twentieth-century Whitehall. There are two possible courses in meeting the enemy: either every available man must repair to do battle at the landing place as soon as the beacons are fired, or the defending force must be withdrawn from the area of the bridgehead and wait at a safe distance until they can mount an organized attack. There is merit in both plans.

It is a good idea to tackle the enemy before they get a firm foothold and land their artillery. The fury of the inhabitants is greatest when the beacons are fired, and delay might cool their ardour. Moreover, everybody knows how vulnerable men in small boats are; and also that once the enemy has made a landing he will fight desperately to retain his position, knowing that retreat may well mean destruction. Finally, any state with religious divisions holds potential traitors; and the longer the invader is unopposed the more time there is to organize a fifth column.

On the other hand, a confused multitude of untrained men rushing to the beaches will almost certainly do themselves great

[1] Lansd. MSS. 1225, f. 19b.

harm, and none to the enemy. Therefore, is it not better to drive away the cattle, and take up defensive positions at strategic points? If their food is thus denied them, and our navy controls the seas, the enemy cannot survive long.

All things considered, writes Digges, there must be no disorderly running to the seashore. On the other hand, the enemy must not be allowed to land unmolested. If he is, there will be great panic and the people will leave the coastal towns. To drive away the cattle might make sense in a place like Ireland, where there is little other food, but England is a rich country where the houses are full of provisions and the barns full of corn—unless, of course, the queen commands that all should be wasted with fire. A scorched earth policy is premature, however. It will be very unpopular and should be used only as a last resort.

England is fortified by a trench or ditch—the Channel. This natural advantage must not be thrown away. We have both her majesty's royal navy and merchant vessels to hold the sea. Men landing out of small boats are in great danger, and if a storm blows up the sea alone will give victory to the defenders. Again, men armed with guns can readily shelter in trenches on the shore, and with the help of billmen and swordsmen they can do great execution. Any of the enemy who are not drowned, slain, or repulsed, can easily be dispatched by those waiting on the shore.

Therefore—Digges at last arrives triumphantly at his recommendation to the commander-in-chief—we must have it both ways. The enemy must be attacked as he lands; and forces must be held in reserve inland for a more substantial onslaught later.[1]

In his essay 'The Earl of Essex as Strategist and Military Organiser (1596–7)' Mr. L. W. Henry examines Essex's projected military reforms and his strategic theories in the light of a paper written by the earl after his expedition to Cadiz, in which he argues in favour of a small and efficient army, and also urges the establishment of an English base somewhere in Spain. Mr. Henry points out that Sir Julian Corbett,

whose emphasis on Essex's interest in military reforms is perhaps among the signal examples of belated historical justice, was the first

---

[1] *Stratioticos*, 369–76. Digges's conclusion is attacked at length by Sir Thomas Wilford in *A Military Discourse* (published in 1734), on the grounds that experience shows that a resolute enemy cannot be prevented from landing and that the defender must not dissipate his strength in attacking the enemy as he lands.

historian to see the importance of his new system. Only up to a point, however, can his judgment be allowed to stand that 'Essex must be credited with being one of the first men who tried to give England an army in the modern sense'. It seems clear that nothing was further from Essex's thoughts than anything in the nature of a standing army: his organization was intended to last until the intended result was forthcoming—a speedy and certain end to the war—and the destiny of his small skilled army was connected with the decisive application of sea power through his projected blockade.[1]

This conclusion is perfectly sound; and it is reinforced by consideration of the many schemes for army reform put forward by lesser men than Essex, all of which proposed more or less drastic reorganization of the militia, and none of which envisaged a standing army as the term is now accepted.

Essex's proposals stand out among the others, however, for several reasons. They were based on his experiences in the amphibious attack on Spain in 1596. They were severely practical. They were put forward by someone whose word carried weight. Above all, they were related to his belief that what was wanted was a small efficient force, that the amorphous militia had served its purpose, and should be relegated to a minor role in the nation's defences. In Corbett's words:

> The end in view was to provide an army of six thousand trained men which could be mobilised at any moment. For this purpose the country was divided into what we should now call regimental districts. Where a county was rich and populous enough to furnish a regiment it formed a district by itself. London also formed a separate district with a regiment of four hundred and fifty men, that being the usual strength of them all.[2]

The new organization was, however, superimposed on the militia as it then existed. It did not replace it. This was a fundamental weakness, as the new 'superintendents of the forces' found themselves working side by side with the lords lieutenant, the deputy lieutenants, and the commissioners of musters. The two organizations were not complementary: one weakened the other. Nevertheless, the troops for the Islands expedition of 1597 were largely chosen from the new regiments, and formed probably the most efficient force to leave England in Elizabeth's reign. The *esprit de corps* engendered by Essex's personality was

---

[1] *E.H.R.* lxviii. 390. [2] *The Successors of Drake*, 162.

probably largely responsible for this, however, rather than any special virtue in the new form of organization.

The real interest in Essex's scheme lies in the use he would have made of his efficient small army. He believed that it would be possible to plant it in a fortified town on the coast of Spain, and to maintain it there indefinitely to provide a base for English ships to harry the commerce of Spain, and so bring the great dictator to his knees. This would not be a costly enterprise. With luck, it could even be self-supporting. The theory of this is admirable, but there must be some doubt as to how it would have worked out in practice. Even if an English force could have been established in a Spanish port—as indeed one was in Cadiz in 1596—it does not follow that it could have remained there indefinitely. The very reasons which attracted Essex to such an enterprise would have made it essential to Philip to liquidate the base at any cost; and while the effort needed to do this might have been considerable it is doubtful whether it would have materially weakened the Spaniards. And to the extent that the whole of the English naval and military effort had been concentrated on this single objective, its neutralization would have left England herself at the mercy of the invasion which would certainly have followed the elimination of her base on the Peninsula. But this is speculation. Essex never got his base.

The strategist needs room and time for manœuvre. In Elizabeth's reign these were available in plenty only in Ireland; and only Lord Mountjoy, the last and best of her commanders-in-chief there, seized with both hands the opportunities offered. Dr. G. A. Hayes-McCoy has provided an admirable study of these events in his essay on strategy and tactics there in the latter part of the reign.[1] He likens the rebel Tyrone to Fabius Cunctator. Except for the fatal final encounter at Kinsale he contrived never to fight a pitched battle. 'His engagements were skirmishes designed to impede the enemy's advance, large-scale ambushes which grew into battles, sudden raids, the cutting off of outlying garrisons.'[2] The parallel English strategy was the exact opposite of this. Three phases are distinguishable. The first —from 1593 to 1597—when the lord deputy would lead an expedition into enemy territory, carry out some destruction

---

[1] 'Strategy and Tactics in Irish Warfare, 1593–1601', in *Irish Historical Studies*, ii. 255–79. [2] Ibid. 263.

there, plant a garrison, and withdraw. The second phase was when Lord Burgh organized attacks by two armies from different directions; and in the third, Mountjoy employed the principles developed by the earlier lords deputy. He went about his job in a much more workmanlike way, however.

First, he carefully prepared his ground by providing garrisons capable of supporting one another close to the enemy's border. . . . Secondly, he systematically destroyed the enemy's corn and food supplies wherever he could find them. Thirdly, he continued the campaign through the winter of 1600–1, never lifting the pressure on Tyrone for a moment. Fourthly, he took full advantage of the English sea-power and was thus greatly assisted by the most important single disposition of the age, which was the lodgment effected by Docwra at Derry on 16 May 1600.[1]

The Irish tactics in the battle of Kinsale were an object lesson in what not to do; and they won the battle for the English. Before it began Mountjoy was stationed between an Irish army larger than his and the town of Kinsale held by the invading Spaniards; but partly because the Irish troops had brought the art of hit and run in warfare to a high level at the expense of their experience of pitched battles, partly because of mistakes made by Tyrone, who ought to have continued to keep the English at arm's length and fight a war of attrition, and partly because the Spaniards in the town neutralized themselves by sitting tight when the battle was on and refusing to catch the English between two fires, what looked like a probable English defeat turned out to be an overwhelming victory for them.

The incompetence of the Irish on this occasion must not be allowed to detract from Mountjoy's success. 'He entered this dangerous campaign with the serenity of mind which is one of the first virtues of a commander. . . . He maintained an admirable balance throughout. Every decision of the smallest importance was his, and his was the full responsibility. . . . His good nerves and reasoned temerity preserved him from disaster and carried him to victory.'[2] His immediate predecessor, the Earl of Essex, had all the opportunities but made nothing of them; and his failure only strengthens Mountjoy's claim to be the greatest of Elizabeth's generals, the greatest strategist and tactician, and indeed the greatest all-rounder.

[1] Hayes-McCoy, op. cit. 269.   [2] Cyril Falls, *Elizabeth's Irish Wars*, 318.

XIII

THREE CAMPAIGNS

A. SCOTLAND, 1560

BEFORE she had been many months on the throne Elizabeth had to face up to her first big military decision. What should she do about the threat of invasion from north of the border?

The Queen of Scots was also Queen of France. She could not be in two places at the same time, so her mother Mary of Guise ruled in Scotland in her stead. There were French forces on Scottish soil, and there was the manifest danger of complete French domination there. If that came about, England would lie cradled powerless within the arms of a nut-cracker formed by the French armies across the Channel to the south, and the catholic Scots and French to the north. Happily for Elizabeth, all Scots were not catholics. A powerful group of the protestant nobility, including the shrewd Maitland of Lethington, spurred on by John Knox (the least human and least divine churchman of the age), sought to depose Mary of Guise and sweep out the French influence.

The Privy Council had been worried about the situation on the Border for some time. The defences there were anything but strong. The commander of Berwick and the wardens of the marches were responsible for the security of the northern frontier, but it was difficult to keep Berwick—the key defence point—fully efficient. Food was a constant problem. The surrounding countryside was not very productive and supplementary supplies had to be brought from as far away as London. It was reckoned in October 1559 that stocks of food would last until about March of the following year, but the commander, Sir James Crofts, thought them inadequate, no doubt having regard to the possibility of a siege. The surveyor of victuals was sent off to London to give the Privy Council a first-hand account of the food situation and to get their authority to buy provisions in the counties he passed through on the return journey. Shortage of food set a limit on the size of the garrison. When the Council decided that the potential threat from Scotland called for an extra 4,000 men, the number had to be halved to limit the strain on food supplies. The recruits were as usual levied from counties near where they were to serve, except that the most northerly counties were not tapped, since they were in any case supposed to be ready to take the first shock of invasion. Money was also a difficulty. Crofts reported that the men were owed £15,000. Unless they had some pay they would be unable to buy heavier clothing for the approaching winter.[1]

Outside Berwick the position was even less satisfactory. The defences of the frontier depended on the competence and loyalty of the wardens of the marches for the time being. When the Earl of Northumberland was summoned to London from his duties as warden a willing successor could not be found. Sir Ralph Sadler was ear-marked for the job but he did his best to wriggle out of it. He suggested that Sir James Crofts should have the east march, next to Berwick; Sir John Forster, the middle; and Lord Wharton, the west.[2] Whatever happened he himself did not want to be landed with any of them. He had no local estates and therefore could not look to his own retainers for support in policing the frontier.[3] The queen, nevertheless, insisted on appointing him to both the east and the middle wardenships, using flattering terms that would have melted the heart of most men[4] although Sadler still considered that he had suffered a grave injustice. In the event, the Earl of Northumberland swore him in as his deputy. This was the last straw. It was a piece of sharp practice that left the emoluments of the wardenships in the earl's hands, but transferred all the expenses and hard work to Sadler.[5] He was a man of considerable resource, however, and contrived to arrive at the position which he had originally recommended, or something like it, by getting Sir John Forster to take on the middle march as *his* deputy, and Sir Ralph Grey the east. When he did a tour of the marches he found things in a sorry state. The men of the border country

---

[1] *For. Cal. 1559–60*, 13, 73, 114, 141.
[2] *The State Papers and Letters of Sir Ralph Sadler*, ii. 8.
[3] Ibid. 82; *For. Cal. 1559–60*, 89.
[4] *Sadler Papers*, ii. 65.   [5] *For. Cal. 1559–60*, 115.

were a lawless crew not much interested in defending the rest of England.

These then were the barriers against invasion. A garrison strained to the limits even in time of peace; a fickle assortment of feudal retainers to defend the frontier; and immediately behind them to the south a semi-feudal region of uncertain religious and political loyalty.

As the weeks passed it looked more and more as if the French were going to win Scotland outright. Tension mounted. A party of French and Scots landed from some ships near Eyemouth for rest and refreshment. Within hours it was rumoured in Berwick that they planned to fortify Eyemouth—a direct contravention of the treaty of 1550 under which the fortifications there had been demolished. This would be the most serious threat yet to England's security. The alarming news was passed on to London right away, with the warning that there had been no time to verify the report; and before Sadler could explain to the Privy Council what had really happened, the queen had reacted strongly. So direct a threat simply could not be borne. If necessary the French were to be attacked and thrown out of Eyemouth, which the treaty of 1550 fully justified. Cecil also wrote to Berwick. The news about Eyemouth had roused them all. There was general agreement that the French threat must now be taken seriously. Would to God that some had shown more foresight![1]

On 16 December the queen told Berwick that she had ordered the recruitment of 4,000 infantry. Two thousand were already on the way and the rest would be levied as quickly as possible. Part of the force was to be taken into the town, and part spread along the frontier. She even went so far as to name the leaders of the invasion force. The Duke of Norfolk would be supreme commander of all the troops north of the river Trent; and Lord Grey of Wilton would replace Sadler as warden of the marches, with command of the forces on the frontier, under Norfolk's general command. This news was in due course joyfully received by Sadler, who had found his short spell as warden financially crippling. But the announcement that Grey would become warden only of the east march clearly worried him. He urged Cecil to make quite sure that Grey was given both east and

[1] *Sadler Papers*, ii. 173; *For. Cal. 1559–60*, 174, 177, 185.

middle marches, so that he himself would not be saddled with any part of this unwelcome and expensive office.[1]

There was a great scarcity of arms and equipment in the counties where the men were being levied, but large quantities were sent north from London to be issued for ready money at fixed prices. William Winter was to be dispatched forthwith with a fleet to carry food and munitions to Berwick. He was then to proceed to the Forth to cut off any French ships trying to get through with reinforcements. If the opportunity offered he was to attack them, contriving if possible to give the impression that he was acting without orders from the queen.[2]

Cecil also wrote to Sadler and Crofts. The French preparations had reached alarming proportions, and must be nipped in the bud. The first essential was to gain control of the Firth of Forth: then, if the Scottish rebels would play their part, to send in say 2,000 cavalry and 4,000 infantry to capture Leith. Grey would have charge of the invasion force. What did Sadler and Crofts think of this proposition?[3]

They agreed wholeheartedly that the French should be dealt with now rather than later, when they could be much stronger; and if the navy were sent it would be difficult for the French to augment their forces. They suggested, however, that 1,000 infantry from Berwick should join the proposed force when it entered Scotland; and they doubted the wisdom of sending so many cavalry. It would be difficult to feed the horses at this time of year. There were a number of other points which the professional soldiers thought the secretary of state had not taken fully into account. Carriages would be needed for the heavy guns, and the number of siege guns suggested by Cecil—a mere five or six—was quite inadequate. Further, timing was of the utmost importance. The Scottish rebels could not afford to keep their troops in the field for any length of time, so it must be arranged for the English army to join up with them at Edinburgh the instant that they were fully assembled. If the Scots were to give effective help, the queen would have to take many of them into her pay. In fact, money would be the key to the whole situation.[4]

The government was not yet committed to intervene; the

---

[1] *Sadler Papers*, ii. 183.   [2] Ibid. 176–9.
[3] Ibid. 179.   [4] *For. Cal. 1559–60*, 216.

way to a peaceful settlement must be kept open as long as possible. But surely invasion could not be long delayed. The Council put up a carefully reasoned case to the queen. Although the French had made peace with England after Mary Tudor's war, they would keep it only so long as it suited them; but, nevertheless, it might be foolish to take them on singlehanded. It was just as easy for that country, organized as a military state, to make war after a year of peace, as it might be necessary for England, organized for peace, to make peace after a year of war. The French had only men and money committed in Scotland. England would be risking not only men and money (both of which were scarcer than they had been in the past) but also the Crown, the realm, and everything that went with them—which was too dreadful to contemplate. On the other hand the French were not yet established in Scotland in great strength, and could still be defeated by a small army. It might be a different story in the spring. The chances were that by then the French would have mastered Scotland, and would turn south.

It was recognized that intervention in Scotland might bring down the whole weight of the French military machine on England; and Spain was standing by to make capital out of any conflict between England and France. The country must therefore be put on a war footing. Lords lieutenant must be appointed in the maritime counties, the militia put in readiness, and those gentlemen who owned houses near the sea coast proceed to them forthwith. If any lacked arms and equipment they could have them from the government at reasonable prices. A royal army must be provided to guard the queen, so that if the worst came to the worst there would be a last-ditch stand round the sovereign.[1]

The invasion plan was finalized on Christmas Eve 1559. It was evolved with considerable misgiving. Despite an optimistic suggestion that the French could be driven from Scotland within a month, the weaknesses revealed by the first general musters of the reign left grave doubts in the Council's mind about the effectiveness of any army they could put in the field; and to invade Scotland was to issue an invitation to other countries to invade England. Agreement was difficult. At first seven members of the Council spoke against the proposals. At the end

[1] Ibid. 220.

of the day two still remained unconvinced that anything more than clandestine aid for the Scottish rebels was called for. Cecil mentioned this difference of opinion in a letter to Sadler. Most of the Council wanted an immediate showdown; but some preferred to wait and see, while keeping everything in readiness for invasion.[1]

The queen accepted the majority view. The French preparations for war were so great, their ability to conquer Scotland so apparent, that she felt impelled to 'rouse herself from her dream of peace' and hasten to the defence of her northern frontier. On Christmas Day the Duke of Norfolk was given his instructions. He was to keep the peace of the northern parts; to organize their defences; and above all to do what he could to drive a wedge between the French and the Scots. His second in command had already been appointed. Now, Sir George Howard, master of the armoury, was given command of the heavy cavalry. Sir Henry Percy, brother of the Earl of Northumberland, had the light cavalry.

Norfolk's most difficult job was to weigh up the military situation in Scotland. How strong were the Scottish rebels? Could they possibly expel the French without help from England? Action by the English army was to depend on the answers to these questions: but if Norfolk decided that invasion *was* the proper course he must tell the queen, and hold himself in readiness to order the troops forward the moment he got the all-clear from London. To keep the record straight he must write to the regent Mary of Guise as soon as his preparations were complete, telling her that he was there to defend England's northern boundary and to forestall an attack by the French. He was to make it plain that if the French left Scotland the English forces would be withdrawn.

If the regent sent an unsatisfactory answer the English army was to cross the Border; but not until they had everything they could conceivably need in the way of food, tents, carriages, and equipment to besiege or assault a fortress. Norfolk was to conceal the true purpose of his preparations by spreading rumours that the French were going to attack Berwick as a preliminary to invasion of England. He himself was not to enter Scotland but was to keep a reserve army on the Border in case disaster

[1] *For. Cal. 1559-60*, 220-4.

befell Grey and the French were tempted to head south.[1] He was also given secret orders to take into his confidence only those who were well known to be the queen's supporters. In arriving at military decisions he was to seek the agreement of Lord Grey or Sir James Crofts; in civil affairs, of Sir Thomas Gargrave; and in all important matters, of Sir Ralph Sadler.[2]

The stage seemed now to be finally set for invasion; but still the queen clung to her hope of peaceful settlement. On 30 December she cancelled her earlier instructions to Norfolk. She had decided that he could not very well invade before all the cavalry arrived, which would not be until after the end of January. The infantry who were now assembling were to disperse along the frontier some distance from the Border (where the price of food was too high) and to train in the use of their weapons until the cavalry turned up.[3]

She continued desperately to play for time. She ordered Norfolk to consider with Sadler whether even now it would suffice to keep the navy in the Firth of Forth, and to back it up with one or two other measures. The Scottish rebels might be strengthened enough if some first-rate English captains were to join them secretly, on their own initiative of course, and ostensibly without the approval of the general. A vessel laden with powder, field guns, and ammunition might accidentally be allowed to fall into the hands of the rebels. But there was to be no open hostility. This must wait for a month or two.[4]

In fact nearly three months were to elapse before the order was given to cross the Border. In that time everything possible was done to bolster up the rebels. They were given money, arms, and moral support. In the Forth, Winter did an admirable job trailing his coat, although before long the fictions that he was lying in wait for pirates and acting on his own initiative wore rather thin. The regent complained about his activities to Elizabeth, who promptly agreed that they must be looked into. She told the regent that she had instructed the Duke of Norfolk to make a full inquiry.[5] The unfortunate Mary of Guise, who was no match for Elizabeth at this game—she was tired, and old, with only three months to live—hopefully sent copies of the correspondence to Norfolk and asked him to arrange for the

---

[1] Ibid. 233. [2] Ibid. 237. [3] Ibid. 254.
[4] Ibid. 255. [5] Ibid. 383, 426.

restitution of ships, men, and goods captured by Winter. Norfolk, under whose instructions Winter was now harrying the French, replied politely. He undertook to write to the admiral to find out what he had been up to, and promised that if he were guilty he would be suitably dealt with.[1]

The queen could not stand indefinitely on the brink of war. Sir Nicholas Throckmorton, her able ambassador in France, reported the first rumblings of religious troubles there and urged that in Scotland she should 'beat the iron while it is hot, and show her greatness'.[2] There was pressure too from the Privy Council.[3] So yet another grudging step forward was taken at the end of Feburary when a treaty was signed with the Scottish rebels under which England contracted to send an army into Scotland to expel the French.[4]

Still the queen refused to spring the mine. She told Norfolk on 9 March that she had just heard from the king of France that he was willing to talk things over and redress any grievances she might have had as a result of the French occupation of Scotland. In reply she had sent him an ultimatum. The withdrawal of French troops must begin by 20 March and be completed by 2 April.[5] She was in fact now reconciled to open intervention in Scotland, which was easier to stomach as the French government had their hands full with their own religious upheaval; but she still wanted to keep the door open up to the last possible second for the peaceful withdrawal of the French troops. Therefore Norfolk was ordered to hold the army until 27 March. If there was the slightest chance that the French were coming to heel, the Border was not to be crossed. In the meantime the troops were to be kept at concert pitch.[6]

The French king ignored the ultimatum; and now at last all was set for invasion. Then there was an eleventh-hour hitch. The men must have ready money to buy their food in Scotland. They could requisition victuals in England, and plunder in an enemy territory; but as their objective was to liberate a friendly occupied country they must buy their food at fair prices to avoid alienating the native population. But the treasure chest at

---

[1] *For. Cal. 1559–60*, 456, 466.   [2] Ibid. 352.   [3] Ibid. 471.   [4] Ibid. 413.
[5] Haynes, *A Collection of State Papers relating to affairs in the reigns of Henry VIII, Edward VI, Mary, and Elizabeth, from 1542 to 1570*, 258.
[6] Ibid. 259.

Berwick was empty. Two more days went by until money turned up from London. Even then Norfolk had the greatest difficulty in satisfying everybody; but by getting the regular Berwick captains to agree to forgo their pay (on the understanding that they would have the first call on the next treasure to arrive) he managed to pay everybody else in advance to 16 April.[1]

At last, on 29 March, nearly four months after the army had begun to assemble, the order to cross into Scotland was given— Thank God! exclaimed Norfolk, with deep feeling. There was now nothing for him to do but to await good news from the north, and the arrival of treasure from the south.[2]

Up to this point Elizabeth had been torn between her conviction that the French would not leave Scotland unless they were driven out by force of arms, and her instinctive dislike of violence—not because it was morally wrong, but because it was expensive and there was no guarantee that it would succeed.

It might be expected that as soon as she was committed to invasion she would have thrown all her energies into achieving the expulsion of the French in the shortest possible time. Not so. Even with her army on foreign soil she still hankered after a peaceful settlement. This put an intolerable strain on her general and his council of war, and indeed on the whole of the rank and file. She told Norfolk on 29 March that although she had at last agreed to invasion she hoped that he would contrive to achieve their objective—the departure of the French—without the use of force. He was therefore to seek advice on the conduct of the campaign from Sir Ralph Sadler rather than from those professional soldiers who liked to keep a war going as long as possible in the interest of their own financial rewards.[3] She also wrote to Grey telling him to rely on Sadler. If it were humanly possible to rid Scotland of the French without force or bloodshed, so much the better. Nevertheless, he was to press on. There were to be no unnecessary delays to suit the convenience of the captains. Elizabeth said at the same time—quite irresponsibly, for there was no conceivable reason for such a step—that she might have to withdraw the navy, which would have cleared

---

[1] Ibid. 271, 274.
[2] Harl. MSS. 540, f. 72; Haynes, *State Papers*, 259, 271, 274. [3] Ibid. 272.

the way for all the reinforcements that France could send. This was hardly the best send-off for a simple soldier like Grey.[1]

The queen had taken a calculated risk in appointing him. He had as much experience of active service as any in the running for the job; but this was his sole qualification, and it was weakened by advancing years. At the time of his appointment the queen went out of her way to say that she had a high regard for his military skill, but in secret instructions Norfolk was warned to handle him judiciously and do everything he could to build him up in the eyes of the army—a vote of no confidence which events proved to be well justified.[2] Later on, at a time when things were not going particularly well for Grey, the queen, showing great understanding of his character, wrote him a letter of encouragement. Perhaps she had tongue in cheek, for she used the words 'we see our expectation in you very well performed'. Had Grey been aware of her misgivings about him, he would not have been flattered. The letter went on: 'continue to be as we have always judged you, and you shall find us as good lady to you as you can deserve'.[3]

The Privy Council shared the queen's view of the general, and at this time also sent a letter of good wishes, all part of the campaign to keep his morale high.[4] Norfolk, who saw these letters, decided to follow the party line. He wrote to Cecil on 29 April referring to the undistinguished handling of the army. He went on to say that the secretary of state knew Grey well enough. He himself 'would feed his humour with some gentle letters' but he begged that the queen should be advised to write to Grey to put some heart into him.[5] Although she had already done just this the queen wrote again. This time she told Grey that Norfolk had reported on the excellence of his performance and that both he and the army deserved great praise. She gave him her hearty thanks, and asked him to pass on her gratitude to those captains who had distinguished themselves.[6]

Grey led his men north, happily ignorant of his sovereign's true opinion of him. For the first day or two all went well. The Scots welcomed the invaders as they passed through the countryside. Provisions were readily available at the same prices as

---

[1] Haynes, *State Papers*, 272-3. [2] *For. Cal. 1559-60*, 237.
[3] Haynes, *State Papers*, 289. [4] Ibid. 290.
[5] Ibid. 301. [6] Ibid. 302.

in Berwick—which was surprising. The infantry—now 6,000 of them—spent the first night at Coldingham, 13 miles from Berwick, a good day's march. On the second day they covered rather less than 10 miles and encamped at Dunglass, where they were joined by the cavalry, who had left Berwick a day later because of their greater speed. On the third and fourth days they covered similar distances to Linton Bridge and Prestonpans, where they joined forces with some of the rebels.

The march had been uneventful. The army was divided into the traditional three groups—vanguard, battle, and rearguard (regimental division was still something for the future)—and was organized on the march through the sergeant-major-general (Edward Randall) and his four corporals of the field. Grey's first dispatches were full of confidence. He hopefully planned an ambush as they skirted Dunbar, where there were 200 French troops. They were to be enticed out by a few light cavalry, and then to 'be given a good morrow' by 500 infantry. But the French would not be tempted and there was no more than a mild skirmish when a troop covering the army's flank exchanged a few shots with the enemy. At the end of the march Grey was able to report to the Duke of Norfolk that he had arrived in the neighbourhood of Leith without losing a man; and at the same time to send his compliments to the Duchess, who might shortly be receiving a few French cannon balls from him as a present.[1]

It was not long before the general's tone changed. The Scots had driven their cattle away to keep them from the French and it was almost impossible to find food. What there was was so dear that a single day's rations cost two or three days' pay. Moreover it was difficult to persuade the Scots to accept English silver coins in payment. The miserable weather and sickness were draining men away. If the navy were recalled, as the queen had hinted it might be, the army would also have to withdraw. The navy was needed to carry the heavy siege guns, quite apart from its strategic value in blockading Leith. There was still no sign of the battery of heavy guns coming by sea from London. Two thousand men who were supposed to be on their way to reinforce his army had not appeared, but Leith had a garrison of at least 4,000, and the besieging force would certainly have to be increased.[2]

[1] Ibid. 495.   [2] Ibid. 499.

On top of all this his instructions were so confusing that he did not know which way to turn. The queen had told him that Sadler was to try to get a negotiated settlement. Norfolk on the other hand was pressing him (Grey) both to negotiate with the regent and to prosecute the war. He would try to do his best—if only he knew what he was supposed to do.

However justifiably confused he may have been by conflicting instructions it was Grey's natural stupidity that led him to put forward an alternative to the plan of campaign laid down by the Council. This was that instead of concentrating on the expulsion of the French from Leith and from Scotland he should lay siege to Edinburgh castle. This proposal made sense from the purely military standpoint: the castle was an easier objective than Leith. But what would the Scots think when they saw the invading English army attacking their fellow-countrymen—and the regent—in Edinburgh castle, where the garrison was benevolently neutral, and ignoring the hostile French in Leith? The foolishness of the plan was immediately seized upon by Norfolk, and the queen lost no time in confirming his judgement. Grey was to put the idea of attacking the castle right out of his head.[1]

The army halted at Restalrig, about a mile from Leith; and Grey, giving priority to that part of his instructions which required him to negotiate, sent a trumpeter to the regent asking that a deputation should be allowed to explain why the English army was there and suggesting that they should try to reach a settlement otherwise than by shedding the blood of her friends. A safe-conduct was duly provided and Sir James Crofts, Sir George Howard, and other senior officers went to the castle, it being understood that there would be a truce until the conference was over. The English delegation explained that only the French threat brought them to Scotland. If the regent arranged for the withdrawal of the French troops the English army would also retire. Mary asked for time to discuss this with the commander in Leith, which the English representatives did not like; but they felt that they could not object. It was left that Crofts and Howard would put their proposals in writing, and that there would be another meeting on the following day. Grey's guess was that eventually the regent would agree that

[1] *For. Cal. 1559–60*, 510; Haynes, *State Papers*, 286.

part of the French forces should leave Scotland, and also that she would grant a free pardon to all the Scottish rebels.

But while this meeting was taking place there was trouble at Leith. About 1,000 musketeers, 500 pikemen, and a squadron of cavalry emerged from the town and faced up to the English army. Grey, who had not accompanied the delegation to the regent, pointed out to their leaders that there was a truce and demanded that they should withdraw into the town; to which the French replied that they stood on their master's and mistress's territory and were entirely within their rights. They had no intention of withdrawing to please anybody. Grey sent back his herald with a message that they must either leave the field or take the consequences. Hardly had this been delivered when the French fired a volley at the English troops.[1]

All thought of a truce now vanished and a fierce engagement began. The French at first had the advantage of fighting from higher ground, but after a hard struggle the English displaced them. As the chronicler smugly notes, those that trust in natural advantages seldom can withstand true valour.[2] The French retired to the cover of a chapel, but once again they were displaced by the sheer courage of the English. The artillery in the town then took a hand, and the English brought up two field guns in reply. Their fire broke up the French forces and they began to withdraw. This was the signal for the English heavy cavalry to take a hand in the fight, and they chased the now disorganized French back into the safety of the town. It was estimated that there were 140 French killed; and there were also many English casualties.

The English general did not cover himself with glory in this first encounter with the enemy. No doubt he had hardly caught his breath after the march from Berwick, and no doubt his mind was occupied by the negotiations with the regent; but had he had his wits about him he could have drawn the whole French force (perhaps a third of the garrison) further from the town and then sought to cut off their retreat. A number of the French infantry did in fact pursue some of the English troops so far that they had no hope of getting back to the town. Four of their captains were taken prisoner with their men. The same fate might

---

[1] *For. Cal. 1559–60*, 509.
[2] Sir John Hayward, *Annals of the first four years of the reign of Queen Elizabeth*, 53.

have been arranged for the whole force, which would have
seriously depleted the garrison. Even the chronicler Hayward,
despite his loyalty to Grey, ventures to suggest that if the
English leaders had known their job as well as the rank and file
knew *theirs* a mortal blow might have been struck; but he
defends his hero by reminding the reader that 'the adventures
of war have many hidden fortunes, which neither the counsel
nor courage of men can assure'.[1]

The besiegers had two alternatives. Either they could sur-
round the town on the landward side, use the navy to cover
the entrance to the harbour, and starve it into submission; or
they could concentrate their fire on the walls, and when a
sufficient breach had been made, take it by assault. The former
was likely to be long and costly in terms of wages; the latter
quicker, but risky and costly in terms of men's lives. The council
of war was not sure which was the better plan. Grey considered
that he had insufficient artillery to win the town by assault;[2]
and there was a general feeling in the camp that the army was
not equal to the demands about to be made on it. Expert opinion
held that it would take 20,000 men to capture the town. Norfolk
passed these gloomy forebodings on to the Privy Council in
London. The perimeter of Leith was vast, and the town was
defended by at least 4,000 men. He doubted whether the army
could do much against it.[3] At the same time he wrote privately
to Cecil suggesting that in the long run it would pay the queen to
intensify her efforts against the French, though it might seem
to be an expensive business. It would be cheaper to go all out to
finish the war now than to abandon it and have to face a much
more serious struggle later on.[4]

The damaging effects of the queen's efforts to attain her
objective without the use of force now began to make themselves
felt. On 12 April Norfolk reported that in his opinion the negotiations for a peaceful settlement had done a lot of harm. Some
of the Scottish nobility who might have been expected to join
the rebels were now sitting on the fence until they saw how the
negotiations turned out. Perhaps they had been given the wrong
impression of the English government's intentions; and indeed
if he (Norfolk) had been handling matters at the camp he would

---

[1] Hayward, *Annals*, 54.   [2] *For. Cal. 1559–60*, 520.   [3] Ibid. 523.
[4] Ibid. 524; Haynes, *State Papers*, 284.

have been loth to 'cast such bones' among their Scottish allies. Some feared that England might negotiate a treaty with the regent that would throw them to the wolves; and despairing of any real help from Elizabeth, they might, he thought, buy forgiveness from the regent by offering to help her to drive the English army from Scottish soil.[1] Norfolk hoped that the queen and the Council would apply their minds carefully to this situation. Although he was still waiting to hear from Sir George Howard (who had been sent to London to give the queen a first-hand account of affairs at Leith) just what the queen's intentions really were, he had taken it upon himself to send Sir Ralph Sadler to the camp to hold the position by talking the Scots into a better frame of mind.[2]

Although Sadler was supposed to be primarily concerned with political matters, his first job was to examine the feasibility of an assault on Leith. What was the real difficulty? Was it the terrain, the small firing power of the batteries, or the shortage of men? He was also to discuss with Grey rumours that a large number of his men were absent from the camp tasting the delights of Edinburgh, and to ensure that this was stopped.[3] The general admitted that his men had been frequenting Edinburgh when they should have been on duty, but claimed that the numbers had been exaggerated. So far as assaulting Leith was concerned, it was true that it was difficult to approach, but it could be taken by assault with three batteries. Even with two there was good hope of success; but with only one, there was none. They needed another 3,000 men and 1,000 pioneers for two new batteries.[4]

In the meantime Howard returned from the queen. She agreed that his news was important, but said that it was quite wrong to use the general of the cavalry as a messenger. A letter would have sufficed. Howard brought back her commands that the siege must be prosecuted more vigorously, at the expense of further negotiation for peace on her terms; but still she was split-minded. If the French *did* look like coming to terms, their offers were not to be rejected. The Scots were to be told that she was determined to increase her army and navy rather than let the campaign drag on indefinitely for lack of sufficient strength.[5]

---

[1] Haynes, *State Papers*, 284. [2] Ibid. 288. [3] *For. Cal. 1559–60*, 536.
[4] Ibid. 548. [5] Haynes, *State Papers*, 288.

This was followed by more positive instructions. The queen said that she had gathered from Norfolk's latest reports that the Scottish rebels suspected her efforts to come to agreement with the French. She was 'rather aggrieved' that her representatives should have said anything that perplexed her Scottish allies, or put fresh hope into the enemy. This would give the whole proceedings a most unwelcome contrariety. The criticism of the higher command was unfair. From the very start their orders could hardly have been more contrary, and the queen was certainly not justified in blaming all the confusion on the council of war. However, she was now forced to take a more positive line. Norfolk was to tell Grey that there never had been any question of making a treaty with the French without the full knowledge and consent of the Scots, and that she would never agree to anything that was not in Scotland's best interests. Nor had she ever had the slightest intention that the siege should not be proceeded with as vigorously as possible. She was particularly angry about the suggestion made to the Scots that there might not be enough money available to keep the English army in the field. Even if it were true (which it most assuredly was not) it was quite wrong to discourage them with talk of that kind.[1]

All this was just what Grey wanted to hear; but yet again the queen had to have her say about a treaty. The council of war was not to ignore any offers made by the French if they were likely to bring peace to Scotland. But the whole emphasis was now on action rather than talk, and Grey and his colleagues must have heaved a sigh of relief. The soldiers could now show the politicians the true road to success.

When the council of war received the queen's letter criticizing their injudicious handling of the negotiations with the regent they took umbrage. It had been made abundantly clear from the outset that she wanted the Scottish problem to be settled without force, if possible. Therefore they had quite properly got in touch with the regent right away. Then, when they had all realized that it was not going to be easy to take Leith, they had pressed the rebels to look more favourably on settlement by agreement; and the Scots had been perfectly content with this. Now the queen wanted all their efforts to be directed against the

[1] Haynes, *State Papers*, 291.

town. So be it. They would get on with the assault as quickly as they could.¹

The latter part of April and the first few days of May were devoted to intensifying the preparations for the attack. The work of digging trenches to shelter the besiegers and to facilitate the eventual approach of the assault forces had begun almost as soon as the army reached Leith, but now that the capture of the town was the central objective it was greatly accelerated. Gun emplacements were built and tunnels driven for mines. The labours of the pioneers digging the trenches had to be constantly covered with musket and artillery fire, for the French did everything they could to hamper the preparations. Inspired by the leadership of D'Oysel, the commander of the garrison, their bravery continued unabated. They 'marvellously annoyed' the English troops with their artillery and small shot, and made many sorties. On one occasion a party of them showed singular enterprise. They emerged from Leith dressed as women, and so fascinated and deceived one of the English scouts that he deserted his post to enjoy their company. Never was retribution swifter or more surprising. No sooner was the scout in the midst of the seductive group than they revealed themselves in their true colours; and before he had recovered from the shock of anti-climax, his head was cut off. It was later displayed on one of the church steeples in the town so that his former comrades might see his fate.²

Perhaps this episode, which must have done much for the morale of the garrison, encouraged D'Oysel to take the initiative on a greater scale the following day. Over 1,000 infantry and sixty cavalry made a sortie and surprised the men guarding the forward English positions. While they held the trenches the French took the opportunity of spiking four of the English guns (that is, driving iron spikes into their touch holes, so that the touch powder could not be fired). The alarm was quickly given to the camp, and Sir James Crofts led a force to the rescue. Captain Vaughan and his company showed great valour in recovering the trenches, killing sixteen French in the process. In the night the four spiked guns were taken back to the camp, the touch holes drilled out, and the guns returned to their positions before daybreak; but they had been silenced for a few

¹ *For. Cal.* ii. 574. ² Hayward, *Annals*, 55.

precious hours when they might have been battering the walls. Although the French claimed to have killed or wounded 200, including many captains, Norfolk reported to Cecil that none above the rank of lieutenant had been killed—although the general's son, Arthur Grey, had been wounded. He said with grim satisfaction that this sort of thing would teach the commanding officers to keep their men out of Edinburgh.[1]

There is at least one hint that the work of entrenching was not expertly done, and that this was responsible for the French success. Humphrey Barwick says that he met Mr. Pelham going to examine the ground where the trenches were to be dug. He had not previously met the master of the pioneers, and took it upon himself to give him the benefit of his advice, because he knew that he was inexperienced. He approached him courteously, and said: 'Master Pelham, it were good for you to begin at the foot of this hill, and run straight to yonder hillock.' Pelham immediately took offence, and pointed out that *he* was in charge of the trenches. Barwick said he was sorry he had spoken. When the French made their attack two days later he maintained that they were tempted by the fact that the trenches were unguarded at the ends, and that their sally was much more successful than it would have been had the trenches run into his hill and hillock.[2]

Norfolk was impatient for results, but Grey reminded him of the difficulties. The constant skirmishing might be reducing the strength of the garrison, but it was also impairing his own forces. He admitted that his master of the ordnance had been very slow in getting the guns into position, but pointed out in his defence that the heavy rains had made the ground so soft that it was difficult to move the guns, especially as the horses they had were not up to much. Ideally, the English would have established complete control of the town, and greatly increased the effectiveness of their final attack, by setting up two separate camps, each of which would have concentrated on one sector of the defences. But they had not enough men for this. The next best thing was to erect a fort on some high ground about 600 yards from the walls, which would enable a smaller number of men to command the eastern side of the town, and allow the main force to remove to the south-west side and there make the

---

[1] *For. Cal.* ii. 558.   [2] *Certain Discourses*, 4.

final preparations for the assault. Norfolk, influenced no doubt by the more vigorous line taken by London, quickly agreed with Grey's proposals. He had studied the plan of the fortifications and thought it quite clear that the best approach was from the south-west. The main thing now was to get on with the job as quickly as possible. And for God's sake, he added not unreasonably, send me a report daily, or at least every second day. The news of a recent skirmish had reached London before he had any word of it from Grey, which was most unsatisfactory. He (Norfolk) was being blamed for the paucity of reports from the field. He also grumbled to Cecil about Grey's failure to keep him informed, although there were no fewer than fourteen of Norfolk's messengers at the camp. In fact, although he did not tell Grey, he knew about this particular skirmish from Scottish spies in his pay.[1]

The heavy guns of the French continuously returned the besiegers' fire. Some of them planted on the steeples of the churches of St. Anthony and St. Nicholas were considerably higher than the walls of the town and were particularly menacing; but before the English artillery could be turned against them the council of war had to indulge in a long debate about the propriety of battering sacred edifices. In this discussion, which shows that the innumerable passages in the military writers citing Biblical and classical precedents sometimes had more than academic significance, it was pointed out that Alexander, Tamburlaine, and many other famous leaders had laid down that temples must not be attacked. Euripides had said that only fools would lay waste temples and sacred places. That, said another member of the council of war, was all very well, so long as the buildings retained their sacred nature. If they were profaned and no longer used for religious purposes, they lost the privilege of religion. When they were converted into stores, fortresses, and castles, not only for defensive purposes, but to be used in attack, they must be regarded as new buildings erected for war.

Eventually the ayes had it, and nine of the siege guns were turned on the two steeples. Before long the cannon on St. Anthony's steeple were silenced, although they were a quarter of a mile off—a long range to pinpoint a church steeple at. Then

[1] *For. Cal.* ii. 577, 559, 587.

the gunners turned their attention to St. Nicholas, where they shot a gun and the gunner clean off the steeple. The battery against St. Nicholas continued all day, for it was known that the church was being used as a store, and great damage was inflicted.[1]

On Wednesday, 1 May, Grey was able to report to Norfolk that the climax was nearing. He planned to attack at dawn on the following Saturday. They would make two breaches, one to be assaulted by 3,020 men, and the other by 2,240; but if the first attack failed, it would not be followed by a second. Grey said that he had not enough reserves to risk it. Two thousand four hundred men were to guard the field and the artillery. While the breaches were being attacked Captain Vaughan was to move in from the east and the Scots were to attack from the west. Winter was to send 500 men from the fleet to attempt an entry in the vicinity of the harbour.

This plan came to nothing. The guns went all out on the Friday, but the French repaired the damage so diligently that the wall looked stronger than before. Grey decreed therefore that the breaches should not be attempted on the Saturday. Instead a dummy run was made on the Friday evening to test the town's defences. It was elaborate and well planned. Winter used the fleet to create a diversion at the harbour mouth. A detachment of infantry attacked the trenches held by the French just outside the walls, and at the same time sought to discover the location of the flanking defences. Another attack was launched from the fort recently constructed on the east side of the town, under the command of Captain Vaughan, who had proved himself to be a leader of great ability in the earlier skirmishes. Mr. Pelham approached the citadel on the north-west side of the town with his pioneers.

The two most important parts of this programme were to measure the breadth and depth of the ditches round the town and the height of the walls, so that long enough scaling ladders could be taken in when the real attack was made; and to get an accurate idea of the strength and location of the defences in the flanking walls, so that they could be softened up in advance. Grey was well satisfied on both scores. Those searching out 'the flankers' did a good job in his opinion. Vaughan, who had made

[1] Hayward, *Annals*, 58–60.

a preliminary survey of the ditches a few days earlier, reported that the walls were more than a pike's length high—an elastic estimate which was received uncritically. In the course of this probe there were many skirmishes, with casualties on both sides.[1]

A new zero hour was fixed for Tuesday, 7 May, at 3 a.m., and a new plan of campaign drawn up. The part to be played by the men from the fleet remained the same, and 2,400 (under the command of the general) were again assigned to guard the field, with the support of 900 under Sir James Crofts. Sir George Howard was to patrol the east side of the town with the heavy cavalry; and Sir Henry Percy, with the light cavalry, had the west side. Pelham, the trench-master, was given a roving commission to take his pioneers to sap any places that seemed particularly vulnerable. The east wall of the town was to be tackled by Vaughan with 1,200 English and 500 Scots; the south wall by Captain Wood with 1,050; and the south curtain wall by Captain Carvell with 1,000 men.

So far the plan differed little from the first, but there were highly significant changes in what was proposed for the two breaches (which were the real key to the capture of the town). These give a clue to the irresponsibility of the higher command in their handling of the numbers of men at their disposal. It is impossible to say with any degree of accuracy how many men were actually engaged in the attack on the town. The numbers who left Berwick with Grey, and the later reinforcements, provide only an upper limit, for they were much reduced by weeks of skirmishing, sickness, and above all by desertion. Grey steadfastly refused to order a muster, no doubt because as a professional soldier of long standing he was reluctant to offend his captains by putting their emoluments at risk. There are therefore no muster books to record the true position. Nor do the numbers mentioned in the assault plans afford much help. The first plan was drawn up on the assumption that the numbers actually with the colours were much nearer to establishment (which was 12,644 men, including the Scots) than they really were. For example, the infantry, on whom the main burden of the attack rested, had an established strength of 9,448 (including the Scots); and the first plan deployed on paper

[1] *For. Cal.* iii. 16.

8,860 infantry. This assumed a wastage of only about 600, which was far too low. In planning to throw 9,000 infantry into the attack the council of war were relying on large numbers of men who existed only as names on the paysheet.

Someone must have drawn the general's attention to the dangers of believing the profitable fictions fed to the treasurer-at-war, for the second plan was based on an infantry force of 7,350 men—more than 2,000 fewer than establishment, but probably still much higher than reality. The significant fact is that the decision to attack the town was made on the assumption that the army's actual strength was considerably greater than it really was. When the council of war admitted to themselves that the numbers in the first plan were fictitious, they nevertheless went ahead with it, using at least 2,000 fewer troops than were at first considered necessary.

Grey further impaired his chance of success by dispersing his forces into no fewer than ten separate elements. His motto might well have been 'divide and be conquered'. Moreover, a very large part of the army was charged with the task of 'keeping the field', when the men would have been better employed in attack. This immobilization of much of the besiegers' strength was the garrison's reward for the many sorties they had made. With such a vigorous enemy inside the walls of Leith Grey simply could not risk throwing all his men into the attack. If it failed there was every likelihood that the French would sally forth to finish off the battered remnants of the English army; and then the way to the south would be dangerously open.

Grey summoned the troops on the evening of 6 May to tell them that the attack would be made next morning. The announcement was greeted with enthusiasm by the rank and file; but alas they did not know the fate that awaited them. Some of the council of war seem to have been genuinely satisfied that the breach was ripe for attack; others were eager for action, and had turned a blind eye on the manifest dangers of the operation; and others again, in agreeing that the attack should be launched, were showing a blind courage more fitting for a private soldier than a member of the council of war. Thus Sir John Hayward.[1] In his speech to the men Grey said that he had no doubt of their success on the morrow. Victory was as certain as they were

[1] *Annals*, 63.

certain of their own valour. Every man was to go to his post, and show the same will to execute the enterprise as he had done to undertake it. They had been wasting their time chasing the enemy into their burrows all these weeks if they could not ferret them out now. If they survived the first dangers of the assault, which like a storm would be furious and short-lived, the rest would be easy. And so the troops dispersed, filled with hope of success, to arm themselves, and snatch a few hours' sleep before dawn.

Then occurred one of the strangest incidents of the campaign. Sir Ralph Sadler, Sir James Crofts, and Kirkaldy of Grange went to inspect the breach, and came to the unanimous conclusion that it could not be assaulted successfully. Sadler and Kirkaldy went off to their lodgings, leaving Crofts to tell Grey that in their opinion the attack should again be called off; and this he did. But it had no effect on Grey. The original orders stood. Yet, when the official inquest was held on the failure of the attack, and much might have been made of the fact that it had been launched against their better judgement, none of the three pressed the point. In particular Crofts (who had a very rough time in the weeks after the siege, when he was made scapegoat, and actually spent some time in the Fleet prison) might have been expected in self-defence to lay all the blame at Grey's door. But he accepted responsibility along with the other members of the council of war. Why? The only explanation that suggests itself is uncharitable. He had been exploiting his command to the limit, and perhaps felt that an attack on Grey would provoke a counter-attack on his own malpractices. Sadler, however, had nothing to hide; and there is no explanation of *his* silence other than loyalty to the council of war.[1]

The order to advance was given just before dawn on 7 May. The English forces 'with greater courage than preparation' converged on the town. The key to the whole attack was the state of the breach, which, only a few days before, Grey had admitted to be impregnable, but which had been subjected to continuous bombardment ever since then. The first men to try to scramble up it proved that Sadler and Crofts were right. There was no hope of winning it. Moreover, the defensive positions flanking the breach in the wall were very strong, and the attackers were

[1] Haynes, *State Papers*, 345–8.

subjected to heavy crossfire from them. This was an equally serious error of judgement on the part of the council of war, for it was axiomatic that the flankers should be disposed of before an assault was ordered. In the Spanish army, for example, the troops had the right to refuse to attack if they were not satisfied that the flankers had been adequately dealt with in the preparatory bombardment.[1] Despite the impossible conditions, the English showed great bravery. They clambered over the rubble from the broken wall and met the French in fierce hand-to-hand fighting with pike and halberd. A few of them actually entered the town, but they could not establish themselves, and they had to fight their way out again, or perish.[2]

The other attacks were no more successful. The attempts to scale the walls which had not been bombarded were hampered by the surrounding ditches. The French had anticipated the attack and diverted the river which flowed through the town. Instead of dry ditches the attackers found moats which would have been difficult enough to cross even had there been no other hazards. Equally disconcerting was the discovery that when Vaughan had reported that the walls were more than a pike's length high he had spoken the truth: but he had not said by how much more. The scaling ladders, which had been made for twenty-foot walls, turned out to be six feet too short. Perhaps someone had forgotten to add in the depth of the ditch. The contingents charged with the task of climbing the walls were doomed to disaster. They provided sitting targets, not for the French soldiers who were mainly occupied at the breach, but for the 'sutlers and trollops' of the town, who hurled boulders and blocks of wood with devastating effect.

The Frenchmen's harlots, of whom the most part were Scottish whores, did no less cruelty than did the soldiers: for besides that they charged their pieces and ministered to them other weapons, some continually cast stones, some carried chimneys of burning fire, some brought timber and impediments of weight, which with great violence they threw over the wall upon our men, but especially when they began to turn their backs.[3]

The garrison was later made to pay for this help from the women. When there was a suggestion that the women and children

---

[1] Williams, *Briefe Discourse*, 22.   [2] Hayward, 64.
[3] J. Knox, *History*, ii. 67.

might be allowed to leave the town because of the shortage of food, Norfolk said that by the grace of God this would not be suffered. The women had done the English troops 'much woe' at the assault. They would now square the account by eating up the town's scarce rations.¹

Sir John Hayward provides a graphic picture of the fury of the assault:

> The cannon were discharged continually on both sides. The small shot went off from the flankers, walls, and trenches so thick that it seemed for a time a very hell. Nothing was seen but fire and smoke, nothing was heard but roaring of shot. The earth, the air, the heavens seemed to be turned into a cloud, casting forth continual thunder and lightning.

Alas, the courage of the men did not compensate for the incapacity of their leaders. They had to withdraw after two or three hours in this inferno, leaving their dead and wounded behind. 'How easily valour falleth to the ground, when it is not guided by the eye of wisdom.'²

The attack had been an utter fiasco. First reports put casualties at 1,000 or more, but this was too high. The final English verdict was round about 200, but this was probably too low. Humphrey Barwick met one of the French captains after the siege and asked him what the French version was. He was told that after the assault the garrison commander had ordered the English dead to be stripped and their outer clothing to be brought to the market place and counted. This gave a total of 448 killed, excluding any bodies that lay too far beyond the walls to be collected by the garrison.³ A figure of round about 500 killed is probably nearer the truth.

There were now only two things to be done. The town must be starved into submission; and there must be an inquest into the failure of the assault.

As soon as he heard the alarming news Norfolk sent 400 men from Berwick to reinforce the besieging army (leaving a mere 600 in the garrison there) and set in motion the levy of a further 2,000 in his lieutenancy.⁴ In the confusion immediately after the

---

[1] Haynes, 319. [2] *Annals*, 64.
[3] *Weapons of Fire*, f. 15b. [4] Haynes, 304.

repulse it was doubtful whether the English army would be able to keep the field. The men were exhausted not only by the attack but by the ordinary duties of watch and ward which had stretched them to the limit. There was no question of a second assault. Many of their best captains and men were lost. Powder and ammunition were running low. Their bows and arrows were completely spent.[1] Grey decided that they could just hang on, provided that reinforcements were sent quickly. The new plan of campaign was to tighten their grip on the town, and wait patiently for surrender.

In fact, before the garrison could be brought to formal capitulation, negotiation won the day. The secretary of state was sent to Edinburgh with other commissioners to meet the French and hammer out a settlement, for it was now tacitly accepted by both sides that stalemate had been reached. Finally, after discussions which Cecil claimed to be more difficult than the assault on Leith, an agreement was reached which gave the English side all that they wanted. The French were to leave Scotland. Their fortifications were to be destroyed. Henceforth both France and England accepted a policy of non-intervention in Scotland.

The inquest was less easily settled. Everyone was wise after the event, and none himself was to blame. Grey accepted no responsibility for the defeat, but apportioned the blame equally between the rank and file, and his commanding officer, the Duke of Norfolk. But for the duke's constant urging he would have bided his time, and captured the town when he was ready. In breaking the news to the queen he was careful to attribute the plan of campaign to his council of war, and to remind her that he had orders from above to get a move on. He also referred to the 'want of courage' in some of his men.[2] He made the same points to Norfolk rather more forcibly. They had gone all out for a quick victory, which the duke had urged them to do often enough, although they were inadequately prepared; and they had been let down by the disorder and cowardice of the men, who were raw soldiers and not equal to the 'hot work' which an attack on a town so well defended as Leith called for. Only the more experienced troops from the garrison of Berwick had acquitted themselves with distinction. (This letter was

[1] *For. Cal.* iii. 25.   [2] Ibid. 31.

in fact signed by several members of the council, but it is difficult to believe that all considered it to be a fair statement of the facts.)[1]

Norfolk did not take this lying down. He had already provided advance protection for himself by pointed criticism of his subordinate's shortcomings. Only a day or two before the attack on Leith he had observed in a letter to Cecil, the strong man of the Privy Council, that the general had plenty of courage, but courage was not enough: 'every man that can lead a band of horsemen is not for so great an enterprise'.[2] He now reported that Grey was saying that he would never have ordered the attack if he (Norfolk) had not pressed him. This was of course nonsense. He had never mentioned the need for speed since the army approached Leith. In fact he had never given Grey any advice at all. Everything had been left to the general, who was a better judge of what the situation demanded than anybody sitting in Berwick. Moreover, he had promised to inform the duke when the attack was fixed. He had not done so, and had even written the day after the assault without mentioning it. Surely this proved conclusively that the decision belonged to Grey and to no-one else?[3]

The supreme commander conveniently forgot about some of his earlier correspondence. On 23 April he had written to Grey approving the assault plan, in which he wished to amend nothing except 'to hasten the matter'.[4] Three days later he advised Cecil to abandon all thought of negotiation, and see that Grey concentrated on the assault. He considered that Leith was not particularly strong, and that they would not find in it half the 4,000 which 'these fearful men' (i.e. the council of war) predicted.[5] On 29 April, nine days before the assault, he reported to Cecil that things were now moving forward at Leith. The past slackness had not been for want of his 'often calling on' Grey; and if things had been handled with proper expedition earlier, Leith would have been won a long time ago.[6]

Grey dispatched Francis Killinghall to the queen to give her his version of the assault, and to describe the present state of the army. He was to make it clear that there was no question of mounting a further assault. In particular he was briefed to

[1] Ibid. 25.   [2] Ibid. 21.   [3] Haynes, 305.
[4] *For. Cal.* ii. 577.   [5] Ibid. 588.   [6] Haynes, 301.

explain that Grey would never have attempted the attack had he not been forced into it by instructions from Norfolk; and how, if only the army had obeyed orders, they would have won their objective. Norfolk was worried by this move, but he felt that he could not stop Killinghall from going to London. Grey and the rest of the council of war would take it amiss if 'he were to write their opinions for them'. But he sought to counter the move by sending his own envoy, Sir Nicholas L'Estrange, who, he told Cecil, would be able to show the Privy Council where the truth lay. L'Estrange had a list of questions the answers to which would overthrow all Killinghall's 'painted tales'.[1]

The queen sent Sir Peter Carew to Leith to get at the truth about the failure of the assault, and report on the prospects of capturing the town. He was to cross-examine all the higher command, so framing his questions that none who might be at fault would get the idea that he was under suspicion. In particular, he was to try to find out whether the whole of the council of war had agreed that the assault should be made. His conclusion on the first point was devastating. The whole affair could not have been worse handled if they had tried. As to the state of the garrison, it was clearly in great difficulty. For three weeks the men had had no meat, and their only drink was water. Their main rations were a pound of bread daily, and a salt salmon divided between six once a week. There was no chance of relief by land. Carew had never seen a town of that size so well besieged by so few men. The only hope for the garrison was that an occasional boat might get through the naval blockade on a stormy night.[2]

The queen and the Privy Council were more concerned with the removal of the French threat than with settling arguments between the supreme commander and the general. Elizabeth's first reaction to their squabble—before she had a chance of listening to Killinghall and L'Estrange—was simply to express regret that the success had been no greater, and to make it clear that there was to be no question of withdrawal; but after she had heard both sides of the argument she delivered a more profound judgement. She was satisfied that there had been great negligence in the army in Scotland, or even something worse; and she was unwilling to commit the conduct of further

[1] *For. Cal.* iii. 31, 34. [2] Haynes, 310, 346.

operations to those who hitherto had been at fault—unless it was certain that they would mend their ways. She reminded Norfolk that the responsibility for the conduct of affairs in Scotland was his, and ordered him to repair to the camp forthwith to carry out an investigation on the spot. He was to take over the command from Grey, if that seemed necessary in the light of his findings: if not, Grey was to be left to get on with the job. But whatever Norfolk did, he was to be careful not to impair Grey's honour.[1]

Norfolk had no wish to go to Leith. It was much easier to criticize the failures of his subordinates from a safe distance. But he could not refuse to obey the queen's command, and therefore played for time. He would be happy to go to the camp, provided that he had enough men to accomplish whatever was required of him. Because he was so young, he must have a wise, honourable, and grave council of war, the composition of which he left to the Privy Council. In the meantime he would prepare himself to do the queen's bidding; and once he had shown his face in Leith he would rather be torn by wild horses than leave without complete victory.[2] In fact he succeeded in playing out time. Before his reluctance to accept new responsibilities had manifested itself in London, the peace negotiations were well under way, and the pressure was removed from the army.

Although victory in Scotland was achieved at the conference table, the army did play its part in making the final settlement possible. The assault on the town had resulted in a resounding victory for the defenders but they could derive little comfort from this. It became increasingly clear that the reinforcements needed to maintain the resistance of the garrison were not going to get through in time. Even if they reached the Forth they still had to contend with the royal navy; and any increase in the strength of the defenders would have increased the problem of keeping them fed. As it was, the morale of the garrison remained high right to the end and encouraged the French commissioners to take a tough line. It was only when Cecil threatened to break off the negotiations and make preparations for a second assault that the French threw their hand in. So a small part of the victory did belong to the army.

The campaign in Scotland was typical of Elizabeth's later

[1] Ibid. 307–8.   [2] Ibid. 312.

'offensive defensive' campaigns. It was an inglorious episode, however, and in particular it was marred by the presence of the Duke of Norfolk in the chain of command. With a supreme commander linking the Council with the army in the field who was neither great soldier nor administrator, but an unconscionable self-seeker, the machine could not conceivably work well. Norfolk (who at one stage of the campaign had the impertinence to accuse Sir James Crofts of approaching as near to treason as any man could without actually slipping over the edge) had his just deserts twelve years later when—'a victim of his own inordinate ambition and crooked ways'[1]—he was himself executed for high treason. Grey, his partner in crime in the Scottish campaign—an old man who, as Norfolk rightly said, should never have been entrusted with the command—died before he could inflict further damage on the morale of the English army.

B. FRANCE, 1589

The campaign in Scotland in 1560 had been a cautious attempt to meet the enemy on foreign soil; and it set the pattern for most of the campaigns of the reign. It was not until 1585, however, that Elizabeth committed herself again to armed intervention abroad, when she dispatched the Earl of Leicester to the Netherlands to help the Dutch against their common enemy, Spain. Four years later she agreed to send a small army to Normandy to help the new king of France. The protestant Henry of Navarre had succeeded to the throne a few months earlier, but found his claim disputed by the French catholics and their allies. Elizabeth first helped him with money (as she had first helped the Scottish rebels nearly thirty years before) and then, because she could not run the risk of a Spanish victory in France, sent troops to join the motley crew of Scots, Swiss, and Germans whom Henry had gathered to help him to secure his position on the throne.

The man chosen to lead the expedition was Peregrine Bertie, the second Lord Willoughby, who was summoned to court to hear the queen's commands on 9 September 1589. He was only 34 but had already proved himself in the Netherlands (where he had succeeded Leicester as commander-in-chief) to be a

---

[1] J. B. Black, *The Reign of Elizabeth*, 120.

leader of distinction. No-one was ever better briefed for his job. In addition to his formal commission from the queen he had a separate set of instructions from her, dealing mainly with the political aspects of the expedition, although they also touched on military affairs; and he had instructions from the Privy Council devoted mainly to his management of the army.

The queen reminded her general of the 'sundry disorders' lately committed by captains and officers, and warned him that there was to be none of this in the expedition now under preparation. She also stressed that in an army composed of several nationalities the danger of quarrels among the rank and file was particularly great—especially when they were of different religions—and asked him to be very careful on this point.[1]

The queen's command that he should come down very heavily on any captains indulging in corrupt practices was echoed by the Privy Council. In recent times many had been more concerned with their profits than with their reputation. On this occasion any who dared to sell their discharge to the soldiers were to be severely punished. They must be degraded as being infamous persons unfit to bear arms, and imprisoned for any period that Willoughby and his council of war thought appropriate. To make it easier to detect fraud strict attention was to be given to the taking of musters, and also to the care of arms, which too often in the past had been sold. All weapons were to be well looked after and in due course returned to the counties that had supplied them, unless of course it could be proved that they had been lost in battle. Rations provided for the voyage to France were to be carefully husbanded, and any surplus remaining was to be sold without loss to the queen. The amount of gunpowder issued to the companies was to be noted so that the cost could be deducted from the men's pay. The fact that the rank and file would be rubbing shoulders with those of the catholic faith made it very necessary to lay down clear instructions about spiritual matters. The general was to ensure that there was public prayer in the whole army at least once a day, and preferably twice. All officers and men were to attend; and there was to be no change in the form of the Litany, nor in the Common Prayer of the Church of England.[2]

The army had a nominal 4,000 men supplied equally by

[1] S.P. France, 20, f. 61. [2] *Dom. Cal. Addenda, 1580-1625*, 283-4.

London, Kent, Sussex, and Hampshire. There was at first some confusion between the Privy Council and the county authorities responsible for levying the recruits on the actual size of the force. The queen had offered 4,000 troops to the French king, and the four local authorities were simply told to provide 1,000 men each. The Lord Mayor of London, for example, was required to assemble 2,000 men, out of whom 1,000 would be selected for service in France. Of the men chosen, 600 would be pikemen, and 400 would carry fire-arms.[1] (There would be no archers.) The work of assembling the troops had been in hand for some time, when Burghley, who as usual was deeply involved, revealed that he had been assuming there would be an allowance for dead pays at the rate of 10 per cent. Each county would therefore supply only 900 men. Lord Buckhurst, who as lord lieutenant of Sussex was in charge of recruitment there, had worked on the assumption that the full number of 1,000 would be needed; and when it dawned on him that he had to provide only 900 he told Burghley that he had in fact already bought food for the larger number—which was just as well, as it was better to have too much than too little. He added that in any case, when the officers were counted in, provisions would be needed for nearly 1,000. This shows that the idea of dead pays at 10 per cent. was as yet by no means automatically accepted by the counties; and it also shows a rare failure of the Privy Council, which for all practical purposes means Burghley, to convey precisely to the local authorities what the Crown had in mind.[2]

The difficulty in assembling even a small force is best seen through the eyes of one of the local authorities. The original instructions were quite clear—subject only to the point already made about dead pays. The lord lieutenant is to have the men levied and properly equipped. He is to have enough ships ready at the appropriate port (Dover for the troops from London and Kent, Rye for those from Sussex, and Portsmouth for those from Hampshire) to proceed to Dieppe on 20 September. He is to provide an initial supply of ten days' victuals for the voyage and the first few days in France; and he is to appoint free-lance victuallers to supply a second month's rations, which will be shipped in time to reach Dieppe before the initial quantities are exhausted. This sounds simple; but it was not so in practice.

[1] *A.P.C.* xviii. 88–89; S.P. France, 20, f. 45.   [2] S.P. Dom. 226, no. 62.

In the first place the time-table went awry. D-day was first changed from 20 to 24 September, and then it was postponed again. Ideally troops were shipped away from the port of assembly the instant they were ready. It was a costly business to feed them, the longer they waited idle in the town the more likely it was that riots would break out, and the opportunities for desertion were greatly increased. Buckhurst prided himself on the efficiency with which his subordinates had levied the Sussex contingent. It was ready to move on the 20 September, and now he would have them on his hands for another four days—which period was to be further stretched, although he did not know it when he made his protest to London. His diligence in collecting the men so quickly was now proving to be a disadvantage. The ships (whose masters were never keen to carry troops) would have to stand by waiting impatiently for their cargo. The presence of nearly a thousand hungry men in the town would push prices up, and the unfortunate soldier would not be able to feed himself adequately.

Buckhurst also reported that he had been able to arrange for rations to be supplied on the lines proposed by the Council. He had had no difficulty in getting hold of enough butter and cheese, but time had been too short to kill and barrel any beef.[1] He had found three substantial men who would supply food for the second period, and he had no doubt that they would do a job. Transport was going to be a problem, however. It had been 'marvellous difficult' to find enough casks for the provisions for 'the first push', and all the available ships had been ear-marked to carry the soldiers. It seemed to him that London could find all the ships needed—and all the food and the casks to pack it in—at a day's notice, when Sussex could not do it in ten. The postponement of the troops' departure meant that the loaf bread which had been provided would probably go mouldy.[2] Buckhurst also feared that the officers, who were well provided with money to buy their own food, would encroach on the supplies laid in for the men, and thus drive prices up further.[3]

Shipping continued to be a major difficulty. The postponement of D-day meant that the tide would be too low at Arundel, Chichester, and Newhaven (from which the men were originally to have been shipped) to allow the big transports to leave. The

[1] Ibid., no. 41. [2] Ibid., no. 62. [3] Ibid., no. 69.

whole force would therefore have to leave from Rye, and the men would have to march there from the other centres. It had been assumed that the masters would be prepared to carry the troops for 2s. a head, or even less,[1] but Buckhurst thought that it would be very difficult to arrange this, although it would help if he were able to offer them ready money. He was eventually able to report that the Mayor of Rye had 'with much ado' persuaded the masters and mariners (the latter seem to have had a say in the matter) to accept the Council's figure of 2s. a man.[2]

The slowness of communications was always a problem, but Buckhurst was put in an unusual difficulty when a gentleman carried a letter to him from the treasurer-at-war in London, and forgot to hand it over. It contained information about money to pay for shipping, uniform, and the first ten days' rations for the Sussex contingent; and being left in ignorance of what the treasurer had in mind the lord lieutenant was forced to make quite different arrangements of his own. Before he knew what was supposed to happen he wrote to Burghley, and to the secretary of state, Walsingham, with 'great grief' complaining that there was as yet no sign of Sir John Burgh, who was to lead the Sussex contingent, nor of any of his captains, nor of the treasurer-at-war or his deputy. This he feared was likely to give rise to much discomfort and confusion among the assembled troops, and he shuddered to think what the outcome might be. The soldiers had begun to assemble on 23, 24, and 25 September and were having to support themselves in the absence of the treasurer-at-war and his staff. This had bred great discontent. As soon as the delayed letter reached him he knew where he stood. The missing money was in the safe-keeping of a gentleman at the sign of the Gilt Cup in Cheapside awaiting collection by his representative. If only he had known this in the first place a lot of trouble would have been avoided.[3] Buckhurst, who had said some harsh things about the treasurer-at-war in his earlier letters, now hastened to say that he was blameless, and that the whole fault lay in the messenger who had so carelessly kept the letter in his pocket.

Buckhurst ventured to suggest to the Privy Council that the

[1] A.P.C. xviii. 113, 116. [2] S.P. Dom. 226, no. 62.
[3] Ibid., no. 70.

queen's allowance of ½*d*. a mile for conduct money was 'marvellous little'. The men could not march more than 10 or 12 miles a day wearing armour. The distance from Lewes to Rye was 30 miles, which meant that the troops would only have 5*d*. a day for the journey, whereas the county authorities considered that the right figure was 8*d*. a day. The county had in fact paid the men at this rate, and he would therefore suggest that the queen's allowance should be paid over to Sir John Burgh so that he might have some cash in hand to provide his men with anything they lacked in the way of equipment.[1] The lord lieutenant also reported with some pride that every recruit had been given a present of 20*s*. by the county over and above the wages and allowances provided by the queen.

There was some trouble in satisfying the officers of the Sussex contingent that the men were adequately equipped. Sir John Burgh's deputy, Captain Cosbie, found fault with the lord lieutenant for not ensuring that all the men were suitably armed. When he inspected them he found that some had white burgonets (steel caps covering part of the face and cheeks), some black, and some had old-fashioned morions with a high crest, which were now most unpopular. What Cosbie wanted was that all the men should be uniformly fitted out with morions of the new Spanish fashion. Buckhurst told him that there simply was not time to re-equip the whole force, and added not unreasonably that the mixed bag of burgonets and morions supplied would serve just as well on the battlefield as the Spanish morion, even if they did not make quite as brave a show on the march. But 'to content his humour' he allowed Cosbie to select from his private armoury 148 of the new Spanish morions, which left him with none.

Captain Cosbie was equally unhappy about the armour of the pikemen. There were hardly any corselets of 'the new fine shape'. Most were of the type which the Privy Council had ordered the county to provide, a fact which the justices of the peace quickly pointed out in answering Cosbie's objections. Buckhurst himself, however, half agreed with the captain. He admitted that the corselets supplied were more flat-bellied than the new shape, but he expected that they would withstand the push of the pike just as well as the other. He was upset when

[1] Ibid., no. 70.

Cosbie ordered the men to throw away their pouldrons, vambraces, and tasses (shoulder, arm, and thigh plates respectively), and keep only their head-pieces and cuirasses (breast-plate and back-plate). It was ever thus with new captains, Buckhurst told Burghley, and he humbly submitted that it would pay the Privy Council to provide the county authorities with patterns of armour which they could have copied. This alone would enable them to provide what was really wanted.

There was no limit to Cosbie's grumbling. Stockings were scarce in Sussex, but they were available in London in unlimited quantities at the very reasonable price of 1s. 2d. the pair. Two thousand pairs should have been bought in London. His beloved Spanish morions were also freely available in London.[1]

At last the men were ready for embarkation, but there was still no sign of their leaders, which meant a further delay of two or three days. On Sunday, 28 September, Buckhurst wrote to Burghley late at night saying that he hoped that by now all the men were safely embarked. He had done his best for them. They should be all right for food on the voyage, although his fears about the loaf bread had been justified. It had already begun to go bad. He had been unable to find anyone in Rye to bake biscuit (which kept much better than bread) in time to be of any use. However, the men had plenty of beer, and if they did run short of food on board ship perhaps they would be less likely to be sea-sick.[2]

The lord lieutenant's optimism about the troops' departure was not justified. They spent two days on the transports waiting for a favourable wind, during which time many 'grew sickly'. So at the special request of the captains and the masters of the vessels they disembarked 'for their better ease and safety'. Twenty-four hours later they re-embarked. This time the wind, which had been 'directly contrary', changed enough for the fleet to put to sea.[3]

Similar difficulties had arisen in the other places where the levies were being assembled. The Council had proposed that Dover should provide the rations for the men from Kent, but the lieutenant, Lord Cobham, maintained that Dover was too poor to help. If that were indeed so, said the Privy Council in

[1] S.P. Dom. 226, no. 73.   [2] Ibid, no. 70.
[3] Ibid., no. 76.

reply, then let Sandwich, whose inhabitants had always been very willing to send food to the enemy, take the job over.[1] The gentlemen of the Kentish contingent proposed to take with them many horses, but the port officers were instructed not to allow any to be shipped without special licence from the queen or six members of the Privy Council, as the country could not afford to lose too many horses.[2] The general was allowed eight, and six of the principal officers two each.[3] The Hampshire contingent were woefully short of equipment. At first they had only twenty muskets between them, though they were able to scrape up half a dozen more. When they were all set to embark it was suddenly discovered that there was no money to pay for the hire of their transports—from Portsmouth—and the lord lieutenant had to dip into his own pocket.[4]

The grouping of the force of 3,600 into county regiments had a precedent in the army levied to meet the Armada in the previous year, and shows that the idea of 'regimentation' was now well established in the mind of the Privy Council. But regimentation by county was in a sense forced on the Council on this occasion. The army was needed quickly, and there was no time to spread the burden of finding men equally over a large number of counties. In any case most other counties were at this time under pressure to send men to Ireland and the Netherlands. The Council therefore had to get the army for France from the few counties nearest the scene of action—which would be the first to suffer if Spain did gain control of the French coast and mount an attack on England—and the number required from each was so large that it was natural to think of it right from the beginning as a regiment, rather than as an aggregate of companies, which it would have been had twenty or thirty counties contributed to it. Each had a colonel and lieutenant colonel. Willoughby himself was colonel of the London regiment, in which he had a company nominally 200 strong (most of the others were 150), which gave him a bonus of twenty dead pays over and above his pay as general, plus, of course, anything that the company clerk was able to make for him on the side. The high marshal was Sir Thomas Wilford, who was colonel of the Kent regiment and also had his own company,

---

[1] *A.P.C.* xviii. 92.   [2] Ibid. 119–20.   [3] Ibid. 121–2.
[4] *Dom. Cal. Addenda, 1580-1625*, 286.

as did the other two colonels, Sir John Burgh (the Sussex regiment) and Sir William Drury (the Hampshire).

The other principal officers followed the usual pattern. There was still a sergeant-major-general with his four corporals of the field; master of the ordnance; muster-master; provost marshal; and treasurer-at-war, with a staff of four clerks. There were four quarter-masters.

Willoughby was anxious to have some say in choosing his captains, although he accepted that he must limit his choice to men approved by the Privy Council. He suggested some fifty men who he was satisfied would do a good job, and asked that he should be given discretion to appoint men from his short list —unless there were any the Council wanted to strike off.[1] In fact, the final choice was made by the Council.[2] There were six companies in each regiment, most of which were 'to be paid' as 150 men, and 'to be believed' as 135.[3]

Arms and equipment were provided for each man by the local authority, or at least they were supposed to be. Replacements, however, were provided from the Tower of London. These included 100 muskets, 200 calivers, and 300 pikes. Other stores which came from the ordnance office were 5 lasts of gunpowder, 6 tons of lead for shot, large and small melting ladles, match, shovels, spades, and scales for weighing out the gunpowder.[4] The Council laid down in advance how the companies were to be armed.[5] The official proportions in a company nominally 100 strong were: 15 musketeers; 15 calivermen; 10 halberdiers; 50 pikemen; and 10 dead pays. Companies nominally of 150 had 23 musketeers; 22 calivermen; 15 halberdiers; 75 pikemen; and 15 dead pays.

The expedition ought to have been called off at the eleventh hour. The English ambassador in France, Sir Edward Stafford, had been watching the situation there very carefully, lest Henry's position so improved that he had no real need of help from England. Towards the end of September just this happened; and with the king's agreement Stafford rushed a dispatch to Willoughby to try to catch him before he embarked his troops.

[1] S.P. France, 20, f. 32.
[2] *H.M.C. Ancaster*, 288.
[3] S.P. France, 31, no. 55.
[4] S.P. Dom. 226, no. 43.
[5] Ibid., no. 27.

The dispatch was to be taken to the general 'wheresoever he be, with all speed for life'; and it was stipulated that a copy should be immediately taken to all the ports where men were about to embark for France.

The message reached Willoughby the following day at Dover as he was on the point of leaving, and if the queen had known of it there is not the slightest doubt that she would at once have called off the enterprise. The general was mentally committed to the expedition, and he was not to be denied his hour of glory. Without making any effort to seek the views of the queen or the Privy Council he allowed the operation to proceed according to plan. He himself set sail with the London and Kent regiments.

The queen was only mildly displeased with his precipitate action, which had lost her the chance of saving a considerable sum of money, and the lives of many of her subjects. As he was now in France, he might as well stay there to find out if Henry had real need of his help. If he had not, the force could return on the same ships.[1] The Council wrote to the ambassador at the same time telling him that the queen had approved of his suggestion that the expedition should be held up, but that it was now too late. He was therefore to discuss the next move with Willoughby when they met; and if it seemed advisable to keep the English army in France for the month for which the queen had contracted to pay, well and good.[2] While the queen and the Council were making up their minds what to do in this situation, urgent messages were sent to Dover, Rye, and Portsmouth to ensure that any troops that had not yet left should be held.[3] This meant a further short delay at Rye and Portsmouth; but at the beginning of October the whole expedition assembled in Dieppe. Henry, who had assumed that no English army would now come, was highly gratified.

The troops went into camp a mile or two from Dieppe and there remained for the next few days trying to get themselves into some sort of order. The general was badly disappointed in the state of the Sussex and Hampshire regiments, and expressed his displeasure to the Privy Council. The Council in turn ordered the justices of the peace who had been responsible for equipping the men to appear before them in London to explain why 'such evil choice had been made' both of the men and their

---

[1] *A.P.C.* xviii. 144.   [2] Ibid. 145.   [3] Ibid. 146.

equipment.¹ By Sunday 5 October the army was in good enough shape to parade before the French king in battle array 'in very good and strong manner'. Henry showed himself very pleased with them—as well he might be, adds the chronicler, considering what a sorry state he was in before the English army came on the scene.² Willoughby at this time had some discussions with the king at which it was agreed that the English force should be at his disposal—and be paid for by him—for a second month.

On 11 October the campaign began in earnest. The army struck camp, and with Willoughby at their head marched eight miles inland. This was the first of a series of the hardest marches by any English army of the time, which took a far greater toll of officers and men than all their encounters with the enemy. Between 11 October and 19 November—forty days—the army marched a total of 227 miles; and in the whole campaign they covered about 400 miles. This may not seem a great distance but it must be remembered that the men were marching in armour which, even when the component parts discarded by Captain Cosbie are taken into account, was still a heavy load, and carrying their weapons—a twenty-foot pike, or a cumbersome fire-arm. Moreover, the weather steadily deteriorated with the approach of winter. The muddy ground made walking difficult, and the cold lowered the men's resistance to disease. But it was the intensity of the campaign more than anything else that proved to be the undoing of the English troops. In the first forty days, for example, they were allowed to rest only on twelve; and resting meant simply that they were not actually marching or fighting. They still had to perform the duties of watch and ward. They still had to struggle with the elements, and the hostile French peasants, who regarded the English as their traditional enemies. In fact it seems likely that more casualties were inflicted on the English troops by the people they were supposed to be helping than by those they were fighting against.

The king's first objective was Paris, about 80 hard miles from Dieppe, which the army reached on 21 October. A day or two of strenuous fighting gained them a foothold in the suburbs, and

---

[1] *A.P.C.* xviii. 166; S.P. France, 20, f. 93.
[2] Cott. MSS., Galba E VI, ff. 413-19.

in the view of the English higher command they were placed to launch an attack on the city proper, if the king had been prepared to bring up his artillery. But Henry had no wish to risk a serious engagement in the capital. If he were successful it might be at the expense of great damage to property, which could lose him some support; and if he failed it would be a serious setback to his cause. So he withdrew and began a great circular march which took his force south-west to Vendôme and Tours, then north-west to Le Mans and Falaise, and finally back to the coast at Caen, where the remnant of the English army was allowed to return thankfully home.

There were only four other engagements of any note: at Vendôme, Le Mans, Alençon, and Falaise. The army reached Vendôme on 6 November and made a successful surprise attack on the suburbs in the evening, in which thirty or forty of the enemy were killed. Next day the king held a parley with the garrisons in the town and the castle, and demanded their surrender; but they refused to yield. The besiegers therefore entrenched themselves near the castle and set up two batteries—one consisting of five cannon, and the other of two culverin. On 9 November the batteries went into action at sunrise, and by noon two breaches had been made. The garrisons sounded a trumpet asking for a parley, but the king considered that they had already been given a chance to surrender, and pressed on with the assault. The chronicler records that the English forces were valiant enough, but he is honest enough to add that there was no great resistance. Most of the booty was taken by the French; all that the English got was an abundance of wine.[1]

The next objective was Le Mans, which was attacked on 18 November. The initial attack was carried out by quite a small force, and was so successful that if any troops had been ready to back it up the town would have fallen there and then. The assault plan on this occasion was that the English should attack from one side, and the French from another. The English had to cross the river to get to their position, and were carried there on horses provided by the French. While the battery was in progress to provide a breach for the French assault, Willoughby arranged for the construction of 'float bridges' made of barrels and ladders, so that the English might cross the river to the

[1] Add. MSS. 4155, f. 59b.

town wall and attempt to scale it. They made some progress with this ambitious plan, but it was the battery that won the day. Eight guns fired a total of 800 rounds, and although they had made only a small breach it was decided to order the assault by the French and the 'scalado' by the English; but before the action could begin the enemy asked for a parley. The king agreed only because his stock of cannon balls was running low, and after the parley the garrison was allowed to depart—the officers with their horses, arms, bag, and baggage, and the men with their arms, bag, and baggage, their matches extinguished, and their drums and ensigns left behind. The English chronicler, ever loyal, says that the townspeople said that they would never have considered surrender if it had not been for the threat of an English attack.

The ingenuity which the English general had shown at Le Mans was repeated at Alençon at the beginning of December. The town's defences were protected by a deep river, and only accessible by a drawbridge. Willoughby and the marshal, Sir Thomas Wilford, devised an 'engine'—some sort of grappling device at the end of a rope—which was used to draw down the drawbridge and give the English troops access to a fort, where they found about thirty-five of the enemy, who were put to the sword. A few others were 'taken to mercy' and kept prisoner. Unfortunately the engine was lost in the darkness. The idea had been to use it to pull down another drawbridge which gave direct access to the town. The enemy reacted strongly to the English attempt and subjected Willoughby's men to heavy fire. Several were killed, and Mr. Pelham was shot 'through the belly', but not fatally. He was able to tell Burghley a fortnight later that he had stood in great hazard of his life for a few days, but he had made a good recovery and hoped to live to serve Burghley again with the venture of his life. He also hoped, as did most who were absent from court for any length of time, that his reputation there was not suffering.[1]

While Willoughby was employing his unorthodox tactics the king's men carried out a traditional escalade, 'thinking to have the sacking and spoil of the town'. They were, however, driven back with heavy losses. But in spite of this, once again the garrison capitulated without making any great effort to hold out.[2]

[1] S.P. France, 20, f. 277. [2] Add. MSS. 4155, f. 62b.

Falaise was the last town to be attacked while Willoughby's force remained with Henry. The usual plan was followed. The cannon played on the castle walls on Christmas eve, Christmas day, and half through St. Stephen's day. Two breaches were made, one in the main wall, and one in a tower. On this occasion the main English force was several miles away, but the principal officers and gentlemen joined in the assault. The breaches proved to be quite inadequate. One was so narrow that it was difficult to get into it; and to get to the other it was necessary for the men to climb one by one up six or seven feet of wall. The general opinion was that twenty good soldiers could have held the breaches indefinitely. One man inside was worth a company outside. But the attacking force entered without resistance and opened the main gates. The only man who put up a fight was a musketeer in the tower which was battered. He was stationed at a loophole at the top of the tower and kept up a steady fire on the attackers. Five cannon were trained on the tower, and fired simultaneously. The whole structure collapsed into the moat, taking the soldier with it. He was captured alive, and later imprisoned by the king.

This was the end of the fighting for the English; but it was not the end of their misery. One captain reported to Walsingham that he did not think they had lost more than 100 men in battle; but there had been very heavy casualties through continual travel, cold, wetness of weather, ill diet, want of hose, shoes, and apparel. Originally they had eighty or ninety pikes in a company: now they were down to thirty. The musketeers had suffered just as badly.[1] This theme was constantly echoed by the general himself. He told Burghley that sickness and lack of clothing were bad enough, but it was far worse having to forage in a country where all the ancient hatreds of the English were being revived. When those who escaped sickness and the enemy's sword went even a short distance from their companies in search of food the country people, with the help of the neighbouring gentry, set upon them and cut their throats.[2] If the army was not recalled soon, the queen would lose her troops, their arms, and the king's thanks.[3]

Despite the miserable conditions there was still enough energy among the principal officers to carry on the private feuds

[1] S.P. France, 20, f. 241. [2] Ibid., f. 245. [3] Ibid., f. 249.

without which no Elizabethan campaign would have been complete. When the English contingent paraded before Henry in the neighbourhood of Paris two of the colonels, Sir William Drury and Sir John Burgh, had a violent quarrel as to who should have precedence. Willoughby summoned the council of war to try to smooth things over, but the two became implacable enemies, and later had a second quarrel, when they agreed to settle their differences by a duel. Willoughby stepped in again and extracted promises from both men that they would have no further dealings with each other while the campaign lasted. All might have gone well had it not been that one day, almost on the eve of embarkation for England, Drury, who was leading the army, left his position to talk with some ladies and gentlemen who had come to watch them. He stood with them while the whole force passed, and then in returning to his position at the head of the column he found himself next to Burgh, who was in charge of the rear. He could not resist saying something offensive, and the fat was in the fire again. They again challenged each other, and went off to fight the duel that for many days had been hanging over their heads. In the fight Drury was so seriously wounded that when the surgeon was called in he advised that his arm should be amputated. This was duly done; but Drury died two days later—to the great grief of the whole army, with the possible exception of his adversary.[1]

There was a suggestion that 800 of the survivors should stay on in France in the king's service, but fortunately this was dropped. The shattered remains of the four regiments made their way back to England as soon as ships could be found for them at Caen.

There was little to be enthusiastic about in the inquest on this expedition. The two outstanding points about it are that it should never have taken place, and that the troops suffered more than in any other enterprise. Willoughby must have many times regretted the impetuosity which drew him across the Channel at a moment when the fate of the expedition lay in his hands. The accounts inevitably make out that it had been a great success. It is recorded, for example, that the king was deeply indebted first to Almighty God, the giver of all good

[1] Add. MSS. 4155, ff. 63b-64.

things, and then to Her Majesty, the Queen of England.¹ The mere sight of the English troops had encouraged him and without their help he could not have made such rapid progress. This is simply not true. Henry would have achieved just as much if Willoughby had taken the chance he was offered and abandoned the enterprise before it began. There was little serious fighting, and while the English troops acquitted themselves well when they were called on it is clear that the French would have got on quite satisfactorily without them. Of the twenty-odd places that were won during the campaign all but four gave in without a struggle: and it is hardly likely that the mere presence of the English element in the army had much bearing on this—although there were those who claimed that the dreaded name of the English was still worth something.

Henry was statesman enough to show gratitude for the help he had had from Elizabeth, however he really felt. The journal compiled by Willoughby's orders has something to say about the attitude of the French as a whole. In spite of the outstanding services rendered by the English army 'the French nation could scarcely afford us a good word'. The author of the journal suggests that this arose more from the traditional dislike of the French for the English than from anything that the troops did on the campaign. If anything, the English were too eager for the fray, and thereby tended to steal the thunder of the French troops; and for this reason not a single French account even mentioned that there was an English force in Henry's army.

C. SPAIN, 1596

The expedition to Spain in 1596 was very different from the two campaigns described above.² In the earlier years of the reign the maxim that attack is the best form of defence had been grudgingly accepted and acted on by the queen and her Council; and their 'offensive defensive' wars—in Scotland, the

---
¹ Ibid., f. 65b.
² The authorities for the expedition are numerous. They include several manuscript accounts (Sloane 229 and 1303; Harley 167; Lambeth 185 and 250 being the more important) and printed accounts by some of the participants, which are discussed by Sir Julian Corbett in *The Successors of Drake.* That work deals fully with the expedition, as does E. P. Cheyney, *A History of England*, and W. B. Devereux, *Lives and Letters of the Devereux, Earls of Essex.*

Netherlands, and in France—had been the easier to undertake as they were fought on England's doorstep. But Spain was a long way off. The fate of the Spanish Armada eight years earlier had shown how easily disaster could strike an amphibious expedition —and the half-failure of England's own venture in Portugal in 1589 was not an encouraging precedent. It was known, however, that the Spaniards were organizing a new invasion of England and it might be plain commonsense to get in the first blow. The accent was therefore now much more heavily on the 'offensive'.

The idea of carrying the war into the enemy's territory was first mooted by the ageing lord high admiral, Lord Howard of Effingham, who had been in command of the navy at the time of the Armada. It was taken up with enthusiasm by the Earl of Essex, who saw it as a glamorous project in which he himself occupied the swashbuckling leading role, and also as an enterprise that was strategically right. After much heart-searching it was adopted by the queen and the Privy Council, and the preliminary work—the provision of ships and victuals—was put in hand in December 1595. The destination of the expedition was still kept top secret.

The enterprise was also different in that it was largely financed by Essex and Howard, who hoped to recover their outlay in booty. The officers for once had the chance of making a fortune out of the enemy rather than out of the men they commanded; and even the common soldiers had some hope of showing a profit.

It was important to have seasoned men on so hazardous an expedition. The Netherlands Government were therefore asked to agree to the temporary withdrawal of 2,000 of the veteran English troops there, and also to help with their own ships and men. They agreed, with some reluctance, only after Sir Francis Vere, the English commander in the Netherlands, had brought all his eloquence to bear on them. In reporting success to Essex Vere said that the Earl's enthusiasm for the scheme had fired his own imagination, but as he did not know precisely what was contemplated he was finding it difficult to work things out in his own mind. If the idea were to land in Spain, and remain there a long time, they would have to capture some place that could be fortified. He thought there were two possibilities—Corunna and Cadiz. The former would be the harder to take, and once captured it would be less of a thorn in the Spaniards' side. It was in mountainous country and not well placed for harassing the coast. Cadiz, on the other hand, was ideal. It was admittedly further away, and had a more difficult climate; but it would be a perfect base for threatening the Spaniards both by land and sea. But neither place would serve for 'more than a summer's bravery' unless the queen were prepared to enter wholeheartedly into the enterprise. If Essex were going to lay the foundation of a great work he must be adequately equipped.

Despite his ignorance of what was in the wind, Vere's professional mind seized on what seemed likely to be the problems and tried to find solutions for them. They must recruit someone for their army who was familiar with the coast of Spain, but happily there were plenty of them to be had in England. They must also remember that the absence of a cavalry unit of any size would prove a great handicap. In hilly country the enemy could so arrange it that the invader would always have to be on the march, seeking an elusive adversary, and this would be particularly burdensome without cavalry. Their absence in the field could be compensated for to some extent if the army were equipped with some of the short stakes that the English archers had used in times gone by as their defence against horsemen. He could cite four or five battles in which they had come in useful. Essex might laugh at the reintroduction of these old-fashioned devices, but he was sure they would help. There were probably stocks of them in the Tower, but if not they could be made cheaply enough. Vere said he could not remember how Essex wanted the men he was bringing from the Low Countries to be organized. Were they to be put in 100s to make companies, or were they to be divided into smaller groups to become parts of regiments? In his own view the veterans should be mixed with the newcomers.[1]

By March 1596 the arrangements for the expedition were in full swing. The fleet, which was to include the leading ships of the royal navy, vessels contributed by London and many other ports, and a contingent from the Netherlands, was to be divided into five squadrons, one Dutch, and the others commanded by the lord admiral, Essex, Lord Thomas Howard, and Sir Walter

[1] *H.M.C. Salisbury*, vi. 86–87.

Raleigh. The lord admiral and Essex were to be joint commanders of the whole expedition. There would be eight regiments of infantry, each under the charge of a colonel who would have no pay or allowances: their reward would come out of the booty in due course. Six of the regiments had 750 men, but those belonging to the generals each had over 1,000. There were to be no dead pays—another indication that the expedition was expected to show a profit. The men, however, were to have the standard 8*d*. a day, 6*d*. of which was supposed to be paid while they were abroad, and the balance when they returned to England. This unusual arrangement, which assumes that the private should be able to save a quarter of his wage while overseas, also suggests that it was hoped that the army would be to some extent self-supporting.[1]

A firmer indication of the nature of the project was revealed in instructions from the Privy Council to the commissioners of musters in the last week of March. The queen had appointed the Earl of Essex and the lord high admiral to be 'lieutenant generals and governors of her majesty's navy and army now intended to be employed out this year for the necessary service of her realm'. No mention was made yet of the destination of the expedition, but it was now clear enough that it was going to be a combined operation.

The enterprise was in fact a classic example of how to deceive the enemy, and how profitable successful deception could be. It was quite impossible to conceal preparations on such a vast scale, but an equally satisfactory alternative was to lead the Spaniards to believe that the objective was totally different from the true one. This was done by Lord Burghley with his accustomed subtlety. Sir Francis Drake was at this time with a fleet in the West Indies, and Burghley arranged for it to be known among the Spaniards that the new force was designed to support Drake on his return, or that it might be going to invade Brittany, or that it might be to prevent Spanish help from getting through to the rebels in Ireland. The results exceeded Burghley's wildest hopes. The first news the Spaniards had that Cadiz was the target was when they saw the sails of the English fleet approaching from the west.

The two commanders-in-chief were given full power to

[1] *Dom. Cal. 1595–7*, 190–1.

appoint senior officers to levy soldiers anywhere in the country, so long as they kept the deputy lieutenants in the picture. The counties were, however, not required on this occasion to contribute towards the cost of levying and equipping the men. It would be too much to expect them to help in financing an expedition which had as one of its main objectives the enriching of the senior officers. Essex and Howard would between them bear the cost of recruitment. The Council let it be known, however, that the generals were considerably out of pocket, and they expressed the hope that the counties would be prepared to volunteer some financial assistance. No-one was to be taken from the trained bands, nor was any servant to be recruited without his master's consent.[1]

Partly because of his financial interest in the venture and partly because he was an organizer by instinct Essex closely supervised the work of recruitment. He was anxious that nothing should be left to chance. It was not enough to issue commissions to his colonels to raise men in the shires. He must himself write to the deputy lieutenants saying that although they would be hearing separately from the Council about raising men it would advance the queen's service and also demonstrate their love for him if they would find the men quickly and do what they could to ensure that they were well equipped. He reminded them that he had sunk a lot of money in the project.[2]

By Easter things were nearing a climax. The generals were at Dover, and many of the ships were assembled there. Then the unexpected happened. The withdrawal of part of the English force in the Netherlands had encouraged the Spaniards to take the initiative and invade France. This was a setback, as it revived doubts about the wisdom of sending an army so far afield as Spain, when the immediate threat was only a few miles away across the Channel. The alternative of diverting the force to France commended itself to some, including many in Dover who could hear the Spanish guns with alarming clarity, and saw with apprehension the glass shaken from their windows by the vibration.

The queen was inevitably attracted by the possibility of recovering Calais for England, and after some hesitation decided to send Essex into France. He was given a new commission: to

[1] *A.P.C.* xxx. 307.   [2] *H.M.C. Salisbury*, vi. 117.

be lieutenant general of 6,000 men sent to the relief of Calais—
and only for this purpose, so many other burdens lay upon her
and the realm. The original plan had been to levy 3,000
in England, to whom were to be added 2,000 from the Low
Countries. Now, however, the total force was increased to 6,000,
the extra 1,000 to be found in London and the home counties—
the usual source of supply when troops were needed in a hurry.[1]

On 14 April Essex received a plea from the French king to
come as soon as possible. The next day was crowded with
excitement. In the morning Essex was authorized by the queen
to proceed to Calais. In the early afternoon three regiments
marched into Dover—Essex's own and those of Sir Thomas
Wilford and Sir Conyers Clifford, which synchronized perfectly
with the decision to go to France. In the evening the troops were
embarked and later the senior officers joined them. Then, just
as the signal to weigh anchor was about to be given a vessel
arrived from France. The news was serious. Calais had fallen
the day before, after a furious assault in which the governor
and the garrison had been put to the sword. The French still
held the citadel, however, and Henry reckoned that they
could survive a few days longer. But Essex decided that there
was now no point in crossing the Channel. He must seek further
guidance from the queen and Council. The troops were disembarked.

Next day the excitement continued. Ships were sighted, and
it was concluded they must be Spanish. First the successful
thrust into France, and now a naval attack on England. The
fleet was hastily manned again and put out to sea. But it was a
false alarm. The vessels were Dutch, and once again the fleet
put into Dover.[2]

This was the end of the expedition to help Henry. For the
time being the Spaniards were to be left unmolested in Calais,
and the plan to strike at the heart of Spain was reinstated. The
centre of activity moved to Plymouth, where the greater part
of May was devoted to training the men. This was not part of
a set programme, but it was the obvious thing to do while the
final preparations were being made—and until the queen finally
gave her permission to leave. Sir Francis Vere, the high marshal,
who was perhaps the most competent English soldier of the time,

---

[1] *Dom. Cal. 1595-7*, 202-3.   [2] Lambeth MSS. 250, f. 344.

welcomed the opportunity to lick the new troops into shape. The raw levies were trained side by side with the veterans from the Low Countries, and the results (which Vere attributes, no doubt reasonably, to his own efforts) were impressive. The marshal's opinion was backed up by an eyewitness, who when he saw the men drawn up in battle formation was most favourably impressed, not only with their 'countenance and promptness'—they were the handsomest men he had ever seen—but also with the state of their equipment. The officers were equally impressive. The richness of their clothing surpassed anything he had ever seen. There were 500 gentlemen smothered in feathers, and silver and gold lace—most of them 'green-headed youths' eager for adventure and the rewards it would bring. Essex was a born leader and inspired every man in the army from the humblest private to the mightiest colonel—except of course those of the rival faction. He won himself a 'wonderful regard' among the troops. Led as they were by a lion, so must they work lion's effects against the Spaniards.[1]

The sort of squabble among the leaders that had led to the death of Sir William Drury on Willoughby's expedition to France in 1589 manifested itself among Essex's staff before the force left Plymouth. Sir Edward Cooke, who was a supporter of Sir Walter Raleigh, quarrelled at dinner with Vere, when everyone present had drunk more than was good for him. A member of the Raleigh faction became so violent in his support of Cooke that he had to be sent from the room. Essex feared that the expedition might be marred by incidents like this, and laid it down that Vere would have precedence over Raleigh on land, and that Raleigh would be second-in-command to the two generals at sea—a sensible compromise that probably pleased neither side.[2]

While a final decision about the expedition was still awaited Essex told the Privy Council that he would not argue for or against it. He was content to leave its fate to the queen. But there were several important questions to be answered. What would happen to the £30,000 worth of food which the queen had provided? What would London and the many other seaports that had sent ships to the fleet think if all their trouble

[1] Thomas Birch, *Memoirs of the Reign of Queen Elizabeth*, ii. 8–11.
[2] Ibid. 10–11.

came to nothing? Would they be as willing to help when next their services were required? He and the lord admiral had provided five months' victuals out of their own pocket. What would they do with them if the expedition were called off? There were also political implications. France might be driven to make peace with Spain, if England failed to help her either by sending a force across the Channel, or by seeking to strike at Spain on her own territory. Then, think of the effect on the insolent rebels in Ireland when they saw that all the English preparations were but smoke, and all their threatenings but wind. Finally, he considered that there was no point in sending only the fleet, as some had advocated. They obviously could not establish themselves on land without a land army. Essex may have been content to leave the decision to the queen, but his questions leave no doubt as to his own view as to what should be done.[1]

At last the long-awaited decision came. The all-clear was given. Both generals had a letter from the queen giving them 'licence to depart, besides comfortable encouragement'. Essex's letter, however, was 'fraught with all kinds of promises and loving offers, as the like since he was a favourite he never had'. The queen also composed a prayer for the troops, and a second for her private use. The latter, which concluded 'we humbly beseech Thee with bended knees, prosper the work and with the best fore winds guide the journey, speed the victory, and make the return the advancement of Thy glory, the triumph of their fame, and surety of the realm, with the least loss of English blood', was copied to Essex by Sir Robert Cecil so that he also would be able to use it.

Burghley, who always thought of everything, considered it essential that it should be made clear to the world at large that the English cause was just. He drafted a declaration to be issued over the signatures of the two generals, that the queen was sending them with a royal army 'against such mighty forces as are advertised from all parts to be prepared by the King of Spain and which are likely to be mightily increased'. All those who were not natural-born subjects of Spain were requested to remove their ships and belongings from the harbours of Spain and Portugal, and return home. If they wanted to, they could

[1] Birch, ii. 18.

come to the English fleet, where they would be made most welcome. Any who did not take advantage of this warning, and remained within Spain, would be deemed to be aiding and abetting the Spaniards' next enterprise against England, and would be held to be enemies of the queen.[1]

The embarkation of the troops, always a slow process, was completed on 31 May; and on that day Essex sketched out a plan of campaign more daring than the plan approved by the queen—so daring that he arranged for his letter to be delivered to the Privy Council only after the fleet had been at sea for several days and could not be recalled. It would bring great honour to the queen, and strengthen the realm if the expedition inflicted damage on the Spanish fleet, or brought home treasure; but how much better to leave a thorn sticking in the King of Spain's foot—a permanent English base on the Spanish mainland. Were that achieved the queen would hear no more of Philip's threats against Ireland, his attempts on the French coast facing England, or his galleys in the Channel. The whole of Christendom would be delivered from his tyranny at a single blow.

Two objections might be urged against any scheme so ambitious. It would be risky, and it would be costly. So far as the risk was concerned, it was not a question of hazarding the whole state in a defensive war, but only a single force chosen for the purpose. Further, the army would be more secure than it would be in France or the Netherlands, for there would be no question of exposing it to attack in open country. It would be lodged so well that not all the efforts of Spain could drive it out. Nor did the project have to cost the queen much. If the right base were chosen, and the war skilfully handled, the enterprise would not only pay for itself but show a profit. In a short time a great part of the golden stream from the West Indies might be diverted from Spain to England, and the queen might be able 'to give law to all the world by sea'.

Essex concluded by saying that the Council would no doubt want to know what place he had in mind, how he would propose to capture and hold it, and precisely what advantages would accrue to the queen. All this he would deal with in a later dispatch. Meantime would they mull over the proposition and, if

[1] *Dom. Cal. 1595–7*, 208.

they thought that it had possibilities, put it to the queen? He would be glad to submit the scheme in greater detail, and the Council might rest assured that he would put nothing forward that did not have the blessing of his council of war. He apologized for writing at such length, and also for using the hand of a secretary. He had begun the letter in the morning, when there was nothing much happening, but it had had to be finished in the midst of all the excitement of getting ready for sea, when he himself had to go from ship to ship urging on the preparations.

Nothing, alas, was to come of this plan. The council of war, even if it had been wholeheartedly in favour of it, had insufficient authority to endorse a strategic step of such magnitude. To have had any hope of success Essex ought to have cleared it with the queen and Council before the expedition left England; but the chances are that they would have been no more in favour of it than the council of war when it was put to them at Cadiz, although for different reasons. Only Essex, his henchman Vere, and one or two others had the vision to see how the power of Spain might be contained at a small cost.

At 4 a.m. on 1 June the lord admiral fired a single cannon. This was the signal to move. His own squadron 'confusedly' followed his lead, and the other squadrons weighed anchor during the day. The wind was unfavourable, however, and they anchored again near the shore—so near that would-be deserters might be tempted to swim for it, and the order was passed round that none was to leave his ship on pain of death.

The queen and the Privy Council had provided no firm instructions about the expedition's objective. It was simply to strike a blow at Spain, and it was left to the commanders-in-chief to decide how best this could be done. While they were waiting for the wind to improve Essex and Howard summoned the council of war 'to resolve what enterprise was fittest to be undertaken for the annoyance of the Spanish king'. The consensus of opinion was that the enemy would be hardest hit by an attack on Cadiz, which confirmed Vere's earlier verdict. It was the easiest town to surprise, it was wealthy and held out promise of rich booty, and there were one or two other places nearby that might be attacked at the same time. The generals agreed. In the interests of surprise the ships would keep well off the coast until they reached Cape St. Vincent, which was to be the rendezvous for any that got separated from the main fleet. So that there would be no misunderstanding all the captains and masters were given sealed orders (written out by the secretary to the council of war), which were to be opened only if they lost touch with their squadron, requiring them first to proceed to Cape St. Vincent, and if they found no other vessel of the fleet there, to go on to Cadiz with all possible speed. Any who opened his orders prematurely was liable to the death penalty.

At last, on 3 June, the wind changed and the fleet was able to head south. It included the lord admiral in the *Ark Royal*, supported by the *Lion*, the *Dreadnought*, the *True Love*, and the *Lion's Whelp* of the royal navy, and twenty-two other vessels, among them armed merchants, hoys, and flyboats carrying victuals and horses; Essex, with twenty-eight vessels, of which five were from the navy, including his own flagship, the *Due Repulse*; Lord Thomas Howard, with twenty-five vessels, of which four were from the navy; and the rear admiral of the fleet, Sir Walter Raleigh, in the *Warspite*, with three other ships of the royal navy, and a total of twenty-three in his squadron. There was also the Dutch squadron, which had three warships, and twenty-three vessels in all. This gave a total of 126 vessels. There was also 'great store of ships and barks from divers parts that followed the fleet upon their own adventures for purchase and pillage'.[1]

The admirable preparation of the men was paralleled by the care with which the instructions for managing the fleet were drafted. Common prayer was to be said twice daily, unless the exigencies of the service prevented it. No man was to discuss religious matters, except to resolve some doubt in his mind, and even then he must refer his difficulties to one of the chaplains. High and mystical matters were not to be argued with anyone who had no professional qualifications. Before the men retired for the night psalms and the Lord's Prayer were to be said. The usual offences were listed in the disciplinary code: swearing, brawling, dicing, picking and stealing. The more serious cases were to be referred to the generals so that 'martial law' might be inflicted on the offender. Fire hazards were always a menace on wooden ships where candles were the main source of artificial

---

[1] Sir William Slingsby, *Relation of the Voyage to Cadiz*, 46–50.

light, and they were specially provided for. No lighted candle was to be carried except in a lantern. If fire did break out (which God forbid!) other ships in the vicinity were to send men to help the victim.

There were also detailed sailing instructions. It was particularly necessary in the case of a maritime expedition that all concerned should know precisely what the arrangements were going to be. Communication between ships was much more difficult than between the component parts of an army on land; and there was every chance that the ships would become separated at night or in a storm. Vessels were to keep to their squadrons and to refrain from giving chase to any ships they sighted unless they were ordered to do so by the admiral of their squadron. They were all to keep well apart, and in particular the bigger were to be careful about taking the wind of the smaller; but if any smaller ship became becalmed through its own fault the captain or master was to be severely punished. A council of war on one of the generals' ships was summoned by 'a flag of counsel of the red cross' at half mast on the mizzen mast. In fog ships were to give warning of their whereabouts either by sounding a drum, shooting, or lighting a flare.

Special care was to be taken to avoid straining the topmasts. If any were broken, the service would be greatly hindered. But if any vessel *did* break a mast or spring a leak, the captain was to summon help by firing a cannon during the day, and at night by showing two great lights one above the other about six feet apart.[1] The watch was to be set every night at 8 p.m. by sounding either trumpet or drum. Thereafter there was to be strict silence. One third of the soldiers were to be on guard duty every night; and in port there were to be special precautions in the forecastle and beakhead 'for fear of cutting of cables', which was common in hot countries.

In fact the fleet sustained hardly any damage on the voyage south. The *Mary Rose*, one of the ships of the royal navy, commanded by Sir George Carew, the master of the ordnance, broke her main yard an hour or two before dawn on 6 June, and duly summoned help by giving the pre-arranged signal. The damage was not too serious, however, and was quickly repaired. The only other accident of note was when the *Swiftsure*—another

[1] S.P. Dom. 257, no. 45.

ship of the royal navy, in Raleigh's squadron—broke her topmast when the wind suddenly got up, fortunately without injuring any of the crew. But once again the damage was soon made good.

It was absolutely vital that the Spaniards should be taken by surprise. Not even the captains and masters of the ships were allowed to know their destination. If any were unlucky enough to fall into the hands of the enemy they would not be able to give anything away—provided, of course, that they destroyed their secret orders. On several occasions the fleet ran into ships that might have revealed their movements to the Spaniards, but in every case they were chased and captured before they could do any harm. The narrowest escape of all was when one flyboat got away after an engagement with the *Swan* (one of the armed merchantmen, which was damaged in the encounter), and was then caught only after a long chase by the *John and Francis*, under the command of Marmaduke Darell, the victualler. Had this vessel reached Lisbon she would have given a precise account of the size and composition of the English fleet, from which the strength of the army could have been deduced. Moreover, the news that the fleet had bypassed Lisbon, which was considered by the Spaniards to be the most likely target for an English attack, would have led to the conclusion that Cadiz must be the real objective. The enemy would have had time to send reinforcements to the garrison, and also to take steps to safeguard their shipping there.

Not only did the English fleet save themselves by the efficiency with which they picked up the stray vessels that crossed their path, but they were able to get news of the Spanish merchant fleet. According to Sir William Monson, who was captain of Essex's ship, the *Repulse*, this was of the greatest importance. Had it not been known that the majority of the ships at Cadiz were merchantmen it would have been difficult to get the English leaders to agree to an attack on the shipping in the bay.

The news which the commanders-in-chief were able to pick up from the ships they intercepted must have made their mouths water. There were only four of the twelve apostles, Philip's great men-o'-war with a tonnage of a thousand-plus, and about twenty galleys, guarding more than forty merchant vessels, many of them about to leave with merchandise for the West Indies—all innocently awaiting the arrival of the English fleet.[1]

On 11 June the 'selected council' (i.e. the council of war proper, as distinct from the 'general council', which included the captains and masters of the principal ships) met to discuss how they should approach Cadiz, which were the best places to put the army ashore on the island of Leon (where the town stood), and how the warships and the galleys should be tackled. There was a great deal of discussion and many different opinions were offered, but no firm decision was reached. It was left that there would be a further meeting of the council when they had reached their destination and saw more clearly how the land lay.

Later on the same day the 'flag for the assembly of the general council was hung forth upon the shrouds' of the flagship to summon the captains and masters to a conference. The purpose of this meeting was to arrive at the best estimate of the position of the fleet and the course they should follow; and the debate reflects the uncertainty of sixteenth-century navigation. There was no agreement when the captains were asked what they thought their latitude was; but it was eventually decided—perhaps by averaging their divergent estimates—that they had reached the forty-second parallel. It was also estimated that they were about 30 leagues west of the nearest land, and that the correct course for doubling Cape St. Vincent was now 'south and by east'. The captains returned to their vessels with orders to steer accordingly.[2]

Four days later the selected council met again on the flagship of Lord Thomas Howard's squadron, the *Merhonour*, to consider the plan of campaign. The main business on this occasion was to work out the detailed orders for landing the troops, which were duly agreed upon and sent to the admirals and colonels. The extraordinary good fortune that had attended the voyage so far manifested itself again on 18 June. At dawn it was observed that a strange vessel was innocently sailing in the middle of the fleet. This was as great a shock to the higher command as it must have been to the master of the vessel, who awoke to find himself surrounded by one of the biggest naval expeditions of the age. If the interloper contrived to get away the chances were that the news of the English fleet's movements—which had

[1] Harl. MSS. 167, no. 209. [2] Lambeth MSS. 250, ff. 348-9.

been miraculously kept secret right to the eleventh hour—would now be broken to the Spaniards. The unhappy new arrival, which turned out to be a merchantman from Waterford in Ireland, did her best to get away, but was captured after a brief engagement. She had left Cadiz only the day before and her master was able to give up-to-the-minute news of the situation there. The authorities had not the remotest idea that an English fleet was only a few miles off; and the richly laden merchant vessels were still there.

This was indeed wonderful news, and there was great rejoicing among the English leaders as they got down to making their final plans. The selected council was summoned again and had a long discussion in which various proposals were examined in detail. There were three broad alternatives. Some favoured simultaneous attacks on the Spanish ships and on the town of Cadiz. Others thought that they ought to go for the ships first. The less time the Spaniards were given the less chance would they have of destroying them and their rich cargoes to prevent them from falling into the hands of the English. Others again advocated attacking the town first and holding the navy in reserve. (When they reached Cadiz Essex preferred an immediate attack on the Spanish ships, but at first the lord admiral thought it too risky.) In the end of the day it was agreed to make the town the first objective—a potentially disastrous decision.

The fleet reached Cadiz early on the morning of 20 June and anchored outside the bay, which has all the appearance of being a great natural harbour. It is formed by a long narrow neck of land—several miles of it, but less than half a mile across at its narrowest point—which protrudes from the island of Leon (which is for all practical purposes part of the mainland) to enclose a vast expanse of water. This is cut almost in two by a second promontory running across it from the mainland proper, and leaving only a narrow passage between the outer and inner bays. The navigable area, however, in both bays was very limited and left little room for the bigger ships to manœuvre. The town of Cadiz is planted right at the tip of the outer peninsula, commanding the broad entrance to the outer bay.

Soon after the fleet had come to anchor the plan to land the army was set in motion. The landing-craft—the ships' longboats, pinnaces, and barges specially made for the purpose—

were got ready. The men were armed and equipped. The
musketeers were given their issue of powder and match. The
first batch of the assault force lowered themselves into the boats,
but before the signal to shove off could be given the sea 'went
marvellous high, and the wind was exceeding large'. A strong
force of Spanish infantry and cavalry appeared on the shore
eagerly awaiting the arrival of the invaders. It would clearly
have been madness to carry on with the attempt, which would
have been hazardous enough under ideal conditions, and was
suicidal with the weather as it was. Four Spanish galleys were
lying in wait for the assault craft; and the sea was now so rough
that many of the boats that escaped from the galleys must have
sunk before they reached land. As it was some of the barges sank
while still sheltered by their parent vessels. One carried eighty
armed men, and despite their heavy equipment, which made
swimming impossible, only eight perished; but it would have
been very different away from the help and protection of the
fleet. Those who did reach the shore would have been cut to
pieces by the Spaniards, who were waiting for them behind an
effective barricade of wine barrels filled with sand.

Yet Essex could not be persuaded that the plan must be abandoned, and the initiative surrendered to the navy. He insisted on keeping the men in the boats, despite the danger, in the forlorn hope that the weather might improve. Already there were signs of the trouble that divided leadership brings. On this critical day when the success of the whole expedition hung in the balance, the lord admiral was on one vessel with his principal naval officers, and Essex was on another with the army higher command. Sir Walter Raleigh was sent 'to and fro betwixt them'—hardly the best way for a council of war to arrive speedily at the right decisions. Raleigh himself considered that the proposed landing would be disastrous. He pointed out to Essex that 'he thereby ran the way of our general ruin, to the utter overthrow of the whole army, then our lives and her majesty's future safety'. It was finally agreed to abandon the assault on the beaches, and instead to enter Cadiz Bay as soon as the tide served.

Disaster had been averted, but only by the narrowest of margins. In 1588 the English had been helped by bad weather at the right time: now a sudden fierce storm had saved the English higher command from itself. Luck was still with it. The only damage to the enterprise was that the Spanish ships in the bay had been given a whole day to put themselves in readiness for attack.

Those who were conscious of the value of speed wanted the attack to be made that evening, but Raleigh was quite firm about this. It took so long to get the men back on the ships again that most of the day had gone. The engagement must be deferred until dawn next day. Essex tried to insist that he should have the honour of leading the ships in, but the whole council of war opposed him, partly because the queen's wish that her favourite should not be exposed to particular danger was well known, and partly because it was considered that he would prejudice the chance of success. In the event Raleigh was selected to lead the attack, and he took up his position at the head of the English line just outside the range of the Spanish guns, ready to go in the following morning.

Sir Francis Vere had to be in the picture, however. He had already suggested to Essex that as he had a 'floaty' ship (i.e. one that drew little water) he should go in first, which led the general to say forcibly that he was damned if Vere would go in before him. Vere, nevertheless, decided to weigh anchor and steal a march on Raleigh. But this was easier said than done. 'The wind was so great and the billow so high' that his men could not turn the capstan to hoist the anchor, and several were thrown against the ship's rails and injured. Vere was not to be stopped by a trifle like this, however, and ordered the cable to be cut. He then crept nearer the entrance to the bay, so that on the morrow he would be well placed to steal a march on the rear-admiral.

Raleigh has left his own account of the competition to lead the attack. There was a suggestion that Lord Thomas Howard should have the honour of taking the lead, to which Raleigh replied that he would normally have been very happy to give way to one who both had precedence in the navy and was a nobleman whom he much honoured; but on this occasion he was bound by his duty to the queen to give and not receive the orders. He weighed anchor 'at the first peep of dawn' and made for the Spanish fleet well ahead of the other English ships. He was first fired on by the fort at the end of the peninsula, then by the guns on the wall of the town, and then by the galleys within the outer harbour. He disdained to return their fire, and proudly records that his only reply to each shot from the enemy was a 'blurt' with a trumpet.[1] The galleys were wasps and beneath contempt. It was the great *St. Philip* he was after, one of the twelve apostles that had helped to seal the fate of the *Revenge* six years earlier, when Sir Richard Grenville had held out single-handed against the Spanish fleet for fifteen glorious hours. Raleigh records, with becoming modesty: 'Always, I must without glory say for myself that I held single in the head of all.'

The battle then began in earnest. The best account is given by Sir Julian Corbett in *The Successors of Drake*, where he reconstructs the engagement in great detail. It was a resounding victory for the English ships, based on better seamanship, and great superiority of gunnery, which the extraordinary indiscipline of the principal English officers did not cancel out. The movement of the fleet 'resolved itself at once into a scramble amongst the leading galleon captains to get first at the enemy, followed by desperate attempts to jockey each other out of the fighting line. So wild was the race, so contradictory the accounts of the competition that it is difficult to know exactly what happened'.[2] According to Raleigh (whose anxiety to outdo his fellow commanders was not matched by his bravery in the action) he exchanged broadsides with the Spaniards for almost three hours; then, fearing that he would be sunk, he went to Essex to ask permission to board, as it made just as good sense to be set on fire in a boarding attempt as it did to remain where they were and be sunk. Essex agreed, and said that whatever Raleigh decided to do, it had his approval. While this conversation was taking place Vere contrived to get ahead of Raleigh's flagship, because, according to Raleigh, he considered that his honour had been touched by remaining so long behind. Lord Thomas Howard, who had failed in his bid to take the lead, also took advantage of Raleigh's absence from his ship to creep ahead of him in the *Nonpareil*. When Raleigh got back he found that he was now only third in the line. This was outrageous. He promptly slipped anchor and thrust between Vere and Lord Thomas, and went further ahead than them all. Then he swung broadside across the channel, effectively blocking the others.

[1] See p. 30, above.   [2] Corbett, op. cit., 79.

He thought he had made sure that none would 'outstart' him again that day. But he had not reckoned with the resourceful lord marshal. Vere surreptitiously sent a boat across to Raleigh's vessel and had his men fasten a cable to it—the idea being that he could then winch himself on, and perhaps head the rear-admiral again. Vere's ostensible reason for this surprising manœuvre was that his own ship was facing in such a way that he could use only his 'chasing pieces'—the guns pointing ahead —and not his broadside. Raleigh soon spotted what his rival was up to. 'When we had leisure to look behind us the marshal had secretly fastened a rope to my ship's side to draw himself up equal to me; but some of my company advertising me thereof I caused it to be cut off and so he fell back into his place.'

This was Vere's first naval action, and his conduct throughout seems to have been that of the enthusiastic and not wholly inept amateur. He records that he was most anxious to appear willing to embrace the occasions that offered themselves; and that he had made up his mind to press on, knowing that he had good men behind him, and that many hands would make light work. His ship's company, however, 'either wiser or more afraid than myself, on a sudden unlooked for by me, let fall the anchor and by no means would be entreated to weigh it again'. The professionals had decided that the amateur had gone far enough.

At last the superiority of the English guns began to tell. The four apostles were 'by negligence and fear' run aground and abandoned by their crews. The *St. Philip* and the *St. Thomas* were set on fire by the Spaniards, and fortunately blew up before they could be boarded, although one pinnace approaching the *St. Philip* did catch fire. The *St. Matthew* and the *St. Andrew* were boarded before they could be fired, and were later sailed to England, where they joined the royal navy. Raleigh has left a vivid picture of the end of the battle:

> The spectacle was very lamentable on their side, for many drowned themselves and many half-burnt leaped into the water, very many hanging by the ropes' ends by the ship's side, under the water even to the lips, many swimming with grievous wounds strucken under water and put out of their pain; and withal so huge a fire, and such tearing of ordnance in the great *Philip* and the rest when the fire came to them, as if any man had a desire to see hell itself, it was there most lively figured. Ourselves spared the lives of all after the victory;

but the Flemings, who did little or nothing in the fight, used merciless slaughter, till they were by myself and afterwards by my lord admiral, beaten off.

The English and Dutch losses were slight. Apart from the pinnace which was set on fire by the holocaust on the *St. Philip*, the only ship lost was a Dutch flyboat on which an accidental fire exploded the powder store. Of the 100 men on board only three or four escaped. The losses of men in the action—mostly through 'great shot'—were round about forty.

The English now had command of the sea; and they could use it in one of two ways. They could round up the forty or fifty merchantmen that had retired to the inner bay, and which were now virtually defenceless, and possess themselves of their valuable cargoes; or they could put the army ashore and attempt to capture Cadiz. There was an element of urgency in both possibilities. If they did not pursue the Spanish merchant ships it was likely that their cargoes would be removed, and the ships sunk or burned. If they left Cadiz alone, there was every likelihood that it would be reinforced. The logical course at this point would have been to divide the force into two parts—a naval element which Howard would have led in pursuit of the merchant ships, and a land element which Essex would have led against Cadiz. Quite a small force could have controlled the narrowest part of the peninsula on which Cadiz stood, so long as the English fleet controlled the bay on one side, and the sea on the other; and reinforcements could thus have been kept away from the town, at least until the Spanish merchant ships were dealt with, and the whole of the force was available for an assault on Cadiz.

Essex, on a sudden impulse, decided to take a force ashore. Sir William Monson pointed out that it would be more profitable to go after the Spanish ships right away, but Essex, who had been denied his land enterprise the day before, was not going to be stopped now. It was relatively easy to go ahead without holding a full council of war, as there was a ready-made plan for the landing—it had been drawn up at sea on 15 June—and all the general had to do was to instruct the lord marshal and the sergeant-major-general (whose job it was to get the troops ready for action) to put it into operation.

The landing arrangements were, however, complicated by three factors. First, there were not enough boats to carry the whole of the assault force at once, and some method of selecting the first wave had to be devised. Second, it was impossible to carry a whole regiment in one ship, and in practice some carried men from two regiments. Third, when Essex made his snap decision to invade, the ships themselves were dispersed. The first two points had been provided for. The initial wave was to be limited to a third of the land force, which was the number the boats could carry at one time; and where there were men from two regiments in the same ship they were to be assigned to the first assault in equal numbers. It was hoped in this way to keep the size of the regimental units in the first landing roughly equal. The problem of the dispersal of the fleet had not been legislated for and Vere and Clifford (the sergeant-major-general) had therefore to take their men where they could find them.

The original plan laid down that the best men in each regiment should be included in the one-third that was to be landed first; but they were not to carry their ensigns with them. This is an interesting decision, for as a rule the ensign was supposed to be the focal point in the most desperate fighting. The same rule applied when the whole force had been landed. It made sense when the whole army was ashore that the ensigns should remain where the majority of the troops were, as it was there that the final rallying point would be if the assault looked like being defeated; but this hardly applied at the stage where one-third of the force was on the beach, and two-thirds still in the safety of the ships, where there was no need to have the ensigns as a rallying point. The implication may be that the landing was originally expected to be so hazardous that the first wave would have only a slender chance of success, and the ensign—the heart of the army—must be kept intact for a later effort.

The colonels were all well aware of the details of the plan, and must have passed them on to the captains and men on the last few days of the voyage. All that was needed was the order to proceed; and this Essex gave on his own responsibility. Although the plan was complex it was executed with meticulous accuracy. While the men were entering the boats Essex and Vere went ashore to examine the beach and determine on what breadth of front the assault craft should approach, as the idea was that the line of the assault should correspond to the width of the beach. Then Essex and the lord marshal returned to the ships to superintend the organization of the assault craft, and to lead them shorewards. Essex, accompanied by 'gentlemen adventurers and choice men', rowed some distance ahead of the main force which followed, 'deeping their oars' in time with the drum, and maintaining a general silence 'as well of warlike instruments as otherwise', so that the drumbeat might be clearly heard. The leading boat in each file carried a St. George's flag, or a white pennant, to act as 'guide and director' to those behind; and all were enjoined to follow a very precise 'order of march'—'no boat thrusting out of a hinder rank into a former, nor shrinking out of the former into a hinder'.

It is a matter of speculation how effective this method of assault would have been, as it was not put to the test. There was not a Spaniard in sight when they reached the beach, and they were able to form themselves into regiments without let or hindrance. The speed with which the Englishmen had moved was too much for the enemy. Neither the burning heat of the midday sun, nor the 'deep, dry, sliding sand' along which they had to struggle in their heavy armour, and which was 'as tiresome and as painful as may be', held them up. The Spaniards had been well placed to meet the original attempt to land the army, which had been frustrated by the weather; they had then been caught off balance by the successful attack on their shipping; and now before they had time to recover from that blow—while their ships were still burning in the bay—here was an English force landing in good order, when it might well have been expected that they would pause to catch their breath after a day and a half of continuous action.

As soon as the Spaniards saw what was happening they rushed a cavalry and infantry force in the direction of the landing-place, but it was too late. The Englishmen were well established, and their boats had returned to the ships to pick up the second wave of assault troops. The landing had been made from within the bay on the northern side of the peninsula, which meant that Cadiz now lay to the right, or west, of the English force. There is some disagreement about the strength of the first wave but it was probably just under 2,000 men. Essex sent Sir Conyers Clifford, with about half the force, to the east to establish himself across the narrowest part of the peninsula and prevent reinforcements coming from the mainland to build up the strength of the garrison in Cadiz. This clearly had to be done, as they saw men hurrying in the direction of the town when they landed. They were probably civilians seeking refuge, but there was no doubt that sooner or later a military force would follow them, and this must be prevented.

In fact Clifford failed to carry out his orders, either because he misunderstood them, or because he lost his way, or because he wanted to achieve something more spectacular than a mere defensive action, however important it might be. Instead of halting at the narrowest part of the neck of land, which was only an arquebus shot across, and could easily have been defended, he marched his men several miles further on until they came to the bridge joining the island of Leon to the mainland, where they were held up by the garrison in the castle commanding the bridge. They exchanged shots with the castle, and succeeded in partially wrecking the bridge. Here they remained for the next twenty-four hours and then unfortunately decided to return to the town. This was the moment the galleys had been waiting for. Although their oars made them more mobile than the rest of the Spanish fleet they had no hope of getting past the English ships in the bay. There was another escape route, however—through the long narrow channel between the island of Leon and the mainland, and under the bridge which Clifford had been threatening. So long as the English were in the vicinity the galleys dared not attempt the passage; but as soon as Clifford withdrew they seized their chance and slipped through to the open sea.

Essex's idea was to establish a camp somewhere in the vicinity of Cadiz, as it was generally agreed that the town could not be taken without a battery; and it would take time to land the heavy guns and get them into position. But before any decision could be taken about the location of the camp a combined infantry and cavalry force sallied from the town to test the strength of the invaders. An attempt was made to encourage the Spaniards to overreach themselves by sending forward a small number of pikemen and musketeers with orders to take to their heels when they came to blows. This was duly done, but the timing went awry, for the Spaniards saw the trap in time, and fled back to the town 'with far swifter legs than manly courage'. Those in charge of the gates panicked and shut them before all their comrades were inside; but those who were left behind promptly saved themselves from the pursuing English by scaling the ramparts.

The excitement of the chase, and the sight of the Spaniards scaling the walls without much difficulty, stimulated Essex and Vere to greater things. They were now no longer interested in setting up camp, as it seemed that there was a good chance to take the town there and then by assault, without a preliminary battery. Once again the English were moving faster than they themselves had thought possible; and once again the Spaniards were caught off balance.

The town was surrounded by a very deep dry ditch, but the rampart rising from it was in the course of construction, and still sloped gently. It was up this rampart and over the wall that the Spaniards who had been shut out of the town had scrambled; and if they could get in that way, so could the English. But the Spaniards had guessed that they would be followed and were now on the wall behind the rampart, awaiting developments. Without pausing to think about the wisdom of the move or arrange a co-ordinated attack some of the English captains boldly led a group of veterans from the Low Countries up the slope, while their companions below kept the enemy occupied with musket fire. They gained the top of the rampart, and found that the wall could be reached from it without much difficulty; and after some fierce hand-to-hand fighting succeeded in establishing themselves on the wall. Despite his usual anxiety to be in the forefront Essex waited until a sizeable group was on the wall before he, accompanied by members of his entourage, followed them up the wall. They were not out of the wood yet, for they were caught between the tower guarding the gates and a second tower, both occupied by enemy musketeers.

They clearly could not remain where they were: either they must retreat, or go forward. The latter meant jumping down 'a pike's length' into the town—say 18 or 20 feet. Once again, Essex found it difficult to take the lead. Twenty feet is a long way down, and to do him justice his armour made the jump more difficult. He stood irresolutely while most of the others took their courage in both hands, and jumped. He might have stood there indefinitely, or until he was picked off by one of the Spanish musketeers, had it not been for the initiative of his henchman Vere. The marshal had been trying to find an easier way into the town while the others were scaling the rampart. He had sent one party round the ditch in search of another gate, which in fact they found, and managed to force; but although they tried to get this news back to Vere the messenger never got through and the marshal concluded that the attempt must have failed. He therefore himself collected a number of men and led a desperate attack on the main gates: after meeting stubborn resistance, they broke them down. There was no longer any need for Essex, still hovering on the brink, to risk his neck, and although the loyal Vere says that he was one of the first over the wall, a more reliable authority says that as soon as Essex saw that the gates were opened, not ten paces away, he turned 'straight from the leap' and entered through the broken gates.

Once in the town, Essex again allowed his impetuosity to cloud his judgement. Instead of pausing to gather a sizeable force from among those who had entered through the main gates, over the wall, and through the sally-port which Vere's men had forced, he rushed on to the market-place with a handful of men, where anything might have happened, had not Vere followed at a slower and surer pace. The marshal was careful to collect all the stragglers he came across into a single body, and they fought their way into the market-place through tough opposition. There they joined forces with Essex and the thirty or forty men supporting him, and between them managed to get a foothold in the town hall. Vere suggested that Essex should make it his headquarters, and see that it was properly defended, while he himself went off to 'assure the rest of the town'. This he did, although he claims that he was 'but slackly and slenderly followed' by the English troops who were already allowing their greed for spoil to interfere with their duty.

Gradually the resistance was overcome, after a good deal of hard house-to-house fighting, and by nightfall only one or two strong-points held out—the castle, and parts of the old town. Next day the castle surrendered, and victory was complete. It had been achieved with a surprisingly small force, extraordinarily quickly. When Howard came ashore about dusk on the day of the attack he found the fighting virtually over; and as things turned out there is no doubt that he would have been better employed against the Spanish merchant ships. But he could not be expected to divine that things were going so well for Essex and Vere, nor can the latter be blamed for not keeping the admiral informed of the progress of the assault. Events had moved so quickly that there was not time even for this. The English triumph was so swift that even their own commanders could not keep up with it.

The English remained in Cadiz for a fortnight, looting, negotiating ransoms, and discussing whether they should get out, or try to stay there. Essex and Vere were in favour of remaining in possession of the town, at least until the queen's wishes were known; but they were in a minority. The council of war decided to leave. Thirty men were chosen from each regiment to set fire to the town, and the troops were re-embarked. Essex, always anxious for the limelight, was last on board. The fleet paid a visit to Faro, where they found no opposition and also to Corunna, where a reconnaissance was made by a ship manned by sailors dressed in Spanish clothing—no doubt part of the booty from Cadiz—to avoid suspicion. No enemy ships of any significance were there and the idea of raiding the harbour was abandoned. There was then a half-hearted suggestion that they should try to intercept the home-coming West Indies fleet, but this fell through. Nearly everyone except Essex wanted to get home; and the majority view prevailed.

The inquest on the Cadiz voyage was the biggest of the reign. The higher command had had a tremendous victory within their grasp—which they must all have realized in the weeks that followed their departure from the town—and all deemed it necessary to put out their own version of events and to saddle someone else with the blame. In fact, only an official version was published at the time, and the manuscript accounts which are available at the present time were denied to the public by government order.

By far the most interesting paper on the expedition was written by Essex himself, and is now among the manuscripts of the British Museum. This paper begins as a straight defence of Essex's conduct as general. The expedition might seem to have failed in four respects; but there are satisfactory defences to criticisms on these lines. This part of the essay has been known all along (it was printed in 1720, for example) but the rest of it has only recently come to light.[1] The four criticisms of the expedition which Essex records are: that no attempt was made to seize the Indies fleet in Cadiz bay; that the town was abandoned, when it might well have been held indefinitely; that the idea of intercepting the Spanish fleet returning from the Indies was not carried through; and finally that there was no attempt made on the other Spanish ports, when the main success of the expedition had been in the destruction of enemy shipping.

Essex provides a detailed reply to each of these points. He admits that the Spanish merchant ships should have been taken. Indeed he himself had urged the lord admiral to get on with this important task. He sent messages through Sir Anthony Ashley (who was acting as secretary to the council of war) to see that some ships were sent to take over the Spanish merchantmen. This could have been done quite easily at the beginning, as their crews were ashore (a fact which prisoners later confirmed); and even if the crews had been on board they would have had no time to decide how to save the ships from the English. If only Howard had gone in to the attack as soon as they reached Cadiz they would have engaged both the men-o'-war and the merchant fleet at the same time; and having defeated the former, they could easily have taken over the latter with their valuable cargoes intact. The Spanish galleys would also have been captured. But by not moving quickly enough the English command gave the enemy time to man their ships and provide them with all the munitions they needed. Despite all Essex's efforts to persuade the 'sea commanders' to go after the merchant ships when he launched his attack on the town they refused to move. The enemy were given a generous forty-eight hours in which to withdraw to the inner harbour and destroy themselves.

There is no doubt that the failure of the English higher command to follow up their victory over the Spanish warships was an act of criminal neglect. The self-destruction of about forty of the King of Spain's merchant vessels was a notable triumph; but how much greater would the Spanish disaster have been if those ships had been captured intact and sailed

---

[1] See L. W. Henry, 'The Earl of Essex as Strategist and Military Organiser, 1596–7', *E.H.R.* lxviii. 363–93.

back to England to supplement Elizabeth's sea power. Essex himself must accept responsibility for the situation that led Howard to neglect his obvious duty. If he had paused for a moment before impetuously launching the land attack on his own authority, and summoned a short session of the council of war, the English force could have gone after both objectives as part of an agreed plan. Events proved that the small force Essex took ashore with him was able to capture the town. This was more than he could reasonably have expected to achieve. The realistic plan would have required Essex to carry out a holding operation on the peninsula, which would have prevented any build-up of the Spanish troops in Cadiz: and indeed this is all that he had in mind at first. The balance of the land force and the ships of the royal navy would have found it easy enough to possess themselves of most of the Spanish merchantmen. But in the absence of any consultation the admiral had no idea what Essex was up to on land; and he had to join him there—whether to ensure that any kudos arising from the attempt was shared by the naval element in the expedition, or whether he genuinely believed that his support might be needed, is immaterial. The essential fact is that Howard wasted his effort on land, and Essex's impetuosity was to blame.

Sir William Monson, who was captain of Essex's ship, provides a balanced summing-up of the Earl's behaviour. His 'forwardness and carriage merited much, yet if it had been with more deliberation and less haste, it would have succeeded better'. If Essex were still alive he would be the first to admit that he (Monson) had advised him to be master of the ships rather than of the town. They would have afforded both wealth and honour. The earl's sudden decision to land and his message to Howard to attack the ships should have 'been resolved by a mature deliberation'.[1]

It is easy enough, however, to clear Essex of the other three charges. He certainly wanted to remain indefinitely in Cadiz, in spite of strong opposition from the naval commanders—especially the lord admiral—who maintained that there could be no question of remaining because of shortage of victuals and other provisions; and as he himself pointed out his instructions required him to follow the advice of the council of war. The

[1] T. Lediard, *Naval History*, 339.

latter body was equally to blame for the failure to intercept the home-coming Indies fleet, and to raid more of the enemy's ports. The fact of the matter is that the naval commanders had done so well out of the Cadiz affair that there was little incentive for them to attempt anything more. Essex alone put the national interest above private considerations, or at least considerations of private finance.

XIV
CONCLUSION

EARLIER judgements of Elizabeth's handling of military affairs have been unfavourable. Sir Charles Firth says that the military system which the Tudors bequeathed to the Stuarts was completely inefficient.[1] While this is entirely true as far as it goes, it leaves on one side the efforts of Elizabeth and her Privy Council to make the system more efficient.

More sweeping is Sir J. W. Fortescue, to whom Elizabeth was no more than a selfish and incapable woman:

> She hated straight dealing for its simplicity; she hated conviction for its certainty; above all she hated war for its expense. She loved her money as herself, and to these twain she would sacrifice alike the most faithful servant and the most friendly State. . . . In truth, throughout the long reign of Elizabeth we feel that in military matters, one effort, and only one was made, namely, in Carlyle's words, to stretch the old formula to cover the new fact, to botch and patch and strain the antiquated web woven by the Statute of Winchester, and newly dyed by the Statute of Philip and Mary to some semblance of the pattern given by the armies of France and Spain.[2]

Thirdly, Sir Charles Oman draws a dismal and accurate picture of the inefficiency of army organization,[3] but again makes no real attempt to assess the difficulties which the Crown faced.

The three judgements might have been more favourable had these difficulties been given greater weight. Sir John Neale in his study of the finances of the troops in the Netherlands in 1586–7 points out that the government was seriously handicapped by the general's incompetence, by the failure of the Dutch to bear their agreed share of the expenses, and by the deeply rooted corruption in the forces. He suggests that other expeditions may have been similarly affected, which is of course perfectly true.[4]

---

[1] *Cromwell's Army*, 1.   [2] *History of the British Army*, i. 130, 133.
[3] *Art of War in the Sixteenth Century*, 373–6.   [4] *E.H.R.* xlv. 373.

CONCLUSION

Corruption was certainly the biggest problem. The fraudulent supply of uniform in Ireland was the most spectacular single transaction, but there must have been others which would be equally astounding, had they ever come to light. Fraud among the merchants was all the more reprehensible, as in tendering for contracts they no doubt left themselves a generous profit margin. Figures quoted above[1] show that one merchant was making as much as 40 per cent. above what his competitors regarded as reasonable; and profiteering at this rate was probably rife in most branches of organization.

The lords lieutenant served the country well enough. They were all wealthy men who did not need to resort to corrupt practices, and their only fault was occasional inefficiency. But the sheriffs and justices of the peace acting as commissioners of musters were often delighted to forget their obligations to the Crown in return for a cash payment. The key figure in the financial administration of the army, the treasurer-at-war, was corrupt as often as not. It may be argued that the government should have ensured loyal service from its employees, either by appointing honest men or by paying others enough to make dishonesty unnecessary. Neither method was feasible. There was not enough money in the exchequer to satisfy the greed of the dishonest, nor were there enough honest men to fill the administrative posts.

Above all the captains were uncontrollable. Without exception they subjected their companies to an infinite variety of exploitation. They encouraged men to buy their way out of the army, hired substitutes to satisfy the muster-master (if he were not prepared to be a party to the deception), and pocketed the subsequent pay of the missing ranks. They sold the arms and equipment of dead and discharged soldiers. They conspired with the clothing suppliers to receive cash instead of uniform, while the troops went unprovided for. When the government tried to help the private through the dead-pay fund, they promptly seized the opportunity of further lining their own pockets. In short, there was no limit to the devices they employed for cheating the government and preying on the private soldier.

The fundamental trouble was that the system of payment had its roots in the traditional methods of raising troops (the

[1] p. 97.

commission of array and the indenture), which made the captain much more directly responsible for the management of his men than he needed to be in the circumstances of the latter part of the sixteenth century. The more modern methods of recruitment, in which the state rather than the individual captain had the primary responsibility for finding men, should have been accompanied by a parallel transfer of financial power in the army; and this transfer should have been made long before Elizabeth's time. But no-one was far-sighted enough to see this, and the captains naturally clung to their traditional rights. In the middle of the sixteenth century the system was too widely accepted to be altered without a tremendous upheaval. The exploitation of the rank and file was the captain's lawful due, sanctified by long custom. The damage had been done, and could not readily be repaired.

The fact remains that on paper the financial machinery had all the checks and balances needed—given that those operating it were not all dishonest. The same is true of the systems for supplying uniform, equipment, and food, for mustering the men, and for levying them in the first place. They were as watertight as they could be, having regard to the limitations imposed by the methods of recording, copying, book-keeping, and accounting which were then available; but having regard also to the standards of honesty, they simply could not work. No system is foolproof if the whole of the human element in it is utterly corrupt.

The second major problem was the change in weapons. The introduction of fire-arms elsewhere in Europe put England temporarily at a disadvantage, for there was much reluctance to put aside the long-bow, the nation's traditional weapon. This is quite understandable. In the hands of a properly trained archer the bow was accurate at more than a hundred yards' range, could be discharged six times a minute, and took little harm from wet weather. On the other hand the sixteenth-century fire-arm was inaccurate even at short range, had a much slower rate of fire, and was very fragile. Above all it was much more costly, and the gunpowder and match on which it depended might be made useless by rain. So strong was the case for the bow that in discarding it and substituting 'weapons of fire' the Privy Council showed courage as well as foresight.

A third important difficulty was the steady increase in the military effort after 1585. From that year to the end of the reign annual recruitment for foreign service was well over 5,000, greater numbers being required in the closing years. Had there been a lull, it might have been used to put the organization of the forces on a sounder basis; but there was no lull. The Crown was given no breathing-space in which to develop a new military system based on recent experience. It had to struggle on as best it could with what it had.

Finally, the nation became more and more war-weary as the reign progressed. Some citizens may have founded their objection to the Crown's military policy on constitutional principles, but there were many more who did not trouble to take their stand on the constitution. The evasion of military service by one device or another became more frequent as time went on. Burghley sadly exclaimed that the country was weary of the ceaseless expenditure of money and life in foreign service. The Privy Council became apprehensive at the hostile attitude of the people. By the end of the century it was well-nigh impossible to raise money for troops. In 1600 Gloucestershire was unable to find enough for half a dozen cavalry for Ireland. Sums raised for troops from the legal profession, gentlemen, knights—all fell short of the amount required. No fewer than eleven counties failed to pay a single penny. In London—which was the nearest England had to a military cornucopia—150 musketeers had to be changed to pikemen to save expense; and even so it was still found impossible to provide the men with armour.

It is difficult to arrive at even a rough estimate of the annual cost of the army, but it increased from a relatively modest sum at the beginning of the reign to a crippling burden at the end. Even the basic military establishment was costly. For example, the garrison town of Berwick had to be maintained whether the country was at war or peace, and this normally cost about £15,000 a year; but when capital works had to be undertaken the figure was much higher. Between 1563 and 1567, when the fortifications were being rebuilt, it averaged £40,000 a year. The cost of the military establishment in Ireland was small enough at first (less than £30,000 a year), but at the close of the century it reached what were then astronomic proportions—£415,000 in 1601. The total cost of the Irish establishment between 1595 and 1603 was over £1,800,000. From 1585 the cost of maintaining the English troops in the Netherlands was a big new drain on the exchequer: £23,000 in 1585; £100,000 the following year; and £175,000 the year after that. But these are simply the easily identifiable costs. To complete the picture innumerable other expenditures must be brought into the account. Items taken at random through the reign include: purchases of saltpetre (1559) £15,000; gunpowder (1577) £20,000; provision for the secret service, to be spent as the queen directed (1585) £13,000; the lieutenant of the ordnance (1590) £21,000; and so on. Military expenditure represented a very large proportion of the total budget, and it could not have been increased without landing the state in bankruptcy.[1]

Earlier writers have held the queen solely responsible for the failures in military administration. She was clearly the villain of the piece in Fortescue's eyes, parsimonious and shortsighted. She did nothing to improve organization: 'but when we turn from the queen to the people, we perceive the energy of a very different force. The English army was not created by a sovereign or a minister: it created itself in despite of them.' There is no doubt that much of the responsibility for what was done, or left undone, belonged to the queen. It was she who took the final major decisions—to invade Scotland, or send troops to the aid of Henry IV, for example—and not always with the unanimous support of the Council. She undoubtedly controlled broad strategic policy, listening of course to the advice of her principal ministers; and the successes and failures at this level were hers and hers alone.

But the shaping of the weapon that was to be used to attain these broad strategic ends was inevitably the practical responsibility of the Privy Council rather than the queen. Even a male sovereign would have found it difficult, at a time when military science was changing rapidly, to control the development of the army and at the same time devote proper attention to other matters of state; and however masculine she might be in outlook, Elizabeth had no experience of the battlefield. She could not give an expert opinion as to whether a single musketeer was worth more than three archers, as did Sir Roger Williams; nor could she conclude, as did Captain Cosbie, that infantrymen

[1] F. C. Dietz, *English Public Finance, 1558–1641*.

should discard pouldrons, vambraces, and tasses in the interests of mobility. These were technical matters which could be assessed only by those members of the Privy Council who had experience of active service, and who were in touch with the livelier minds among the captains. There is plenty of evidence that they pondered deeply the problems of modernizing the forces. Perhaps the most notable occasion was in 1569 (long before the 'war period' began), when they tried by gentle persuasion to get the country as a whole to accept that the day of the fire-arm had arrived, and to work out in partnership with the government arrangements for the provision and storage of the new weapons. That nothing dramatic resulted from this approach was not the fault of the Privy Council, but of the majority of the people. It was difficult to drive them on at a greater pace than that of their own choosing, however desirable the goal. This count alone is enough to throw grave doubts on the reasonableness of Fortescue's assessment that it was the people and not the government who were behind the development of the army.

What then did the queen and Council achieve against the background of universal corruption, unwillingness to contribute towards the ever-increasing cost of the army, and anxiety to avoid military service at any price? The introduction of fire-arms has already been mentioned. Then, there was the development of the trained bands, and a deliberate attempt to tighten up the militia generally. The Council took an ever closer interest in the behaviour of the local authorities in military affairs, especially after England's open intervention in the continental war in 1585. It became more exacting in its demands, less generous when appeals were made against compulsory service. At the same time it showed a new and humane approach in its attitude to the rank and file. There are many instances of genuine sympathy for the lot of the private—the pension legislation, for example, and expressions of admiration for the part he played, which have all the appearance of coming from the heart, although they no doubt contained the inevitable undercurrent of propaganda.

In the eyes of most military historians the greatest shortcoming of Elizabethan policy was the failure to provide a permanent paid army. Fortescue correctly points out that by

Elizabeth's time war had become a profession, and could no longer be regarded as a mere appendage to the everyday life of the citizen.

Now, therefore, if ever, (he exclaims) was the time for the establishment of a standing army in England. She was menaced by foreign enemies on all sides, and in perpetual peril of intestine insurrection. There was unceasing trouble in Ireland, and eternal anxiety on the Scottish border. The forces of the shire had been proved to be worthless, and the service was not only inefficient but unpopular; the people came unwillingly to the muster, and would gladly have paid to be relieved of the burden.[1]

All this is true, except the last few words. All the indications are that the people would have been no more willing (assuming that they were able) to give their money to the state to provide a standing army than they were to give personal service in the militia. The whole community was either unable or unwilling to support the soldiers disabled on the foreign expeditions—a much smaller body of men than would have been needed for a permanent army.

The possibility of an Elizabethan standing army, nevertheless, remains a fascinating question. The germ of a permanent organization is perhaps seen in an institution peculiar to Ireland —a reserve of officers and men known as the pensioners, who in return for their pensions were obliged to reside in Ireland and hold themselves available in case of emergency. They had no fixed establishment, but their strength was usually round about fifty. It is not suggested that this body of reservists constituted anything approaching a standing army; but at least it shows that the government made some slight attempt to introduce an element of permanency into the forces.

Many schemes were put forward for the reorganization of the militia, but none of them really provided the basis of a standing army as it is known today. The most interesting line of thought is that developed by the Earl of Essex, who argues in favour of a small efficient army. 'Monstrous unwieldy bodies' cannot be governed properly, and nothing can last that cannot be governed.[2] (This idea would have been acceptable to many, for there were plenty of Biblical and classical precedents for the

---

[1] *History of the British Army*, i. 130. [2] B.M. Loan 23, f. 160b.

triumph of the small army, and the Elizabethan pundits loved their precedents.) Essex did not go so far as to suggest that his small force should be made permanent (in his particular case this would have been deemed near to high treason), but it would have been the logical next step.

The promise of increased efficiency was an incentive to reduce the size of the national force; but there was at the same time a natural tendency in this direction, because of the growing need for specialization. The idea that every able-bodied man between the ages of 16 and 60 should be liable to serve in the army was a relic of the days when the community's ability to defend itself did in fact depend on the efforts of every able-bodied male citizen. This is true of course only of a most primitive society. With the increasing sophistication of warfare so the numbers of actual combatants in relation to the total population is progressively reduced. Even in Elizabeth's time only something like one-tenth of the population was eligible for military service; and the forces in the field at any given moment were never more than about one-tenth of those liable to serve—say 20,000. But the selection of the one man in ten needed to produce that number was never organized on a systematic basis.

The idea of specialization, however, was just beginning to emerge. Mary Tudor's 'act for the taking of musters' refers in the preamble to the levy of men who were 'most able and likeliest to serve in the wars'; and the theory certainly was that the commissioners of musters should choose the best material—whatever the practice. Although there was never any formal division of the population into those who would be required to serve in time of war, and those who would not, or who would be regarded as the second line of defence, the institution of the trained bands was a step in the direction of specialization. This was inevitable, if only because the increasing complexity and cost of weapons meant that not every man could be fully equipped. The men of the trained bands were kept together in separate companies at the successive shire musters: so that for the first time there was a thread of continuity in the county forces. It was very slender, of course; and it was weakened as men moved about the county and became liable for service in a different place; but at least some faint semblance of permanence was brought into the militia.

The government, however, never contemplated setting up a permanent force. There was too much to be said against it. It would have been costly, and it would have meant a constant threat to the regime, or at least so the Council imagined. Moreover, they were forced to live from hand to mouth in the military sphere in the last twenty years of the reign. A standing army, could have been created in this period only at the expense of interrupting other military activity for perhaps two or three years; and this interruption could not be afforded.

Of the achievements of Elizabeth's army in the field there is little to be said. Her troops were involved only in one great engagement—the battle of Nieuport—where they acquitted themselves well in an auxiliary role. For the rest, it was a matter of laying siege, or defending a town, of marching and skirmishing, with hardly ever an encounter that merited the name of battle. The three combined operations—the Portugal expedition in 1589, and those to Cadiz in 1596 and the Azores in 1597—were the most spectacular enterprises of the reign; and they are, of course, reminders that England's defences were based on the power of the navy rather than the army.

It is difficult to give a simple verdict on the rank and file. While the great majority were unwilling conscripts, who made the worst possible fighting material, there was always a minority of a better type—young gentlemen, yeomen, yeomen's sons, and craftsmen, who in the opinion of Sir John Smythe went willingly, nay eagerly to the wars, and were the force and flower of the kingdom. The Earl of Essex, on the other hand, provides a devastating comment on the private soldier. He accepts that men of judgement and those that have a sense of honour (i.e. the officer class) will gladly give their lives in the defence of their country—that is sweeter to them than conquest abroad. It is without question, however, that the common and baser sort are incapable of the noble considerations that incite and inflame courage. They are artificers and clowns who apprehend almost nothing but what they see before them.[1] This is much too sweeping. At the siege of Leith it was the men who covered themselves with glory in an assault that had been bungled by the higher command—Essex's men of judgement—and there are other cases where the despised privates distinguished themselves.

[1] B.M. Loan 23, f. 161.

CONCLUSION

But it must be admitted that these are isolated examples. However much the government might preach that its wars were 'just, honourable and defensive' it never really succeeded in convincing the rank and file that by helping the state they were also helping themselves—any more than it convinced those who were taxed to provide ever-increasing quantities of uniform, equipment, and munitions that their money was well spent.

Any doubt on this point must surely be dispelled by the inquest ordered by the Privy Council into the 'abuses committed by captains and officers' in the army assembled to face the Spanish invasion attempt of 1588. It might be supposed that at this one moment of supreme military crisis, when the liberty of every Englishman was at risk, none would imperil the national cause by seeking to line his own pocket, or to save his own skin. But no. Soldiers deserted, often taking arms and equipment with them. Captains released men for a few shillings a head; and they cheated out of their pay those who remained with the colours.[1]

Had a major campaign been fought within England the picture might have been different. The deceits and stratagems practised at all levels in military organization might have been swept away; and the manifest need to fight for survival might have created an efficient and honest army. But as it turned out, no Englishman was ever required to give his life 'for his sacred sovereign and dear country' on an English beach. Elizabeth's army was not to be tempered in the fires of total invasion. The opportunity of a finest hour never came.

The Crown may have overstepped its rights in its handling of conscription; but the citizen got his own back with something to spare through his profoundly uncooperative attitude to military service, if he were a private, and his merciless exploitation of the Exchequer if he were an officer. He emerged a clear winner in his contest with the Crown; and his victory—more sweeping than any on the field of battle—sadly tarnishes the glorious golden image of the Elizabethan age.

[1] *H.M.C. Foljambe*, 61.

APPENDIXES

No. 1. *Levies in England and Wales for Service Abroad, 1585–1602*[1]

Year	Total	Destination
1585	7,500	Netherlands
1586	4,870	Netherlands
1587	4,800	Netherlands
1588	6,000	Portugal
1589	4,850	France
1590	4,250	Ireland
1591	8,425	France and Netherlands
1592	2,490	France
1593	3,025	France
1594	4,800	France and Netherlands
1595	1,806	Ireland
1596	8,940	Cadiz and Ireland
1597	8,835	Ireland and Azores
1598	9,164	Ireland and Netherlands
1599	5,250	Ireland
1600	4,885	Ireland
1601	12,620	Ireland
1602	3,300	Netherlands

No. 2. *Origin and Destination of Troops levied in the Welsh Counties between 1585 and 1602*[2]

County	Ireland	France	Netherlands	Total
Anglesey	251	..	..	251
Brecknock	825	..	30	855
Cardigan	500	..	30	530
Carmarthen	960	..	30	990
Carnarvon	566	..	..	566
Denbigh	980	75	..	1,055
Flint	765	75	..	840
Glamorgan	970	..	30	1,000
Merioneth	450	..	..	450
Monmouth	901	..	30	931
Montgomery	621	75	..	696
Pembroke	610	..	30	640
Radnor	530	75	..	605

[1] Only the principal destination of the troops is shown in this table, but in most years considerable numbers went to reinforce the English armies in the other theatres of war. There are no satisfactory figures for 1603.

[2] The figures for the Netherlands in this table are derived from an order in the state papers for 'two hundred men from the six south shires of Wales' (S.P. Dom. Eliz. 181, no. 3). There is no record of the numbers levied from the individual shires, and the total has therefore been equally divided between the counties.

No. 3. *Origin and Destination of Troops levied in English Counties between 1585 and 1602*

County	Ireland	France	Netherlands	Total
Bedford	419	250	600	1,269
Berks.	469	480	675	1,624
Bucks.	636	380	675	1,691
Cambridge	572	150	450	1,172
Cheshire	902	..	150	1,052
Cornwall	595	350	..	945
Cumberland	..	..	..	..
Derby	773	..	75	848
Devon	1,490	750	150	2,390
Dorset	470	600	260	1,330
Durham	..	..	..	..
Essex	1,199	800	1,100	3,099
Gloucester	1,692	500	400	2,592
Hampshire	641	1,400	525	2,566
Hereford	1,110	..	300	1,410
Hertford	539	600	675	1,814
Huntingdon	398	150	50	598
Kent	750	2,250	1,600	4,600
Lancashire	1,346	..	300	1,646
Leicester	547	150	..	697
Lincoln	1,345	300	300	1,945
London	1,600	4,420	3,495	9,515
Middlesex	195	250	600	1,045
Norfolk	900	450	600	1,950
Northampton	1,059	450	600	2,109
Northumberland	..	..	..	..
Nottingham	737	150	..	887
Oxford	544	440	650	1,634
Rutland	220	50	..	270
Shropshire	871	138	..	1,009
Somerset	1,194	1,200	460	2,854
Stafford	648	..	75	723
Suffolk	1,100	450	700	2,250
Surrey	85	200	550	835
Sussex	500	2,060	550	3,110
Warwick	761	150	475	1,386
Westmorland	..	..	..	..
Wiltshire	795	350	560	1,705
Worcester	1,151	..	..	1,151
Yorkshire	1,810	400	400	2,610

No. 4. *Indenture for Troops*[1]

THIS Indenture Tripertite made the Fift day of August in the Three and Fortieth yere of the Raigne of our Souereigne Ladie Elizabeth by the grace of god Queene of Englande Fraunce and Irelande

[1] Exchequer Accounts, Q.R., bundle 65, no. 5 (2).

defendour of the faythe etc. Betwene Sir Thomas Lucy knight high Sheriff of the Countye of Warwick Sir Thomas Leigh and Sir Edwarde Greuill knightes and Richard Darney Esquier Commissioners with others for musters in the saide countye of Warwick of thone partie And Tymothie Fieldinge gent. of thother partie. Witnesseth that the said Commissioners by vertue of letters to them and others directed, Aswell from our said souereigne Ladye the Queenes Matie as also from the Lordes of her highnes most honorable Privie Counsell have according to the tenor of the same leavyed and mustered out of the said out of the said [sic] Countye Fiftie able men to supplie her Maties forces in Irelande and also have leavied the some of Three pounds and ten shillinges for every man. Whose names and surnames with the places of their habitacions are in these present Indentures mencioned and expressed which men the said Commissioners delivered at Stratford uppon Avon in the said countye the day of the date hereof to the charge of the said Tymothie Fieldinge to conduct them to the Port of Bristoll. And there to deliver them over to such captaines as shall be sent thither by her Maties privic Counsell to receave them by Roll Indented subscribed by him the said conductor And which said money is levied and sent up to her Maties Exchequer according to the tenor of her Maties and their Lordships said letters.

> Knighlowe hundred
> Richard Burdett of Bulkenton, and 13 others.
>
> Barlichway hundred
> Michael Piggot of Rolaington, and 10 others.
>
> Hemlingeforde hundred
> Richard Pope of Chastocke, and 13 others.
>
> Kynton hundred
> William Poole of Tanworthe, and 10 others.

In Witnes whereof to the first part these Indentures remayninge with the said Commissioners the said Tymothie Fieldinge hath putte his hande, and to the seconde part remayning with the said Tymothie the said Commissioners have put their handes, And to the third part to be sent to the Privie Counsell the said Commissioners have lykewise putte their handes the day and yere above written.

THO. LUCY   EDW. GREUILL

No. 5. *Prayer for the Troops*

A PRAYER for the good successe of her Maiesties forces in Ireland.

Almightie God and most mercifull Father, which by thine holy Worde declarest thy selfe to be the first ordeiner and continuall upholder of all Princely power and right, and by thy terrible iudgements against Core, Dathan, and Abiram, in opening the earth to swallow up them and theirs, And which like vengeance poured upon Absalom, Achitophel, Adoniah and Sheba, diddest manifest to the whole world, how much thou hatest all resistance and rebellion against thy Diuine ordinance: Vouchsafe (we humbly beseech thee) to strengthen and protect the Forces of thine anointed our Queen and souereigne, sent out to suppresse these wicked and unnaturall Rebels. Be thou to our Armies a Captaine, Leader, and Defender. Let thine holy Angels pitch their Tents round about to guard them, and give them victorie against all such as rise up to withstand them. Let not our sinnes (O Lord) be an hindrance to thine accustomed mercies towards us, neither punish our misdeeds by strengthening the hands of such as despise thy Trueth, and have wickedly cast off the rightfull yoke of their due allegiance: That so thy blessed Handmayde our dread Souereigne, may always reioyce in thy Salvation, And we her loyall subiects still haue cause to magnify thy glorious Name, and to offer to thee with ioy the sacrifices of praise and thankes-giuing in the middest of the great Congregation. Grant this (O most righteous Lord God of Hosts) we beseech thee through Jesus Christ our only Sauiour and Redeemer. Amen.

> Imprinted at London by the Deputies of Christopher Barker, Printer to the Queenes most excellent Maiestie.
> Anno 1599

No. 6. *Soldiers' Oath*[1]

The oathe to be ministered unto the souldiers upon their enteringe into Paye.

Wee doe sweare and promise to doe all loyall true and faythefull sarvice unto the Queene of Englande her most Excell. majesty: and unto the provinces and citties united in theis countries and their associates, under the charge and obedience of the Right exelent the Earle of Leicester Governor generall of the said provinces and citties and their associates, and of her majesties Army and forces within the same: And all lawfull and due obedience unto the Governor and to any other superior that shall have charge under him for the governement in this Army: And further we do endevore our selves to keep and fulfill all such lawfull ordinances as his Exelencie hath or shall set forth and establish for the better orderinge of this Army as much as concerns us, so long as we shall serve under him, so help us God by Jhesus Christe.

[1] Harl. MSS. 168, f. 109b. Cf. S.P. Holland, Eliz. 18, f. 105.

No. 7. *An Admonition before the Musters*[1]

SOULDIERS and brethren, as by longe experience we haue fonde the greuious inconueniences whiche are chansed by reason of the fraudes, and abuses in the musters, and that thereby townes, and places of great importance are loste, the meanes and reuenewes of the Countrije unprofitably spent, being the principall cause that the poore and vaillant soldiers, to the great greife of his Excell^{cie} very ill payd whiche might be remidied, by remouing the saide abuses: I praye you and by vertue of the charge I haue, I doe ordeyne you generally and perticulerly uppon the othe, which you haue taken to his Excell^{cie}, and the Countrie to declare freely if ther be among you any passevolant, borrowed soldiers, Burgers, victuallers, freebutters or others not beinge in standinge seruice under your Companije, and that dothe not orderly keepe, watche, and warde and every waye goinge withe you to the warres, for suche be unworthie to be accounted amongst valiant soldiars and stand you in no steede, then[2] to charge you with more trauayles watche ward and centinels, and for one howre and make you stande twoe. Also doe cause you to loose your honor if necessitie cause you to meete the enemye, when as for the smal nomber whiche is in your Companie, you are forced to tourne your backes to the Enemye, or geue place, wheras if your companie weare stronge and compleat of good and valiant souldiars, you should be often able to beate and defeate them, to your great honor and aduancinge: and especially to the honor of God and prosperity of your countrie, so many yeares alreadie afflicted. Wherfore I pray you once againe to reveale them to the end dewe punishment may be done. I doe also commande all them that are not in standinge seruice bound to this company, that they depart this muster uppon payne that being knowne to be hanged as Villaynes without grace or fauour.

No. 8. *Oath for Musters*[3]

AN Oth before the muster particuler.[4]

We sweare and promisse that all the persounes and names which we present in the rolle by us deliuered, be soldiars in standinge and actuall seruice of our companye, watching and wardinge euery one in his degree. And that they are bounde to followe the company

---

[1] S.P. Holland, Eliz. 18, ff. 144–144b.   [2] 'but', marginal note.
[3] S.P. Holland, Eliz. 18, f. 144b. The oath was taken by the captain, lieutenant, and clerk of the company.
[4] Marginal note.

APPENDIXES 295

every wheare, and there whether the same maye be sente. Also that we have not borrowed nor taken any soldiers in seruice, or sett them in the rolle but those whiche haue had absolute and dewe pasport of ther Captaines or otherwise haue bin free. And finallie that in no sorte, directly or indirectlie, we pretend by this muster to defraude his Excel. the country, or any other body.

No. 9. *Examples for Musters Certificates*[1]

PRECEDENTS of Billetts for receaving and discharginge of souldiers to be delivered by the Commissioners of Musters resident, unto the Captaines.

To Captaine: A:B: on of the Captaines in her majesties paye now resident in the garrison of C:

Theis shall testifie that D.E. hath taken his oath and is this present xth day of August anno RR Elizab: xxix° admitted and entered into your bande, wittnes my hand.

These shall testifie that D.E. your souldier beinge orderlie discharged this xth of September accordinge entred in my Muster Bookes, witnes my hand.

Theis shall testifie that D.E. your souldier beinge dead or ronne away without licence the xth September as hath been orderlie approved, is accordinglie entered in my Muster Bookes, witnes my hand.

Theis shall testifie that D.E. having pasporte beringe date the xth of September to returne before the xxth of October next ensuinge is accordinglie entered in my Muster Rolles witnes my hand.

Theis shall testifie that I have receaved from the commissarye resident of the garrison of Flushinge the Muster Rolle of Captain G. whose Bande is entered into this Garrison of H. this present 12th day of February, witnes my hand.

No. 10. *Warrant for Payment*[2]

SIR PH. SYDNEY, knight.

Theis are to require you to paie unto Sir Phillip Sidney knight captaine of a cornet of c. launces for his owne enterteignment at viii^s per diem, his Lieutenant at iiij^s per diem, his Guydon at ij^s per diem, one Trumpet, one Clarcke and one Surgeon at xx^d per diem le peece, fourscore ten launces, and ten dead paies at xviij^d per diem

---

[1] Harl. MSS. 168, f. 109. Cf. S.P. Holland, Eliz. 18, f. 104b.
[2] Add. MSS. 5753, f. 277.

le peece for iij^{c}xxxiiij daies, beginning the xijth day of November, 1585, and ending the xjth day of October last past the some of two thowsande eight hundred twentie twoe pounds six shillings sterling. Provided allwaies that yow doe not only defaulk the some of Thirteene shillinges and foure pens sterlinge checked within the said tyme, but allso all former Imprests to him delivered and all victualls and munition, together with all other deductions defaulcable upon this Account by certificate from the ministers thereof approved by the captaines hand. And theis together with his Acquittance confessing the receipt of the same shalbe your sufficient warrant in that behalf. Geven at Gravenhage the viijth day of November Anno Reginae Elizabeth xxviij°

R. LEYCESTER.

To Richard Huddilston esquier, her majesties Threasurer at Warres.
Ex. Tho. Digges.

ij^{m}viij^{c}xxij^{li} sixe shillings.¹

Ex p. Edmond Hunte.

No. 11. *Receipt for Payment*²

RECEYVED by me Captayne Edwarde Cromwell at the hands of the ryght worshipfful Rycharde Hudleston esquyre treasurer at wares for her majesty in the Lowe Countryes the some of thirtye and eyght pownds ster. monye to be deffaulked owt of the first paye or impreste made to me and the companye under my leadynge wyttnes whereof I have subscrybed this quyttance with my owne hand. Datted the 8 daye of September anno dom. 1586. ED. CROMWELL.

No. 12. *Leicester's Disciplinary Code*³

LAWES and Ordinances set downe by Robert Earle of Leycester, the Queenes Maiesties Lieutenant and Captaine Generall of her Armie and Forces in the lowe Countries: meete and fitte to be obserued by all such as shall serue her Maiestie vnder him in the said Countries, and therefore to be published and notified to the whole Armie.

Forasmuch as there is not any gouerned Estate, which in peace or warre can be accounted sure, or preserued from dishonour and ruine, vnlesse it be supported and borne up by Justice duely administred, and discipline orderly obserued: And for that no man can

---

¹ Marginal note. ² Add. MSS. 5753, f. 252.
³ From the printed copy in the Bodleian Library. This code also appears in Add. MSS. 30170, f. 35, and 38139, f. 16b.

be so ignorant as not to knowe that honor, fame and prosperitie, doe duely followe that common Wealth or Nation, wherein good lawes are established, the Magistrate ministring Justice is duely regarded, and the people fearing to offend, are drawen under the rules of Justice and obedience: And seeing that martiall discipline aboue all thinges (proper to men of warre) is by us at this time most to be followed, aswell for the aduancement of Gods glorie, as honourablie to gouerne this Armie in good order: And least that the euill inclined (pleading simplicitie) shoulde couer any wicked facte by ignorance: Therefore these martiall Ordinances and Lawes following are established and published whereby all good mindes endeuouring to attaine honour, may stand armed, and receiue encouragement to perseuere in well doing, and such as are inclined to lewdnesse, be warned from committing offences punishable. Which being embraced with carefull respect, and followed with obedience, doe promise good order and agreement amongst our selues, with victorie and good euents against our enemies.

1. First, euery chiefe Magistrate, Captaine, inferiour Officer, Souldiour, Pioner, or what person els receiuing her Maiesties paye in Fielde or Garison, shall solemnely sweare, and by corporall othe be bounde to perfourme the under written Articles, so farre as to eache in their seuerall qualities shall appertaine: the violating or breaking whereof, is to be punished by the Generalles direction, according to the quality of the offence.

2. Forsomuch as the holy Name of our most mightie and inuincible GOD, with all reuerence ought to be regarded, and that destruction is pronounced to such as blaspheme or abuse the same: it is therefore ordeined and commanded that no person whatsoeuer, either in common conference or communication, or for any cause whatsoeuer, shall blaspheme being thus admonished, or take his Name in vaine, upon pain of losse of v. s. to the releife of the poore for the first offence: for the seconde, fiue dayes imprisonment: for the third losse of his place and wages.

3. And because the continuall and unspeakeable fauours of our Almightie God, by our unthankfulnesse may be taken from us, and that no good euent of any action can be expected, wherein God is not first principally honoured and serued: It is therefore especially ordeyned and commanded, that all persons whatsoeuer, shall upon generall warning giuen either by sound of Trumpet or Drum, repaire to the place appointed, where the Diuine seruice is to be used, there to heare the same read and preached, unlesse for the present by sicknesse or other seruice he be impeached upon paine to lose his dayes wages for the first, two dayes wages for the second, and so to be encreased by the discretion of the Judge, and for euery such

default in the Souldier, aswell the Captaine as his inferiour officers, to be punished with like penaltie.

4. And seeing it well beseemeth all Christians, especially such as professe the militarie seruice, to passe away the time in matters requisite for their profession: And because no time can be more vainely spent, then that which is consumed in unlawfull games, besides the breeding of much contention, and quarrelles: And for that there be many allowable and commendable exercises for all sortes of men to use: Therefore it is streightly commanded, that no priuate Souldiour or inferiour Officer shall frequent the playing at Dice and Cardes, nor any other unlawfull games, upon pain of two dayes imprisonment for the first time, and for after committing the like, to be further punished by the Judges discretion.

5. And for that it often happeneth, that by permitting of many vagrant idle women in an armie, sundry disorders and horrible abuses are committed: Therefore it is ordeined that no man shall carrie into the fielde, or deteine with him in the place of his garrison, any woman whatsoeuer, other than such as be knowen to be his lawful wife, or such other women to tende the sicke and to serue for launders, as shall be thought meete by the Marshall, upon paine of whipping and banishment.

6. And insomuch as clemencie amongst men of warre in some respects is a singuler vertue: It is ordeined that no man in any part of this seruice that he shall doe, shal lay violent handes upon any woman with childe, or lying in childebed, olde persons, widowes, yong virgins, or babes, without especial order from the Magistrate, upon pain of death.

7. What person soeuer that shall be commonly giuen to drunkennesse or riotously behaue himselfe, shall be banished the Armie.

8. Whosoeuer shall conceale, or in any sort keepe secrete Treason, any dangerous Conspiracie, or other practice which may be hurtfull, and may concerne the perill of her Maiesties person, or of her General, or the estate of the Armie, and shall not with all diligence reueale the same either unto the Generall, or some other Officer of especiall trust, shall incurre the paines of death with torments.

9. No man shall haue speeche or conference, send message, deliuer or receiue letters to or from the enemie, or any of his confederates, either secretly or openly, without manifesting the same presently unto the Generall or Marshall, or having former authoritie so to doe upon paine of death.

10. No man being in this seruice shal depart ye Campe or place of Garrison for any cause whatsoeuer, without the Generals especial Pasport, or other head Officer authorized, upon pain of death.

11. No man shall breake out or leaue the order of his **ranke**,

being once ordered in the fielde by the Marshall or Sergeant Maior, without some great occasion first made knowen unto the saide Officer, upon paine of losse either of life or limme, at the discretion of the Generall or of the Marshall.

12. No man appointed to watch or warde, shall shun or depart the place, neither shall sleepe, or neglect his duetie therein especially after the watch is set and the woorde giuen, unless he is orderly relieued, or for some great occasion enforced, with licence of his Captaine or Officer, upon paine of death.

13. No man shal bewray the watchworde to the enemie or to any other, or giue any other woorde than is deliuered by the Officer, upon paine of death with torment.

14. No man shal raise any mutinie, or procure unlawfull assemblies upon priuate, secrete, or hidden purpose, whereby to disturbe the peace and quiet of the Armie, upon paine of death.

15. No man shall lift up his weapon against the Magistrate his Captain or Officer, upon paine of death.

16. No man shall quarell, brawle, or make any affray within the Campe or Toune of garrison, upon olde malice, or newe occasion whatsoeuer, but shall complaine to the Officer, who is to decide the cause and punish the partie offending, upon paine of losse of life or limme, at the discretion of the Generall or Marshall.

17. And whereas sundrie nations are to serue with us in these warres, so as through diuersitie of languages occasion of many controuersies may arise or happen to growe: It is therefore ordeined, that if any person of English nation shall finde him selfe agriued with any wrong profered him by any foreiner, that then without profering further reuenge he shall signifie the same unto his Captaine or other officer, whereby order may be taken so, as no further quarrell growe thereof, but that quietnesse in all respects may be preserued, upon pain of such punishment as the head officers shall thinke meete, either by losse of life or limme.

18. No man appointed to the defence of any Breach, Trench, or Streight, either Captaine or Souldiour, shall willingly leaue it, or upon any false or imagined cause or excuse, shall absent himselfe from the place, without sufficient warrant, upon paine of death.

19. No Captaine, officer, or other person, shall receiue or entertaine any other mans Souldiour or seruant, without consent of his former Captaine or Master, neither shall entice another mans Souldiour from him, upon paine of losse of a Monethes wages, and to restore the partie to his former Captaine or Master.

20. No man shall enrolle his name under two Captaines, nor muster in seuerall companies at one time, or otherwise pass in another mans name, or lende Armour, weapon, or other furniture

upon the muster day, whereby to abuse her Maiestie, and weaken the present seruice, upon paine of a moneths imprisonment, and banishment.

21. No man shall embezill or diminish any of his Armour, weapon and furniture, which is appointed him by his Captaine, unlesse he can prooue that he lost the same in seruice: And that no man shall take in pawne any Souldiours weapon or furniture, upon paine to the Souldiour of loss of his place, and to the other that shall take it in pawne, the losse of the double value.

22. No man shall play away, engage, or lende away his furniture, but shall alwayes keepe his Armour and weapon cleane and seruiceable, upon paine of being discharged.

23. No man shall deceitfully take away his companions prouision, victuals, or furniture, upon paine of imprisonment.

24. No person traueyling, lodging, or abiding in any the Tounes or Countires of her Maiesties friendes or Allies, shall in any wise exact or take by force from the people either victuall or other goods whatsoeuer, without present payment, or other sufficient order to the iust satisfaction of the partie, upon paine of death.

25. No man shall forestall any victuals brought for the Campe or place of garrison, but suffer the same peacefully to come into the Market place, there to be rated and priced by the Marshall or his officer, before he buy the same, upon paine of death.

26. No man shall robbe or spoyle any Shop or Tent, or any victualler or Marchant comming for the relief of the Campe or garison, but in all good sort shall entertaine and defend them, upon paine of death.

27. No Souldiour commanded at any time to take victuals for certaine dayes, shall exceede the same dayes, or spend the same otherwise then according to the proportion and time allowed him, upon paine of imprisonment or other such punishment as the lawfull officers shall appoint.

28. No man shall distress or spoyle any person standing on her Maiesties partie, or being under the Generals protection, upon paine of death.

29. No man shall disobey or transgresse any Proclamation made by Drumme or Trumpet, set foorth by the generall, upon such paine as he shall set foorth.

30. No man shall resist the Prouost or his other officer in apprehending of any malefactour, but if need require, shall ayde and assist him therein, or otherwise if by such occasion any escape be made it is ordeined that euery person by whose defaulte the escape was committed, shall suffer like punishment that the parties so escaped shoulde have endured.

31. No man shall molest or trouble any person beeing under his owne regiment, or the leading of any other, once placed by the Marshall forrier, or Harbinger in the Campe or Toune, but quietly to permit and suffer euery one to enioye his seueral roume or lodging, unless it be by mutuall consent and agreement, neither shall any man lodge out of his Captaines quarter without licence, upon paine of imprisonment.

32. No man contrarie to order shal set on fire or burne any house, milne, or corne, nor at dislodging or remoouing shall set the Campe on fire, without speciall commaundement from the Generall or other head Officer present, upon paine of death.

33. No man without great occasion shall make Alarme, but if any chaunce to arise, then shall euery man presently repaire in all haste unto his appointed place, unless some true excusable cause do hinder him, upon paine of death.

34. No man shall harbour or receaue into his lodging any person being a stranger, or of our owne nation not being enrolled in her Maiesties paye, but shall presently acquaint the Generall or Marshall with his name, countrey, the time of his coming, and business, upon paine of imprisonment, and losse of his place and wages.

35. No man shall talke or haue conuersation with any Trumpeter or Drummer of the enemies, or other sent in message, but such as be appointed by the Generall, upon paine of death.

36. No man shall attende upon the cariages, but such as are appointed to that charge, neither linger, or loyter behind with them to ride or ease themselues, unlesse it be such as by sicknesse, hurtes, or other infirmities knowen to the officers, to be permitted so, upon paine of imprisonment and loss of wages.

37. No man shall attempt to goe a foraging, without the officer appointed for that purpose deliuer them a sufficient guarde for their defence, upon paine of death.

38. No Captaine shall sende foorth any men to doe any enterprise, without knowledge of the Generall, or chiefe officer appointed hereunto, upon paine of losse of his place.

39. All priuate Captaines, being no head Officers, shall watch and warde with their Ensignes, unlesse it be by speciall leaue, upon paine of the losse of a months paye, and for the second time, loss of his place.

40. Euery Souldiour shall present such prisoners as are taken, to their Captaine immediately at their return to the Campe, and none shall either kill them, or licence them to depart, without commaundement or leaue from the Generall, or other head Officer thereunto appointed, upon paine of being disarmed, and banished the Campe.

41. Euery Souldier at all times in seruice shalbe obedient and faithfull, aswell to their Captaines as other inferiour Officers, and not to refuse direction of any under whom they are appointed to serue, upon paine of imprisonment, and losse of a moneths wages.

42. Euery man shall support and defende his owne Ensigne both night and day, and shall resort unto the same upon the first warning, and not depart untill it be brought into safetie, upon paine of death.

43. Euery souldier shal diligently obserue and learne the sound of Drums, Fifes, and Trumpets, to the end he may know how to answere the same in his seruice.

44. No man shall slaughter or kill any beast of what nature soeuer within the Campe or Garrison, but in such places as are appointed for that purpose, nor shall suffer the garbage to remain unburied, neither shall any man trouble or defile the waters adioyning, but in the lower part of the streame some good distance from the Camp, upon payne of imprisonment.

45. No man shall ease himselfe or defile the Campe or Toune of Garrison, save in such places as is appointed for that purpose, upon paine of imprisonment, and such further punishment, as shall be thought meete by the chiefe Officers.

46. No Captaine shall sell or raunsome his prisoner without license of the Generall, and shall not suffer them to depart without making the high Marshall priuie to the same, upon paine of losse of his prisoner, and imprisonment.

47. If any man doe take a prisoner or hostie, he shall immediately after hee is returned unto the Campe or Toune of Garrison, make his Captaine or Gouernour acquainted therewith, and the Captaine shall declare the same unto the Marshall, who euery eight dayes shall make certificate thereof unto the Generall, upon paine of imprisonment, and further punishment as the Generall shall set doune.

48. In Marching by the fieldes, no man at the putting up of any Hare, or other beast shal make any shout or crie, whereby to disquiet or stay the rest of the bands, but to use all quietnesse and silence in their march, upon paine of imprisonment.

49. No man shall giue up or deliuer unto the enemies any place left to his charge or keeping, upon paine of death.

50. If any man flie to the enemies, or be taken upon his departure towards them, he shall suffer death.

51. Any Captaine finding any Souldiour of what band or company so euer, which hath transgressed any of these Lawes and Ordinances, may take him and bring him unto the Marshall to be punished.

52. That who soeuer shall be enrolled into paye after the othe be ministred to others and he not present, and if afterwards he shall

transgresse any of these Ordinances, he shall be as well punishable by vertue of these Articles, as if he had bene present at the first.

53. That no Captaine shall receiue or enroll any person into his paye under him, but that he cause the sayde Souldier to receiue the othe, as is set doune in the first Article, upon paine to the Captaine for not obseruing the same, of losse of a months paye.

54. That no person whatsoeuer shal passe by any other way either in Toune or Campe, but at the ordinarie gates and passages, upon paine of death.

55. All other offences and Actes that may tende to disorder not comprised within these articles, shalbe subiect to such manner of punishment, as the Lieutenant Generall shall inflict upon them, as if it had been specially expressed and set doune.

INDEX

Absence without leave, 145, 167.
Agincourt, battle of (1415), 102.
Alençon, town of, 247, 248.
Alexander, 225.
Anglesey, levies in, 92, 290.
Aniseed, 90.
Antonio, Don, of Portugal, 15.
Aquavitae, 90.
Archers, 91, 103, 108;
    at siege of Leith, 113-14;
    equipment of, 116-17;
    no longer trained men, 114.
Archery, 102-5.
Ark Royal, 261.
Armada, Spanish, 14, 15, 16, 31, 32, 70, 71, 82, 127, 243, 252.
Armour, 9 n., 17, 65, 118, 162;
    illegal sale of, 125, 163;
    proving of, 121;
    standard patterns proposed, 120, 242.
Armourer, 49, 125, 176.
Armoury Office, 119, 120.
Arms, 7, 8, 20, 58;
    illegal sale of, 126;
    issue of, 237;
    provision of, 124-5, 211, 244;
    replacement of, 126, 244;
    storage of, 110-12.
Army:
    English:
        case for standing army, 1, 285-8;
        constitutional position of, 1-5, 9-13;
        cost of, 283-4;
        feudal, 1-5, 12, 19, 50;
        foreign service, 2;
        specialization in, 287.
    French, 1, 207;
    German, 1;
    Spanish, 1, 14, 15, 92, 95, 159, 193;
    Swiss, 1.
Arquebus, 9 n., 17, 107, 109-10, 111.
Arrow, 2, 17, 107, 111, 116, 201, 232.
Arrowhead makers, 103, 105.
Artillery, 49, 125, 196, 210;
    export of, 119;
    supply of, 121;
    types, 122;
    use of, 122-3, 224, 225-6.
Artillery Garden, 121.
Arundel, 239.
Ascham, Roger, 105.
Ashley, Sir Anthony, 277.

Auditor, 136, 144, 147, 157;
    duties of, 146.
Azores, 16, 46, 288;
    levies for, 290.

Babington, Uriah, 96, 99, 101.
Bacon, 88, 89.
Bacon, Sir Francis, 73-74.
Baeshe, Edward, 77.
Baldric, 175.
Ballyshannon, 89, 179.
Bandolier, 121, 125.
Bann, river, 89.
Barber-Surgeons, Company of, 174-6.
Barnstaple, 64, 69.
Barret, Robert, 21, 41, 53, 106, 118, 197-8.
Barwick, Humphrey, 113-14, 117, 224, 231.
Bastard musket, 125.
Battle formations, 50, 53, 196, 257.
Beacons, 70-71, 202.
Beans, 82, 88.
Bedfordshire, levies in, 291.
Beecher, William, 97.
Beef, 78, 82, 87, 88, 239.
Beer, 78, 82, 84, 86, 88, 90, 170, 242.
Belt, 116.
Bergen-op-Zoom, 155.
Berkshire, 71;
    levies in 291.
Berwick, 1, 75, 92, 128, 154, 159, 160, 207, 209, 210, 212, 215, 217, 227, 231, 232, 234;
    governor of, 43;
    maintenance costs of, 283.
Bill, 17, 29, 114, 195;
    cost of, 115.
Billets, 135, 163, 170.
Bills, army:
    'training in use of hand-guns' (1571), 9 n.;
    'making, proving and marking of calivers' (1572), 9 n;
    'furniture of armour and weapon' (1580), 9 n.;
    'captains and soldiers' (1588), 6-9;
    'horse, armour, and weapon' (1588), 6-7, 9;
    'reform of abuses by soldiers and others' (1597), 9 n.;
    'for increase of people' (1597), 6-9.

Bills (*cont.*)
'musters, soldiers, and other things' (1601), 7–9.
Biscuit, 88, 242.
Blandy, William, 41.
Blasphemy, 161, 163.
Bodley, Sir Thomas, 74.
Bolton, John, 97.
Bolton, Thomas, 97.
Bowstaves, 103, 104, 107, 119.
Bowstrings, 107, 111.
Bowyers, 103–5, 121;
unemployment among, 104.
Bracer, 116.
Bread, 76, 82, 83, 88, 89, 183, 234, 239, 242.
Breaking rank, 161, 164.
Brecknockshire, levies in, 290.
Breeches, 92.
Brill, 151.
Bristol, 62, 66, 69, 83, 101, 125;
commissioners of musters in, 165;
mayor of, 68, 70, 83, 87–88, 101, 165;
mutiny at, 168.
British Museum, 276.
Brittany, 15, 66, 96, 148, 254.
Brogues, 94, 95.
Bromley, Robert, 96, 99, 101.
Buckhurst (Thomas Sackville), Lord, 89, 93, 112, 126, 152, 238;
instructions to, 45;
issues free gunpowder, 129;
on dead-pay system, 156;
recommends hospitals in Ireland, 181.
levies regiment for France, 238–42;
Buckinghamshire:
commissioners of musters in, 114;
hospital in, 182;
levies in, 62, 291.
Bullets, 58, 106, 111, 121, 145.
Burgh, Sir John, 240, 241, 244, 250.
Burgh, Thomas, Lord, 47, 94, 167, 206.
Burghley (Sir William Cecil), Lord, 47, 115, 119, 120, 139, 141, 183, 240, 242, 254;
proclaimed traitor by Smythe, 10;
organizes shire muster, 112;
and siege of Leith, 209–25 *passim*.
negotiates with French, 232;
relations with local authorities, 238;
justifies attack on Spain (1596), 258.
Burgonet, 117, 241.
Butter, 79–88 *passim*, 239.
Byrde, John, 100.

Cadiz, 15, 32, 53, 203, 205, 252–79 *passim*, 288.
Caen, 151, 247, 250.
Calais, 13, 14, 80, 255, 256;
siege of (1346), 174.

Caliver, 9 n., 49, 108–10, 111, 114, 121, 124, 125, 244.
Caliverman, equipment of, 117.
Camarada, 142, 194.
Cambridgeshire, levies in, 166, 291.
Camp, 47, 48, 49, 50, 132, 162, 196, 245, 273.
Cannon, 122, 247, 249.
Cannoneer, 49, 57, 58, 59, 175, 184.
Canterbury, 32;
Archbishop of (John Whitgift), 59, 92;
levies cavalry, 31–32, 71–73;
prayer for troops, 32.
Canvas, 121.
Cap, 92, 119.
Cape St. Vincent, 260, 261, 264.
Captain Pill and Captain Skill, 29–30.
Captains, 22, 162;
administer oath, 164;
appointment of, 21, 45, 56–57, 244;
Barret on, 21;
distribute uniform, 101;
duties of, 54;
issue pay, 143;
malpractice of, 29, 52, 54–56, 66, 99, 100, 134, 136, 139–41, 145, 166, 237, 281, 289;
Rich on, 21;
Smythe on, 55.
Cardiganshire, levies in, 66, 290.
Carew, Sir George, 171–2, 262.
Carew, Sir Peter, 234.
Carey, Sir George, 99, 101, 148, 150, 151–2.
Carmarthenshire, levies in, 290.
Carnarvonshire, levies in, 290.
Carpenter, 49, 121.
Carriage-master, 49–50.
Carter, 121.
Carvell, Captain, 227.
Cassock, 92, 94, 95, 98, 118.
Catcher, Richard, 97.
Catcher, Thomas, 97.
Catholic league, 15.
Cavalry, 49–50, 61, 65, 253;
cost of, 30;
demilances, 118;
light horse, 118–19;
men-at-arms, 118;
provision of, 30–33.
Cecil, Sir Robert, 10, 32, 258;
on military pensions, 186–8.
Chain of command, 2.
Chain shot, 171.
Chandos (William Brydges), Lord, 92.
Charcoal, 127.
Charles I, 23.
Chatham, 123.
Cheapside, 168, 240.

INDEX

Cheese, 78, 83, 86–89 *passim*, 170, 183, 239.
Cheshire, levies in, 291.
Chester, 62, 64, 66, 68, 69, 83, 101, 124, 125, 140;
  mayor of, 68, 83.
Chichester, 239.
Chickens, 82.
Chivalry, 3, 200.
Christchurch (Dublin), dean of, 59.
Churchwarden, 185.
Cider, 76.
Cinque Ports, Warden of, 8, 20.
Ciphers, 73–74.
Clergy:
  criticized by Privy Council, 31;
  exempt from musters, 24;
  provide cavalry, 30–32, 71–73.
Clerk of company, 45, 136, 144, 243;
  corruption of, 142, 145, 166;
  duties of, 143, 144–5;
  pay of, 128;
  proposed change of status, 145.
Clerk of check, 144, 145.
Clifford, Sir Conyers, 256, 271, 272–3.
Climate, effect of on troops, 182–3, 249.
Clinton (Edward Fiennes de), Lord, 14.
Clowes, William, 177;
  on amputation, 177–8.
Coat, 92.
Coat money, *see* Uniform.
Cobham (William Brooke), Lord, 20, 112–13, 242.
Cod, 88, 89.
Code words, 74.
Colchester, 10.
Coldingham, 217.
Collar, 92.
Collector of Customs, 62.
Colonel, 51, 53, 243, 271.
Commands, *see* Orders.
Commission of array, 5, 23, 282.
Commissioners of grain, 81.
Commissioners of musters, *see* Musters.
Communications, 70–75, 225, 240, 244, 245, 262.
Commutation, 3.
Company, 54;
  composition of, 113–15, 244;
  size of, 54.
Concordatum fund, *see* Pay.
Conduct money, *see* Movement.
Conscription, *see* Recruitment.
Constable, 19, 26–27, 63, 132, 185;
  Rich on, 29–30.
Constable, Sir Robert, 199–200.
Conway, Sir John, 169, 170.
Cooke, Sir Edward, 257.
Cooking utensils, 89.
Cooper, 121.

Corbett, Sir Julian, 203–4, 268.
Cork, 83, 87;
  dean of, 89.
Corn, 78, 87.
Corned powder, *see* Gunpowder.
Cornwall, 62;
  levies in, 72, 291.
Corporal (company), 22, 57–58, 135–6, 155.
Corporal (of the field), 50–52, 217, 244.
Corrupt discharge, 17, 125.
Corselet, 113, 117, 119, 120, 125, 241.
Corunna, 15, 252, 276.
Cosbie, Captain, 241, 242, 246, 284.
Council in Ireland, 88, 100, 126, 167.
Council of the North, 14.
Council of war, 46, 50, 137, 215, 222–37 *passim*, 250, 260, 261, 264, 270;
  secretary of, 261, 277.
Court martial, 164.
Coventry and Lichfield, Bishop of, 30.
Cowardice, 57.
Crécy, battle of (1346), 2, 102, 107.
Crofts, Sir James, 207, 208, 210, 213, 218, 223, 227, 229, 236.
Cross-bow, 3.
Crowbar, 121.
Croydon, 71.
Cuirass, 118, 242.
Culverin, 122, 247.
Cumberland, levies in, 291.
Cutlers, 125.

Dagger, 116, 117, 160.
Darell, Marmaduke, 263.
Davies, Robert, 69.
Dead pay, *see* Pay.
Demi-cannon, 122.
Demi-culverin, 122.
Demilance, *see* Cavalry.
Demobilization, 36–40.
Denbighshire, levies in, 290.
Denmark, 94.
Denys, Sir Maurice, 152.
Deputy lieutenant, 112, 255.
Derbyshire, levies in, 62, 64, 291.
Derry, 206.
Desertion, 17, 36, 63, 67, 160, 165–7.
Desmond (Gerald Fitzgerald), Earl of, 16.
Devonshire, 62;
  levies in, 72, 291.
Dieppe, 77, 238, 245, 246.
Digges, James, 137, 138.
Digges, Leonard, 36, 41.
Digges, Thomas, 36, 41, 47, 93, 136–9, 146, 152, 195–7, 202.
Disabled soldiers, 37, 63, 183–8.
Discharged soldiers:
  Thomas Digges on, 36;

INDEX

Discharged soldiers (*cont.*)
  menace of, 38;
  re-employment of, 26, 36;
  Rich on, 39–40;
  Sutcliffe on, 36.
Disciplinary codes:
  1562 (France), 159–60;
  1570 (Scotland), 160;
  1585 (Low Countries), 161, 296–303;
  1589 (France), 163;
  1591 (France), 163–4;
  1600 (Ireland), 163–4, 165, 192–3.
Discipline, 159–73.
Dispatch riders, 47, 71, 73, 74, 75, 151.
Docwra, Sir Henry, 182, 206.
Dorsetshire, 21–22, 71, 74;
  levies in, 291.
Doublet, 92, 95, 116, 117.
Dover, 1, 238, 242, 255, 256.
Downs, 202.
D'Oysel, Henri, 218, 223.
Drake, Sir Francis, 15, 23, 176, 254.
Dreadnought, 261.
Drill, 34 58;
  books, 189;
  Edmondes on, 191–3;
  Smythe on, 189–91.
Drum, 11, 161, 170, 192, 193, 196, 262.
Drummer, 57, 58, 117, 171, 175, 176, 190.
Drunkenness, 160, 161, 164, 172.
Drury, Sir William, 160 244, 250, 257.
Dublin, 68, 69, 171, 180, 181.
Dublin castle, 171.
Due Repulse, 261, 263.
Dunbar, 217.
Dunglass, 217.
Durham, levies in, 291.
Dutch, 14, 35, 77, 138–9, 145, 236, 261, 270.
Dysentery, 94, 183.

Edinburgh, 210, 221, 224.
Edinburgh castle, 160, 218.
Edmondes, Sir Clement, 191.
Edward I, 23.
Edward III, 2, 4, 4 n., 5, 11, 174;
  military legislation of, 4–5.
Edward IV, 174.
Edward VI, 6, 17, 23, 77.
Eels, 89.
Eggs, 89.
English Channel, 70, 75, 203, 255.
Elizabeth I, 1, 2, 4, 13, 14, 15, 17, 23, 25, 27;
  encourages breeding of horses, 33;
  issues general's commission, 44;
  attitude to knighthood, 46–47;
  care for discharged soldiers, 188, 285;
  authorizes invasion of Scotland, 209–13;
  composes prayer for troops, 258;
  criticism of her military policy, 284.
Ensign, 57, 58, 164, 271.
Ensign-bearer, 57, 190.
Ensign-pole, 57.
Equipment, 7, 8, 58;
  design of, 120;
  statutory provision of, 17.
Erington, Nicholas, 68.
Escalade, 248.
Essex, 111, 112;
  levies in, 27, 291.
Essex (Robert Devereux), Earl of, 15, 16, 38, 47, 94, 115, 129;
  as commander-in-chief, 43, 46;
  on Cadiz expedition, 53, 252–79 *passim*;
  master of ordnance, 123;
  disciplinary code of, 163;
  failure in Ireland, 206;
  advocates base in Spain, 259;
  advocates small army, 286–7;
  criticizes private soldier, 288.
Euripides, 225.
Europe, 1, 2, 5, 13.
Exchequer Court, 8, 150.
Expeditions:
  France (1589), 14, 37, 47, 53, 59, 75, 79, 107, 236–51;
    objectives of, 236;
    recruitment for, 237–8;
    preparation of Sussex contingent, 238–42.
    'regimentation', 243–4;
    crosses Channel, 244–5;
    principal engagements, 246–9;
    inquest on, 250–1.
  Low Countries (1585), 14, 35, 76, 92.
  Portugal (1589), 15, 37, 58, 172, 176, 252;
    'regimentation', 53;
    provision of arms for, 124;
    desertion from, 166.
  Scotland (1560), 13, 52, 66, 75, 89, 93, 159, 207–36;
    French threaten border, 207–9;
    invasion preparations, 209–13;
    English army enters Scotland, 215–18;
    Leith besieged, 219–36;
    assault on Leith, 226–31;
    inquest on assault, 231–6.
  Spain (1596), 15–16, 53, 251–79;
    preparations, 251–5;
    proposed diversion to France, 255–6;
    troops assemble at Plymouth, 256–7;

departure from England, 258–60;
Essex's objectives, 259–60;
voyage to Cadiz, 260–5;
naval engagement, 267–70;
attack on Cadiz, 270–6;
inquest on results, 276–9.
Eyemouth, 209.

Falaise, 247, 249.
Falcon, 122.
Falconet, 122.
Faro, 276.
Felling-axes, 121.
Fife, 192.
Fifer, 176, 190.
Finch, Sir Moyle, 148.
Fire-arms, 102, 113, 114;
cost of, 115–16, 282;
disadvantages of, 106–7;
increased provision of, 109;
loading of, 106;
military experts on, 106–9;
Privy Council favour, 109, 282;
rate of fire, 128, 282;
replace long-bow, 114–15, 282;
storage of, 110–13;
training in use of, 110, 111, 194–5.
Firth, Sir Charles, 280.
Fish, 82.
Fitzmaurice, James, 16.
Fitzwilliam, Sir William, 171.
Fleet prison, 11, 229.
Fletchers, 103, 105, 121.
Flintshire, levies in, 290.
Fluellen, 14.
Flushing, 46, 68, 151, 179;
burgomaster of, 96;
Governor of, 56.
Forage-master, 49–50, 162.
Foreign service, *see* Recruitment.
Forster, Sir John, 208.
Fortescue, Sir J. W., 153, 154, 280, 284, 285.
Forth, river, 210, 213.
France, levies for, 243, 290.
Full pay, *see* Pay.
Furbisher, 121.
Fyrd, 1, 12.

Gaming, 58, 101, 102, 160, 161, 162, 261;
effect on archery, 104–5.
Gargrave, Sir Thomas, 213.
General, 50, 51, 162, 174;
Barret on, 41;
commission of, 44–47, 237;
location in battle, 47;
qualities required in, 41–43;
Rich on, 41, 45.
General of foot, 46, 49, 174.

General of horse, 49, 174.
Gentlemen volunteers, *see* Recruitment.
Germans, 1, 236.
Gilbert, Sir Humphrey, 14.
Glamorganshire, 71, 92, 168;
levies in, 65, 283, 291.
Gloucestershire, 71, 92;
levies in, 65, 291.
Goite, John, 69.
Greenwich, 10.
Grenville, Sir Richard, 268.
Gresham, Sir Thomas, 119, 124.
Grey, Arthur, 224.
Grey, Sir Ralph, 208.
Grey, William, Lord Grey of Wilton, 13, 209–36 *passim*;
as commander-in-chief, 42;
character of, 216.
criticizes his troops, 232.
Gun carriage, 122.
Gun-founders, 121.
Gunmetal, export of, 119.
Gunmakers, 125.
Gunnery, 122–3.
Gunpowder, 58, 108, 120, 125, 143, 145, 199, 244, 282, 284;
consumption rates, 109;
corned powder, 106;
export of, 127;
import of, 126;
issue of, 128–9, 144, 237;
manufacture of, 127;
provision of, 110, 111;
storage of, 127–8;
testing of, 121;
touchpowder, 106.

Hail shot, 102, 171.
Halberd, 17, 114, 121.
Halberdier, 244.
Hampshire, 64, 71, 112;
levies in, 63–64, 115, 238, 291.
Harbinger, *see* Quarter-master.
Harwich, 68.
Hastings, battle of (1066), 2, 5.
Hat, 92.
Hayes-McCoy, Dr. G. A., 205.
Hayward, Sir John, 42, 219, 220, 228, 231.
Hedging bills, 121.
Heigham, Sir Thomas, 46.
Helmet, 17.
Henry II, 4.
Henry V, 159, 174.
Henry VII, 1, 7, 33, 159.
Henry VIII, 1, 18, 23, 33, 103, 104.
Henry II (of France), 225.
Henry IV (of France), 15, 236, 238, 244–56 *passim*, 284.
Henry, Mr. L. W., 203–4.

Herald, 200, 219.
Herefordshire, levies in, 291.
Herring, 88, 89.
Hertfordshire, 187;
  commissioners of musters in, 111;
  levies in, 63, 291.
High constable, 179, 185.
Holliday, William, 99.
Honourable Artillery Company, 1.
Horses, 17, 18, 118, 164, 243;
  breeding of, 33–34;
  export of, 33;
  post, 77;
  sizes, etc., 33, 34 n.
Hose, 92.
Hospitals, 38, 164, 179, 180–2;
  in Buckinghamshire, 182;
  in Ireland, 180–1;
  in London, 38;
  in Low Countries, 180;
  at Lough Foyle, 182.
House of Commons, 6, 7, 8, 9, 21, 60, 186–7.
House of Lords, 6, 7, 8, 9,
Howard, Charles, Lord Howard of Effingham, 8, 15, 20, 252, 253, 255, 258, 260, 270, 275, 277, 278.
Howard, Sir George, 212, 218, 221, 227.
Howard, Lord Thomas, 253, 261, 264, 267, 268.
Huddilston, Richard, 148, 149, 150.
Huguenots, 13.
Hungary, 27.
Hunsdon (Henry Carey), Lord, 14, 155.
Huntingdonshire, levies in, 291.

Imprest, *see* Pay.
Indenture, *see* Recruitment.
Invisible writing, 74.
Isle of Wight, 70, 155.
Ireland:
  cost of army in, 283–4;
  levies for, 243, 390.
Irish ague, 180.
Irish sea, 75.

Jack, 17, 116, 117, 119.
Jacket, 92.
Jacquerie, 27.
Jersey, Governor of, 20.
John, 5.
John and Francis, 263.
Jolles, John, 96.
Justice of the peace, 9, 19, 20, 22–23, 29, 32, 36, 38, 39, 62, 63, 65, 71, 111, 133, 186, 281;
  asked to provide extra fire-arms, 110;
  criticism of, 9, 21;
  exempt from musters, 24.

Kent, 110, 112;
  commissioners of musters in, 116;
  levies in, 72, 238, 242, 291.
Killinghall, Francis, 233, 234.
Kinsale, battle of, (1601), 205–6.
Kirkaldy of Grange, 229.
Knight marshal, 37.
Knighthood, 46–47.
Knollys, Sir Francis, 201.
Knox, John, 13, 207.
Kyffin, Maurice, 68–69, 141.

Ladder, 226, 230.
Lamb, 82.
Lambeth, 72.
Lancashire, 187;
  levies in, 64, 291.
Lancepresado, 194.
Land's End, 69.
Lane, Sir Ralph, 52, 141–2.
Laundress, 161.
Lead, 244.
Le Havre, 13, 27, 45, 74, 152, 154, 160, 165, 175, 184.
Leicester (Robert Dudley), Earl of, 14, 35, 45, 46, 70, 76, 78, 80, 92, 139, 152, 165, 166, 177, 179, 202, 236;
  as commander-in-chief, 42–43, 280;
  devises dead-pay scheme, 155;
  disciplinary code of, 161, 296–303.
Leicester, George, 81, 97.
Leicestershire, levies in, 291.
Leith, 13, 93, 210;
  siege of (1560), 13, 75, 89, 113, 118, 142, 152, 153, 165, 217–36 *passim*, 288.
Le Mans, 247, 248.
Leon, Island of, 265, 273.
L'Estrange, Sir Nicholas, 234.
Lewes, 241,
Lieutenant, 57.
Light horse, *see* Cavalry.
Limerick, 165.
Lincolnshire, levies in, 64, 291.
Ling, 87, 88.
Linton Bridge, 217.
Lion, 261.
Lion's Whelp, 261.
Liquorice, 90.
Lisbon, 263.
Liverpool, 69, 80.
London, 28, 66, 73, 75, 101, 104, 109, 119, 127, 210;
  corporation of, 38, 174;
  levies in, 28, 62, 68, 113, 238, 256, 283, 291;
  Lord Mayor of, 29, 168, 174, 175, 176, 238;
  Tower of, 10, 115, 127, 253.
Long-bow, 2, 17–18, 26, 86, 114;

INDEX

Ascham on, 105;
  encouraged by statute, 102-3;
  increased cost of, 102, 115-16;
  military experts on, 106-9;
  price control of, 104;
  provided for children, 103-4;
  rate of fire, 282;
  replaced by fire-arms, 52, 282;
  Wilford on, 107-8.
Lord Chancellor, 147.
Lord Chief Justice, 100.
Lord deputy (of Ireland), 42, 55, 76, 124, 171.
Lord lieutenant, 20, 38, 48, 49, 62, 117, 133, 211, 281;
  commission to, 19;
  control of, 20;
  organizes musters, 132;
  powers of, 19;
  supersedes justices, 19.
Lough Foyle, 89, 179, 182.
Lough Swilly, 89.
Low Countries, levies for, 243, 290.
Lucar, Cyprian, 59, 122.

Machiavelli, 199.
Maitland of Lethington, 207.
Malines, 119.
Mantle, 93-94.
Manwood, Sir Roger, 11.
Marching, 58, 61;
  day's march, 61, 164, 217;
  formations, 190, 196;
  training for, 58, 61.
Margate, 202.
Marriage, 160.
Marshal, 46, 49, 50, 51, 172, 174, 196, 243, 270, 272;
  duties of, 47-48, 164.
Martial law, 48.
Mary of Guise, 207, 212, 213, 218.
Mary Rose, 262.
Mary Stuart, 14, 207.
Mary Tudor, 4, 8, 17, 23, 128, 183, 211, 287.
Master gunner, 121.
Master of ordnance, 46, 49, 50, 144, 174, 196, 244.
Master of victuals, 30, 49.
Match, 58, 106, 121, 143, 145, 244, 282.
Melting ladle, 121, 244.
Men-at-arms, *see* Cavalry.
Mercenaries, *see* Recruitment.
Meredith William, 148.
Merhonour, 264.
Merionethshire, levies, in 290.
Middleburg, 67, 150.
Middlesex, levies in, 29, 187, 291.
Milford, 69, 210.
Military law, 48, 159, 164, 165, 172.

Military tenure, 4.
Militia, 1, 2, 4, 12, 18, 20;
  statutory basis of, 17.
Milk, 76.
Mining, 200.
Minion, 122.
Monson, Sir William, 263, 270, 278.
Monmouthshire, levies in, 65, 290.
Montgomeryshire, levies in, 61, 290.
Moors, 27.
Morgan, Sir Matthew, 23.
Morgan, Captain Thomas, 138.
Morion, 117, 120, 125, 241, 242.
Mountjoy (Charles Blount), Lord, 16, 47, 56, 89, 100, 156;
  as commander-in-chief, 43, 206;
  as strategist, 199, 205-6;
  disciplinary code of, 163, 165.
Movement, 61-69;
  conduct money, 61-63, 241;
  cost of, 67-68, 240;
  difficulty of, 64, 66-67, 242;
  on land, 61-66;
  on sea, 66-68, 238-40;
  transport controllers, 68-70, 125.
Munster, 83.
Musket, 49, 52, 107, 114, 116, 121, 124, 125, 243, 244.
Musket arrow, 115.
Musket rest, 121.
Musketeer, 108, 155, 244, 249, 283;
  equipment of, 117;
  training of, 195.
Muster master, 19, 35, 100, 136, 144, 145, 147, 166, 244;
  corruption of, 134;
  difficulties of, 137-9;
  good and bad, 136-7;
  pay of, 128.
Muster rolls, 36, 132, 134, 186;
  surveyor general of, 131, 186.
Musters, 20, 25, 30, 125, 193, 237, 287;
  admonition before musters, 294;
  certificates, 295;
  commissioners of, 10, 18, 22, 23, 62, 64, 106, 109, 112, 131, 132, 168, 254, 281;
  general, 7, 12, 131-2;
  importance of, 142;
  in Ireland, 139-42;
  in Low Countries, 138-9;
  in militia, 17, 130-4;
  irregularities in, 131, 136, 138, 139-41, 160;
  on active service, 130, 134-6;
  procedure for, 132-3;
  statutory basis of, 17, 130;
  oath for musters, 294.
Mutiny, 162, 168;
  at Bristol, 165, 168;

Mutiny (*cont.*)
  in Ireland, 171–2;
  in London, 168;
  in Ostend, 79, 169–71.
Mutton, 82.

Nails, 121.
Navy, 66, 78, 210, 215, 217, 235, 253, 259.
Neale, Sir John, 280.
Netherlands, *see* Low Countries.
Netherstocks (stockings), 92.
Newcomen, Robert, 84.
Newgate prison, 27.
Newhaven, 239.
Nicholson, Edmund, 124, 125.
Nieuport, battle of (1600), 288.
Nîmes, 200.
Norfolk, levies in, 62, 291.
Norfolk (Thomas Howard), Duke of, 75, 168;
  commands invasion of Scotland (1560), 209–36 *passim*;
  proposes dead-pay allowance, 154.
Norman conquest, 2, 4, 19.
Normandy, 15, 66, 79, 115, 148.
Norreys, Sir Edward, 67, 169.
Norreys, Sir John, 15, 23, 35, 63–64, 66, 68, 138, 165, 168, 176, 201.
  on enlisting rogues, 28.
Norreys, Sir Thomas, 171.
Northamptonshire, levies in, 291.
Northern rebellion, 13–14, 16, 52.
Northumberland, levies in, 291.
Northumberland (Thomas Percy), Earl of, 14, 208, 212.
Nottinghamshire, levies in, 291.
Nurses, 161, 180, 181.

Oath, 163, 164, 173, 293;
  administration of, 164.
Oatmeal, 83, 87, 88, 89.
Oman, Sir Charles, 280.
O'Neill, Shane, 16.
Orders, 190–3;
  'inarticulate', 193;
  sealed, 261;
  transmission of, 192;
  typical commands, 190–2.
Ordnance office, 119, 121–4, 128, 244;
  in Ireland, 111, 124;
  master of, 123, 128, 144;
  regulations for, 123;
  reorganization of, 123–4.
Ostend, 28, 29, 79, 95, 166, 183.
Oxfordshire, 71;
  levies in, 28, 62, 113, 291.

Padstow, 69.
Pale, 167.

Paris, 107, 246–7.
Parliament, 5–6, 18;
  encourages archery, 102, 106;
  interest in army, 5–9.
Passes, 164, 165, 166.
Paulet, Sir Amyas, 20.
Pay, 5, 52, 54, 57, 59, 128, 168;
  concordatum fund, 151–2;
  dead pays, 51, 55, 59, 115, 151, 153–8, 238, 243, 244, 254, 281;
  full pay, 143, 171;
  imprest, 143;
  issued by captains, 143, 144;
  lendings, 143, 170;
  by poll, 151, 152–3, 157;
  receipt for payment, 295;
  system out-of-date, 281–2;
  transferred through merchants, 150–1;
  warrant for payment, 295–6.
Peas, 82, 88, 89.
Peers, exempt from musters, 24.
Pelham, William, 152, 224, 226, 227, 248.
Pembrokeshire, levies in, 65, 290.
Pensioner reserve, 286;
Pensions, military, 184–8;
  financing of, 185;
  legislation, 60;
  payment of, 186;
  value of, 185–6.
Percy, Sir Henry, 212, 227.
Perrot, Sir John, 76.
Philip II, 11, 14, 15, 53, 70, 71, 258, 263, 277.
Physical fitness, 194.
Physicians, 174, 181.
Picardy, 28, 148.
Pickaxe, 121.
Pig, 82.
Pigeons, 82.
Pike, 17, 86, 113, 114, 116, 117, 125, 195, 230, 244;
  cost of, 115;
  handling of, 190–1, 194.
Pikeman, 119, 241, 244, 249;
  equipment of, 117–18.
Pioneers, 25, 49, 56, 137, 164, 174, 197, 223, 226, 227.
Plague, 13, 184.
Plumber, 121.
Plymouth, 201, 256, 257.
Poole, 66;
  Mayor of, 66.
Pork, 82, 88, 89.
Portland, 201.
Portsmouth, 238, 243, 245.
Portugal, 15, 23, 258;
  levies for, 290.
Pouldron, 117, 118, 125, 242, 285.

Powder flask, 121.
Poynings, Sir Adrian, 159, 160.
Prayer for troops, 292–3.
Preacher, 57, 58, 168, 175;
  pay of, 59, 128.
Prestonpans, 217.
Prisoner, 58, 151, 162.
Private soldier, 59;
  blamed for failure at Leith, 232;
  criticized by Essex, 238;
  desirable qualities, 60;
  Rich on, 39–40.
Privy Council, 6, 10, 11, 23, 26;
  appoints captains, 56;
  attitude to overseas service, 11–14;
  control of military affairs, 18, 284–5;
  develops trained bands, 285;
  discharges employed men, 26;
  encourages use of fire-arms, 109–12, 285;
  exempt from musters, 24;
  military committee of, 18;
  recruits vagabonds, 28;
  relations with commander, 46.
Proclamations, 18;
  returned soldiers (1562), 184;
  breeding of horses (1565, 1568, 1580), 34;
  carrying of fire-arms (1579), 110–11;
  price control of board and lodging (1588), 82;
  illegal sale of weapons (1588, 1589), 125;
  export of food (1588, 1591, 1597), 81;
  unlawful assembly of discharged soldiers (1589, two), 37–38;
  examination of discharged soldiers (1591, two), 38–39, 184;
  illegal use of handguns (1600), 102–3.
Projectiles, 122.
Promotion, 56.
Proof master, 121.
Provost marshal ('civilian'), 37–39, 49.
Provost marshal ('military'), 48, 49, 53, 164, 168, 172, 244.
Punishments, 125, 163, 171, 172.
Purveyance, 77.

Quadrant, 122.
Quarles, James, 99.
Quarrelling, 160.
Quarter-master, 49, 244.

Radnorshire, levies in, 28, 66, 290.
Raleigh, Sir Walter, 9, 253–4, 257, 261, 263, 266, 267, 268, 269.
Randall, Edward, 217.
Randolph, Thomas, 89.
Ransom, 3.

Rations, 55, 58, 69, 78, 142, 214, 237, 237, 239, 242, 278;
  distribution of, 84–85, 145;
  poor quality of, 29, 77, 170;
  prices of, 48, 67, 76, 79, 82, 88;
  smuggling of, 79–80, 81, 243;
  storage of, 86–87;
  supplied by contract, 80–81, 82–83, 85;
  transport of, 87–88;
  typical issues, 88–89.
  See also under individual foodstuffs.
Reaping hooks, 121.
Receiver of Taxes, 62.
Recruitment, 17–40, 282, 283;
  authorized by queen and Council, 23;
  cavalry, 30–32, 71–73;
  by commission, 5, 23;
  conscription, 8, 26, 288, 289;
  gentlemen volunteers, 25, 44, 154, 155, 156, 157, 169, 249;
  indenture, 5, 23, 64, 65, 66, 69, 70, 282, 291–2;
  of Irish citizens, 34;
  liability for service, 8, 23, 287;
  masterless men, 26, 28;
  mercenaries, 1, 2, 5;
  military experts on, 26–29;
  minimum age, 8;
  money fiefs, 3–4;
  recusants, 24;
  replacements, 34–36;
  rogues and vagabonds, 25–29;
  service overseas, 11–13;
  Shakespeare on, 22–23;
  surgeons, 175;
  trained bands, 24–25, 112, 114, 285, 287;
  volunteers, 11, 14, 25–26, 37, 53.
Regiment, 51–53, 59, 243, 244, 253, 254;
  Barret on, 53;
  size of, 52;
  Smythe on, 52.
Restalrig, 218.
Revenge, 268.
Rich, Barnaby, 21, 26, 29, 39, 41, 45, 76, 108, 192.
Richard II, 159.
Roberts, Professor Michael, 198.
Robinet, 122.
Rochester, 123.
Romans, 27, 142.
Rope, 121.
Rouen, siege of (1591), 23, 172.
Russell, Sir William, 76.
Rutland, levies in, 291.
Rutland (Roger Manners), Earl of, 92.
Rye, 27, 238, 240, 242, 245;
  Mayor of, 240.

Sack, 90.
Saddle, 119.
Sadler, Sir Ralph, 208, 209, 210, 212, 213, 215, 218, 229.
St. Andrew, 269.
St. Matthew, 269.
St. Philip, 268, 269, 270.
St. Quentin, battle of (1557), 174.
St. Thomas, 269.
Saker, 122.
Sale of equipment, 17
Salmon, 89, 234.
Saltpetre, 122, 199, 284; manufacture of, 126-7; testing of, 121.
Sandwich, 68, 243.
Scales, 89, 244.
Scotland, 6, 13, 16, 52, 66, 94.
Scots, 236.
Scouring-stick, 106.
Scout-master, 49.
Scythes, 121.
Secretary of state, 10, 77, 138.
Sergeant, 57-58, 172, 195.
Sergeant-major, 50, 196.
Sergeant-major-general, 46, 50-51, 52, 53, 217, 244, 270.
Shakespeare, William, 14.
Sheriff, 19, 20, 32, 39, 62, 65, 281.
Sherley, Sir Thomas, 95, 96, 138, 148-50, 155.
Shirt, 92.
Shoes, 92, 93, 95, 96, 98.
Shooting-glove, 116.
Shot, 110, 121, 122, 125.
Shovels, 121, 244.
Shrewsbury (George Talbot), Earl of, 64.
Shropshire, levies in, 291.
Sick leave, 179-80.
Sickness, 145, 161, 165, 179, 182, 183.
Sidney, Sir Henry, 151.
Sidney, Sir Philip, 41, 176-7.
Skull, 116, 117, 119.
Sleeping on duty, 164.
Smith, 49, 121, 124.
Smith, Sir Thomas, 74.
Smithfield, 29.
Smythe, Sir John, 10-13, 27, 52, 55, 106, 107, 108, 114, 115, 116, 117, 118, 188-91, 288.
Southampton, 125.
Southwark, 72.
Somersetshire, 71; commissioners of musters in, 10; levies in, 291.
Spades, 121, 244.
Spain, 1, 11, 14, 17, 46, 131, 205; levies for, 290.
Specialization, 24, 134, 287.
Spies, 151, 285.

Squadron (of cavalry), 54.
Staffordshire, levies in, 291.
Stafford, Sir Edward, 244, 245.
Star Chamber, Court of, 10, 38, 156.
Statutes:
  Assize of arms (1181) (military service), 4;
  Statute of Winchester (1285), (military service), 4, 280;
  1 Edward III, st. 2, c. 5 (military service), 4;
  1 Edward III, st. 2, c. 7 (payment of troops) 4-5;
  1 Edward III, st. 2, c. 15 (military service), 5;
  18 Edward III, st. 2, c. 7, (payment of troops), 5.
  4 Henry IV, c. 13 (military service), 4 n;
  1 Richard III, c. 11 (bowstaves), 103;
  11 Henry VII, c. 13 (export of horses), 33;
  3 Henry VIII, c. 3 (archery), 103;
  3 Henry VIII, c. 5, (pay, etc.), 23;
  6 Henry VIII, c. 2 (archery), 103;
  27 Henry VIII, c. 6 (breeding of horses), 33;
  32 Henry VIII, c. 13 (breeding of horses), 33;
  33 Henry VIII, c. 9 (archery and unlawful games), 103, 104;
  2 & 3 Edward VI, c. 2 (reformation of captains and soldiers), 6, 17;
  2 & 3 Edward VI, c. 3 (purveyance), 77;
  4 & 5 Philip and Mary, c. 2 (horse, armour, and weapon), 7, 8, 17, 109, 113;
  4 & 5 Philip and Mary, c. 3 (musters), 8, 17, 130-1, 280, 287;
  8 Elizabeth I, c. 8 (breeding of horses), 34;
  8 Elizabeth I, c. 10 (bow prices), 104;
  13 Elizabeth I, c. 14 (bowstaves), 103, 104;
  14 Elizabeth I, c. 5 (demobilization), 36-37;
  31 Elizabeth I, c. 4 (illegal sale of armour, etc.), 125;
  35 Elizabeth I, c. 4 (disabled soldiers), 184;
  39 Elizabeth I, c. 1 (husbandry), 7;
  39 Elizabeth I, c. 17 (resettlement of soldiers and sailors), 39;
  39 Elizabeth I, c. 21 (disabled soldiers), 184;
  43 Elizabeth I, c. 3 (disabled soldiers), 184.
  See also **Bills, army.**
Stealing, 160, 162, 164, 172, 261.

INDEX

Stephen, 5.
Stockings, 92, 93, 95, 96, 98, 242.
Strategy:
   defence against invasion, 201–3;
   Essex on, 203–5;
   Mountjoy as strategist, 205–6;
   scorched earth policy, 203.
Striking superior officer, 162.
Stringers, 103, 105.
Styward, Thomas, 196.
Suffolk, levies in, 25, 291.
Sulphur, 122.
Surgeons, 57;
   Clowes, William, 177–8;
   dissatisfaction with, 178;
   equipment of, 176;
   inexperience of, 176;
   pay, 128, 178–9;
   recruitment of, 174–6.
Surrey, levies in, 27, 29, 192.
Sussex, 71;
   levies in, 238, 239, 291.
Sussex (Thomas Radcliffe) Earl of, 14.
Sutcliffe, Matthew, 5, 26–27, 34, 41, 43, 44–45, 143, 157–8, 200–1.
Swan, 263.
Swearing, 145, 161, 163, 261.
Swiftsure, 262.
Swiss, 1, 236.
Sword, 113, 116, 117, 125, 169;
   supplied by armoury office, 120.

Tactics, 34, 198–201.
Tallow, 121.
Tamburlaine, 225.
Target, 120.
Tasses, 117, 118, 242, 285.
Thames, river, 202.
Throckmorton, Sir Nicholas, 214.
Tilbury, 14, 31, 52, 82, 125.
Touchboxes, 121.
Touchpowder, *see* Gunpowder.
Tower Hill, 127, 168.
Trained bands, *see* Recruitment.
Training, 130, 193–8, 256–7;
   Barret on, 197–8;
   cost of, 133, 195;
   Digges on, 195–7;
   importance of, 130;
   in marching, 195–6;
   Rich on, 193;
   Styward on, 196;
   Sutcliffe on, 193–4;
   textbooks, 197–8;
   use of weapons, 111, 133, 194–5, 213.
Transport, *see* Movement.
Travis, John, 84.
Treasurer-at-war, 38, 50, 54, 95, 101, 128, 130, 136, 144, 145, 146, 147, 157, 228, 240, 244;
   corruption of, 149–50, 281;
   duties of, 150;
   emoluments of, 147, 148;
   good and bad, 146–7.
Treasurer (lord high), *see* Burghley; Buckhurst.
Trench-master, 48, 49, 50, 227.
Trenches, 197, 223, 224, 226, 231.
Trent, river, 209.
True Love, 261.
Trumpet, 161, 193, 247, 262.
Trumpeter, 171, 176.
Tyrone (Hugh O'Neill), Earl of, 16, 82, 156, 205–6.

Uniform, 126, 142, 143;
   coat money, 61, 91–92;
   colour of, 72, 91;
   corruption in supply of, 99–101, 150, 281, 282;
   cost of, 97 n., 100;
   distribution of, 98–99, 101, 145;
   in Ireland, 93–95, 101;
   officers' outfit, 93;
   poor quality of, 100;
   privates' outfit, 92–93;
   provided by contract, 95–98;
   resold by soldiers, 98.
Utrecht, 172.

Vambrace, 117, 118, 242, 285.
Vaughan, Captain, 223, 226–7, 230.
Veal, 82.
Vendôme, 247.
Venetians (trousers), 92.
Venice, 75, 92, 103.
Vere, Sir Francis, 46, 74, 193, 252–76 *passim*.
Vice-admiral, 46.
Victuallers, 29, 169, 197, 238.
Victualling commissaries, 81, 84.
Victualling contracts, 80–82, 85.
Victualling merchants, 78–82.
Victuals, *see* Rations.
Volunteers, *see* Recruitment.

Wadding, 106, 122.
Wagons, 61, 81, 127, 162, 164.
Wales, levies in, 62, 72, 290.
Wallop, Sir Henry, 93–94, 148.
Walsingham, Sir Francis, 35, 47, 152, 240, 249.
Wardrobe office, 96, 97, 98.
Warspite, 261.
Warwick, 110.
Warwick (Ambrose Dudley), Earl of, 13, 14, 20, 45, 74, 154, 163, 165, 175, 177;
   disciplinary code of, 159–60;
   master of ordnance, 123.

Warwickshire, levies in, 62, 291.
Watch and ward, 58, 98, 135, 160, 162, 170, 232, 262.
Watchword, 58, 162.
  betrayal of, 163.
Waterford, 264.
Wendon, Thomas, 10.
Wernham, Professor R. B., 15 n.
West Indies, 254, 259, 264, 276.
Westminster, Palace of, 7.
Westmorland, levies in, 291.
Westmorland (Charles Neville), Earl of, 14.
Wharton, Thomas, Lord, 208.
Wheat, 81, 82, 86.
Wheelwright, 49, 121.
Whitehorne, Peter, 199.
Wildfire, 107, 199.
Wilford, Sir Thomas, 107–8, 120, 243, 248, 256.
William I, 2, 5.
Williams, Sir Roger, 14, 45, 53, 61, 77, 108, 172, 173, 210, 284.
Willoughby (Peregrine Bertie), Lord, 46, 56, 113, 120;
  as commander-in-chief, 43, 45;
  in France, 15, 75, 114, 236–57 *passim*.
  in Low Countries, 45–46, 96, 145, 166, 169.
Wills, 164.
Wiltshire, 71;
  levies in, 62, 65, 291.
Wimbledon, 71.
Winchester, Bishop of:
  Bilson, Thomas, 32;
  Cooper, Thomas, 31–32.
Winter, William, 210, 213–14, 226.
Withholding pay, 17.
Women, 163, 164, 172, 179;
  at siege of Leith, 230–1.
Wood, Captain, 227.
Woolwich, 123.
Worcester, 62.
Worcestershire, levies in, 291.

Yeomen of the guard, 1.
York, 14.
Yorkshire, levies in, 291.
Youghal, 83.

Zutphen, battle of (1586), 176.

REPRINTED LITHOGRAPHICALLY IN GREAT BRITAIN
AT THE UNIVERSITY PRESS, OXFORD
BY VIVIAN RIDLER
PRINTER TO THE UNIVERSITY